EUROPE IN THE SEVENTEENTH CENTURY

Europe in the Seventeenth Century

DAVID MALAND, M.A.
High Master, The Manchester Grammar School

SECOND EDITION

Macmillan Education

London and Basingstoke

First edition 1966
Reprinted 1966, 1967, 1968, 1970, 1973, 1975,
1977, 1978, 1980, 1981, 1982
Second edition 1983

Published by
MACMILLAN EDUCATION LTD
Houndmills Basingstoke Hampshire RG21 2XS
and London
Associated companies throughout the world

Printed in Hong Kong

British Library Cataloguing in Publication Data
Maland, David
    Europe in the seventeenth century.—2nd ed.
    1. Europe—History—17th century
    I. Title
    940.2'52   D246
    ISBN 0–333–33574–0

CONTENTS

I   THE SEVENTEENTH CENTURY

VI LOUIS XIV: A STUDY IN ABSOLUTISM

VII WESTERN EUROPE 1660–1714

VIII SWEDEN AND THE STRUGGLE FOR SUPREMACY IN THE BALTIC 1600–1700

LIST OF PLATES

ACKNOWLEDGEMENTS

The publishers gratefully acknowledge the following sources
of the photographs reproduced in this book:

Mansell Collection: Plates 1a, 1b, 2, 3, 4a, 4b, 6b
Dr. Eva Frodl-Kraft, Vienna: Plate 5
Photographie Giraudon: Plate 6a
M. Jean Roubier, Paris: Plate 7a
Mr. A. F. Kersting: Plates 7b and 8

LIST OF MAPS

LIST OF MAPS

EUROPE
IN THE SEVENTEENTH CENTURY

I

THE SEVENTEENTH CENTURY

ECONOMIC DEVELOPMENT

The Peasantry and Food Production

Most Europeans in the seventeenth century were peasants, though their status, their legal rights and their terms of tenure varied greatly from one region to the next. East of the Elbe where serfdom prevailed they were at their worst, subject to the jurisdiction of their landlords, burdened with heavy labour services and with little or no personal freedom.[1] In western Europe serfdom was less common — though it was not abolished in the royal estates of Portugal until 1702, and there were perhaps a million or more serfs in France, a tenth of the peasant population — but there existed many degrees of bondage short of serfdom itself, not all of them always preferable to it. The number of landless labourers, for instance, had grown considerably since the sixteenth century; men condemned to eke out an existence by selling their labour in an age when forced labour was too often available and when there were few industries other than farming to offer them employment. More fortunate in the greater security of their life but denied personal freedom, were most of the Danish peasantry, along with a substantial minority in other western countries where landlords, attempting to combat the price rise of the previous century, were cultivating their demesnes more intensively and thus demanding greater labour services than in the past. Since the lords were judges in their own case the peasants had little success in pleading their customary rights, and their freedom was consequently invaded.

[1] Chapter VIII, p. 403 on Brandenburg; Chapter IX, p. 417 on Austria; and Chapter X p. 465 on Russia.

On the other hand, there were many, perhaps the majority in France and Spain, who were free of manorial control in all but minor matters, however irksome, provided they shared their crops with the lord, paying from one-fifth to one-half of their produce.[2] Freer still were those who had commuted all services for a rent charge, though the landlord might also be at greater liberty to raise their rents and to secure their eviction. On the fringe of the peasantry, if not of it, were the peasant proprietors who had won possession of their own smallholdings. In France there were a million, or so, grouped mostly in the north and west and especially around Paris, working their land at a profit to supply the growing population of the capital. An independent peasantry of this type was also to be found in Holland, though a few kilometres away the peasants of Overijssel suffered under heavy feudal burdens. In Sweden where the peasantry enjoyed social freedom and political powers unheard of in the rest of Europe, these privileges might none the less have been reversed had it not been for the triumph of Charles XI over his nobles.[3] Indeed, apart from the rough division of European peasantry into those east and west of the Elbe, the range of serfdom was too great, the variations in gradation too subtle, too fluid and too uncertain, to be trapped within a generalisation.

Whatever changes for good or ill occurred in the status of the peasant, none took place in his methods of work, nor did he see any reason why they should. Ignorant and hidebound by tradition, he grew food principally for his own consumption, and there was little incentive to do otherwise. Throughout most of Europe stretched the great open fields, bastions of a primitive economy, which determined the time-honoured progression of the manorial calendar, preventing the adoption of new crop rotations, and compelling adherence to traditional methods of cultivation. As they had done for centuries, teams of oxen scratched the earth's surface with wooden ploughs; as always cereals were the staple crop, especially rye, oats and millet which yielded more per hectare than wheat. Since cereals exhausted the soil it was necessary to leave land fallow one year in three in the north, one year in two in the south, and even two years in three in

---

[2] In France this service was known as *métayage*, see Chapter VI, p.300.

[3] See Chapter VIII, pp.396–7

particularly infertile regions. In any given year, therefore, two-fifths of Europe's arable land was unproductive.

Variations from traditional procedures were uncommon, their causes various. One novel development took place in Ireland where the adoption of the potato was welcomed by an impoverished people who could grow sufficient potatoes to sustain them on half the land, and with half the effort, required to keep them in cereals. In Holland too cereals were abandoned, but from reasons of wealth, not poverty: enriched by trade the Dutch could afford to import the cereals they required, mainly from Danzig, while they themselves developed the market-gardening of fruits and vegetables, and grew barley and hops for brewing, root crops and clover. These last crops gave nitrogen to the soil and winter feed to the cattle which, being stalled throughout the winter, not only supplied their owners with better milk and meat but with more organic fertiliser than could be found in the rest of Europe. Such intensive cultivation on a similar scale was only to be found elsewhere in the Ile-de-France and in Kent, where the demands of a rapidly expanding population in both Paris and London had to be met.

Away from the pressures created by population density there was little change, nor could any be expected until the landlords themselves desired it. The peasant was generally ignorant and poor. It was only the noble who had opportunities to inform himself on agriculture by travel and by reading; who had the power to enclose land; who had the wealth to drain it, to fertilise it and to experiment. Though it involved no revolutionary innovation in crop rotation and farming technique, none the less a most important development was taking place in Bohemia, Austria, and above all in Poland, where the tradition of self-sufficiency was being smashed by some of the nobles. The demand for corn in the west, the expanding population of Vienna, the perennial necessity to supply armies at war in Europe, were being exploited by landlords who used their monopoly of political power to secure for themselves commercial monopolies and trading privileges. They increased both their demesnes and the labour services of their serfs; they built granaries to store their surplus produce, and barges and rafts to ship it down the tributaries of the Danube and the Vistula.

Generally, however, the environment of court and camp, and

the association of commercial farming with the stigma of the
bourgeois, worked against the practice of successful estate
management: it was Madame de Sévigné's cousin who explained
to her that tenants neglected the land unless 'you get yourself
exiled [i.e. from Versailles] and then you will be able to keep an
eye on them'. Where the English were to excel was in the fact that
their social system gave to the improving landlord, who had the
capital with which to experiment, a prestige which stimulated
imitation by lesser men. Interest in agrarian matters was already
more widespread in England than in any other country, and
though there was much extolling of the Netherlands — the most
famous of agricultural works was Hartlib's *Discours of Husbandrie
used in Brabant and Flanders* (1652) — the English in fact were not
so backward as their own writers supposed. The number of
improving landlords was increasing steadily; market-gardening,
land drainage, such as the immense schemes of the Duke of
Bedford in the fens, and the use of root crops were expanding
under the influence of a growing population and a landlord class
who had the leisure, the capital and the interest to devote to their
estates. It was this environment which made possible the rapid
acceptance of the ideas of Tull, Bakewell and Townshend in the
next century, and thus paved the way for English primacy in
agriculture.

Population and Prices

The failure to achieve a general improvement in methods of food
production was the most important factor determining the size of
Europe's population in the seventeenth century. Political
arithmetic, as demography was significantly termed, was in its
infancy; it was only the more commercially minded governments
who took pains to discover the statistics of their populations, and
the evidence they collected was often unreliable. The sale of
government annuities, for example, despite the informed advice
in Holland of Christiaan Huygens on the mathematics of
probability, and the compilation of the first reasonable life-table
by Edmund Halley in England, was more of a Treasury gamble
than an actuarial calculation.[4] For the most backward countries,

---

[4] As late as 1810 the municipality of The Hague sold life annuities at a rate which
did not vary with the ages of the persons during whose survival they were payable.

such as Spain, the estimates of historians are likely to be based on nothing more reliable than a Venetian ambassador's guess.

Accepting the estimates which are available, it appears that the population increase of the sixteenth century petered out early in the seventeenth, and that numbers thereafter remained more or less static. Scandinavia, including Denmark, varied but little about the two million mark; Brandenburg-Prussia remained slightly below this, the United Provinces rather above it; Italy held steady at about 13,000,000, Poland at 16,000,000. France rose from 16,000,000 to 19,000,000 and Austria from 5,500,000 to 7,500,000, but both examples are misleading since the increase was derived less from any change in birth or death rates than from the territorial acquisitions made by both countries throughout the century. Great Britain, alone, rising by one million to 7,500,000, provides evidence of a real increase based upon increased prosperity, just as the economic decline of the Iberian peninsula explains the estimated fall in numbers there from ten to eight millions. National statistics are deceptive in two ways; they are meaningless for many purposes without some indication of the density of the population,[5] and they fail to indicate all manner of local variations which, to the historian, might be significant. Towns for example often kept fairly accurate records of their population, and there are interesting conclusions to be drawn from the growth of London, Amsterdam, Paris and Vienna — London and Paris both exceeded 400,000 by 1700 — which relate to the increased power enjoyed in Europe by the states of which they were the capital cities. Too hasty a generalisation, however, is silenced by the reflection that Madrid also increased its population.

The general stability of the total figure of Europeans was not affected by the local fluctuations which occurred. Emigration would reduce numbers in one particular region only to create increases elsewhere, and there is evidence of considerable redistribution of the population across Europe. Religious persecution drove at least 200,000 Huguenots into the haven of Protestant states such as Holland and Brandenburg: warfare stimulated emigration from war zones, the Rhineland or the

[5] Density figures, quoted in G.N. Clark, *The Seventeenth Century*, are: Italy, 44 souls per square kilometre; Netherlands, 40; France, 34; England and Wales, 30; Germany, 28; Spain and Portugal, 17; Denmark, 15; Poland with Prussia, 14; Sweden, Norway and Finland, 13.

Leipzig plain, to more happily placed areas: equally there was emigration from regions of declining economic importance to more flourishing centres; more than a hundred of the richest merchants of Cologne emigrated to Frankfurt with their families between 1594 and 1637, while in France at the end of the century over 4,000 Catholic weavers left Normandy to seek better employment in England. Plague, unlike emigration, had only bad results. Sometimes it struck with devastating effect, killing for instance 130,000 in Naples in 1656: nine years later 100,000 died in the Great Plague of London: Danzig suffered severely in 1653, 1657 and 1660, as did Amsterdam and Frankfurt in both 1664 and 1666. Amid these major disasters the constant and universal incidence of the plague must not be ignored, since its persistent toll of the population was of greater significance than its periodically spectacular killings. Most spectacular of all in its effects, however, was warfare. Though comparatively few Europeans died in battle, the movement of armies brought famine, typhus and syphilis. Contemporaries always laid great stress on the depopulation caused by war, and if they tended to do so frequently in pleas for reduction of their taxes, no one could doubt that the Thirty Years War in Germany, the campaigns of 1650-60 in Poland, the devastation of the Palatinate in 1688 and the struggle for Spain after 1700, collectively reduced the population of Europe — though no two authorities would agree on an estimate.

Emigration, plague, warfare, causing tremendous fluctuation in particular localities, exercised a check upon the population as a whole; but since there were always some survivors, the losses wrought were made good by a sharp increase in the birth rate. The entire population was governed in fact by one simple rule: its size was directly determined by its supply of food. Far worse than an epidemic or invasion was the incapacity of European farming, apart from rare exceptions as in Poland and England,[6] to produce and to store a surplus against the inevitable years when the crop failed, not merely locally, but throughout the continent. Between 1648 and 1652, for example, the harvest failed in one country after another across Europe, adding economic distress to the political factors which brought or threatened revolution in

[6] See above, p.6. Though the Dutch produced no surplus, their commercial facilities ensured the regular importation of food.

those years:[7] there were further general failures in 1660–3, 1675–9 and, in the worst crisis of all, 1693–4.

The failure of the harvest whether local or general was a disaster for all who lived at subsistence level, and these comprised the great majority of Europeans. Such folk might survive one bad year by selling their goods and chattels — if there were any rich enough to buy them — in order to purchase food imported from other regions; but if the crops failed generally, or if they failed two years together, then famine resulted. Many died directly from starvation. Thousands more were so weakened by malnutrition that they fell prey to the first illness to attack them. At such periods in the seventeenth century the death rate doubled or trebled and there were practically no births to offset it. The countryside was more immediately affected than the towns, since these had the means to lay in supplies and to buy further afield, but they too suffered when the famine was widespread. The famine of 1693, for example, caused food prices to rise so sharply that in Beauvais in northern France a family of five, even though they were all employed in weaving serges, could afford to buy less than half the bread it needed. Before the next harvest the father and two children had died: 'From a particularly fortunate family, because everyone worked, only a widow and an orphan remained because of the price of bread.'[8]

The harsh fact was that the population of Europe was pressing hard upon its means of subsistence, and since they were unable to produce greater supplies of food most Europeans suffered from undernourishment, poor health and a low expectation of life. One-half of all the babies born in the seventeenth century died within twelve months of birth; those who survived childhood might hope to live from 48 to 56 years if they were wealthy, and therefore comparatively well fed; if they were not, their expectation was between 30 to 40 years. For society as a whole the average expectation of life was 22 years.

Whereas famine accelerated the death rate and reduced the number of births, a series of good harvests produced an immediate parallel rise in births and a decline in deaths. The overall picture is therefore one of wild fluctuation in detail,

[7] See Chapter VIII, p.387 for Sweden and Chapter IV, p.221, for Spain.
[8] See P. Goubert, *Beauvais et les Beauvaisis de 1600 à 1730*, Paris, 1960.

determined primarily by the success or failure of the harvest, around a fairly constant mean. The same pattern is true also of the movement of prices, and for the same reason. In the sixteenth century the steady growth in numbers and the influx of American bullion had caused a steady rise in prices; in the seventeenth the population increase was checked, the influx of bullion fell off, and prices were again regulated by the harvest. Good harvests resulted in cheap food, and since money was thus released to purchase other goods, production was stimulated to the benefit of all classes. Conversely, a bad harvest not only caused starvation among the poor but compelled even the wealthy to economise in order to maintain their standard of housekeeping: industry and trade were consequently depressed.

On a European graph prices continued to rise steadily to 1625, fell to some extent by 1650, and held this level until a new rise began after 1700 — but such a general outline is wholly misleading. Europe was not an economic unit. The basic pattern was accompanied by startling variations from region to region, caused not only by the harvest, but also by the action of regional governments. The operation of tariffs, the sale of monopolies, and the debasement of the coinage[9] produced so many disconcerting fluctuations in the general pattern of European prices that merchants and manufacturers were filled with uncertainty and pessimism. This more than anything explains the fact that although the scale of economic activity continued to increase, the general rate of expansion was considerably less than in the sixteenth century with its mood of confident optimism. Because of the uncertainty of monetary values, the field of enterprise contracted; fewer new companies were founded, and established ones began to limit their activities as the investor, the merchant and the industrialist chose to take fewer risks.

Industry and Technology

If the uncertainties caused by price fluctuation checked the rate of industrial growth in Europe, there was none the less a degree of expansion stimulated by the needs of warfare, and the demand for luxuries which an increasingly wealthy middle class was able to afford. Remarkably, none of this expansion was accompanied

[9] See Chapter IV, pp.208–9, for the effect of this upon the Spanish economy.

by any significant change in methods of production, despite the fact that in the history of science the seventeenth century was a revolutionary era. Technological progress continued to depend upon the development of empirical methods by practical men, and science probably gained more from technology than she gave in return, at least before 1750.

In a few specialist fields only did the technologist benefit from scientific research: the study of pendular oscillation was applied by Christiaan Huygens to improving the measurement of time, while the study of the atmosphere contributed a great deal to pioneer work on the steam engine. This began when Galileo and his pupil Torricelli were asked by Cosimo II de Medici of Florence to account for the failure of his engineers to construct a suction pump capable of lifting water from a depth of 15 metres in the mines. In 1644 Torricelli announced his discovery of atmospheric pressure, and ten years later at Magdeburg, the immense forces exerted by it were demonstrated by von Guericke in a famous experiment with iron hemispheres.[10] In a subsequent experiment von Guericke showed that, when a partial vacuum was created below a large piston working in a cylinder, the combined force of fifty men could not prevent the atmospheric pressure driving the piston into the cylinder. Here, therefore, was a means of harnessing atmospheric pressure as a source of power, if only some simple means could be found of repeatedly creating a vacuum.

Huygens in all seriousness proposed to achieve this by means of gunpowder explosions, but fortunately his assistant, Denis Papin, achieved his object more simply and more safely by condensing steam in a cylinder: 'Since it is a property of water', he wrote in 1690, 'that a small quantity of it turned into vapour by heat has an elastic force like that of air, but upon cold supervening is again resolved into water, so that no trace of the said elastic force remains, I concluded that machines could be constructed wherein water, by the help of no very intense heat, and at little cost, could produce that perfect vacuum which could by no means be obtained by gunpowder.' The first machine to apply this principle in practice was *The Miners' Friend*, 'an engine to raise water by force', demonstrated by its inventor, Thomas Savery, at Hampton Court in 1698. A better machine, invented

[10] On all this see below, pp.41–3.

independently by Thomas Newcomen, appeared in 1712, capable of lifting 45 litres of water 45 metres through tiers of pumps, and so successful did it prove in the collieries and tin-mines of Great Britain that within fifteen years it was also in use in the Spanish Netherlands, France, Sweden, Germany, Austria and as far afield as Hungary.

The other inventions of any industrial significance were not adopted so speedily, nor did they owe their creation to scientific discovery. The stocking-frame, for example, developed in 1589 by an English clergyman, William Lee, was so unpopular in England that its inventor left for France — only to meet with a similarly hostile reception. The truth was that, unlike the steam pump which created opportunities for employment in mines hitherto flooded, labour-saving devices in the textile industry were suspected of causing unemployment: consequently it was not merely the workmen who rejected them but the local authorities too who banned their use in order to prevent riots and the spread of vagabondage. Industrialists themselves were not greatly exercised; since there was no shortage of cheap labour, labour-saving devices were not worth the trouble and expense, and the fate of the stocking-frame was shared by the ribbon loom, a device invented in Danzig by which the simple movement of one bar sufficed to produce six narrow weaves simultaneously. Introduced into London in 1616 and Leyden in 1620, it provoked such opposition that finally its use was banned not only in England and the Netherlands, but throughout Austria and the Holy Roman Empire. Even as late as the eighteenth century the city of Basle prohibited an attempt to harness it to water power.

Important though these inventions might be for the future, their impact on Europe in the seventeenth century was negligible. They represented the exception rather than the rule; technology not only made few advances on positions gained in the later Middle Ages, it was hardly considered by most business men as a potential factor in improving production and in making bigger profits. The major industries of building, shipbuilding, metallurgy and textile manufacture, and the local crafts of the smith, the joiner and the miller, remained basically unchanged save for the empirical refinement of existing practices. In shipbuilding, for example, there were interesting developments but no sensational advances. While trading ships altered little in size and shape — even the great East Indiamen of 800 tonnes were not of unprecedented size — warships lowered their poops, cultivated larger, lower lines and occasionally attained to 1,500 tonnes: this of course was as large as the resources of the age could permit, since the *Sovereign of the Seas*, for instance, built for Charles I of England, required the destruction of two thousand oak trees, covering fifty acres of woodland. Design was largely a matter for rule of thumb: the midships section of a well-known ship was often reduced to scale and used as a model for others, but there was little attempt to modify design for novel purposes, except among the Dutch, who saw that experiment could be commercially profitable. Their herring *busses*, for example were decked over and enlarged so that after the fish had been caught, coopers and salters could prepare the catch for market long before returning to port: the *fluitschips*, too, were a triumph of design; transports with rigging simplified to need less crew, they were planned to carry goods swiftly and succeeded so brilliantly that their owners could fit in one extra voyage to the Baltic every year.

The endemic nature of warfare in the seventeenth century, and its greater scale, prompted a general assault on Europe's mineral resources.[11] At the siege of Magdeburg, for example, Tilly expended 12,000 to 18,000 cannon balls every day for a period of two months; yet even though the demand for cast iron increased so much the technique of smelting was still handicapped by its dependence upon charcoal, since no way was found to employ less expensive fuels without increasing the carbon impurities in the metal. Within this limitation, the pattern of production changed considerably. In 1600 England was the primary producer of iron in Europe; by 1700 she was producing 17,000 tonnes a year, but Sweden had overtaken her during the Thirty Years War with an annual production of 45,000 tonnes of which 30,000 were exported. The German states together increased their production to 30,000 tonnes, France reached 25,000 and Russia sprang from 5,000 to 20,000 during the single span of Tsar Peter's reign.[12] England's primacy was only to be recovered as a

[11] See Chapter VIII, p.381, for example, on the exploitation of copper-mining in Sweden.

[12] See Chapter X, p.466.

result of the secret experiments in coke-smelting which the
Darbys of Coalbrookdale first began in 1706.

The conservatism of European industry in the seventeenth
century is partly explained by three separate factors. Both in the
social esteem and in the profits it offered, industry took second
place to commerce and hence it rarely attracted the most
acquisitive and ambitious minds. More important than this, the
basic problem was the commercial one of finding new markets; a
contrast to the nineteenth century, for example, when the
problem was to produce goods more swiftly and more cheaply
than anyone else. Consequently there was little emphasis on
productivity as an end in itself: indeed, the greater part of
industrial production was designed for the maker's own use.
Europe was essentially an agrarian community, there was little
profit from farming to devote to the purchase of commodities
other than food, and as a result it was left to most men to use the
local raw materials in their spare time to make their own cloth
and to fashion their own tools and furniture. A few who found in
this a more congenial occupation than tilling the fields set up as
specialists, but their activities were severely limited by the cost
and difficulty of transporting their products beyond their own
locality. Very few had the skill, the capital and the enterprise to
manufacture goods for markets elsewhere, and Colbert found it
necessary in his plans to stimulate productivity[13] to compensate
for these deficiencies by drawing upon the resources of the state
itself.

The third and most important factor restraining technological
and industrial experiment was that, given the capitalist, whether
an industrial entrepreneur, an association of individuals, or a
state-backed joint-stock company, there remained the problem of
industrial control. It was difficult, often impossible to persuade
workers to adopt new techniques in order to sell their products
more competitively outside their region. The industrial organisation known as the cottage or domestic system suffered greatly
from this disadvantage. In theory the capitalist provided the raw
materials and distributed them among the workers in their own
homes, who then produced the goods according to his
specifications and returned the finished product to him for sale in
local or distant markets. But in practice the sanctions left to the

[13] See Chapter VI, pp.317–23.

employer were often inadequate. Because the domestic worker was usually in a position to derive an alternative livelihood from the land, since industrial activity was often a part-time occupation, he was sufficiently free to work as he pleased, even to the extent of withdrawing his labour without necessarily ruining himself. This was very important because of all those involved in the industrial process the worker was the least likely to comprehend the need for change in methods of production.[14]

A possible solution, though one generally beyond the means of the seventeenth century, was to establish factories employing full-time labour, so that the worker was not only supervised more closely, but, being thus more dependent upon his employer for his livelihood, became more amenable to discipline. This, however, was discouraged by the cost of building a factory and of supplying it with machinery; only where the nature of the product was such as to demand close supervision and the concentration of highly skilled workers was there any economic incentive for large workshops. While small-scale metal production might still be carried on at home, the manufacture of cannon required the establishment of a factory: similarly the *Manufactures Royales* were initiated by Colbert to perform specialist functions, such as the great works at Abbeville set up by the Van Robais to produce luxury cloth, but they were an expensive venture scarcely typical of industry in general during the seventeenth century.

Commerce

Despite the discoveries of the fifteenth and sixteenth centuries and the spectacular efforts of individuals and companies to establish trading stations across the world, most merchants were still primarily concerned with the transportation of goods from one region to another in Europe. But if the geography of European trade remained much the same, its control was passing into very different hands, and the seventeenth century witnessed the final stages in a long process by which the Italian republics and the Hanseatic cities, both based on the shores of inland seas,

[14] See the case of the Widow Falempin, and Colbert's failure to bring French domestic workers within the aegis of a nationally regulated textile industry, in Chapter VI, p.319.

lost their monopolies to the states on the Atlantic seaboard. The Italians had controlled Europe's trade with the Levant, not only for the Mediterranean produce of wines, oils and fruits to be purchased in Aleppo, Beirut or Jaffa, but also for the spices and silks shipped overland from the Indian ocean. The opening of the new route to India around the Cape had done them less harm than they had feared: their problem was to compete with English, French and Dutch interlopers in the Mediterranean itself. They were handicapped by the growth of Turkish naval power in the previous century which had destroyed much of their trade, and their banking houses had been drained of wealth by the bankruptcies of successive Spanish governments. In the seventeenth century, therefore, though their cities retained much individual importance, their days of collective pre-eminence were over.

In conscious imitation of the Italians the member cities of the Hanseatic League, stretched around the shores of the Baltic and along the west coast of Scandinavia, had succeeded by the fifteenth century in controlling all trade between their shores and the markets of Germany, England and the Netherlands. They trafficked in wares less exotic than the Italians' but no less valuable, exporting corn and naval stores, and monopolising both the cod fisheries off the Lofoten Islands and the herring grounds of Scania: salted fish was in great demand, and in a good year the catch frequently exceeded 13,000 tonnes. Wealth had given the Hanse political power: they had made possible the Yorkist invasion of England by Edward IV and they supplied aid to Gustavus Vasa's rebellion,[15] but they could not withstand the rise of strong national governments in Denmark, Sweden and, ultimately, Brandenburg and Russia, which destroyed the concept of commercial co-operation in the Baltic and substituted a long struggle for military supremacy. In addition there was the competition of the Dutch who broke into the Hanseatic enclave to fish for herrings, and whose competitive techniques outstripped those of their rivals. They invented a new process for salting, and their herring *busses* were equipped to process the catch at sea. Worse still, the herrings themselves had turned fickle and deserted the Baltic for the North Sea. Hanseatic towns like Stralsund and Danzig still enjoyed a measure of prosperity in the

15 See Chapter VIII, p.371.

seventeenth century, though both suffered from Sweden's expansion, but the bulk of the Baltic trade fell into the hands of the Dutch, the French and the English. The last Diet of the Hanseatic League met in 1669.

The first effective challenge to the supremacy of the Italian and Baltic towns had come from Antwerp. As Bruges, her local rival and a Hanseatic base, was left stranded by the silting-up of the river Zwyn, Antwerp became the Staple for the English Merchant Adventurers and replaced Venice as the European copper market; moreover, as the effect of the overseas discoveries began to take place, she became the market for the colonial produce of the Spanish and Portuguese empires. With the Dutch revolt and the blockade of the Scheldt, however, she lost her trade and influence to Amsterdam, but not so swiftly as to allay all Dutch fears of her recovery if liberated from Spanish rule in 1645.[16] Amsterdam's pre-eminence, and with it the commercial supremacy of the Dutch, coincided almost exactly with the limits of the seventeenth century. As every prince attempted to erect his own Versailles, as every court hastened to adopt French fashions in dress and deportment, so, in matters of commerce, it was the Dutch who were the exemplars of Europe. Unfortunately for them they were the first to suffer from successful imitation, and competition from England and France began to make inroads into their monopoly of the carrying trade.[17] Amsterdam, however, yet remained unrivalled as the very hub of European commerce, its principal money market and exchange.

No commercial venture could succeed without capital, and this was generally provided by the partnership of two or more individuals. Such a relationship was essentially a personal one, often restricted to the operation of a single voyage or expedition, and by its very nature could not survive indefinitely. In place of this type of regulated company, an association of traders, the English by 1600 had developed the joint-stock company, an association of capital. Its merit was that it attracted the capital of investors who knew nothing of commerce, but whose interests were safeguarded by an elected board of officials. Shareholders

[16] See Chapter V, p.282–4.

[17] Dutch supremacy was the cardinal feature of commercial history in the seventeenth century. V, pp.241–8 and 282–4. See also Chapter VI, pp.321–2 for a study of French commercial companies.

might sell their stock, the stock might fall in value, individual officials might resign or die, but the joint-stock company itself could remain indifferent to such events: it had achieved a type of immortality. The Dutch swiftly appropriated the idea from England, and the rest of Europe from the Dutch. The joint-stock company was of particular value in undertaking a sustained series of long range commercial ventures, such as those of the East and West India Companies, which were far beyond the pockets of any group of individual merchants. It was also a useful device for the encouragement or control of trade by the state.[18]

Nevertheless there is a danger of confusing the spectacular with the normal; the joint-stock company for all its significance was still a rarity. Just as the bulk of trade was still essentially confined within the boundaries of Europe, so it was that the individual merchant, backed by his family or a few partners, remained the typical figure in seventeenth-century commerce.

POLITICAL THEORY AND PRACTICE[19]

Warfare, Absolutism and Political Philosophy

In the Middle Ages political theory and feudal practice assumed that states were not so much political organisms as interchangeable items of inheritance. Territories were only superficially united in the person of one prince since effective central control, except on occasion in England and Sicily, was prevented by the autonomous powers vested in local feudatories, ecclesiastical princes and corporate towns. In the sixteenth century the empire of Charles V provided a classic example of this: not only did he inherit the Habsburg lands in Austria, the combined thrones of Castile and Aragon and the Duchy of Burgundy, but within these separate states his title was further fragmented as, in the Netherlands, Duke of Brabant, Count of Flanders or Marquess of Antwerp. This personal empire was even then an anachronism: the trend in the sixteenth century was already towards the

[18] See Chapter VI, pp.321–2, for examples of state direction.

[19] Since this section generalises much of the material described in subsequent chapters, cross-references for all topics would be distracting, and references will be made only where they seem necessary to assist an understanding of the text.

so-called 'New Monarchy' from which evolved some of the absolutist concepts of the seventeenth century.

The source of absolutism in Europe has been traced to the revival of Roman law in the twelfth century. Customary law arose from the complex gradations which had evolved in western European society; since this society was essentially hierarchic, one man's lord another man's vassal, it laid down no harsh dividing line between bond and free, between ruler and subject. Roman law, on the other hand, recognised neither the indeterminate status of the villein nor the disjunctive nature of medieval sovereignty. The villein was thus condemned to serfdom, since if he was not wholly *liber* he must be deemed wholly *servus*, and the sovereign declared absolute: 'Quod principi placuit legis habet vigorem.' Yet though the villein lost his freedom straightway, four centuries supervened before the prince became absolute; consequently some more immediate explanation of seventeenth-century monarchy must be found.

The answer probably lies in the extended scope of warfare after 1500. Operations were on a larger scale than in the past, the number of men under arms increased, campaigns were more prolonged, so that a revolution was necessary in the organisation and equipment of armies. Novel problems of recruitment and finance arose which could only be solved by strengthening the powers of the prince so that his decisions might be obeyed unquestioningly by all his subjects everywhere. Since the machinery of state was not only rudimentary but was also in the hands of the great noble families, it was necessary to follow the suppression of regional franchises and class privileges with the creation of an efficient bureaucracy, loyal to the prince who alone gave it its authority. Moreover, since rebellion endangered security and made it impossible to mobilise the country's resources, domestic faction and religious dissent had first to be silenced before effective preparations could be made for war. Ideally,[20] therefore, the European state best qualified to wage successful war was the one in which central direction, administrative uniformity and efficiency had been established.

A philosophical justification of this political development had gained ground steadily since the Renaissance. Unlike the

---

[20] For a summary of what tended to happen in practice see below, pp.27–8, 297–300.

political philosophy of the Middle Ages the new concept was wholly secular. It paid only lip service to the notion of monarchy by divine right and it regarded the state as a self-sufficient entity, a law unto itself, with its own morality — *raison d'état*. The anarchy of the Italian wars prompted Machiavelli to demonstrate that a strong and stable community could only be secured by princely absolutism. In a similar environment, that of the French wars of religion, Bodin expounded in his *Six Livres de la République* a similar doctrine, prescribing an absolute monarchy exercising, 'supreme power un-restrained by law over citizens and subjects'. Such a philosophy justified the disregard of established rights and customs, and the destruction of rival authorities within the state, on the grounds of expediency and national strength.

So too in England during the civil war of the seventeenth century Thomas Hobbes gave classic expression to this theory in his *Leviathan*, a book which was all the more effective for its air of scientific infallibility. Hobbes indeed owed much to his scientific interests. Fired by the new enthusiasm for mathematical modes of reasoning, he tried to apply Descarte's *esprit géométrique*[21] to society at large, to construct a political philosophy as exact as a geometric proof. He agreed that if Euclid aroused as much passion as did politics, then people would argue equally as much over geometry, but he believed that by the application of a rational technique a similar science of politics was practicable. He agreed with Galileo that all explanations expressed in terms of substantial form or essential nature were tautological.[22] A pellet of wax sank or floated not according to its essential nature, but to its specific gravity. Similarly, man did not create the state because he was a political animal, as Aristotle maintained, but because his reason taught him that only thus could he avoid violent death. Life in Hobbes's state of nature was, 'solitary, poor, nasty, brutish and short', an atomistic view of equally competitive individuals constantly striving with each other, which clearly reflected the corpuscular theory of matter of his fellow countryman Boyle. At bottom, of course, the emotional basis of Hobbes's lay not in science but in his experience of the civil war, which he then identified with life in its natural state: 'Hereby it is manifest that during the time men live without a common power to keep them all in awe they are in that condition which is called war, and such a war as is of every man against every man.'

In these circumstances it was only to be expected that Hobbes should seek to establish security of person and property, and in doing so should be willing to pay heavily in terms of personal liberty. He thus defined his new concept of the state, combining total responsibility with total power: 'This is that great Leviathan, or rather (to speak more reverently) that Mortall God, to which we owe under the Immortal God our peace and defence.' In this state morality is no longer the basis of law, but law — the sovereign's decree — is the basis of morality. Hobbes did in fact allow for considerable modification of this totalitarian principle, since he established the origins of the sovereign power in the doctrine of popular consent, and always recognised that 'the obligation of subjects to the sovereign is understood to last as long and no longer than the power lasteth by which he is able to protect them'. Hobbes's utilitarian philosophy was too hedonist and too materialist for his contemporaries wholly to accept. Nonetheless, the divorce of political theory from theological belief was becoming increasingly clear, and the seventeenth century witnessed the gradual secularisation of political standards. Even Bossuet, with his *Politique tirée des Propres Paroles de l'Écriture Sainte*, merely used scripture to refute the Protestant apologists of rebellion, and to corroborate his own views which were clearly derived from the political circumstances of seventeenth-century France.

Also secular in outlook was Grotius, the Dutch polymath who fled from Holland after Oldenbarneveldt's execution, and whose most famous work, *De Jure Belli et Pacis*, was published in Paris in 1625. Though his plea for international law was backed by massive and detailed quotation not merely from legal authorities but from the Bible and the Fathers, it is evident that his most vital source of inspiration was the Stoic concept of natural law, a concept essentially rational and secular. Moreover he too was fascinated by the scientific advances of his day and, like Hobbes, believed that ethics and politics were potentially demonstrable sciences. To this end he sought to provide a chain of reasoning sufficiently exhaustive, sufficiently systematic, and backed by every conceivable authority in order to convince mankind of his urgent thesis, that there was a common law between nations, valid in peace and war. His experience of the Dutch revolt and the Thirty Years War gave substance to his humanitarian desire to prevent war from becoming 'nothing but a riot of fury as though authorisation had been given for every sort of crime'. Consequently he tried to apply the rules of right reason, of natural law, to the actions of sovereign states. As for the states themselves, Grotius assumed that their rulers were wholly responsible for their actions: 'That power is called supreme whose acts are not subject to another's jurisdiction in such a way that they can be rendered void by the decision of another human authority.'

The evolution of a political philosophy under the pressure of a changing environment is best seen in the work of Spinoza, a fellow countryman of Grotius, better known for his more general philosophical works.[23] Like Hobbes and Grotius he tried to make his reasoning as cogent as a mathematical proof — the *more geometrico* — but he shifted his basic premises too radically to succeed in this. He began by extolling an idealist view of democracy but, as the friend and admirer of Jan de Witt, and living in a society which promoted security, liberty, commercial expansion and a flourishing culture, he began to consider the attractions of benign oligarchy. In 1672 all this was rudely shattered by the power of absolute France: from that moment there was little to distinguish Spinoza's attitude from Hobbes's. Since nothing seemed comparable to the virtues of peace and security, the function of the state, defined in the *Tractatus Politicus* (1677), 'is purely and simply to guarantee peace and security.' Spinoza continued: 'It follows that the best state is that in which men live their lives in concord and in which their rights are inviolate', but these rights were not to be tolerated if their operation weakened the guarantor of security, the Sovereign. The clear-eyed disillusionment of the philosopher is reflected in his dictum, 'It is not wisdom but authority that makes a law.'

Absolutism

The basis of political practice in the seventeenth century was the identification of the state with the sovereign, a view expressed

23 See below, p.67.

characteristically by Louis XIV: 'When you are working for the good of the state you are working for yourself; the good of the one constitutes the glory of the other.' To achieve this the prince had first to control the separate units of medieval society — the Estates, the great noble households, the church and the corporate towns. If the federal nature of this society presented a challenge, it also offered a means of attaining control since, so self-regarding were these separate units, the crown could play off one against the other, especially by offering to one group alone the opportunity to win rewards in the royal service which were not otherwise available. In eastern Europe, where there was no powerful middle class to set against the nobles, the rulers of Russia and Austria secured the nobles' loyalty by granting to them greater powers over their serfs, a concession which in no way weakened the crown. This was true also of Brandenburg, but here the Great Elector went further, following a practice begun in Sweden by Gustavus Adolphus, and gave the nobles an entirely new function in the state as leaders of the administration.

One feature common to the growth of absolutism in every country, except of course in England and Poland where absolutism made no headway, was the eclipse of the Estates, since the very existence of popular assemblies challenged royal supremacy. Some of them, as in Aragon, might control taxation; others, in Castile, served simply as sounding boards for public opinion, but whatever their function they naturally sought to extend it. 'The more you rely on such bodies', wrote the Great Elector to his son, 'the more you lose your authority since the Estates are always trying to weaken your sovereign power.' The Austrian Habsburgs shared his view. They took advantage of their conquest of Bohemia to annihilate the powers of the Estates, and even that most powerful and independent of assemblies, the Hungarian Diet, was brought under control by 1720: dependence upon Vienna was the price of Hungary's liberation from the Turks. In France the Bourbons solved the problem by dispensing altogether with the States-General except on one occasion, in 1614, which significantly enough was a moment of royal weakness after the assassination of Henry IV. The reduction of the provincial Estates, achieved already in the *pays d'élections*, was completed in the *pays d'état* by Richelieu and Louis XIV. Paradoxically, the Swedish *riksdag* survived, but only in order to strengthen the absolutism of Charles XI and Charles XII against the ambitions of the *rad* to establish a permanent oligarchy. The government of the United Provinces was less of an exception than might appear, since in this case it was the States-General which became the sovereign, exercising an increasing measure of control over the separate provinces of the Union of Utrecht. For all their propaganda the regents of Holland and the princes of Orange, who contested control of the States-General, worked continually to strengthen its authority at the expense of local assemblies and urban councils.

The destruction or weakening of popular assemblies was not enough: it was equally important to ensure control of the Church which, as the second estate and with claims upon men's deepest loyalties, represented a rival authority within the state. 'Rex est in regno suo imperator', ran the dictum of Roman law: henceforward, as the monopoly of Rome was replaced by royal monopolies across Europe, the monarch was also to be pope. If the prince became a Protestant, as in north Germany, Sweden and Denmark, he could then appropriate ecclesiastical revenues and secularise monastic lands: equally important, he could control appointments to benefices, supervise the policies of his clergy and make the national Church serve his needs. But Erastianism of this sort was not confined to Protestant princes. If he remained a Catholic, the prince could none the less insist upon a greater measure of control over his clergy. Orthodoxy did not entail submission to Rome, and a feature of the Counter-Reformation had been the compacts made between the papacy and such states as Bavaria and Austria, by which the prince was guaranteed greater powers in return for his suppression of heresy. Kings of France had in any case enjoyed absolute control over the appointment of their clergy since the Concordat of Bologna (1516), and, as the *régale* crisis demonstrated,[24] they were accustomed to rely on their support against the rival authority of the pope. So too in Spain, where the Inquisition was virtually a department of state and where papal bulls were promulgated only with royal permission, their Most Catholic Majesties enjoyed absolute authority over the Church.

The Churches were particularly dependent upon the state for success in their struggle with their rivals. Lutheranism was

[24] See Chapter VI, pp.304–6.

established solely by the action of princes, and the Counter-Reformation owed its successes as much to the prince as to the priest. The conflict of denominations endangered the state and thus the sovereign was as eager as his clergy to suppress heresy. Nor was his interest confined to rival Churches. The seventeenth-century ruler disliked all signs of nonconformity and diversity within the established church of his state, and the Jansenists in Catholic France suffered as severely from the secular authorities as did the Arminians of Calvinist Holland. The goal of political absolutism precluded toleration: the individual was allowed to worship freely only where the prince was not supreme, and wherever toleration had been granted there was a strong tendency for it to be revoked, as it was in Bohemia (1621), in Hungary (1678) and in France (1685), as the powers of the sovereign increased. Tolerance could only make its way unofficially when the conflict of sects had abated, as in Holland after Gomarist rigorism had become a spent force, or in England when the political circumstances of 1689 made toleration of a sort advisable: in either case it was toleration by Protestants of other Protestants. There was no truce in the rivalry of Protestant and Catholic.

The absolute power which princes sought to acquire could not be exercised through the traditional offices of state, since these were too closely wedded to the medieval system from which they had sprung. Consequently their titles were abolished, their powers emasculated or their functions transformed. This is what happened in East Prussia where the independent and powerful *Oberrathe* became, in the Great Elector's words, 'councillors and servants who derive their power only from their lord; without his will and his approval they have no power to do or to decide anything in his affairs, except in conformity with their instructions'. These great officers of state should not too readily be acclaimed as martyrs to the cause of absolutism. The liberty they championed was too often a cloak for inefficiency or for their own tyranny in local affairs. Their place was taken by men of outstanding brilliance, not merely subservient to the crown but distinguished by their comprehensive grasp of the essentials of administration. Such men, the epitome of bureaucracy, shared the same outlook whatever country they claimed their own: in the committees of the Holland Estates, in the Viennese Chancery, in the *conseil du roi*, in the *Reduktion* commissions, in the *Generalkriegs-kommissariat*, they strove after uniformity, good order and the rational exploitation of the states' resources. Without them the absolutist assumptions of the seventeenth-century prince would have been worthless.

Mercantilism: Political Economy

Warfare and bureaucracy imposed so great a burden on the royal exchequer that no sovereign could survive unless the economic resources of his state were exploited to the full. Since his power to tax at will was valueless if there were no wealth to be taxed, the creation of wealth became a matter for government direction. There was also a strong argument for unifying territories by economic as well as political ties by the introduction of a single currency, of standard weights and measures, of improved communications and of uniform regulations for trade and industry. Wealth, moreover, encouraged civil peace: the most significant fact about Bacon's dictum, 'money is like muck, not good except it be spread,' is that it comes not from his essay on *Riches* but from that on *Seditions and Troubles*. This clear-sighted analyst of politics knew well that poverty was a potent cause of rebellion, and thus the sovereign was required to concern himself with his people's material welfare as a necessary means of defence.

For these reasons the seventeenth-century ruler had a vested interest in promoting the economic welfare of his state. To do so he evolved a system of direction, regulation and encouragement which has been generally termed the 'mercantile system' or 'mercantilism', a term invented in the eighteenth century as a generalisation about the previous century's practices and beliefs in these matters. It has been held these practices were simply the extension, on a national scale, of the regulations governing the economy of the medieval towns, the paternalism of the guilds being replaced by the paternalism of the state. But this was not the full story. Medieval economic thought was dominated by religious ideas of a 'just price', by a desire to protect the artisan from unfair competition, and by the notion that an adequate livelihood and a fair return for honest work were ends in themselves. The seventeenth-century state, on the other hand, was organised for the acquisition of power, and this demanded the endless exploitation of national resources. The mercantilist sought to increase the wealth of his country immoderately, and without moral limitations, so that the exchequer might replenish itself unceasingly from the accumulating wealth of the taxpayers: his purpose was not primarily to enrich the public at large but to force the economy into the service of the state.

A principal characteristic of seventeenth-century political economy was the identification of military and political power with the possession of gold. It seemed to explain, for example, the momentary ascendancy of Spain, and mercantilists therefore concentrated on measures designed to acquire greater supplies of the previous metals — hence the use of the term 'bullionist' to describe their policies. They believed that gold was a limited commodity which was a view encouraged to some extent by the ever-decreasing proportion of gold and silver to copper in the shipments from America to Spain by 1600, and that its acquisition was possible only by theft or commercial competition. Colbert, moreover, drawing close parallels between the wealth and the power of Venice in the past and of Holland in his own day, believed that commerce itself nourished national greatness, and he shared with his contemporaries the notion that commerce too was limited in its volume. Despite the fact that greater opportunities for trade were being opened up in America and in the Far East, this view was substantially sound at the time, for the bulk of European trade was within Europe itself,[25] and the steady inflation of the previous century which had stimulated economic activity had been checked. To expand their trade states would therefore have to fight.

Commerce was in any case an aggressive occupation, especially in an age of insecure craft and mutinous crews, of pirates and wreckers, and the respectable merchant slipped easily from commerce to contraband, from trade to theft. In its search for the constituents of power, the seventeenth century merely added one further hazard, national exclusiveness or commercial war. If trade had to be filched from the foreigner, governments were quick to fashion their weapons. Government agencies were established, as the *Kommerzkolleg* in Vienna and the Council of

[25] See above, p.15, and, for a detailed study of Colbert's application of mercantilist ideas, see Chapter VI, pp.317–23.

Trade in London, to direct the strategy of the operation: state companies were formed, as the Dutch West India Company and the French *Compagnie du Nord*, to drive their rivals from selected areas: tariffs were imposed and goods proscribed, as in the Navigation Act of 1651 and the Methuen Treaty of 1703, in order to deny home ports to foreign ships or to boycott an enemy's exports. When all this failed, governments turned to war. The Dutch fought the English three times for essentially commercial reasons. When the two combined against France, the French tariffs of 1667, the success of the *Compagnie du Nord* in the Baltic by 1688, the threat of a French monopoly of Spanish trade in 1702, were potent factors in the resultant wars against Louis XIV, whatever other issues were involved. Colbert was clearly justified in his report of 1669 that, 'le commerce cause un combat perpétuel en paix et en guerre entre les nations de l'Europe, à qui en emportera la meilleure partie. Les Hollandais, Anglais et Francais sont les acteurs de ce combat.'

The mercantilist thus constructed an economic system geared to the needs of warfare: in the words of the contemporary dictum, 'Trade is the source of public finance, and public finance is the vital nerve of war.' Any benefits which accrued to the individual by the regulation of industry or trade were incidental to the prime purpose of mercantilism. It was not concerned with the creation of prosperity for its own sake, nor with the raising of the standard of living as an end in itself: its purpose was political. Colbert, naturally enough, became so enthusiastically involved in his projects to revitalise industry that he clearly forgot this on occasion, but he never failed to recognise that even the interests of the economy were subordinate to those of the state in its struggle for power. Tariffs designed to stimulate the export of manufactured goods in place of raw materials could not be kept artificially low when the cost of warfare forced the Treasury to raise all taxes indiscriminately, and subsidies to newly established industries took second place to military expenditure. The periodic depreciation of the currency during the last decades of Louis XIV's reign prejudiced the success of industry, the continual recourse to higher taxation restricted consumption and expenditure, and regulations for the good of industry frequently became mere devices for taxing the worker.

It was thus the weakness of mercantilism in practice that,

while it recognised that economic growth was a vital prerequisite to the pursuit of power, and that governmental direction was often necessary to promote this growth, the onset of the very wars which these policies were intended to sustain resulted in their being abandoned and, frequently, in national insolvency.

The Limits to Absolutism

The absolutism of seventeenth-century government must not be equated with totalitarianism. Arbitrary though the powers of the absolute monarch might be, and considerably more comprehensive than those wielded by his predecessors, they were yet meagre by modern standards. In the imposing façade of power there were significant flaws. In the first place there was the insurmountable difficulty of communication. The time taken for an order to be sent from Paris, Brandenburg, Madrid, Stockholm, Moscow or Vienna to royal officers in Languedoc, Cleves, Catalonia, Livonia, Siberia or Transylvania, and the difficulties involved in calling these far-flung agents to account, explain the impossibility of maintaining absolute control over the administration until the age of modern transport and communication. Local officials were only too ready to ignore despatches whose contents they disliked, and it could take many years before the central government discovered that its orders were not being implemented. The vagaries of the postal services then provided offenders with the excuse that their orders had never arrived.

Though the expansion of bureaucracy was a feature of the century, the absolute monarch still had only a few servants on whom he might implicitly rely. His councils were staffed with men whose obedience and loyalty were never in doubt, but there were very few officials to enforce his policies away from the centre of government. No matter how hardworking they were, such men could not exercise that supervision over every member of society which is the prerogative of a modern civil service, since many of the functions which today devolve upon the central government or its provincial agents were then fulfilled by the traditional local authorities. Even in France, where the work of men like Colbert did so much to bring the body of the population under the aegis of the royal councils, it was the local *parlement*, the local noble or the local corporation which still acted as the authority most

directly affecting the daily life of the average individual. It was
unlikely that such bodies would openly oppose the decrees of an
absolute monarch, but their enforcement of them might be
ludicrously ineffectual. The activities of royal intendants and
inspectors were thus confined to checking the grosser abuses of
local authorities and to dealing with openly recalcitrant individuals. Even the intendant, or his equivalent outside France,
might tend to escape royal control by overlong residence in a
particular province so that he too acquired a parochial attitude to
the dictates of the central government.

Instead of ruling a society of individuals whose equality only
served to expose them uniformly to the power of his government,
the seventeenth-century monarch governed a society whose
hierarchic structure afforded bastions of privilege to protect the
separate classes from the full force of his power. He might
strengthen his authority by playing off one class against another,
but he could not destroy the privileges of a class if these were
jealously guarded or vigorously upheld. French nobles were
excluded from the administration and their ability to wage
private war destroyed, but Louis XIV at his greatest did not dare
to tax them as he taxed his peasants. Similarly, the *junkers* in
Brandenburg, the *boyars* in Russia and the nobles of the
Danubian Monarchy did not acknowledge the augmented
powers of their sovereigns until they themselves had been
confirmed and strengthened in their social privileges. Serfs apart,
every stratum of society was hedged about and protected by
time-honoured privileges, and though the prince might arbitrari-
ly strike at individuals, and even reverse individual traditions, he
could not challenge classes as a whole. Only when a class was in
decline, as in the north German towns, or had been defeated in
war, as in Bohemia, could its traditional privileges be overthrown. Absolutism, in short, was remarkably ineffective in a
society based upon privilege, and the governments of the
seventeenth century had far less direct impact upon the daily
lives of their subjects than their successors in the egalitarian
societies of the modern age.

By the end of the century there came a significant trend in
political thought away from royal absolutism. The state had
emerged as the central concept of political theory: this of course
might be linked, as in the writings of Bossuet and Hobbes, with

the concept of royal absolutism, but there arose an alternative notion that the prince himself might not always serve the best interests of the state. *Raison d'état* might then be invoked, not for the prince but against him, and even Hobbes had recognised that when the sovereign failed to protect his subjects they were free to rebel. Fénelon, a man who experienced the full rigour of Louis XIV's power, appealed to a visionary past in which the aristocracy had provided a form of government which had best served the interests of the people. Though in this respect he was wholly out of touch with the realities both of the past and of the present, his denunciation of the king's personal policies as running counter to the nation's interests is most significant. In a letter to the Duc de Chevreuse in 1710, he wrote: 'Our misfortune arises from the fact that the war has hitherto been the affair of the king alone, who is ruined and discredited. It is necessary that there should be spread throughout our nation an intimate conviction that it is the nation itself that in its own interests bears the burden of this war.'

This deliberate separation of the sovereign and the state, in contrast to the generally held identification of the two, was repeated early in the following century by Montesquieu, who wrote of England: 'I call it free because the sovereign, whose person is controlled and limited, is unable to inflict any imaginable harm on anyone.' In England the reaction against absolutism had reached its climax in the Glorious Revolution of 1688, its permanent expression in the parliamentary settlement of 1689–1715, and its philosophical justification in the writings of John Locke. 'For all power given with trust for the attaining an end being limited by that end, whenever that end is manifestly neglected or opposed the trust must necessarily be forfeited, and the power devolve into the hands of these that gave it, who may place it anew where they shall think best for their safety and security. And thus the community perpetually retains a supreme power of saving themselves from the attempts and designs of anybody, even of the legislators, whenever they shall be so foolish or so wicked, as to lay and carry on designs against the liberties and properties of the subject.'

The emphasis was shifting from the rights of the king to the rights of his subjects: the maxim, 'quod principi placuit legis habet vigorem', was being offset by another, 'lex est quod populus romanus constituebat', which represented the obverse side to Hobbes's theory of the social contract. Its essence was to insist upon government as the action of society, delegated perhaps to one man but always revocable. The government acts as a trustee, and this fiduciary concept is also the basis of Fénelon's demand, 'Is the flock made for the shepherd or the shepherd for the flock?' There was very little thought along these lines outside France and England, perhaps because elsewhere the centralised state was only just being established, but once monarchy had become absolute in Austria, Prussia and Russia, there were strong hints of this same concept behind the behaviour of the Enlightened Despots of the eighteenth century.

THE SCIENTIFIC REVOLUTION

New Methods and New Aims in Scientific Discovery

In the Middle Ages scholars were concerned less with the exact description of natural objects than with the construction of philosophical and logical systems: 'This kind of degenerate learning', wrote Bacon, who was one of the first to attack it, 'did chiefly reign among the schoolmen; who having sharp and strong wits and abundance of leisure, and small variety of reading, but their wits being shut up in the cells of a few authors (chiefly Aristotle their dictator), as their persons were shut up in the cells of monasteries and colleges, and knowing little history, either of nature or of time, did of no great quantity of matter and infinite agitation of wit spin out unto us those laborious webs of learning which are extant in their books.'

But Bacon was less than just: the classical scientists, Aristotle, Galen and Ptolemy, had already provided explanations of the material world[26] which satisfied so fully the demands of common sense, and which were then so smoothly integrated into Christian theology by St Thomas Aquinas in the thirteenth century, that to question them was not only to question common sense but to venture into heresy. As a result scientific study in the Middle Ages was mainly the literary transmission of classical science,

26 For these explanations see below, pp.39, 43, 47.

experiments being conducted only to demonstrate accepted truths. Albertus Magnus of Cologne, who is credited with the close study of natural history in the twelfth century wrote of the ostrich: 'It is said of this bird that it swallows and digests iron, but I have not found this myself because several ostriches refused to eat the iron which I threw them.' There were very few who wrote like this. The majority preferred their bestiaries stuffed with biblical exegesis and little natural history, following St Augustine's dictum that it mattered less whether an animal existed than what it symbolised.

Mathematicians at Oxford in the twelfth century and at Paris in the thirteenth began to query some of the principles of Aristotle's physics, the weakest element in the corpus of classical science and when Duns Scotus and William of Occam, two English Franciscans of the fourteenth century, had exposed serious flaws in the philosophy of Aquinas, the way was prepared for further inquiry. Occam was particularly important for his belief that nature does everything in the simplest manner, and his famous Razor, 'entia non sunt multiplicanda praeter necessitatem', was a plea for the rejection of unnecessary hypotheses. Under his influence Parisian scholars came close to the modern theory of impetus, and it might have been thought that a major breakthrough in science was to be expected by the time of the Renaissance. Curiously enough, though art and literature, politics and philosophy were immediately affected, the impact of the Renaissance on science was principally to reinforce the authority of the ancients, since it was they who were held up by the humanists as models of perfection. Nevertheless, the recovery of classical texts did lead to some discoveries in science: the full text of Aristotle on biology, his best subject, had never been accessible to medieval scholars, nor had the original text of Galen on medicine. Moreover, the revival of Platonic and Pythagorean concepts of the universe at variance with those of Aristotle, as well as the rediscovery of Archimedes, whose teaching did not fit into any of the accepted systems of thought, made it possible, as at the University of Padua, for Aristotle to be challenged: and it was no accident that there, in one of the few centres of relatively free thought, both Galileo and Vesalius were professors.

The great developments in Renaissance art did much to stimulate the study of anatomy, perspective and natural history, and Leonardo da Vinci, who combined the scientist's curiosity with the artist's eye has been acclaimed the symbolic figure of the scientific revolution. This he was not. He experimented widely, he brought a freshness of observation to accepted doctrines, but he had neither the experimental method — the methodical collation of material and the systematic verification of hypotheses — the mathematics, nor the means of measurement which were to be among the great achievements of the seventeenth century. Why the seventeenth century should have been so vital a period in the history of science is a complex problem. Certainly the long-term effect of both the Renaissance and the Reformation was to encourage a questioning spirit among many scholars, but a greater factor was the invention of printing, which allowed men throughout Europe to become immediately aware of the work of their contemporaries. Collaboration at a distance was now possible, and the pace of scientific advance no longer depended upon the chance concentration of scholars in one favoured place. Above all, the one development that made possible the scientific revolution was the tremendous technological advance in the manufacture of precision instruments of observation and measurement, which furnished mankind with the telescope, the microscope, the micrometer, the barometer, the thermometer, the pendulum clock, and balances, no longer accurate to 1 grain but to $\frac{1}{500}$ of a grain.

This remarkable and necessary addition to man's scientific equipment resulted from the increasing amount of accurate investigation into nature carried on by men outside the universities, in spheres where no inherent reverence for authority precluded investigation, and where the demands of practical problems compelled the formulation of new questions and answers. Artillery attacked the physics of Aristotle at its weakest point by compelling the study of ballistics. The sternpost rudder, which replaced what had virtually been an oar lashed to the stern, made ocean-going less hazardous in the sixteenth century and thus prompted a demand for better means of navigation. Mariners, therefore, became knowledgeable in the study of compasses and magnetism, of astronomy and tides. Men employed in land drainage also studied the tides, and it was Stevin, a Dutch engineer and mathematician, who produced in 1590 the first scientific tide table: others, engaged in mining and metallurgy, studied the properties of metals, the mechanics of the pump, and the problems of hydrostatics and ventilation. So it was that away from the traditional centres of learning the scientific revolution owed its greatest impetus to the practical problems, solutions and equipment evolved by countless foundryworkers, instrument-makers, mariners, miners, smiths and engineers — some well versed in Euclid, others illiterate, but all alike driven by the profit motive and curiosity to experiment in their work.

One man who profited much from the experience gained by sailors, and also from his own extensive practical knowledge of mining and metallurgy, was William Gilbert, Fellow of St John's College, Cambridge, and physician to Queen Elizabeth I. Spending hours in the company of craftsmen, especially of Robert Norman, a retired mariner and compass-maker, he was prompted by them to examine the nature of magnetic variation, and the problem of the compass needle which tilts at various angles according to its position on the earth's surface. Gilbert made a model of the earth, a *terella*, out of lodestone, a magnetic rock, and placed upon it a series of small iron needles. These behaved exactly like compass needles. Not only did they point to the *terella's* north pole, they also dipped at various angles in different places, horizontally at the equator, vertically at the pole. From this Gilbert demonstrated that the earth itself was a magnet with its magnetic poles near the geographic North and South Poles, and that between these poles there flowed lines of magnetic influence which governed the behaviour of the needles. In his *De Magnete* (1600), the first learned work to appear on experimental physics, Gilbert at one stroke transferred the whole subject of magnetism from the empirical to the scientific, though he did not fail in the dedication to acknowledge his initial debt to those 'who look for knowledge not in books but in things themselves'.

This attitude was shared by a more famous Englishman, Sir Francis Bacon, Lord Chancellor to James I. He himself performed no experiments, until one winter's day in 1626 he left his coach to gather snow to stuff into a dead fowl that he might observe the effect on the preservation of the flesh: the result was a chill from which he died. His true importance was as the powerful advocate of what he called experimental philosophy:

'Men have sought to make a world from their own conception and to draw from their own minds all the material which they employed, but if, instead of doing so, they had consulted experience and observation, they would have had the facts and not opinions to reason about, and might have ultimately arrived at the knowledge of the laws which govern the material world.' Bacon believed that systematic experiment was the new instrument, the *Novum Organum*, in the investigation of nature: its revolutionary value was symbolised for him by the picture on the title-page, a ship under full sail passing the Pillars of Hercules, the limits of the ancient world.

Bacon's forecast of how scientific work ought to be carried on was largely mistaken. He believed that if nature were examined sufficiently intensively and systematically, the resulting mass of data would, when correctly tabulated, automatically demonstrate the general laws of nature. This in fact never happened: the great achievements of science were made, not by such collations on a massive scale, but by intuitive guesses, by the leap in the dark, and above all by the rare ability to reconsider accepted facts in a novel way. Experiments were then conducted to satisfy the new hypothesis, or to demonstrate its adequacy. It was Bacon's enthusiasm rather than his logic which counted. As he said, 'he rang the bell which called the wits together'. It was, too, his insistence upon experiment which served a vital purpose in urging men to accept the validity of the results arrived at, whether they liked them or not — such as the experiment of Torricelli's on atmospheric pressure[27] which demonstrated the creation of a vacuum in despite of Aristotle's contention that a vacuum could not exist. Experiment was urged with equal enthusiasm by Torricelli's master, Galileo, who opposed all arguments based on *a priori* assumptions: 'I know very well that one single experiment or conclusive demonstration produced against them is enough to batter to the ground these and a thousand other probable arguments.'

Another Baconian concept of importance was the necessity of collaborating among those engaged in scientific studies. For this purpose, in his visionary Utopia, the *New Atlantis*, he proposed a House of Solomon, an institute for organised co-operative research, not only of scholars, but of technologists and craftsmen,

[27] See below, p.42.

so that intellectual activity should not be confined to the universities, which were to be distrusted as strongholds of orthodoxy. Both these desires were ultimately satisfied by the foundation of the Royal Society. From informal beginnings in the Philosophic or Invisible College which met variously after the Civil War at Gresham College and at Wadham College, Oxford, it was established in 1662 under royal patronage. Its business, in the words of Robert Hooke, was to 'improve the knowledge of natural things and all useful Arts, Manufactures, Mechanick practices, Engines and Inventions by Experiments — (not meddling with Divinity, Metaphysics, Moralls, Politics, Grammar, Rhetoric or Logick)'.

On the Continent similar societies were already in existence, as in Italy, where the *Accademia Secretorum Naturae*, founded as early as the sixteenth century, was succeeded at Rome by the *Accademia dei Lincei* — the lynx-eyed. Galileo's association with this society, though intellectually stimulating, proved ultimately fatal, since the Inquisition began to investigate its members after Galileo's clash with the pope,[28] and despite the patronage of Federigo Cesi, Duke of Aquasparta, it was then closed. In 1651, however, Federigo's brother, the Grand Duke of Tuscany, founded a successor, the *Accademia del Cimento* — the experimental academy — under his own protection in Florence. The older societies had been nothing more than fraternities but the Florentine academy existed for the purpose of co-operative experiment. Several of Galileo's pupils, Torricelli among them, did much useful work there, and their results were published after 1667 in the *Saggi di Naturali Esperienze fatte nell' Accademia del Cimento*. Their work, like that of the Royal Society, was enthusiastic but undirected, their results interesting but inconclusive and lacking in coherence. Other Italian societies sprang up, the *Accademia Fisico-Matematico* at Rome (1667), the *Accademia del Scienza* at Naples (1695), and the rest of Europe was not to be outdone. In France the informal Thursday gatherings at the homes of Mersenne and Montmar of men like Gassendi, Pascal and Descartes — the *Académie Libre* — were eventually superseded in 1662 by the formation of the *Académie des Sciences*. Colbert showed much interest in its activities, particularly in its practical study of textiles and industrial techniques, but state direction was deadening,

[28] See below, p.53.

especially after the appointment of Louvois in 1683 as its protector, and men of ability were not attracted to it. In Germany the *Collegium Naturae Curiosum* specialised in medicine at Schweinfurt; Joachim Jungius, a biologist, founded the *Societas Erneutica* at Rostock in 1662, and, ten years later, students at Altdorf formed the *Collegium Curiosum sive Experimentale*. Leibniz realised a life-long ambition when in 1700 an academy was established at Berlin; a similar ambition of Peter the Great resulted in the Academy of St Petersburg in 1725.

Experiment, singly or in collaboration, was not however the most important feature of the scientific revolution, and chemistry, the science most responsive to experiment, made the least progress of all. The new instruments which encouraged experiment had quite another result, since without them men were geared for ever to the qualitative investigation of the world associated with Aristotle, compelled to enumerate the qualities of objects, to classify them accordingly and to explain phenomena in terms of their qualities: with the new instruments it became possible to establish the physical quantities of matter. Sanctorius, the inventor of a medical thermometer and of improved balances, was fascinated for hours on end by weighing himself and taking his temperature under all kinds of conditions, carefully recording his results. But if the development of tools to undertake quantitative investigation was important, equally so was the discovery of means to express the results of this type of investigation. This means was mathematics. 'Science', wrote Isaac Barrow, a professor of mathematics at Cambridge, 'is to study the sensible realm so far as it shows quantitative continuity, and mathematics is the art of measurement.'

Descartes, who denied the validity of the senses in revealing the hardness, roughness or any other quality of material objects, insisted that the nature of matter consisted in its extension in space: thus its mathematical quantities, its length, breadth, weight, mass and so on were the only ones worthy of study. Galileo went further still in stressing the function of mathematics in science by claiming that all the data produced by experiment and observation was valueless unless interpreted mathematically. 'Philosophy is written in this grand book, the universe, which stands continually open to our gaze. But the book cannot be understood unless one first learns to comprehend the language and read the letters in which it is composed. It is written in the language of mathematics, and its characters are triangles, circles and other geometric figures, without which it is humanly impossible to understand a single word of it; without these, one wanders about in a dark labyrinth.' That this is true was demonstrated by the verbal complexity of medieval scholars who wrestled with problems of impetus and motion without the aid of a mathematical language. This language — notation — was both simplified and amplified in the seventeenth century. Decimals were introduced, along with algebra, equations, logarithms and slide rules; the mathematics of probability and of centrifugal force were examined; coordinate geometry, Descartes's invention, made it possible to express the motion of a point by means of a formula, the infinitesimal calculus went a stage further by studying the point's rates of change in position. So it was that the seventeenth century was not only one of the greatest periods of progress in mathematics, but the period in which mathematical knowledge had the greatest influence on science.

The Structure of Matter

Medieval theories about the nature of matter, based on Aristotle and adapted to suit Christian theology, represented a curious amalgam of two different approaches, physical and metaphysical. The physical analysis concentrated upon the four elements revealed by the process of combustion: a twig, for example, when it burns is resolved in flame, smoke, moisture and ash — four elements which Aristotle generalised as fire, air, water and earth. These elements were believed to possess properties which accounted for their action. Earth and water had gravity, air and fire levity; and mixed up with this was the theory of the four primary qualities, heat, cold, dryness and humidity, so that fire was characterised as hot and dry, earth as cold and dry, air as hot and moist, water as cold and moist. The fusion of the elements thus produced different materials, and the mingling of the primary qualities resulted in secondary qualities like softness or acidity. The alternative approach to matter was metaphysical, a distinction being made not between the separate elements but between Form and Matter. Form was believed to be the active agent, the principle which determined not merely shape but the entire organisation of Matter: Matter was the passive agent, that which is organised by Form. Such a distinction was necessarily metaphysical since it was quite impossible to demonstrate it physically by combustion, by dissection or by any other experiment. In Christian theology there existed a hierarchy of Forms. God was Pure Form: from Him there descended the nine grades of angels down to man, and thence through the animal, vegetable and mineral grades to mere Matter, about which, since it had no Form, nothing could be said. Form determined the properties of material objects. Wood therefore floated in water because its Form dictated its activity — in other words it was its nature to float, an explanation which was both tautological and meaningless.

Whatever the method of inquiry, whether physical or metaphysical, whether things behaved according to the properties of their principal element or because of their Form, the tendency was to endow matter with attributes which explained its behaviour, as though matter was capable of self-direction. Usually these explanations were anthropomorphic, given in human terms such as horror of a vacuum. The falling stone accelerated because it was jubilant at returning home; things went where they belonged in the universe, and comets, earthquakes and other interferences with the natural order were ascribed to the power of supernatural forces. What could be demonstrated by experiment thus seemed reasonably satisfying, and what could not, and therefore required faith for its understanding, did not strain men's reason too greatly since men are essentially sympathetic to anthropomorphism.

The first to destroy the whole overburdened structure of tortuous verbosity and wishful thinking was Galileo, who performed an experiment with a ball of wax. First he placed the ball in a bowl of water, where it sank; then, by dissolving salt in the water, he caused the ball to rise. Thus were confounded all existing theories as the action of the wax ball was interpreted no longer in terms of elements, properties of Form, but of specific gravity.

True to the tradition of Renaissance learning, scientists began to search the writings of classical antiquity for alternative explanations of the nature of matter, and found what they sought in the neglected philosophy of Democritus, the first Greek atomist, who held: 'In truth there are atoms and a void.' On this the seventeenth century based its *corpuscular* philosophy, though Descartes, the first in the field, rejected the concept of the void. The universe for him was composed of infinitely indivisible matter, existing in unbroken continuity without any intervening space or vacuum. Motion was therefore something imparted by one corpuscle to the next, like the behaviour of individuals jammed in a crowd. Gassendi, his colleague in the *Académie Libre*, insisted on retaining the theory of the void, claiming that atoms were indivisible particles of the same primary material, differing from each other only in shape and size, and separated from each other by a vacuum. In England the theory was further developed by Robert Boyle, a founder of the Royal Society, who, like Gilbert, had gained much from contact with craftsmen, and who claimed that it was they who had taught him all his chemistry. In conscious rejection of all university notions based upon *a priori* reasoning he entitled his book, published in 1661, *The Sceptical Chymist*. Matter was reduced, not to the four elements but to minute particles which joined together as corpuscles: everything could then be explained by the formation of atoms into different systems with different motions. 'Bodies exhibit colours not upon the account of the predominancy of this or that principle in them, but upon that of their texture and especially the disposition of their superficial parts; whereby the light rebounding thence to the eyes is modified.'

Though their attacks on medieval theories were effective, Boyle and his colleagues failed to propound a clear alternative in their place, as Joseph Friend, professor of chemistry at Oxford, shrewdly complained in 1712: 'Chemistry has made very laudable progress in Experiments; but we may justly complain that little Advances have been made towards the explication of 'em... No body has brought more Light into this Art than Mr Boyle ... who nevertheless has not so much laid a new Foundation of Chemistry as he has thrown down the old.'

Nevertheless, one of the most important investigations of the seventeenth century was that which led to the recognition of the pressure of air. The fact that water rushed into the barrel of a pump when the piston was drawn back was previously explained by Aristotle's theory that, since nature abhors a vacuum, the water poured in to prevent a vacuum being created. When lift-pumps came into extensive use for mine drainage Galileo was asked to explain·why they could not raise water from a depth of more than 10.35 metres. So arbitrary a limit to nature's abhorrence of a vacuum seemed curious at least, and it was Galileo's pupil, Torricelli, who suggested the answer in 1643. A column of water 10.35 metres high was clearly too clumsy an object for experiment, and so he filled a glass tube, a metre long, with mercury and, turning it upside down, placed the open end in a trough of mercury. The mercury level in the tube fell to about 80 centimetres. As mercury is 13.6 times as dense as water, the 80 centimetres of mercury in the tube corresponded to the 10.35 metres of water in the lift-pump, thus demonstrating that both the water and the mercury were being balanced by the weight of the atmosphere. But what was also demonstrated was the fact that as the mercury fell in the tube, a vacuum was actually created above it, since there was no means by which air could enter the tube. 'We live submerged at the bottom of an ocean of the element air', wrote Torricelli, and, noting that the height of the mercury in the tube varied slightly from day to day, ascribed this to changes in the atmospheric pressure: 'Nature would not, as a flirtatious girl, have a different *horror vacui* on different days.'

Mersenne, the secretary of the *Académie Libre*, passed on the news of Torricelli's experiment to his members, and to Blaise Pascal in particular. Pascal, an infant prodigy who had produced an original study of conic sections at the age of sixteen, immediately repeated the experiment on a grand scale with 22.6 kilograms of mercury in a 1.2 metre tube. The mercury again stood to a height of about 80 centimetres, but as Pascal was unaware of Torricelli's reasoning about the vacuum created above the mercury he had to arrive at the same conclusion independently. Back in Paris he found a bitter opponent in Descartes, whose atomic theory precluded the existence of the vacuum, and who insisted that some 'subtle form of matter' made its way into the tube. To counter this, and other attacks, from traditional scholastic quarters, Pascal went on to further experiment. Believing the air to be compressed by its own weight as, in a pile of wool, 'the bottom layers would be far more compressed than the middle or top layers, because they are compressed by a greater quantity of wool', he concluded that the pressure of the atmosphere would be less great on the mountain-tops than in the lowlands. A successful demonstration of this was performed by his brother-in-law, who carried a Torricelli tube to the top of the Puy-de-Dôme, the highest point in the Auvergne, observing as he climbed the gradual fall of the mercury in the tube.

Similar lines of research into the nature of the air were followed by Boyle in England, leading to his famous law that 'the pressures and expansions' of any given quantity of air are 'in reciprocal proportion', so that when the pressure exerted on an enclosed volume of air is, for example, doubled or trebled, the air shrinks to one-half or one-third of its original volume. Otto von Guericke, remarkable for surviving the siege of Magdeburg, was to a large extent unaware of the discoveries of his contemporaries, but performed his own experiments along similar lines. Becoming interested in the problem of the vacuum, he tried to create one by pumping water out of a cask, but the air forced its way in past the wooden staves and he did not succeed until he had used a cask made of copper. He then invented an improved air pump and drew out the air from two bronze hemispheres placed together as a hollow globe. In 1651 the Emperor Ferdinand III was invited to Regensburg to witness a dramatic experiment when two teams, each of eight horses, were scarcely able to pull apart the evacuated hemispheres. Equally of value was von Guericke's action in weighing the hemispheres, and, by noticing the change in weight before and after withdrawing the air, thus determining the density of the air.

Living Matter: Medicine and Biology

In the study of the body, great stress had always been laid upon observation since from earliest times doctors had had to examine their patients and to discover connections between symptoms and diseases. But for all that, throughout the Middle Ages, men persisted in observing only what they had been taught to look for: over them all fell the shadow of Galen, physician to the Emperor Marcus Aurelius, and whose teaching had since been integrated with Christian theology. Even a practical experiment was conducted under his dead hand; the purpose of dissection was not discovery but demonstration, and if the results contradicted

Galen's teaching it was assumed that the demonstrator had bungled his job.

In the study of the circulation of the blood, Galen's influence was especially pernicious because it seemed to correspond so well to the facts. Since venous blood has a blue tinge while arterial blood is bright red, he assumed that there were therefore two distinct blood systems, the venous system which nourished the tissues of the body and the arterial system which gave the tissues life. Galen also assumed that all the blood was made in the liver, part of the venous system, and thus his chief problem was to trace the blood from the liver into the arterial system. This he did by finding a connection between the liver and the right auricle and ventricle of the heart, and since he also found a special passage between the right ventricle and the lungs, he believed that once the blood had arrived in the heart it was immediately cooled by air sent up from the lungs. It then passed into the left ventricle, there to be enriched, purified and strengthened by the addition of vital spirits, *pneuma psuchikon*, essential for life. Finally it surged into the body in a kind of tidal ebb and flow, the valves of the heart to some extent restraining the violence of the flow, while the rate of absorption of the blood into the tissues was balanced by the rate at which new blood was delivered from the liver to the heart. The greatest single difficulty about the theory was that the thick fleshy wall between the right and left ventricles, called the septum, appeared impenetrable but Galen insisted that fine pores, invisible to the human eye allowed the blood to seep through: 'These indeed are seen with difficulty in the dead body, the parts being then cold, hard and rigid. Reason assures me, however, that such pores must exist.'

The discovery during the Renaissance of a Greek text of Galen's work revealed the hitherto unknown fact that all Galen's conclusions had been drawn from experiments on animals alone. Consequently, Vesalius, professor of anatomy at Padua, produced his own study of the body, *De Corporis Humani Fabrica* (1543), in which he exposed more than two hundred anatomical errors in Galen, among them the fact that the human thigh bone is straight, not curved as a dog's. The diehard Galenists immediately blamed this phenomenon on the narrow trousers of their day, and attacked Vesalius bitterly; but Vesalius himself was less of a deliberate rebel than a fervent Galenist with doubts.

Above all, he was not satisfied by Galen's views on the septum, but as he could offer no alternative theory he enigmatically commented: 'We are driven to wonder at the handiwork of the Creator, by means of which blood sweats from the right into the left ventricle through passages which escape the human vision.' Four years later, in 1547, there was published a Latin translation of the theories and experiments of a thirteenth-century Arabian doctor who had not only denied the possibility of blood seeping through the septum, but postulated its movement from the right to left ventricles by way of the lungs. Another blow was struck by Leonardo da Vinci, who in his practical way tried in vain to pump air through the pipe which Galen had identified as bringing air from the lungs to the right ventricle. So great however was the authority of Galen that though his work was criticised in detail, no one presumed to challenge his general theories. Even when Fabricius of Padua discovered the existence of valves in the veins, a clear indication that the flow of the blood could only be in one direction— back to the heart — he explained them away as barriers designed to prevent the rush of blood down to the legs.

It was not until the seventeenth century that the spell of Galen was finally broken by William Harvey, a man who shared the empirical philosophy of his countrymen Bacon and Boyle: 'It were disgraceful, therefore, did we take the reports of others upon trust, and go on coining crude problems out of these, and on them hanging knotty and captious and petty disputations. Nature herself is to be addressed; the paths she shows us are to be boldly trodden; for thus ... shall we penetrate at length into the heart of her mystery.' Harvey studied at Padua under Fabricius but found himself unable to accept his explanation of the valves in the venous system; the airpipe through which Leonardo had failed to pump air appeared to him to have all the characteristics of a major blood-vessel; he discovered that creatures without lungs have only one ventricle, which prompted him to consider that if animals with lungs have two ventricles then the second is for the flow of blood into the lungs; lastly he calculated that the amount of blood pumped out of the heart in the course of one hour exceeded the total weight of a man, and that the blood was 'continuously passing into the arteries in greater amount than can be supplied from the food ingested'. From all these things

Harvey concluded that the blood must circulate through the body. 'I began to think whether there might not be a motion, as it were, in a circle. Now this I afterwards found to be true; and I finally saw that the blood, forced by the action of the left ventricle into the arteries, was distributed to the body at large and in its several parts, in the same manner as it is sent through the lungs impelled by the right ventricle in the right pulmonary artery, and that it then passed through the veins and along the *vena cava* and so round to the left ventricle in the manner already indicated, which motion we may be allowed to call circular.'

Harvey's *Exercitatio Anatomica de Motu Cordis et Sanguinis*, published in 1628, was certainly the most vital medical publication of the century, but it was not the only one. Malpighi of Bologna University took Harvey's theory a stage further by discovering the means, unknown to Harvey, by which the arteries and veins were linked. For this he made great use of the microscope and, by studying the tissue of a frog's lung, discovered the tiny capillary tubes which carry the blood through the tissue: 'Hence it was clear that the blood flowed away along tortuous vessels and was not poured into spaces, but was always contained within tubules.' Even more remarkable in some ways were the discoveries of Leeuwenhoek, a draper of Delft, who became fascinated by the new world of discovery opened to him by the microscope. A compound microscope, such as Malpighi used, could only magnify from sixty to eighty times, and the two lenses, being insufficiently ground, caused blur and distortion. Leeuwenhoek fashioned his own, consisting of a single lens, almost spherical, mounted between metal plates. This was extremely difficult to produce but by exceptional skill in setting and grinding his lens he achieved a degree of magnification up to about 300.

Leeuwenhoek studied the capillary tubes observed by Malpighi, but his greatest interest lay in the micro-organisms which he found in drops of liquid. These he termed *animalculae*, 'little animals'; in fact he was observing protozoa, the simplest form of animal life, protophyta, single-celled plants, and bacteria. He derived tremendous pleasure by alarming his acquaintances with sights of the monstrous inhabitants of a drop of fresh water. When he showed a group of ladies the 'eels' in vinegar, they immediately foreswore its use: 'But what if one should tell such people in future', he commented, 'that there are more animals living in the scum of the teeth than there are men in a whole kingdom.' In tartar he found the *animalculae*, 'moving about in a highly amusing way,' with one of the larger ones 'passing through the saliva as a fish of prey darts through the sea'. The study of tartar and spittle obsessed him, and he collected samples everywhere: one such sample however did not prove so exciting as he had hoped. 'I have also taken the spittle from an old man who makes a practice of drinking brandy every morning, and wine and tobacco every afternoon; wondering whether the animalcules, with such continued boozing, could e'en remain alive, I judged that this man, because his teeth were so uncommon foul, never washed his mouth. So I asked him, and got for an answer, "Never in all my life with water, but it gets a good swill with wine or brandy every day." Yet I couldn't find anything beyond the ordinary in his spittle.'

Matter in Motion: Copernicus and Kepler

Although St Ambrose said, 'To discuss the nature and position of the earth does not help us in the life to come', natural curiosity could not be suppressed. From the earliest times the stars had aroused both interest and emotion in mankind, and their study had had practical results in the making of calendars and in navigation — and even in astrology which, if something of a bastard offspring, at least kept its parent in business: 'God', said Kepler, 'provides for every animal his means of subsistence. For astronomers he has provided astrology.' As the Greeks had inherited the vast amount of data of the Babylonians and Egyptians and then rationalised it, so the medieval Church had adopted Greek astronomy and adapted it to its theology. By 1500, therefore, the study of astronomy rested upon three apparently incontrovertible authorities — scholastic theology, Aristotelian physics, and the observations recorded in Ptolemy's *Almagest*. More important still, perhaps, the *Almagest* tallied with common-sense observation. The earth, solid, spherical and immovable, lay at the centre of the universe. Around it the moon, the sun and the five planets were carried upon seven revolving concentric spheres, made of some translucent, crystalline substance. The eighth sphere held the fixed stars; the ninth, the *primum mobile*, imparted motion to the rest; and the tenth was believed to be heaven. The supralunary universe was deemed to be in a state of perfection; that state which the medieval mind wistfully regarded as one in which change and decay were impossible, owing to the addition of a divine quintessence to the existing four elements. Between the moon and the earth, however, there was no such preservative: the moon itself was obviously tainted by dark blotches, comets exploded across the sky in great exhalations of fire, and on earth the four elements existed in restless confusion.

Within this perfectly ordered universe the behaviour of the planets gave cause for concern since each was observed to follow an erratic course. It was for this very reason that Plato had christened them 'planets' — vagabonds — and many attempts were made to reconcile their apparent course with the theory of their uniform circular motion around the earth. Ptolemy suggested that they revolved in epicycles, the centres of which described a uniform circular path; this could be made to fit the observed facts provided that the construction of eighty such epicycles was accepted. Alphonso the Wise of Castile, a medieval patron of astronomy, complained: 'If the Almighty had consulted me before the Creation I should have recommended something simpler.' Such complexity was none the less effective since it accounted for every known irregularity of the planets, and tables composed on this system proved wholly reliable.

Less easy to solve was the problem of motion in the universe. The *primum mobile* was presumed to impart motion in some way to the other spheres, and Christian thought romanticised this by assigning the nine grades of angels to superintend the motion of the nine spheres. Celestial motion was circular because circular motion was deemed 'natural' to celestial bodies, a question-begging answer which went unquestioned in an age which endowed material objects with human aspirations. Terrestrial motion was more difficult to explain. Motion up or down was simple enough, since matter was endowed with the attributes of levity and gravity, but any other type of motion had to be assigned its due cause. This proved to be the weakest point of Aristotelian physics, which taught that since a state of rest was natural to all objects, nothing would move unless compelled to by some agent or force. This failed to satisfy the perplexity of those who pointed to the arrow which continued to fly through the air long after losing contact with its mover, the bowstring. Aristotle's own explanation of this was obscure and inaccurate, and the target of learned criticism from the twelfth century onwards, with the result that by 1500 a concept of impetus was evolved as being something like heat which gradually lost its potency.

The publication in 1543 of Copernicus's *De Revolutionibus Orbium Celestium* was an event of unusual importance. As befitted a canon of Cracow Cathedral, from whose tower he was permitted to observe the heavens, Copernicus was in most respects a medievalist: matter was endowed with aspirations; all bodies sought to assume the shape of the sphere since this was the perfect shape, and circular motion was perfect motion. But for many years Copernicus had also studied in Italy under de Novara, professor of mathematics and astronomy at Bologna, a fervent neo-Platonist whose mathematics was loaded with Pythagorean symbolism. Copernicus was inspired by him with a love for mathematical simplicity. He thus attacked the Ptolemaic universe as too cumbersome and claimed, purely as an hypothesis, that the whole problem might be simplified by assuming the sun to be at the centre. What pleased him was not merely that the number of epicycles could be cut to thirty-four, nor even that, in Pythagorean terms, the light of the universe would now be in its most suitable place, but the elegant simplicity of his proposal: 'It is so bound together both the order and magnitude of all the planets and all the spheres and the heaven itself that in no single part could one thing be altered without confusion among the other parts and in all the Universe.' His theory caused new problems. If the earth were to move around the sun, then its position in relation to the fixed stars would alter every month. Since no such parallactic shift was discernible, Copernicus had to save this theory by putting the fixed stars at so great a distance from the earth that no shift could be expected, but this, though correct, involved concepts of distance so immense that most men found them more difficult to accept than heliocentrism itself. Moreover, when Copernicus settled down to revise the *Almagest* in detail he found it impossible to put the sun exactly at the centre of the planets' orbits,[29] which

[29] Naturally enough, as Kepler discovered, since the orbits are elliptical not circular; see below, p.51.

compelled him to construct another twelve epicycles. Nor were his tables uniformly superior to those of Ptolemy and it was possible for men of the most open mind to choose equally between the two systems.

The most damning weakness of the Copernican system was that it could not be reconciled with Aristotelian physics, for to the mind brought up on this no force in the universe was capable of moving the sluggish earth. Hence the immediate importance of the publication, also in 1543, of a Latin edition of Archimedes, the greatest geometer of classical times, who had imagined how the earth might be moved with a lever. Archimedes had been known by name in the Middle Ages, but the texts were too inadequate and too corrupt to convey the originality of his thought. One of his greatest qualities was an ability to perform mental experiments in order to abstract essential from irrelevant factors, and to present them in mathematical terms. In dealing with fluids, for example, he ignored their taste, their colour and the attributes by which other scientists explained their activity, and considered only their motion. Similarly, having measured objects in air and in water he tried to imagine them unencumbered by either. If Aristotelian physics prevented the serious acceptance of the Copernican theory of heliocentrism then the revival of Archimedean teaching was a significant step towards its re-examination.

One other feature of the sixteenth century, vital to the subsequent revolution, was the work of Tycho Brahe, a Danish noble who studied at the royal observatory in Denmark until, after violent quarrels with his own countrymen, he went to Prague in 1596 at the invitation of Emperor Rudolf II. His observations were unique alike in their accuracy and their comprehension. Equipped with quadrants and direction finders, but without a telescope, he plotted the position of the planets and stars with unrivalled care. Though he accepted that the planets revolved around the sun he was not a Copernican, since he could discern no parallactic shift in the position of the fixed stars and believed that planets and sun together circled the earth. The first man to make a detailed study of the planets at every stage of their orbit, he was perplexed to find that the orbits were never circular. More disconcertingly, in 1572, he observed in the constellation of Cassiopeia a supernova — a star, previously faint, blowing up and gradually burning out — and in 1577 a comet which, far from moving in the sublunary sphere of change and imperfection, followed a track far beyond the moon, as trigonometrical observation confirmed. These observations ended the belief in uniform circular motion, in the immutability of the heavens, and in the crystalline spheres through which the comet must have crashed its way.

In 1600 Brahe appointed an assistant, Johannes Kepler, a poor but brilliant astronomer whose reputation had been made by his *Mysterium Cosmographicum*. A fervent Copernican, inspired by neo-Platonist and Pythagorean theories on the harmony of numbers and shapes, Kepler had been looking for one law to explain the distances between the planets. To his great delight he discovered a rough relationship between their orbits and the five regular solids: if the orbit of Mercury were imagined as a solid shell it would fit inside an octahedron whose points would touch the inner surface of the shell of Venus: Venus in turn lay within an icosahedron whose points touched the inner surface of the earth's shell, the earth lay within a dodecahedron, Mars within a tetrahedron, Jupiter within a cube. Around the cube fitted the orbit of Saturn. To Brahe this was mere romancing but he was struck by the observations Kepler had made, and he put him to observe the orbit of Mars. Within a year Brahe had died, leaving his collection of data to Kepler, who thus possessed more information on the behaviour of the planets than anyone had held before. He at once set out to postulate a theory to explain the motion of Mars in keeping with the recorded observations. This was soon done but, on comparing the positions computed from his system with the corresponding positions observed by Brahe, Kepler discovered a discrepancy of eight minutes of arc. This was negligible: even Ptolemy and Copernicus had been accurate only to ten minutes of arc, but so great was his respect for Brahe's records that Kepler refused to make the facts fit into the theory. 'And thus the edifice which we erected on the foundations of Tycho's observations we have now again destroyed... For if I had believed we could ignore these eight minutes I would have patched up my hypothesis accordingly.'

Kepler's scrupulous regard for eight minutes of arc caused him eight more years of intense labour, but at last he found the answer: the planets move in an elliptical path with the sun at one

focus: as they near the sun they accelerate, as they veer away they
slow down so that a line drawn from the planet to the sun sweeps
out equal areas in equal times. Having published these laws in
his *Astronomia Nova* in 1609, Kepler returned to his mystic
preoccupation with the harmony of the spheres, preparing for
publication his *Harmonica Mundi*. There among discussion as to
whether Mars is a tenor and Mecury a falsetto, was included
almost fortuitously the third of Kepler's laws, that the time taken
by a planet to complete its orbit increases the further it is from
the sun: indeed, the squares of the time of the planets' revolutions
bear a constant ratio to the cubes of their mean distances from
the sun. As for his explanation of the dynamics of the universe, he
derived this from Gilbert's work on magnetism,[30] and assumed
that the sun maintained the planets in rotation by exerting an
effluvium magneticum.

Matter in Motion: Galileo and Newton

The man who paved the way for a more satisfactory explanation
of planetary motion was Galileo, professor of mathematics at
Padua, and a man of many interests who examined practically
every scientific subject under discussion in his day. In the study
of the universe his first great contribution was to convince most
people that the Copernican system, operating by Kepler's laws,
was fundamentally sound. This he did with the help of the
telescope, the chance invention of a Dutch spectacle-maker
between 1590 and 1600, which he copied and improved to a
degree of magnification of thirty. Through this he studied the
heavens more closely than ever before, and published the results
in his *Siderius Nuncius* of 1610. Among many other novelties he
recorded his observations of blemishes on the face of the sun; of
80 stars in the constellation of Orion and of 40 in the Pleiades
where even Brahe had seen only nine and six respectively; of the
four satellites of Jupiter, a Copernican system in miniature; of the
Milky Way which he described as 'nothing else but a mass of
innumerable stars planted together in clusters', not, as believed,
planted at a uniform distance from the earth in the sphere of the
fixed stars. These observations compelled men to reconsider
long-held beliefs, but the Church having successfully integrated

[30] See above, p.35.

Ptolemy into its theology, was reluctant to approve of change, and Galileo deliberately provoked a conflict.

He left Padua in the free territory of Venice for Florence, and then for Rome, the centre of the controversy, having published in 1613 his *Letters on the Solar Spots* and in 1615 a *Letter Concerning The Use of Biblical Quotations in Matters of Science*. The opposition to him however was more powerful than he had suspected. Indeed those who claimed that the moons of Jupiter existed only in the telescope had unknowingly some justification: the danger that so novel an invention might distort the truth was not illusory since spherical aberration, the failure of the lens to give a rectilinear image, was not identified and corrected until 1637, and the cause of chromatic aberration, the light from different colours coming to a different focus, was not analysed before Newton studied the problem in 1671. In 1616 the Church exacted from Galileo a promise to cease his public advocacy of the Copernican system but in 1632, after the accession of a pope whom he believed to be sympathetic, he published his major assault on the Ptolemaic universe, the *Dialogue concerning the Two Chief World Systems*. Though Galileo pretended to state both cases fairly, he portrayed the defendant of the old system as a thick-witted gull, aptly named Simplicio, who obligingly fell into each of his antagonists' logical traps. For this work Galileo was disgraced, the pope mistakenly believing that Simplicio was based upon himself, but in 1633, on an apparently different topic, the *Discourse on the Two New Sciences*, he fulfilled his second major achievement, the destruction of the Aristotelian laws of motion, and with them the last remnants of the medieval world picture.

Galileo realised that if his enemies denied the evidence of the telescope because it conflicted with their concepts of motion, then motion itself would have to be studied afresh. He began by observing the movement of the pendulum, discovering that a long swing took the same time to complete as a short one, and putting his discovery to practical use in the invention of a pendulum clock. Equally practical was his interest in gunnery. It had been proposed by another Italian, Tartaglia, that projection was most efficient at an elevation of 45 degrees and that the trajectory was curved. Galileo identified the curve as a parabola and wondered if the speed acquired by the falling cannon ball was in any way proportional to the time it took to fall. This led to his experiments with metal balls in which he rolled them down grooves lined with polished leather to reduce friction, and found that their final speed varied with the height at which they were released, not with the angle at which the plane was inclined. He also discovered the relationship he sought between the distance and the time, expressing it as $d = \frac{1}{2}at^2$ where a represents the constant acceleration caused by gravity. The formulation of the hypothesis was not new since medieval mathematicians at Oxford had arrived at the same truth in verbal terms: where Galileo broke new ground was first by conducting his experiments and then by expressing his findings in a mathematical equation.

Equally important was Galileo's attack on the problem of inertia. First he rolled a ball down one plane and observed it run up a second until halted by the force of gravity. Modelling himself on Archimedes from whose work he derived his greatest inspiration, he then tried to imagine what the ball might do if gravity and friction were dispensed with. He concluded that it would rise to the same vertical height from which it had started. Finally he realised that if the ball, instead of climbing the second plane, followed a horizontal course, it would continue to roll for ever, seeking to regain its original height. The problem of inertia was thus put in an entirely novel setting. For the first time in history attention was directed not to the causes of motion, but to the forces which cause a body in motion to stop or alter course.

It was Descartes who pointed out that, since Galileo's horizontal plane was one parallel to the curved surface of the earth, the motion of the ball along it was in fact circular. To Descartes, however, natural motion, that is, motion in an ideal Euclidean sense, frictionless and free from interference, had to be in a straight line. Consequently the problem was to discover why the ball in motion along the horizontal plane did not fly off at a tangent to the earth. If Descartes' formulation of the problem marked a significant advance towards the discovery of the truth, his answer unfortunately obscured the issue. Like Aristotle, his metaphysical assumptions underlay his physics: like Aristotle, he drew his illustrations from the immediately recognisable world of common-sense experience. The Cartesian world was dualistic, consisting of Mind and Matter.[31] Matter he defined as *res extensa*,

[31] See below, p.66.

that which is extended in space. By this he meant that colour and taste, for example, were of secondary importance in identifying an object, and that the essence of matter consisted in its geometric characteristics. The universe represented an infinite extension of continuous matter in which there was no room for a vacuum to exist. Motion was imparted by one particle to another, just as the jostling of one individual in a crowd causes the movement of those around him. Moreover, as eddies form in the course of a river, trapping and carrying round a passing leaf, so, in the universe matter forms vortices whose circular motion carries the planets in their orbits. Suction towards the centre of the vortex was thus the cause of deviation from a straight-line path.

To Descartes this represented a satisfying demonstration of his belief in a mechanical universe, and many of his contemporaries found it wholly intelligible. Unfortunately it flouted Kepler's law that the motion of the planets was not circular but elliptical. Borelli in 1665 suggested that it was centripetal force which prevented Galileo's metal ball from flying off at a tangent to the earth, and which kept the earth and the planets for ever circling in orbit around the sun, but until Huygens had published his *Horologium Oscillatorium* in 1673 there was no public explanation of how this force could be calculated. Huygens said that the force required to make a point describe a circle uniformly was equal to $4\pi^2 r/t^2$ for each unit of mass, where t is the time taken to describe the circle. With the aid of Kepler's third law, $r^3/t^2 = C$, he then expressed the force more simply as $4\pi^2 C/r^2$. In other words, the force required to keep a planet in circular orbit was inversely proportional to the square of its distance from the centre. Huygens, however, was not satisfied that his formula held true of elliptical motion, and until this could be demonstrated his work could no more relate to the universe of Kepler's laws than did the vortices of Descartes.

Both the formula and the proof of its application to ellipses had already been discovered independently by Isaac Newton in 1665–6 when, during the plague year in Cambridge he took refuge at Woolsthorpe in Lincolnshire, and worked out the principle of his laws of motion. These, however, were not released to the world until the publication of his *Principia Mathematica* in 1681. His ideas taken singly had mostly been anticipated though he himself had arrived at his conclusions independently, and he was especially ahead of his contemporaries in taking Galileo's concept of inertia as a quality or property of matter in motion, and developing it into a quantitative concept of mass — even though he was later proved wrong in his calculation of mass in terms of weight and density. Of greater importance than the novelty of individual concepts was Newton's ability, his genius, to select from all the varied notions of the age the ones most capable of fitting together; to isolate Kepler's three laws, for example, from twenty volumes of mystical nonsense which enshrined them, and to create an imaginative synthesis sustained by proofs so detailed that no more rigorous a publication than the *Principia* appeared in the whole century.

Newton agreed with Descartes that the important problem was to seek the causes of divergence from a straight line, but he rejected the theory of vortices, preferring to study the operation of a centripetal force than to identify its nature. 'That by means of centripetal forces the planets may be retained in certain orbits, we may easily understand, if we consider the motions of projectiles; for a stone that is projected is by the pressure of its own weight forced out of the rectilinear path, which by the initial projection alone it should have pursued, and made to describe a curved line in the air; and through that crooked way is at last brought down to the ground; and the greater the velocity is with which it is projected, the farther it goes before it falls to the Earth.' He argued that if the velocity were increased sufficiently the stone would then 'reach at last quite beyond the circumference of the Earth', and go into orbit. The moon, he argued, was such a satellite, its motion controlled by the same centripetal force which caused stones to fall upon the earth's surface — a force proportional to the inverse square of the distance. 'And this same year', he wrote in 1666, 'I began to think of gravity extending to the orb of the Moon and having found out how to estimate the force with which a globe revolving within a sphere presses the surface of the sphere, from Kepler's Rule... I deduced that the forces which keep the planets in their Orbs must be reciprocally as the squares of their distances from the centres about which they revolve; and thereby compared the force requisite to keep the Moon in her Orb with the force of gravity at the surface of the Earth and found them answer pretty nearly.'

This comparison of forces, stated so simply, was in fact a task of great complexity. First he had to compute the rate at which the path of the moon as it circles the earth diverges from a straight line, and then to compare this with the rate at which objects fall at the earth's surface. Finally, he had to demonstrate that these rates were in the appropriate ratio according to Huygens's formula. The solution he arrived at in 1666, which satisfied him 'pretty nearly', was not sufficiently accurate for publication in the *Principia*, partly because current estimates of the moon's distance from the earth were unreliable. This was remedied soon after 1680 when a Frenchman, Picard, produced new calculations based on extremely accurate observations, which estimated that the distance between the earth and the moon was sixty times the radius of the earth — this last being calculated at 6,400 kilometres. Another factor which delayed Newton was the difficulty of calculating the force that the earth exerted upon the moon, since he faced the impossible task of calculating the attraction of every point on the earth's surface for every point on the moon's unless he could prove that the earth attracts bodies to it as though all its mass were concentrated at its centre. Once satisfied on this point, he began the formal demonstration of his theory, though even then the work might never have been undertaken had it not been for Newton's colleagues in the Royal Society, whose urgent insistence compelled him to return to problems which had been solved for his own immediate satisfaction at Woolsthorpe fifteen years earlier.

In the *Principia* Newton demonstrated that the moon, on account of the earth's attraction, diverges from a straight-line path at the rate of 0.013 metres in the first second. If Huygens's formula were correct, and if the attraction varied inversely to the square of the distance, then since the distance between the moon and the earth was believed to be sixty times the earth's radius, the attraction must be 60^2 times as intense at the surface of the earth. In other words, a stone should fall at 4.8 metres in the first second — which is in fact the case. The behaviour of an object falling upon the earth and of the moon encircling it were thus attributed to one and the same cause. But Newton was not concerned solely with the forces of attraction between the earth and the moon. He demonstrated that the universe as a whole represented a complex set of mathematical relationships, with each planet exerting influence upon the others, the whole being dominated by the attraction of the sun. To understand this universe he formulated three laws. Any body will remain either at rest or in a state of uniform motion in a straight line unless it is compelled to change its state by an external force: the rate of change of motion will be directly proportional to the external force acting on the body and will take place in the direction in which the force is acting: when a force of attraction exists between two bodies this force acts equally on both — but the motion which it produces in the more massive body is less than that produced in the other.

For all that he revealed the universe in an entirely novel and revolutionary way, Newton's achievement was deceptively simple. He made three reasonable assumptions about the movement of matter under the action of forces, and made a fourth assumption about the one particular force, gravitation, by which motion within the solar system was explained. It was in this simplicity that his genius lay, and also in his ability to give the whole theory a logical, mathematical expression: if as Galileo had said, 'the book of Nature is written in mathematical symbols', it was Newton who deciphered much of the code. The universe was thus demonstrated to be something of a machine whose behaviour could be accounted for by considering the attraction that its various parts exerted upon each other. Unlike a machine, however, the parts acted upon each other across empty space, and this was a notion which horrified Descartes and Leibniz, who could only think of forces being impacted upon bodies, such as by bats upon balls. Newton himself believed that attraction at a distance was only apparent, and that someone might subsequently discover the true nature of the mechanism. For the time being he was content to know that his system worked. 'I have not yet been able to deduce the reason of these properties of gravity from phenomena and I do not frame hypotheses. For whatsoever is not deduced from phenomena is to be called hypothesis; and hypotheses whether metaphysical or physical or of occult qualities or mechanical, have no place in experimental philosophy. In this philosophy propositions are deduced from phenomena, and are rendered general by induction. So impenetrability, mobility, the impetus of bodies and the laws of motions and gravity have become known. And it is enough that gravity really exists and acts according to the law explained by me and suffices for all the motions of the heavenly bodies and of our sea.'

THE INTELLECTUAL REVOLUTION

Philosophy and the Scientific Revolution

So great an accession of scientific data, so revolutionary a transformation in interpreting it, was bound to have a fundamental impact on philosophy. In a later age a generation might well have passed before the men of one discipline succeeded in re-educating those of another, but in the seventeenth century, since there was no formal division between natural science and philosophy — the term 'Natural Philosophy' embraced them both — changes in physics were immediately reflected in metaphysics. With men like Descartes and Leibniz prominent in both spheres, ideas moved swiftly and with dramatic effect.

In the Middle Ages 'natural philosophers' had been preoccupied with the analysis of function and properties: their basic approach was qualitative, their prime achievement classification. Hence the syllogism, the basic tool of medieval logic, made classification appear to be the standard expression of knowledge:

All Xs are Ys;
This is an X;
Therefore this is a Y.

With the syllogism as the model of rational inference, medieval philosophy was thus restricted to terms of definition — of essence, substance and attribute; of essential properties and accidental properties. From this attitude to the world as a museum of things and creatures, eternally divided, distinguished and determined by their Forms,[32] there sprang the notion of hierarchy, since classification was naturally followed by compari-

[32] See above, p.40.

son and grading. Important analogues were made between, for example, the hierarchy of the heavenly spheres and that of earthly society, so that good order on earth came to be considered a reflection of the orderly progress of the planets — 'The heavens themselves, the planets and this centre, observe degree, priority and place.'[33] In consequence, all violent disturbances in society were regarded either as the cause of disturbances in the natural world, or, alternatively, as the result of these.

When Harvey revolutionised physiology by thinking of the heart and the body in mechanical terms as a pump and a system of pipes, and Newton revealed the entire universe as one vast mechanism, the whole structure of scholastic philosophy was discredited. Things could no longer be described in terms of their final causes, their purpose or their attributes, but in terms of their interaction as part of a machine. Physical change was thus explained as the effect of the motion and impact of matter in space; matter itself was regarded as the action of atoms in motion; the difference between one object and another could only be assessed quantitatively in terms of their extension.

Alarmed bewilderment was the immediate reaction to this intellectual upheaval. The world had lost its order: 'The new philosophy puts all in doubt', wrote John Donne in 1611:

> 'The sun is lost and th' earth and no man's wit
> Can well direct him where to look for it.'

It was not surprising that fear of change prompted some to discredit the new science in order to salvage the old philosophy, especially since the Church, by uniting its theology with Aristotelian physics had thus bound itself to theories of matter and motion which were being proved false. The comet of 1572 was shrugged off as a miracle, despite the retort that *miraculum est ignorantiae asylum*; Copernicus's books were put on the Index and in 1616 the Holy Office, in a vain attempt to save the situation, pronounced: 'The view that the sun stands motionless at the centre of the Universe is foolish, philosophically false and utterly heretical, because contrary to Holy Scripture.' This was not altogether the work of bigotry. Churchmen had good reason to be worried about the possible impact of the discoveries. If Donne, an educated man, a poet and an Anglican priest, confessed

33 *Troilus and Cressida*, 1. iii. 85.

himself baffled then the effect on the ignorant might be disastrous. Once the medieval cosmology was uprooted, the popular imagery and conceptions of the world that everyone had taken for granted would be undermined. As it happened this fear was exaggerated; popular imagery remained geared to medieval cosmology for at least two centuries, and is still reflected in statements about the sun rising or in the concept of descending into hell.

Despite the perplexity and fear, there was in fact no question of a serious clash between science and religion. If the case of Galileo had aroused as much interest as his theories, it was the only one of its kind; nor was his treatment at all harsh in comparison to the martyrdom and imprisonment meted out to heretics. Galileo himself deliberately provoked a conflict in order to attack those churchmen who involved the Church in matters on which it was not theologically required to pronounce, and whose wilful adherence to outworn concepts only made it more difficult for the Church to shed its Aristotelian shackles. 'Take note, theologians', he wrote in a note added to his copy of his *Dialogue*, 'that in your drive to make matters of faith out of propositions relating to the fixity of sun and earth you run the risk of eventually having to condemn as heretics those who would declare the earth to stand still and the sun to move — at such a time as it might be physically or logically proved that the earth moves and the sun stands still.'

Those who came to regard the universe, and the human body, as mechanisms were not destroying spiritual values. Machinery was still something rare enough to be wondered at — like the famous Strassburg clock, so complex that even the simplified and miniature model in the British Museum not only tells the time, the day and the phase of the moon, but stages five simultaneous mechanical pantomimes. In this context to consider the universe as a clock was not to denigrate it; on the contrary, by revealing it to be an orderly, intelligible mechanism of the highest degree of complexity and skill they were thereby exalting its Creator. Hobbes alone adopted a wholly materialist view, interpreting the discoveries to mean that 'the universe is material, all that is real is material, and what is not material is not real'. Mind was merely the product of matter: 'There is no conception in a man's mind which hath not at first totally or by parts been begotten upon the organs of sense.' Hobbes's atheism was shared by none. Robert Boyle, who challenged the traditional theories of matter, believed that though the immediate causes of motion in the world might be explained in terms of a mechanism, the ultimate causes were non-mechanical: man's body might be corpuscular, but within it there existed a rational soul, the image of God in man, 'a nobler and more valuable being than the whole corporeal world'. The other scientist-philosophers shared Boyle's assumption, though sometimes in ways that could scarcely have satisfied an orthodox theologian, however willing he was to embrace the new science. Descartes, for example, made the existence of God one of the self-evident propositions upon which his philosophy depended,[34] but his vision of God was scarcely that revealed by Christ. Abstract and impersonal, the divine geometer rather than the loving Father, the Cartesian God was no longer active in the world; and Pascal[35] complained that Descartes brought God into his philosophy in order to start the world and could then find no further use for him. Descartes none the less insisted that his attachment to the Catholic Church was sincere, and, though the Church condemned his writings, he himself made no attack on the Church.

Newton, more than any other man, removed the magic from the universe by replacing the supernatural spirits and mysterious intelligences by his laws of motion: 'The gloriously romantic universe of Dante and Milton that set no bounds to the imagination of man as it played over space and time has now been swept away ... The really important world outside was a world, hard, cold, colourless, silent and dead; a world of quantity, a world of mathematically computable motions in mechanical regularity.'[36] But Newton did not see his universe in such terms. The world of mathematically computable motions was far more romantic and imaginative for him than that of medieval thought — nor was it silent and dead.

> 'What though in solemn silence, all
> Move round the dark terrestrial ball;
> What though no real voice nor sound
> Amid their radiant orbs be found:

[34] See below, p.64.   [35] See below, p.79.
[36] Professor E.A. Burtt, *The Metaphysical Foundations of Modern Science*.

In reason's ear they all rejoice
And utter forth a glorious voice,
For ever singing as they shine:
The hand that made us is divine.'

Joseph Addison's hymn gave fervent expression to Newton's own faith. The removal of outdated mysteries and physically impossible laws did not remove the need for God, 'who being in all places', wrote Newton, 'is more ably by his Will to move the Bodies within this boundless uniform Sensorium and thereby to form and reform the Parts of the Universe, than we are by our Will to move the Parts of our own Bodies.' Unlike Descartes, Newton believed that God was fully active in the universe, partly because this was the teaching of the Church, partly because he discovered certain problems in the daily running of the universe which only God could solve by perennial intervention. It worried him that motion was always being dissipated within the universe; 'by reason of the tenacity of fluids and attrition of their parts, and the weakness of elasticity in solids, motion is much more apt to be lost than got and is always upon the decay.' In addition, the gravitational interaction of the planets caused minor 'perturbations' in the orbit of each, and Newton was not sure if this indicated a stable system in which the variations could all cancel each other out, or if the 'perturbations' were cumulative. The constant intervention of God was thus required to keep the planets in their courses, and to restore motion.

The Cartesian Revolution: Descartes

René Descartes was born into a typically *bourgeois* family of doctors and *officiers*, who sent him to the Jesuit college of La Flèche in Anjou, and subsequently to the University of Poitiers where he graduated in law. He then took everyone by surprise by becoming a soldier, leaving France in 1618 to serve at Breda as a gentleman volunteer in the army of Maurice of Nassau. His pursuits were more scientific than military since the Dutch were then at peace with the Spaniards, and the current vogue among the officers was the creation and solution of problems in military engineering and mathematics, at which Descartes excelled. He left in 1619, travelling in a desultory fashion across Europe for the next ten years as a soldier in the Thirty Years War, though he took part in no major engagements. It was the opportunity to travel and to study human nature which attracted him to the life, and he also enjoyed the long winters between campaigns which allowed him leisure for reflection.[37] In 1629 he settled in Holland, where he wrote three short discourses on physical and mathematical subjects, prefaced by the celebrated *Discours de la Méthode* (1637), the *Meditationes de Prima Philosophia* (1641), and the *Principia Philosophiae* (1644), which he dedicated to Elizabeth, the wife of the Elector Palatine. Another patron was Christina of Sweden, who persuaded him to visit Stockholm in 1649. The climate, however, proved too severe, and his patron too demanding in her insistence upon philosophical instruction at five in the morning. Within a few weeks Descartes caught pneumonia, and died in 1650.

Such a man was scarcely a cloistered scholastic, and his contempt for traditional philosophy was boundless: 'I had become aware, even so early as during my college days that no opinion, however absurd or incredible, can be imagined which has not been maintained by some one of the philosophers.' Since he believed the mathematical and physical principles of the schoolmen to be inaccurate, he also lost all confidence in their philosophy, deliberately trying to clear his mind of all *a priori* assumptions and to subject all traditional authorities to his own independent criticism. In words which almost echoed those of Francis Bacon[38] he wrote: 'We shall not, for instance, become mathematicians even if we know by heart all the proofs that others have elaborated unless we have an intellectual talent that fits us to solve difficulties of that kind. Neither, though we have mastered all the arguments of Plato and Aristotle, shall we become philosophers if we have not the capacity for forming a solid judgement on these matters.'

The new approach was to be established on mathematical lines. Descartes shared none of Kepler's Pythagorean mysticism, and indulged in no rhapsodies about the theory of number, for 'there is nothing more futile than to busy oneself with bare

[37] See for examples Part II of the *Discours*. 'The setting in of winter arrested me in a locality where, as I found no society to interest me, and was besides fortunately undisturbed by any cares or passions, I remained the whole day in seclusion, with full opportunity to occupy my attention with my own thoughts.'

[38] See above, p.32.

numbers and imaginary figures in such a way as to appear to rest content with such trifles'. It was the method of mathematics which fascinated him, and he believed it capable of application to other disciplines. 'These long chains of reasoning all simple and easy, which geometers use to arrive at their most difficult demonstrations, suggested to me that all things which came within human knowledge must follow each other in a similar chain; and provided that we abstain from admitting anything as true which is not so, and that we always preserve in them the order necessary to deduce one from the other, there can be none so remote to which we cannot finally attain, nor so obscure but that we may discover them.'

Armed with *l'esprit géométrique* Descartes set out to establish the first principles of philosophy: 'I thought that I ought to reject as absolutely false all opinions in regard to which I could suppose the least ground for doubt, in order to ascertain whether after that there remained aught in my belief that was wholly indubitable.' A programme of systematic scepticism might thus establish a surer basis for belief than one based on adherence to traditional doctrine. Rigorously he doubted the reality of the world and the validity of the senses, calling into question all experiences and wondering whether or not 'the objects that had ever entered intó my mind when awake, had in them no more truth than the illusions of my dreams. But immediately upon this I observed that, whilst I thus wished to think that all was false, it was absolutely necessary that I, who thus thought, should be somewhat; and as I observed that this truth, *I think, hence I am*, was so certain and of such evidence, that no ground of doubt, however extravagant, could be alleged by the sceptics capable of shaking it, I concluded that I might, without scruple, accept it as the first principle of the philosophy of which I was in search.'

Cogito ergo sum was in no way the conclusion of a syllogism —

> All thinking things must exist;
> I think;
> Therefore I exist —

but a purely intuitive maxim whose very clarity and distinctness made it indubitable: 'by intuition I understand, not the fluctuating testimony of the senses, nor the misleading judgement that proceeds from the blundering constructions of imagination, but the conception which an unclouded and attentive mind gives us so readily and distinctly that we are wholly freed from doubt about that which we understand.' Descartes said, in effect, 'I know I exist because I am conscious that I exist.' Thus consciousness is made the starting-point in the discovery of truth, so that philosophy undertakes the interrogation of the consciousness in order to discover those concepts which are more certain and distinct than anything else. One such concept, for Descartes, was the knowledge of God. 'In the next place, from reflecting on the circumstance that I doubted, and that consequently my being was not wholly perfect (for I clearly saw that it was a greater perfection to know than to doubt), I was led to inquire whence I had learned to think of something more perfect than myself ... accordingly, it but remained that the idea had been placed in me by a nature which was in reality more perfect than mine, and which even possessed within itself all the perfections of which I could form any idea; that is to say, in a single word, which was God.'

Since the existence of God guaranteed that the evidence of the senses was not illusory, Descartes believed he was justified in studying the material world. This, he claimed, was composed of one extended substance, *res extensa*, which might vary in density but was never discontinuous — thus denying the existence of a vacuum — which could only be comprehended by its mathematical quantities of length, breadth and height; which had no life of its own but operated mechanically according to the laws of physics. But human bodies, composed of this lifeless matter have the capacity for thought. Descartes avoided Hobbes's materialist conclusions by making an absolute distinction between mind and body, between *res cogitans* and *res extensa*. This dualism was vital to Descartes's attempt to reconcile the Catholic Church to the advances in scientific knowledge, since it withdrew soul and spirit from the material world, whose investigation was giving rise to controversy, and left them securely in the hands of the Church.

The Church none the less was disturbed by Descartes's philosophy and condemned his works. His equation of matter with extension raised serious difficulties concerning the doctrine of the Creation and of Transubstantiation. His dualism raised equally serious problems about the soul's intimate connection with the mechanism of the body. It could not be part of the body, nor could it be the principle of life within it: 'It is not that the body dies because the soul leaves it but that the soul leaves because the body had died.' Yet it was true that mind and body produced effects within each other; pains in the stomach were related to the mind's clear and distinct desire for food, fears in the mind were reflected in the trembling of limbs. Just before leaving for Stockholm in 1649 Descartes published a less famous work, *Les Passions de l'Âme*, in which he suggested that the soul inhabited the pineal gland at the base of the brain, where it might affect and be affected by the operation of the body. The theory particularly appealed to him since he could find no pineal gland in animals — brute, mechanical creatures without souls.

The Cartesian Revolution: Spinoza and Leibniz

It was Nicholas Malebranche who attempted to make his master's teaching more acceptable to the Church by stressing Descartes's arguments for the necessary existence of God. His *Recherche de la Vérité* (1674) went further by claiming that, since the evidence of the senses is suspect, all knowledge results from the divine illumination of the intellect. Malebranche, moreover, adopted the theory of occasionalism, first published in Antwerp by Arnold Geulincx (1665), in order to solve the problem of body and soul by explaining the apparent interaction between them as the result of divine intervention. *On the occasion* of a man's desire to move his hand, God miraculously causes a corresponding effect to take place in the body in conformity with the desire: he similarly produces experiences in the mind on the occasion of changes in the body. 'Here then was a queer outcome of the new search for truth: miraculous interventions had been banished from the physical universe only to reappear within the narrow compass of the individual human being. God had made the world in such a way that it could run "of itself", but he had made man so fearfully and wonderfully that he could not act or perceive without God's continuous intervention.'[39]

If orthodox minds were only partially reassured by the efforts of Malebranche to make Cartesian philosophy respectable, their worst suspicions were to be confirmed by the development of this philosophy by Baruch Spinoza. Born in 1632 into a family of

---

[39] Professor Basil Willey, *The Seventeenth Century Background*, p.82.

Portuguese Jews who had sought refuge in Amsterdam, he caused alarm by his boldly critical exposition of the Old Testament in which he subjected inspiration to the judgement of reason. In consequence he was excommunicated from the synagogue in 1656, since his views not only scandalised the members but made them afraid lest they cause offence to their Dutch neighbours and hosts, orthodox Calvinists whose views on Holy Scripture were as fundamentalist as their own. Spinoza made a living by grinding lenses, but his fame resulted from his quick understanding of the new ideas in science and philosophy, and from the shrewd analysis of his *Principles of Descartes' Philosophy*. By 1663 when he finally settled at Voorburg near The Hague he was a prominent figure, the friend of many scientists, including Oldenburg, the first secretary of the Royal Society in London, Huygens and Leibniz, and also of men like Jan de Witt and the Elector Palatine — who offered him the chair of philosophy at Heidelberg, which Spinoza refused lest the responsibility of such a post should constrain his freedom of thought. He remained at Voorburg until his death at the age of 45, writing the *Tractatus-Theologico-Politicus* (1670), the *Tractatus-Politico* and the *Ethica*, the last two appearing in print immediately after his death.

Spinoza's thought was greatly influenced by that of Descartes. He adopted *l'esprit géométrique* so literally that the *Ethica* consisted of a system of definitions, axioms, theorems and corollaries, and he accepted the notion of intuitive knowledge, agreeing that, 'he who has a true idea knows at the same time that he has a true idea'. The rigid distinction which Descartes drew between mind and matter did not, however, appeal to him, since he believed that the world as a whole constituted a single substance, none of whose parts was logically capable of any separate existence. The foundation of his system was the idea of God as a substance which exists independently, *causa sui*; God is in fact identified with *natura naturans*, nature which creates, as opposed to *natura naturata*, nature which is created. God's attributes are infinite, but two of them, Thought and Extension, are known to men. Thus the dualism of mind and matter was resolved in the greater unity of God, while the problem of how soul and body interact no longer arose since mind and body were inseparably correlated attributes of one and the same divine substance.

But, since thought and extension were attributes of God — not created by Him but essentially of Him — then there could be no distinction between God and His creation. Such a view, Spinoza claimed, could trouble only those whose anthropomorphic imagination identified God as a person simply because they judged everything in terms of their own experience. Of them he wrote: 'They necessarily estimate other natures by their own ... they consider all natural things alike to be made for their use; and as they know that they found these things as they were and did not make them themselves, they have cause for believing that some one else prepared these things for their use. Now having considered things as means, they cannot believe them to be self-created; but they must conclude ... that there is some governor or governors of nature, endowed with human freedom, who take care of all things for them and make all things for their use.' According to Spinoza they thus had to explain how God could be the author of evil and of suffering in the world, a dilemma which he himself tried to resolve by saying that evil and suffering were merely subjective terms. 'As soon as men had persuaded themselves that all things which were made, were made for their sakes, they were bound to consider as the best quality in everything that which was the most useful to them, and to esteem that above all things which brought them the most good. Hence they must have formed those notions by which they explain the things of nature, to wit, good, evil, order, confusion, hot, cold, beauty, and ugliness, etc.; and as they deemed themselves free agents, the notions of praise and blame, sin and merit, arose.'

Spinoza, however, did not deem men to be free agents. If everything sprang from God's nature, nothing could be independent of it. 'All things are in God and so depend upon Him that without Him they could neither exist nor be conceived; and all things were predetermined by God, not through his free or good will but through his absolute nature or infinite power.' The Cartesian Revolution thus took one more turn. Where Descartes had raised the vitally important questions, 'How do we know things? Is there a fundamental distinction between mind and matter?' Spinoza asked, 'Is God distinct from His creation? Does free will exist?' Determinist and apparently pantheist, Spinoza horrified many contemporaries; but, if there was clearly no place for him in Christianity and Judaism, he was a deeply religious man, and the metaphysical views which aroused controversy were designed principally as the background for his ethical teaching, the release of the mind from mundane things for the eternal love of God.

One of the most brilliant, certainly the most versatile, men of the seventeenth century was Gottfried Wilhelm Leibniz. After training in law he entered the service of the Elector-Archbishop of Mainz as both jurist and diplomat, revising the statutes of the city and proposing schemes for German unity as a defence against the power of Louis XIV. He then became historian-librarian to the House of Brunswick-Wolfenbüttel at Hanover, though his fame spread further afield and both the Elector of Brandenburg and Peter the Great conferred upon him the title of Privy Councillor of Justice, a title he also received in Hanover in 1704. As a theologian he was welcomed equally at Protestant and Catholic courts, even at Rome, and he worked in vain to promote reconciliation between the churches. As a scientist he discovered the infinitesimal calculus independently of Newton and contributed the concept of kinetic energy to mechanics: he was also largely responsible for the foundation of scientific academies at Berlin and St Petersburg. As a philosopher he met and corresponded with Malebranche and Spinoza and, like them, owed everything initially to the inspiration of Descartes.

Like Spinoza, Leibniz sought to unite the separate realities of extension and thought, but he was repelled by Spinoza's notion of them being attributes of one divine substance. His own theory sprang from his great interest in the mathematics of infinitesimals. Extension, he claimed, could not be a reality after all, since whatever was extended was infinitely divisible, and what was made up of parts could not be regarded as an ultimate reality. Since the essential factor in all substances was force, or energy, Leibniz envisaged a universe consisting of centres of force which he termed 'monads'. The monad was 'a simple substance without parts': it was not to be confused with physical atoms since it was metaphysical and without extension of any kind. It was indestructible, unchanging, and completely independent of other monads, 'having no windows by which anything could get out or come in'. Leibniz thus avoided Spinoza's pantheism only to raise a new problem of explaining how things in fact work together in the world. This he solved in a manner reflecting the influence of occasionalism by assuming that the monads operated according to a plan of divine harmony, preordained by God, acting together without actually influencing one another like a set of clocks timed to a master clock.

Monads which lacked consciousness were those of which bodies were composed. Souls were monads of a higher degree of activity since, through the power of the mind, they were capable of knowing the system of the universe. This made them capable of entering into communion with God. Moreover they enjoyed free will, in the sense that their free and spontaneous activity was allowed force in the pre-established harmony of all monads and their states. The world was therefore something more than extension and thought; it was an ensemble of spiritual forces which, in preordained harmony, conformed to the will of God who created the best of all possible worlds.

Monads, as centres of force, could not be static but were capable of development, and by attempting to solve the problem of the mind's development Leibniz became involved in controversy with John Locke[40] over the latter's *Essay on Human Understanding*. The monad, as Leibniz conceived it, was created with innate ideas, the germs of development, while Locke denied the whole concept of innate ideas. 'Our differences', wrote Leibniz, 'are important. The question between us is whether the soul in itself is entirely empty like tablets upon which nothing has been written, according to Aristotle and the author of the *Essay*; and whether all that is there traced comes wholly from the senses and experience; or whether the soul originally contains the principles of several notions and doctrines which the external objects only awaken on occasions as I believe with Plato.' This was vitally important to the followers of the Cartesian method since all certainty was established by appealing to the consciousness. If, however, true and universal ideas were not innate but were acquired through the experience of the senses, then there were no grounds for certainty since Descartes had begun by denying the solidity of everything revealed through the senses. Leibniz agreed that though the senses were necessary for the acquisition of knowledge, yet they could not reveal the full picture. At the best they provided a set of particular, individual

[40] See below, p.73.

truths, but 'All the examples which confirm a general truth, however numerous, do not suffice to establish the universal necessity of that truth, for it does not follow that that which has once occurred will always occur in the same way.'

The Transition to the Eighteenth Century and the Idea of Progress

No one better illustrates the transition from the seventeenth to the eighteenth century than Fontenelle, who was born in the middle of one (1657) and lived through a hundred years to the middle of the next. For much of this time he was secretary to the *Académie des Sciences* and played an important part in the process by which the discoveries of the scientists were made intelligible and were transmitted to the layman. In France, of course, there were many wealthy and leisured families of the *officier* class, who were eager to gain prestige by associating with men of letters, and who were especially welcomed by the scientists as a court of public appeal since they had no vested interest in adhering to the older views. Descartes had deliberately written his *Discours* in French, in order to appeal, as he said, to a reading public which had not been biased by a scholastic education: Fontenelle's *Projet d'une Science Universelle* was also in French, 'which is my native language, because I hope that those who employ only their natural reason will judge better of my opinion than those who only trust to ancient books'.

His most famous work, *Entretiens sur La pluralité des Mondes*, was a discussion between an astronomer and a lady, in which the revelations of the telescope and the new physical explanations of the universe were simplified for popular consumption. In this respect the book was no different from the series of public lectures on geometry, chemistry and astronomy which were becoming fashionable in Paris, but what is so remarkable about its author was the attitude of rational scepticism which presaged the *philosophes* of the eighteenth century far more than it reflected the natural philosophy of the seventeenth. The *philosophes* — men like Montesquieu, Voltaire and Diderot — were prompted by the great advances in knowledge made in the seventeenth century to claim that man's mind had been emancipated from authority, from innate ideas and from revelation. Endowed with the supreme faculty of reason, man was not only autonomous but capable of perfectability. The *philosophes* believed they were emancipating the human spirit by rational enlightenment: the mood, however, was largely secular and ultimately arid since it reduced God to a disinterested first cause, and subjected all authority to a critical scrutiny which destroyed more than it could replace.

Pierre Bayle was another influential writer who provided scientific literature for popular consumption. The appearance of a comet in 1680 had focused attention once again on the popularly held theories of planetary influence on human life, and in particular on the notion that comets had some especial and probably malignant power. Bayle determined to reveal the ignorance and irrationality underlying such beliefs and his *Pensées* were published in 1682. Two years later he began a monthly series of writings on scientific subjects for the general reader, *Nouvelles de la République de Lettres*, and in 1695 he embarked on a task which in its scope foreshadowed the efforts of the *philosophes*. Like them he hoped to assist in the spreading of knowledge by the compilation of a *Dictionnaire historique et critique*: like them, too, his work was largely critical of the Church, discounting revelation and fostering a sceptical spirit which made his book a source of inspiration to the Deists and other opponents of Christianity in the eighteenth century.

Altogether different in character but equally revolutionary in effect was the *Essay concerning Human Understanding* by John Locke,[41] whose rationalist assumptions brought him nearer in spirit to the eighteenth century than Leibniz and others whom in point of time he preceded. The belief that ideas were innate was common to Descartes, Spinoza and Leibniz and went back, as Leibniz said, to Plato, but an age which established an empirical science produced its most modern philosopher in Locke, who denied the innateness of ideas. In doing so, Locke also abandoned the philosophy underlying such a belief, namely the philosophy which postulated the existence of universals. Such a philosophy had already been challenged in part by the nominalists of the later Middle Ages who asserted that universals, for example truth, beauty, or man, are only names which had been invented for linguistic convenience. Locke, however, was even more thorough-going, for he stated that the

---

[41] Locke's political philosophy is described above, p.31.

finite is prior to the infinite, the particular precedes the generalisation, and that knowledge must reject all those beliefs which can only be justified by an appeal to universal concepts. Just as Galileo or Bacon had ignored the general theory until they had built up a system of particular facts and observations, Locke in his *Essay* denied that universal ideas could be evolved except by the acquisition of particular experiences. The mind he compared variously to an empty cupboard or a *tabula rasa*, a clean blackboard, being entirely dependent upon experience for its ideas, and he sought proof of this by showing that children or savages reveal no trace of possessing any universal concepts innately. Complex ideas were merely the sum total of the simple ideas derived from experience.

The interesting point is that Locke, while he attacked the Cartesian or Platonic theory, deliberately avoided any confusion of his own ideas with those of the materialist Hobbes. Hence he refused to derive all knowledge from sensation, taking care to distinguish between sensation and 'another fountain from which experience furnisheth the understanding with ideas', and this source he termed 'reflection'. 'Though it be not sense, as having nothing to do with external objects, yet it is very like it, and might properly enough be called internal sense.' The mind by reflection, therefore, comes to consider the ideas of sensation and builds upon them, and naturally, the sum of the whole can be greater than the sum of the parts. 'When the understanding is once stored with these simple ideas, it has the power of the most exalted wit or enlarged understanding, by any quickness or variety of thought, to invent or frame one new simple idea in the mind not taken in by the ways aforementioned.' As Locke accepted the idea of God he assumed that it must therefore be one of the clearest and most certain of the complex ideas. He was, in fact, a deeply religious man but even in his Christianity he retained his staunch empiricism. He disliked intolerance and distrusted enthusiasm. The enthusiast, he argued, was only too ready to abandon common sense and substitute revelation. Hence 'revelation must be judged of by reason'.

As the seventeenth century broke so decisively with the past, the Golden Age, for the first time in European history, was transposed to the future. The battle between Ancients and Moderns was mostly a literary affair, but ammunition was drawn from most aspects of contemporary culture, not least from science. Corneille, in a preface to *Clitandre*, argued that the Ancients did not know everything, and in view of the discoveries of Galileo, Harvey and Newton it was difficult to refute him. Fontenelle, not unnaturally, made his own contribution to the controversy with two works, *Dialogues des Morts* and *Digression sur les Anciens et les Modernes*, which emphasised the advantages of his own age: 'A man of culture is, as it were, compounded from the distillation of all the cultures of preceding ages. Such a man will have no old age; for men do not degenerate, and there will be a steady accumulation of sanity and wisdom as one age succeeds the other.' Here is a novel concept, not simply of superiority over the Ancients with their misguided notions of motion and matter, but of progress yet to come.

No doctrine of progress could be fully evolved until the zoologists and botanists had arrived at some theory of evolution, which was not to happen until the nineteenth century. Even so, the excitement and enthusiasm created by the new philosophy induced in many a mood of optimism to rival the perplexed pessimism of men like Donne.[42] The most excited, and if not the most characteristic, certainly the most prophetic, voice of all was perhaps that of Joseph Glanvill, who wrote the *Vanity of Dogmatising*. Its title might be prosaic but in the course of the book Glanvill became rhapsodic about the unlimited possibilities of the future. He cited the work of Galileo, Harvey and Descartes — though not of Newton, since he wrote in 1661, as examples of the revolutionary achievements of the age, and continued: 'Should these Heroes go on as they have happily begun, they'll fill the world with wonders. And I doubt not but posterity will find many things that are now but Rumors, verified into practical Realities. It may be some Ages hence, a voyage to Southern unknown tracts, yea possibly to the Moon, will not be more strange than one to America. To them that come after us it may be as ordinary to buy a pair of wings, to fly into remotest Regions; as now a pair of Boots to ride a journey. And to conferr at the distance of the Indies by Sympathetic conveyances, may be as usual to future times, as to us in a litterary correspondence. The restauration of gray hairs to Juvenility, and renewing the exhausted marrow, may at length be affected without a miracle:

[42] See above, p.60.

and the turning of the now comparatively desert world into a
Paradise may not improbably be expected from late Agriculture.'

RELIGION

The Church in the Seventeenth Century

The Reformation, springing from Martin Luther's repudiation of
papal authority in 1521, and the Counter-Reformation this
evoked in the Roman Catholic Church, established the sixteenth
century as an era of violent religious conflict. Justification by
faith alone, the priesthood of all believers, the sole authority of
the scriptures and the sanctity of the individual conscience in
interpreting them, were to remain the characteristic tenets of
Protestantism generally, but the Lutheran Church in particular,
by its emphasis on the individual conscience, became fissiparous.
A new leader had only to arise to challenge the teaching of his
day for a new sect immediately to form around him, its life rarely
being prolonged beyond his own. Of the many sects which broke
away, Calvinism alone was to prove vigorous and effective.
Unlike Luther, who arrived at his doctrines over a period of
many years and whose teaching was not only liable to
inconsistency but was never efficiently collated in his lifetime,
Calvin formulated in the *Institutio* a comprehensive, logically
cohesive theology which served as an invaluable frame of
reference for his followers.

Calvin's doctrine of predestination, that only God's elect were
to be saved, gave tremendous confidence to his followers in the
face of persecution since each confidently assumed his own
inclusion among the elect. Moreover, the international structure
of the Church, centred upon Geneva as a source of inspiration
and instruction, gave them a strength and a cohesion denied to
the members of Lutheran State Churches, each reflecting the
personality of local princes and ministers. Calvin's social
teaching, too, was as positive and as comprehensive as his
theology. In sharp contrast to Luther, whose revulsion from the
mechanical performance of duties, which he associated with the
belief in justification by works, prevented him from laying down

precise rules for his followers, Calvin demanded of his
fellow-elect that they showed by their behaviour in this world
their fitness for salvation in the next. Hence the severe and
comprehensive regulations he laid down, which, in an authoritarian age, attracted many Lutherans who preferred to be told
what to do, especially as Calvin was less conservative than
Luther in his frank recognition of the necessity of commercial life
and his approval of thrift, hard work and sobriety. Less happy for
the future was the possible implication that successful business
men were, by the evidence of God's favour, among the elect while
the poor were damned.

Calvin was more radical than Luther in his repudiation of
Catholicism, rejecting entirely the concept of the Real Presence,
which Luther had tried to preserve by a complicated doctrine of
consubstantiation, and creating an entirely novel administration
in which the consistory of laymen and ministers replaced the
traditional hierarchy of clergy. The Lutheran in consequence
tended to be left in a midway position, exposed to the cross-fire of
both Calvinist and Catholic, especially when the Catholic
Church at the Council of Trent responded to the challenge of the
Reformation by reforming its abuses and restating its doctrine.
Where the Protestant believed in salvation by faith alone, and the
priesthood of all believers, the Catholic Church uncompromisingly asserted the value of good works and the necessity of its
own mediation by means of the confessional and the sacraments.
Thus the dividing-line between orthodoxy and heresy, unwittingly crossed by many Catholics in the early days of the
Reformation, was distinctly drawn, and the Society of Jesus was
formed specifically to recover ground lost to the Catholic Church.
The Jesuit was required to have attained a respectable standard
of education before admission to the Society; he then devoted two
years of his novitiate entirely to a routine designed to develop his
character in holiness and obedience, after which he resumed his
studies for the priesthood. The *Exercitia Spiritualia,* drawn up by
Ignatius Loyola, the Society's founder, trained him not only in
meditation, self-knowledge and humility, but also prepared him
for martyrdom. Though they were not the only champions of the
Counter-Reformation, the Jesuits were remarkable in their
achievements. As skilful debaters, thoroughly grounded in
theology, they recovered many to their Church: as confessors

they gained the ears of rulers, urging them to renew their efforts to fight heresy: as educators they formed the minds of many of the new generation.[43]

The impetus given to the conflict by the Calvinists on the one hand and by the Jesuits on the other, ensured that the controversy was no less bitter, no less intense in 1600 than it had been in Luther's day; and in the Thirty Years War the passions roused by theology burned fiercely. But to the devout and the dogmatic on both sides they did not burn fiercely enough: for them the war proved sadly inconclusive. The denominational frontiers of 1648 differed only slightly from those of 1618 — remaining virtually fixed for the rest of the century — and though religious faith continued to be a vital force in seventeenth-century life it lost its importance as a prime cause of warfare. Consequently, the rival Churches had to come to terms with a state of compulsory coexistence. For this reason the papal bull *Zelo Domus Dei* condemned the peace as 'null and void, accursed and without any influence or result for the past, the present or the future', but it could not alter the realities of seventeenth-century politics. Coexistence did not necessarily imply toleration of a rival faith in one's own country. Most states opposed the existence of religious dissent on grounds of security; a few allowed it to some extent as good for trade. In both cases *raison d'état* decided the outcome, though, generally speaking, the clergy themselves held no brief for toleration.

Reunion, however, was a cause which won a surprising amount of lip-service, and if few took it seriously it was given much publicity by men like Grotius and Leibniz.[44] Exiled from Holland both for his tolerant sympathy with the Arminians and for his friendship with the Catholic Oldenbarneveldt, Grotius had advocated reunion in two books, *Via ad Pacem Ecclesiasticum* and *Votum pro Pace Ecclesiastica*, published in 1642, but to little effect. Leibniz, after his appointment to Hanover, found himself in an unusually tolerant court, his patron, the duke, becoming a Catholic, but his successor marrying the daughter of the Calvinist Elector Palatine. It was easier for him than for Grotius, therefore, to believe that all confessions could find agreement in the fundamental rules of faith provided they gave themselves to

---

[43] Maximilian of Bavaria and Ferdinand of Styria were both pupils of the Jesuits.
[44] For Grotius see above, pp.21–2, for Leibniz see pp.70–72.

honest discussion. By way of a preliminary to this he began a
correspondence with Bossuet, the distinguished French theologian; but Bossuet was handicapped in this, as were all Catholics,
by the dogmas of the Council of Trent, and it was over the
question of the Council's authority that the correspondence
ended. This same point was taken up by another Catholic
bishop, Cristobal de Roja y Spinola, who, sent by the pope on a
mission to rally all German opinion against the Ottoman peril in
1673, became convinced of the possibility of reunion. He wanted
to pave the way for the summoning of a new General Council,
but realised that in order for it to succeed the decisions of Trent
would first have to be suspended. This was not a proposal which
won support, and it died with him in 1695.

Paradoxically, while reunion, an officially respectable guest,
failed to secure admission, toleration, universally reviled, began
to creep in at the back door. It had few advocates. Not only did
Catholics and Protestants abhor each other, but within each
Church intolerance and exclusiveness prevailed whenever a
serious division of opinion arose. Paul Gerhardt, famous for
many Lutheran hymns, left Brandenburg after many conflicts
with the Calvinist clergy, exiling himself to Saxony with the
bitter words, 'I cannot regard the Calvinists as Christians'.
Saxony, because of its traditional link with Luther's University of
Wittenberg, remained the fount of purest Lutheranism — or so it
believed. Others were more critical: 'If things are to go on
according to the intentions of the Elector of Saxony ... we shall
have a new papacy and a new religion', wrote George Calixtus,
but he was a liberal Lutheran of the University of Helmstedt,
who advocated syncretism, the belief that it was more profitable
to establish points of agreement between the Protestant Churches
than to emphasise the disputed ones. He was attacked from all
sides, and elsewhere the supporters of toleration awoke little
response. Nevertheless, though in most countries the limits of
religious freedom were contracting, the practice of unofficial
toleration began to grow haltingly, especially in those areas
where men became less fearful, or more indifferent.

The Churches, however, had serious problems to face other
than their own rivalry or intolerance, for as man's horizons
widened the centre of his interest changed. Trade expanded,
standards of living for the wealthy began to improve, and the

quest for material comfort was redoubled. Men absorbed in the present had less time for the eternal. This was not the consequence of commerce alone but of something more general. While it is true that the sense of God's presence in every act of daily life remained an integral feature of life in general, there were none the less aspects of life which, formerly spiritual, were becoming increasingly secular. The service of the state was an all-absorbing occupation with its own morality; science and philosophy began to move away from theology; international relations eluded the control of the Churches. This last was due in part to the greater control exercised by the State over the Church. The long conflict of the faiths had left the secular State to rise as arbiter between them, while the idea of sovereignty as an attribute of the prince alone left little room for the concept of the Church as an equal partner in the State.

As men travelled throughout the world in search of trade they discovered not only new merchandise but old religions. The *Koran* was already known to Europe, but from further afield such works as the *Analects* of Confucius awoke a surprised response in European minds. Pagans though they might be, Chinese and Indians were seen to have concepts of virtue and morality, of God and of eternity, without ever having heard of Christ. In consequence, the discovery of such unsuspected wisdom in these alien religions induced a relativism which in turn gave rise to scepticism, as La Bruyère commented: 'Some complete their demoralization by extensive travel, and lose whatever shreds of religion remained to them. Every day they see a new religion, new customs, new rites.' It also promoted a tendency to call in question the unique character of the Christian Church, to think of a 'natural religion' to which all religions approximated; this especially since the collapse of scholasticism and the schism of the Reformation seemed to point the moral that no religion had a monopoly of wisdom or of inspiration. 'Who can doubt', wrote the sceptic Bayle, 'that the Church is sometimes more, sometimes less enlightened and that in this diversity of illumination and knowledge, it may quite legitimately have different opinions on the same things.'

Nothing, however, was quite so devastating in its ultimate effect upon the Church than the impact of the scientific and intellectual revolutions. Descartes was implicitly a religious man, convinced of the truth of the Christian revelation, but Cartesianism opened up paths which Descartes himself never thought to tread; nor did his disciple and apologist, Malebranche, fully realise that the Cartesian God was not altogether congruous with the God of the New Testament. Locke never challenged the necessity nor the value of revelation but the relative position he assigned it implied that it merely confirmed what could be acquired in other ways. His successors accordingly deified reason, deposed revelation, and subjected the Scriptures to intensive, and often unsympathetic, scrutiny. Most of this of course took place in the eighteenth century, but long before the damage was done the Church might well have taken effective counter-action. Unfortunately, as an institution wedded to medieval principles of science and philosophy, it seemed more concerned to oppose the revolution than to play a part in it. Scholastic thought continued to dominate Catholic theology as though no revolution had taken place. Protestant response varied greatly. Luther had condemned Copernicus, but his successors were free to reject the ancient cosmology since it was not specifically taught in the Scriptures, for them the sole source of authority. For the Calvinist, in particular, the Cartesian concept of God setting the universe to work according to unalterable laws coincided reasonably well with the doctrine of predestination, and Descartes's ideas were accordingly permitted to be taught in the United Provinces and at Puritan Cambridge.

Nonetheless, no one but Blaise Pascal realised that the challenge of the new ideas had to be met if the victory were not ultimately to go by default to the freethinkers. A gifted mathematician with tremendous powers of imagination and analysis,[45] he abandoned his scientific pursuits after a mystical religious experience in 1654 which entirely altered his life. From then he devoted his time to the preparation of material for a defence of Christianity. His death supervened in 1662 before he could complete it, but his *Pensées* indicated the pattern of his work. His concern being to expose the inevitable weakness of human reason and the necessity of faith, he used the scientists' own regard for factual truth to challenge those who gave reason pride of place over revelation, by demonstrating that human life was in fact entangled in irrational confusion. The endemic misery

[45] See above, p.42.

of mankind indicated man's fallen state from which nothing but the operation of divine grace could raise him. Pascal thus offered an attitude to the rational science of his day which, if the Church had adopted it, might have given it greater strength with which to face the free-thinking assault of the succeeding century. Religion, he argued, was not detachable from the rest of life. 'It illuminates our nature and experience. It draws into a unity the scattered elements in our life. It guides our minds and controls our science, because it alone can unfold the full mystery of nature. It answers the questions which reason can only raise, and it brings us to that fulfilment of life towards which science in its more limited way is struggling. It cannot be set in opposition to reason or science, because it includes yet transcends both.'[46]

The Varieties of Christian Experience

Whatever the difficulties and inadequacies of the Christian Church in the seventeenth century, its spiritual life was both intense and varied. In France during the first half of the century the *dévots*, as they were termed, led a spiritual revival, a natural outcome of the Counter-Reformation though altogether different from the more emotional, almost sensational, movements in Spain and Italy. Its keynote was active Christianity, its inspiration the Cardinal Bérulle, who founded the French Oratory as a means to train clergy; this was, perhaps, the most necessary reform the Gallican Church required since there were few seminaries and the average *curé* was often invincibly ignorant. Bérulle's followers maintained his characteristic blend of devotion and practical action. St Francis of Sales, titular bishop of Geneva, wrote two classic works of devotion, the *Treatise on the Love of God* and an *Introduction to a Devout Life*, persevered successfully against enormous odds to recover the inhabitants of the Chablais from Calvinism, and founded the Order of Visitation, the Visitandines or Salesian Sisters, who were to leave their convents to care for the sick and to teach, an innovation eventually suppressed by the Archbishop of Lyon. The Sisters of Charity, however, founded by St Vincent de Paul, secured permission to work in the world, particularly to alleviate the poverty of the country districts caused by the warfare of the

[46] G.R. Cragg, *The Church in the Age of Reason (1648-1789)*, p.43.

Fronde: The spiritual poverty of these areas especially concerned St Vincent and he established the Lazarist Fathers to assist and to educate the country *curés*.

A movement which aroused St Vincent's bitter opposition, and indeed the pope's too, sprang from the teaching of Cornelius Jansen, bishop of Ypres in the Spanish Netherlands. Jansen condemned the ceremonial of the Church which, to him, merely disguised the fact that man could only be saved by God's grace, which, once granted, resulted in man's love for God and, through love, faith. His *Augustinus*, a study of the saint most drawn upon by Protestants in the sixteenth century, not unnaturally resulted in a system which had much in common with Calvinism, not least in its belief in predestination and in its puritan spirit. Two things in particular — that man cannot fulfil God's commands without the assistance of a special Grace, and that God's grace is irresistible so that there is no withstanding it — proved objectionably pessimistic and determinist to many other Catholics, and not least to the Jesuits. Indeed it was their conflict with them, rather than their own theology, which won the Jansenists their fame. In France the movement was led by Antoine Arnauld, a doctor of the Sorbonne, and by his sister Angélique, Abbess of Port-Royal in Paris. Arnauld's publication of *De la Fréquent Communion* (1643) brought the conflict into the open by criticising the laxity of the Jesuits in the confessional. Their doctrine of probabilism urged the confessor to be lenient if there were good grounds for granting absolution, in order that the morally frail be not for ever barred from the Mass, but it was true that probabilism had often degenerated into a lax casuistry. The Jansenists were not alone in criticising this, but Arnauld's demands were typically rigorous in that the penitent was to be denied absolution until his confessor was absolutely satisfied of his contrition.

Later the Jansenists won the support of Pascal, whose *Lettres Provenciales* eternally branded the Jesuit with the stigma of casuistry, and gave the controversy immortality by the brilliant sarcasm of his style. The Jesuits mobilised their reserves, the movement fell foul of Louis XIV[47] and was proscribed by the popes. Independently of its persecution, the movement degenerated as it lost the impetus of its founders. It tended to become

[47] See Chapter VI, p.310.

associated with the type of reformed sinner who demands a
regimen of unattainable rigour in order to compensate for his
past life by making his present one unbearable. Its puritanism,
originally a valuable and necessary warning against the dangers
of ceremonial, developed into a harsh and narrow doctrine,
reinforced by an unduly pessimistic view of mankind and by the
spiritual pride which often accompanies belief in the predestination of the elect to salvation. This attitude was to be found in the
writing of Pierre Nicole (1625-95): 'All these blind sinners,
abandoned to their passions, are proofs of the rigour and justice
of God which delivers them to the devils who torment them and,
after inflicting infinite miseries upon them in this life, plunges
them into the abyss of eternal torture.' Toleration, denied them
by Louis XIV, was not something the Jansenists were likely to
grant to anyone else. In this respect they resembled the rigorist
Calvinists of Holland who condemned Arminianism.

Arminius, a student of Calvinist theology at Leyden, had
subsequently studied both at Geneva and at Rome, an education
which had confirmed him in his naturally charitable and
humanist outlook. On his return to Leyden he questioned
Calvin's doctrine of predestination since it seemed to him
incomprehensible that God should deny men free will and that
He should preordain most men to damnation. It was an ancient
problem: Arminius could not deny God's prescience lest he limit
God's omniscience, but his humane instincts compelled him to
modify the harsher implications of predestination. 'God has of all
eternity established this distinction among fallen humanity, that
those who renounce their sins and place their trust in Christ are
granted forgiveness of their sins and life eternal; those, however,
who remain impenitent are to be punished. Moreover, it is
agreeable to God that all men should be converted ... But He
compels no one.' The divinity school at Leyden became an arena
in which Arminius was challenged at every point by his rigorist
colleague, Gomarus: 'An eternal and divine decree', he
thundered, 'has established which men were to be saved, and
which were to be damned.' The conflict then turned to the
sources of Calvinist theology as the contestants argued over the
interpretation of sentences, but neither side could allow its
emotional philosophy to be decided by logical discussion. In the
event the appeal was made to force, and the Gomarists were

victorious.[48]

Despite the evils associated with rigid and intolerant dogmatism, the formulation of theology was a necessary process and it had been one of the weaknesses of the Lutheran Church that it had lacked a coherent body of dogma. Under pressure of attacks from Geneva and Rome, the second and third generations of Lutherans undertook to remedy this. Unfortunately their approach was tediously scholastic, and resulted in arid controversy. Preaching, once the greatest strength of the Lutheran Church, became notoriously argumentative about minor points of doctrine. Consequently the Church lost touch with the ordinary people, who looked for a more personal faith, immediately relevant to their own lives. To satisfy this need, a religious revival began which drew its inspiration not only from Luther but from an older tradition of mysticism, established in the fourteenth century. Pietism, as it was termed, owed its foundation to Phillipp Jakob Spener, a Lutheran minister, whose *Pia Desideria* presented a programme of reform in which personal piety and the fear of God were to be the central features, and the sermon to be restored to its devotional character. In addition, he established centres of fellowship, *collegia pietatis*, so that his followers might find by shared experience that faith was less a matter of doctrine than a way of life. If Pietism was characterised by faults of emotionalism and contempt of learning, this was only to be expected in the circumstances, reflecting as it did a passionate discontent with the arid formalism of the official Lutheran Church. In Saxony the authorities made known their disapproval, but Spener at last won the support of the Elector Frederick of Brandenburg, later to become king of Prussia, and in 1694 established the University of Halle, which became a centre from which Pietism expanded in the eighteenth century, not only throughout Germany, but even reaching through its organised missions, the shores of India and America.

Another reaction from formal theology was to be found in the Catholic Church as a result of the mystic doctrines of Miguel de Molinos, a Spanish priest who became famous among fashionable society in Rome. By abandoning all effort, by resigning itself to complete passivity, the soul, he claimed, would lose itself in God and thus attain perfection. But the concept of passivity, of

[48] See Chapter V, p.251.

becoming a vessel filled with God, could easily be corrupted into the notion that such a soul was therefore incapable of sin; from this it was but a short step to suppose that the body containing it could go through the actions of sin without being contaminated. The Catholic Church, moreover, while accepting the fact of mysticism, has always been suspicious of those who insisted on their direct access to God since, strong in their immediate knowledge and experience of God, they become intolerant of authority and frequently dispense with dogmas, rites and the entire priesthood. This, in fact, happened among the nuns whom Molinos directed in Rome when they discarded their rosaries and refused to go to confession or to recite their office. Condemned to lifelong imprisonment by the Inquisition for various propositions in his works and for irregularities in his private life, Molinos yet continued to exert great influence through his most popular work, the *Guida Spirituale* (1675).

The mystic concepts of Molinism appeared in France, under the name of Quietism, through Madame Guyon, a remarkable widow, obsessed with the need for spirituality in religion. Whereas the Church accepted as valid the experience of the great mystics of the past, she affirmed that such communion with God was possible for lesser people who were not acclaimed as saints: by an act of total passivity, the love of God could be directly experienced by a large number of virtuous, but ordinary, Christians. Moreover, in her *Moyen court et très facile de faire oraison* (1685) she claimed that there was no need to ponder the great truths of the Gospel since these were not the proper objects of pure contemplation. The one thing needful was to yield, 'to the torrent of the forces of God'. Her confessor was arrested by Harlay, Archbishop of Paris, and she herself was threatened with removal to a convent as a lunatic until, through the mediation of a cousin among the ladies of Madame de Maintenon, she was released and brought to Versailles. There she won the friendship of Fénelon, whose *Explication des maximes des saints*, published in 1697, distinguished true from false mysticism in a sincere attempt not only to protect Madame Guyon, but also to moderate her own extravagant opinions. Bossuet, however, who could see none of the qualities of Quietism which attracted Fénelon, but only its threat to orthodoxy and authority, appealed both to Rome and to Louis XIV. Though Fénelon was high in the king's favour, and tutor to his grandson, he could not overcome the pathological dislike of nonconformity which inspired Louis's religious policy in general.[49] Madame Guyon was arrested, and finally exiled, while Fénelon was compelled to submit to a papal condemnation of his ideas.

THE AGE OF THE BAROQUE

The Principles of Roman Baroque Architecture

Baroque architecture was born of very diverse parents. As a child of the Renaissance it inherited the classical standards of Vitruvius[50] which had inspired and guided the work of Brunelleschi, Alberti, Bramante and Michelangelo. Since they were men of universal genius not one of them had applied the rules of composition slavishly: their styles had expanded and developed within a common form, and because of their work Renaissance architecture was never allowed to stagnate into mere formalism. Michelangelo had become absorbed by the tremendous struggle between the engineering skill of the architect and the overpowering masses of masonry, and his response marked the transition from the Renaissance proper, as formally codified by art historians, to the Baroque. But the next step was long delayed. If the discovery of Vitruvius had supplied the basic grammar for the language of Renaissance architecture, its later effect was to enable mechanical academicians to preach grammar when they had nothing new to say. After Michelangelo's death in 1564 there ensued such a phase, termed 'Mannerism', in which accepted motifs and rules were handled either too rigidly or too self-consciously. Intellect triumphed over inspiration, and the result was as arid as the sermons of the Lutheran pastors.[51] Just as some Lutheran congregations had therefore embraced Pietism, so Italian architects evolved the Baroque as their protest against the exclusion of the emotions from building.

---

[49] See Chapter VI, pp.302–13.
[50] Marcus Vitruvius Pollio, a Roman architect whose *De Architectura*, written shortly before the birth of Christ, was recovered during the fifteenth century.
[51] See above, p.85.

But Baroque owed even more to its other parent, the Counter-Reformation. It was a style with an avowed missionary purpose. The champions of the Counter-Reformation, after an initial period of ascetism — in reaction to the pagan hedonism they identified in the Renaissance — recruited the fine arts in a new campaign to recover the heretic to the faith. For the Roman Catholic the miracle of transubstantiation made the Real Presence a sacred reality. A church, therefore was not simply a preaching box or a place for private meditation, but the House of God, which in pomp and majesty could not rank second to a temporal palace. The humanist detachment of Bramante's Tempietto in Rome or of Brunelleschi's church of S. Lorenzo in Florence afforded the Church no support in its war with heresy. To sustain the fighting spirit of the Counter-Reformation it was necessary to appeal directly to the eyes and to the emotions of the people by a splendid display of magnificence and drama. Hence, the Counter-Reformation, through the medium of the Baroque, 'overwhelmed heresy by splendour; it did not argue but proclaimed; it brought conviction to the doubter by the very scale of its grandeurs; it guaranteed truth by magniloquence.'[52]

The propaganda values of painting and architecture were first exploited by the Jesuits, and the Gesù, their church in Rome begun in 1568, gave some indication of what was to follow. The interior by Giacomo Vignola is not as he left it, since a great deal was added by way of decoration in the last quarter of the seventeenth century, but the basic structure still reveals his purpose. By means of massive columns, by a heavy cornice running along the nave to carry the eye eastwards, by dramatic lighting and by the bright blue pigment of lapis in the ornate side chapels, he set out to design a church of palatial splendour to reassure the faithful and to silence the sceptic. Materialist in its profuse ornamentation, it is wholly spiritual in inspiration, and within these polarities much of the Baroque was to be defined. The facade by Della Porta was as novel as the interior and equally as important in setting a trend for the future. The features were indeed those of classical architecture, but his treatment of them was revolutionary: pilasters were doubled up to achieve variety and grandeur, while the bold use of volutes, two massive scrolls, to link the first and second stories gave a

52 W. Sypher, *Four Stages of Renaissance Style*.

dramatic unity to the whole. The Renaissance architect had defined and differentiated each part of his composition, articulating the stories by the use of the appropriate orders, to establish a mood of serene mastery and control, of balance and logic. The Baroque architect merged all the parts together in an organic unity so that one form appeared to grow out of another, instead of being placed beside it for some logical principle. Boldness, strength and power became the characteristics of the architecture of the militant Counter-Reformation.

From Michelangelo and the Renaissance, from the Gesù and the Counter-Reformation, sprang the drama and the opulent florescence of Roman Baroque in the seventeenth century. It has horrified the purists, who seem to believe that the conventions of the Tuscan tradition, of Brunelleschi and Alberti, should be frozen for all time, and who have coined the word 'baroque' from the Portuguese for a deformed pearl. It has aroused the suspicion of the northerner, perennially contemptuous yet fearful of the operatic qualities, both sensuous and sensational, of the Latin races. It has frightened the puritan out of his wits. Discomfited by the blatant appeal to his senses, he has sniffed behind the most devout Catholic art to discern latent traces of paganism and idolatry. In fact Baroque architecture is nothing more than an attempt to excite, to uplift and to impress; by the dramatic use of mass, light and colour it seeks to create a sense of grandeur and movement which will overwhelm the spectator.

Since propaganda is the art of public proclamation, the exterior design and decoration of the churches acquired an interest and an importance for the Baroque architect which his predecessors of the Renaissance had not always shared, and though the difference between the two styles is, in this respect, one of degree and emphasis only, it is still a valid one. The classic Renaissance interior of the church of S. Lorenzo in Florence is married to external walls and an incomplete façade which have as much dignity and charm as a warehouse: this example, if an extreme one and the result of chance, none the less reflects the Renaissance architects' preoccupation with the interiors of their churches. The Baroque architect from the very beginning conceived of his church as an integral part of its neighbourhood and could not leave its outer appearance to chance. Hence, when circumstances allowed, he delighted in the siting of fountains and statuary, the planning of squares, colonnades, and flights of steps with ornate balustrades, so that at the dramatic centre of the scene his church might rise. The dome, among the most dramatic of all architectural features, had an especial appeal and was constantly exploited since it gave majesty to the skyline of the church and, almost literally, crowned it in its regal setting.

Of great importance was the façade, the flat surface at the centre of the vista which had to be related to the whole by means of its decoration. To achieve this the accepted rules of the sixteenth century were abandoned. Curves replaced straight lines, and forms swelled and writhed instead of merely standing. The impressive façade of S. Agnese in Piazza Navona at Rome, designed by Borromini and Rainaldi, curves outward to bring it in line with the bases of its flanking towers. The towers themselves are novel in that the first storey is square, the second round, and as such a juxtaposition was inconceivable in classic rules the method of reconciling them by a curiously broken entablature had to be unique also. But so succesful is the dramatic effect that it is only upon examination that the novelty of the individual features is noticed. It is the impact of the whole which counts. For this same reason, the storeys of the facade were rarely articulated by the appropriately decorated capitals and pillars of the Renaissance; in their place the use of giant columns or pilasters, stretching from top to bottom gave a dramatic unity to the façade. Frequently, to enhance this effect and to catch the eye, the columns might be grouped in pairs, or their stonework carved into spiral patterns soaring to the crowning pediment.

The handling of masses, the swelling domes, the spiral columns, the curved façades with their exciting patterns of concave-convex surfaces all indicate the sculptural quality of Baroque architecture, and, like a piece of sculpture, a Baroque church is an organic whole. The exterior was planned as the focal point of the neighbourhood; within, the unity of the decorative plan was equally imperative. If the architect were to succeed in his object of exciting, uplifting and impressing the spirits of the spectators, then he had to stage manage his effects with care. The sculptured figures are not merely placed upon pedestals or in niches along the walls but seem to have grown there, living parts of the organism, blending not only with their setting but also with the painted figures from which at a distance they can scarcely be distinguished. By tricks of perspective, and by exploiting the theatrical nature of the setting, Gaulli could paint the ceiling of the Gesù so that the formal lozenges and volutes of the patterned roof are broken in the centre as though the roof had opened to admit a heavenly host, enraptured in the worship of the holy name of Jesus. Not only is the line of the ceiling broken, it is broken irregularly so that while some of the figures appear against the sky, others seem to be borne upon cloud within the very canopy of the roof. For those who are not too busy protesting at the *trompe-l'œil*, the effect is tremendous.

Where the Baroque succeeds it represents a union of the arts of the architect, the painter and the sculptor, acting in concert to attack the emotions of the spectator. Total effect is more important than obedience to formal rules, and in this respect the Baroque is essentially theatrical, not least in its concealment of structural features behind statuary of stucco work and in its skilful understanding of the dramatic qualities of light. Statues and altar figures were often lit by concealed windows, and the windows themselves were coloured so that the exact hue might be predetermined, as for example, in Bernini's S. Andrea al Quirinale where the panes of the lantern are stained yellow so that even on dull days the light filtering through appears to be sunlight. Like most other features of the Baroque, lighting was first exploited in the Gesù. The nave is lit by windows over the side chapels, but the last one before the crossing was deliberately made smaller in order to admit less light than the others: this serves to heighten the dramatic effect of the flood of light which pours from the windows of the lantern, to illuminate the crossing and to draw the eye towards the altar.

After the Council of Trent had deliberately reasserted the dogma of transubstantiation the need to stress the importance of the altar, and its primacy over all other features, made it impossible to continue the use of the central plan which had been a prominent feature of the Renaissance, since this gave no particular emphasis to the east end. In its place the Baroque exploited the oval, which lent itself to exciting variations in treatment, especially so in the relationship of concave-convex lines. Moreover, and this was the specific function of the oval, its two axes of different lengths gave a more formal definition to the structure, thus creating an awareness of length and breadth which helped to focus the eye more directly upon the high altar.

The Architects of Rome, Vienna and Paris

The chief characteristics of the Baroque — its sculptural quality, its rejection of the restraint imposed by the Mannerists, its fervent championing of the Counter-Reformation — were reflected in the personality of its foremost exponent, Gian Lorenzo Bernini, who was not only a sculptor but devoutly practised the *Spiritual Exercises* of the Jesuits. His father, a sculptor also, brought him to Rome from Naples while still a child and trained him in the Mannerist tradition of the day. This tradition Bernini soon abandoned. Dissatisfied by the taste for multiple silhouettes, an effect which often creates an impression of uncertainty and strain, at once disturbing and disturbed, he preferred to achieve a more dynamic, more dramatic and yet much calmer effect by emphasising a single frontal viewpoint. Between 1621 and 1624, by a series of commissions for Cardinal Borghese, which included the *Rape of Proserpina, David, Apollo and Daphne*, he established a reputation as the finest artist since Michelangelo, whose brooding temperament and latent violence he shared but whose concept of sculpture he rejected. Instead of letting the figure adhere closely to the block, as Michelangelo insisted, he tried to liberate it from its material limitations so that it might break through into the world of the spectator. This in essence was the nature of Baroque; an attempt to shatter the formal distinction between virtual space, created by the artist, and real space, inhabited by the spectator. The audience and the action were thus made one.

Bernini brought to the task a consummate skill, especially with marble; he also exploited the effects created by using coloured lights and mixed materials, as can be seen in his chapel dedicated to Saint Teresa in the church of S. Maria della Vittoria in Rome. The walls are richly faced with marbles of amber, gold and pink, but the spectator's attention is riveted by the heavy coupled columns and the broken pediment which frame the altar: these are projected at an angle to the wall to catch his eye and to lead it within the frame, not to the traditional altar painting but to a

sculptural group of astonishing vigour. Saint Teresa, apparently
rising through the air, swoons in an agony of pain and blissful
ecstasy as the angel raises the golden arrow with which, in the
legend of her vision, he pierced her heart. The effect is heightened
by the diagonal tilt of the group, by the golden light admitted
from a hidden window, and by the golden beams, gilt metal
shafts, which conceal the blank wall of the altar niche. In order to
grant whole-hearted admiration to Bernini's work it is clearly
important to be sympathetic to the legend which inspired it, and
much of the controversy which has raged around the altarpiece
has reflected religious rather than artistic prejudices. One
objective comment, however, seems justified: in contrast to his
penetrating studies of Louis XIV or Cardinal Borghese,
Bernini's treatment of religious themes in general was perhaps
too emotional and too contrived. His David appears too
self-consciously righteous, his Teresa too ecstatic, to be wholly
convincing.

In the altarpiece of Saint Teresa Bernini established an
intimate relationship between sculpture and architecture, as he
had already tried to do in his *baldaquino*, the majestic bronze
canopy he constructed in St Peter's in order to give the greatest
possible dignity and emphasis to the most important high altar of
the Catholic Church. Its four spiralling columns soar one
hundred feet to a canopy which, for all its weight, deceives the
eye by the lightness of its sculptured drapery. But the total effect
is marred by the setting. The unrestrained grandeur and
extravagant detail, breath-taking in themselves, contrast uneasily with the austerity of Michelangelo's walls. Bernini, therefore,
seized avidly upon the opportunity to supply the architectural
background for his own decoration when he was invited to build
S. Andrea al Quirinale in Rome.

The result was a perfectly integrated Baroque church. Bernini
made no deliberate pursuit of novelty: in 1625 he had designed
the façade of S. Bibiana in a manner conventional enough to be
wholly uninspiring, and his subsequent exterior work rarely
broke the accepted conventions. If a curve would do the work of a
straight line then he would use it, as he did in St Peter's Square,
where he transformed a correctly devised classical loggia of
free-standing colonnades by laying them out in an elliptical
curve; but if his treatment of classical forms endowed them with a

new significance, he never abandoned them in the revolutionary manner of his contemporary, Borromini.[53] Hence his façade to S. Andrea al Quirinale is correct enough, save perhaps for the convex portico and for the quadrants formed by two retaining walls on its flanks. Inside, however, his blend of painting, sculpture and architecture is more revolutionary. The ground plan is an oval, set against the façade so that entry is at the most obtuse point of the ellipse, from where the eye can take in the entire church. The three most dominant features are the sanctuary, heavily framed by coupled columns and flooded with light; the figure of Saint Andrew, who soars above it to the gilded dome; the dome itself, ornately decorated with hexagonal patterns in white and gold which diminish in size towards the lantern. The windows of the drum are dramatically alive with the marble figures of god-like young men whose lively nonchalance makes the spectator feel an intruder, while above them angels in stucco hover around the frame of the lantern.

In the history of Roman Baroque architecture Bernini's name is permanently linked with that of Francesco Borromini, though in every important respect the two men were remarkably dissimilar. Borromini, the son of an architect, was first trained in Milan as a mason. From there he went to Rome in 1615 at the age of sixteen to work under his cousin, Carlo Maderno, who had built the nave and façade of St Peter's. It was an auspicious start and he learned much from his cousin, but he was still only a mason in 1629 when Maderno died and was succeeded as papal architect by Bernini. It was not easy for Borromini to serve a man of passionate moods who was only one year older than himself, and, though he avoided any open breach, he resigned his post as chief mason in 1633. Six more years elapsed before he won his first independent commission as an architect. This slow burgeoning of his genius resulted in part from inborn modesty and caution so that he appeared to be diffident and unambitious, but there was a deeper cause. Where Bernini was subject to frequent fits of tempestuous passion, Borromini was the slave to sombre moods of melancholy. Labouring only to glorify God through the perfection of his art, he was perpetually aware of his deficiencies, and, lacking his rival's self-confident *bravura*, the illusion of his own inadequacy preyed upon his mind. In the end,

[53] See next paragraph.

despite nearly thirty years of acclamation as an architect, he destroyed all his drawings in a paroxysm of despair and took his own life.

Despite the hesitancy, despite the inner turmoil which ultimately paralysed his creative spirit, Borromini was in comparison with Bernini by far the more fearless innovator. From his intense admiration for Michelangelo's sculpture he came to believe that proportion was God's special gift to mankind, having its origin in His creation of the human form.[54] Consequently he maintained that none could succeed as architects but painters and sculptors who were familiar with the human body, since they alone would have the ability to fashion buildings into true living forms. In this organic view of architecture he propounded a basic principle of the Baroque, but one which revealed a profound difference from Bernini. There was little in the plans and elevations of Bernini's work at which Vitruvius might have cavilled. His basic structure was classical; it was in his sculptural treatment of it and in his decoration that he was novel and, by classical standards, extravagant. Borromini's extravagance lay in his original and dramatic handling of the basic structure itself; the greater his audacity here, the more restrained became his surface decoration.

His greatest single-handed achievement was the church of S. Carlino alle Quattro Fontane, and one which spanned his working life as an architect from 1638 to 1667. The façade he completed just before his death, and the numerous designs he made in an attempt to integrate the separate parts may have indicated the growing lack of confidence which precipitated his suicide. Whatever the cause, the decoration of the façade — a complicated series of bays, oval windows, Roman sacrificial altars, with columns, statuary and a massive oval portrait to boot — has rarely been considered entirely successful, even by devotees of the Baroque; but few can deny the lively sense of movement it imparts. This is suggested by the pattern of the bays of the lower storey, which are successively concave, convex, concave, creating an undulation which is emphasised and

---

[54] Vitruvius had said, in his rules for sacred edifices, that these buildings should have the proportions of a man. This however was simply to establish a geometrical relationship between a man, a square and a circle. Borromini's view of proportion was more organic.

repeated by the unusually solid entablature between the storeys. The bays above are all concave, but the introduction of a small oval pavilion in the lower half of the central bay gives the effect of balancing, and yet contrasting with, the lower storey. But it is the interior which is one of Borromini's greatest triumphs, and one which almost defies description, it is so personal and so overwhelming. This effect is brought about neither by sumptuous decoration nor by dramatic lighting, but by brilliant mastery of the structure. The plan is an oval, with an oval dome, and with the side and entrance chapels all representing fragments of ovals, so that the complex interrelation, though not immediately apparent, is gradually apprehended by the spectator. As Professor Pevsner writes, 'five compound spatial shapes merge into each other. We can stand nowhere without taking part in the swaying rhythm of several of them ... Space now seems hollowed out by the hand of a sculptor, walls are moulded as if made of wax or clay.'[55] Such is the sensation of motion that one is scarcely aware of the astonishing smallness of the church, the longest axes of which are barely 15.2 metres and 21.2 metres and the whole plan would fit comfortably inside any of the four piers which support the dome of St Peter's; but it is the very smallness which helps to create the illusion of movement, since one has only to move a single pace to find all the features of the interior change their relative position.

The greatest days of Roman Baroque were those of Bernini and Borromini, from 1630 to 1670. Thereafter its influence spread across Europe though the nature of its reception varied greatly from one country to the next. The Spaniards, for example, adapting it to their own techniques and to their own temperaments, arrived at a style which placed more emphasis on colour and ornamentation than can be found anywhere else in Europe. It was an unfair comment, perhaps, on the work of José Churriguera that his name should have been given to extravagances of style which he himself would have rejected. At Salamanca he designed the town hall, decorated the cathedral and laid out a magnificent square surrounded by ninety arcades, thus combining the Baroque's love of colour and decoration with its flair for town planning. The style of his contemporaries and successors, *churrigueresque*, however, became a wild and wayward

[55] N. Pevsner, *An Outline of European Architecture*.

version of *il stilo borrominesco*, in which the principle of decoration
was over-elaborated to such a point that fantasy and intricacy
became ends in themselves. It thus degenerated into mere
eccentricity.

In north Italy the Baroque was adopted in a more orthodox
fashion by Guarino Guarini, an architect who was also a
mathematician, a philosopher and a devout Oratarian. Neither
Bernini nor Borromini had confined themselves solely to
churches, but it was Guarini who demonstrated the peculiar
adaptability of Baroque for secular purposes. The style of the
church militant was easily assimilated to the glorification of
princes, and the dramatic undulations of the Roman façades
were repeated on the palaces of Turin. Guarini to some extent
succeeded in analysing the principles of his style in his *Architettura
Civile* and though it was not published before 1737, engravings
from it were circulating after 1668, and played an important part
in stimulating the exciting growth of German architecture. Asam
and Neumann, its greatest masters, worked mainly between 1720
and 1760, but before the seventeenth century was out the
Baroque was already established in Vienna. The relaxation of
tension produced by the relief of the city in 1683, the pride
engendered among its citizens by the creation of the Danubian
empire, and the sense of triumph achieved by the destruction of
heresy within the Habsburg domains, combined to create a mood
of celebration and self-glorification, of extravagance, expansion
and exhibitionism.

To satisfy this mood, the Viennese imported Italian architects
but these were soon eclipsed by a native rival, Johann Bernhard
Fischer von Erlach, who returned to Austria imbued with *il stilo
borrominesco* after barely three years in Italy. His ideas, stimulated
by his experiences in Rome and Naples, were original and
exciting; and, although they were not published until 1721, the
basic principles he then enunciated in his *Entwurf einer Historischen
Architektur* were those which inspired his work from his
appointment in 1687 as architect-engineer to the Emperor
Leopold. One especially important innovation was his admiration for the exotic; not the flamboyant excesses of Baroque
extravagance, but the styles, hitherto regarded as mere
curiosities, of China and the East. Pagodas and Islamic mosques
were analysed and acclaimed in his book on the grounds that a

barbaric monument deserved as much study and respect as a classical temple: "Artists will see here,' he wrote, 'that nations dissent no less in their taste for architecture, than in food and raiment, and by comparing one with the other they themselves may make a judicious choice.'

The way was thus opened to eclecticism, as for example in the Karlskirche, commissioned by the Emperor Charles VI in 1716. So great is the number of motifs, so varied their provenance, that the church defies purely verbal description. A pedimented portico, supported by six pillars, evokes the mood of ancient Rome, and within the curved recesses of the facade as it sweeps back to join the side towers stand two gigantic columns, modelled on Trajan's. Unlike Trajan's, however, they are surmounted by platforms and cupolas so that they give the impression of minarets. On their flanks stand the side towers, a product of Baroque imagination run riot. Each tower begins as a triumphal archway decked out with coupled pilasters; above the arch, is a square window, shaped in the form of an heraldic blazon; thereafter the line is lost in the bizarre eccentricity of a pagoda roof. It is almost with relief that the eye returns to the centre where, above the façade, stands a Baroque dome on a massive drum: in such an exotic context it seems reassuringly conventional. But an inventory of the features is misleading, since, in the true tradition of the Baroque, it is the total effect which counts, and few can deny the exotic and exciting impressions conveyed by the Karlskirche.

Before his death in 1723 von Erlach had transformed Vienna. The medieval centre he left untouched, since it was scarcely feasible to destroy fortifications which had so recently been tested by the Turks, but by building the Karlskirche to face across it to the Imperial Palace, and by siting his other palaces in a semicircle around them, he gave a focal point for the sprawling suburbs of the city. The Imperial Palace, as befitted its importance in Vienna, represented one of the most distinctive features of von Erlach's style, the secularisation of the Baroque to extol not the divinity of the Godhead but the divine right of the Habsburg monarchy. His original intention was to place the palace on a hill overlooking the valley in which it was eventually built, and, as is shown in the illustrations preserved in the *Entwurf*, to lay it out on a scale to dwarf Versailles, with colonnades, pavilions, fountains and lakes, culminating in an Imperial entrance flanked by two Trajan's columns. The enterprise was too costly and too ambitious, but its more modest successor echoed the classical theme, being clearly modelled on Nero's Golden House which was also featured in the *Entwurf*.

The art of the Counter-Reformation, though it was so eminently suited to the adulation of monarchy in general, could not take root in Protestant soil. It transformed Bavaria during the eighteenth century but made no impact on Brandenburg, and the divisions between the Catholic and Protestant states of Europe were reflected in their architecture. The one important exception to this rule was France: Catholic beyond question, monarchist to excess, the French were never swept away by the tide of Baroque exuberance. Italian models were respected, Bernini was invited to Paris, but the Roman style never became dominant. The classical tradition in France was of more recent date and was therefore the less readily abandoned. Moreover, the austere phase of the Council of Trent, so short-lived in Italy, was ideally suited to the spiritual climate of Louis XIII's reign, to the France of Bérulle and St Vincent. French Catholicism differed from the Italian in two important respects. The Cistercians and the Jansenists re-emphasised the importance of prayer and meditation, and opposed the theatrical quality of Baroque decoration as an unwelcome distraction from spiritual communion. The French, too, had an unusually high regard for the intellect: they respected the rational, which they identified with the classical, and disliked the blatant appeal of Baroque to the emotions. 'Clarity, logic, balance, a happy medium, such were to be the characteristics of the art of this period. It respected antiquity but not too much, taking practical necessities more and more into account, and combining good sense with reason.[56]

None the less, the sky-line of Paris owes much to the intrusion of Baroque motifs. In Jacques Lemercier's chapel of the Sorbonne the ribs of the drum are heavily emphasised, rising across the line of the dome to the lantern where, instead of being rounded off by a gentle cupola, they are drawn vigorously upward by a short spire to point restlessly at the heavens. The effect of this, and of the façade, is both impressive and exuberant, and Richelieu ordered the Place de la Sorbonne to be cleared in

[56] P. Lavedan, *French Architecture*.

order that a better view might be obtained of it — a Baroque device if ever there was one. In 1645 Anne of Austria commissioned François Mansart, the first of a famous dynasty of French architects, to design the convent and chapel of the Val-de-Grâce. Within a year he had run into so many difficulties with his patron and his work that he was replaced by Lemercier, though his plans were largely carried out, in particular those for a dramatic dome whose lofty line was achieved by constructing a false timber dome above the masonry of the inner shell. This same device was adopted by Hardouin-Mansart, François's great-nephew, for the splendid church of Les Invalides which combines classical proportion and elegance with Baroque magnificence. The two storeys of the façade are correctly articulated with Doric and Ionic orders, but not only is the line of the façade advanced in four stages, culminating with the four columns of the portico, but the columns themselves stand freely away from the walls. Above the façade soars the great dome which, for all its air of ordered serenity, is, upon analysis, wholly unconventional. With its double drum, itself a novel feature, it accounts for more than half the total height of the church so that the facade appears to be reduced to the level of a podium; while above the classic line of the dome, for all its Gothic associations, stands a simple spire. But none of this is apparent: the contrasts, the novelty, the medley of features are combined so skilfully that the total effect is one of grace and ordered majesty.

In domestic architecture, the Palais du Luxembourg represented the most typical French palace. Built for Marie de Medici, its main buildings are flanked by two projecting wings to form a *cour d'honneur*, which is closed on the fourth side by a screen. At first this was also to have been the plan for the Louvre, but its history was chequered by many delays and alterations: between 1610 and 1664 the Louvre was extended from two small buildings forming a right angle to an entirely square bloc around a courtyard. The problem was then to design a façade which would be majestic enough for so important a palace, and Bernini was called in in 1665 to solve it. His plans did not reflect the style of his Roman churches. Relying on the effect of unadorned mass, he proposed to leave the basement and ground floor to run the full length of the palace without decoration, to link the second and third storeys by a series of giant columns detached from the walls, and to crown the façade with a terraced roof ornamented with balustrades and statuary. In front of it all he planned to create a colossal square. By 1667, however, after Bernini's return to Rome, his plans had been replaced by those of Charles Perrault. The flat unbroken line of the façade and the balustraded roof were preserved, but Perrault reduced the other features to a more restrained design. The ground floor with regular tall windows, became a podium for a single great storey with a free-standing colonnade of pillars grouped in pairs. Baroque principles were thus reconciled to the classical, rational mood of French architecture, and cool formality took the place of impetuous grandeur.

Traditionally, the rejection of the Baroque in French domestic architecture is identified with the decision to adopt Perrault's design in place of Bernini's, but in this field Baroque influence had never been pronounced. François Mansart had introduced a subdued hint of it when he designed the Orléans wing at Blois with a curved pediment on the third storey, and with two short colonnades to round off the right angles of the courtyard. At Vaux-le-Vicomte, begun in 1657 by Louis Le Vau, the influence was more pronounced, since the ground plan was clearly suggested by that of the Palazzo Barberini designed by Carlo Maderna in Rome. Instead of the solid blocks presented to the public by earlier palaces, with an entrance to the *cour d'honneur* within, Maderna had projected the wings from the façade to create a courtyard exposed to public view, and if the wings at Vaux-le-Vicomte are only slightly projected beyond the line of the façade, the principle of the *cour d'honneur* concealed from the world is none the less rejected. Also typical of the Baroque was the landscaping of the gardens by Le Nôtre so that the flower-beds and pools, framed by two massed groups of trees, lead the eye onward to the culminating point of a grotto. The experience gained at Vaux-le-Vicomte by both Le Vau, Le Nôtre, and by the painter Le Brun, was then applied at Versailles with tremendous effect, until Louis XIV expressed his preference for the classical style.[57] Only in its immensity and its landscaped gardens did Versailles remain in any sense a Baroque creation. The sense of movement was destroyed and, under Hardouin-Mansart's direction, the exciting variations of Le Vau's design

[57] Versailles is dealt with in some detail in Chapter VI, pp.289–94.

were replaced by a façade of immense but uninspiring uniformity; a criticism which reflects the fate of the fine arts generally under the absolutism of Louis XIV.

Painting in the Seventeenth Century

In the fifteenth century the Italian painter learnt to master the parts of the human body. In the sixteenth he learnt to compose a perfect figure from these parts and to find a satisfactory means of linking one figure with another in a group study. In the seventeenth he began to relate figures more successfully to their environment, to visualise the picture as a whole and not merely as the sum of its parts. Rembrandt, for example, 'was no longer conscious of painting a set of definable and therefore separable objects. His eye could pass from a figure to the floor under its feet and the wall behind it and the cloud seen through the window in the wall without being conscious of passing from one thing to another. The whole texture of his picture is one.'[58] Similarly the architects abandoned the rigid articulation of each storey in order to find ways of stressing the unity of the whole building, and also where possible to emphasise its relation to its environment. But the analogy between architecture and painting can be misleading. Though the term 'Baroque' admirably reflects the mood of certain seventeenth-century paintings, it cannot be applied so universally to Catholic art as it is to Catholic architecture. Art which is wholly Baroque is always part of a whole, a detail which loses its meaning when detached from its context in a greater architectural whole. Moreover, the differences between the styles of Rubens, Velazquez and Poussin are too complex to be resolved within a single definition.

The death of Raphael (1520) and of Michelangelo (1564) provoked a crisis in Italian art. Their very excellence inspired emulation, but so great was their genius that their work could not be surpassed. Those who followed their style fell into exaggeration, and even caricature, and what had been a sincere mode of expression degenerated into a set of artificial mannerisms. By the end of the sixteenth century, however, a new way forward was suggested by Annibale Carracci and his brothers. Having fallen

[58] E. Newton, *European Painting and Sculpture*. Rembrandt and the Dutch school are treated separately in Chapter V, pp.260–65.

under the spell of Raphael's work they too set out to recapture something of its simplicity and beauty, but they brought to the task a skill in using colour acquired from a study of the Venetian painters. Where Raphael had concentrated upon line they gave the emphasis to surface, and this distinction between the two styles saved the Carracci from producing mere *pastiches*: it also led to their style being termed eclectic, having as its aim the imitation of all that was best in the Tuscan and Venetian schools.

More to the point, the Carracci were especially concerned to cultivate the ideal of classical beauty. From Giotto's day it had been generally agreed that the art of painting consisted in reproducing the appearance of nature; but as nature was not always attractive the artist began to modify what he saw in the interests of beauty. Raphael, for example, had said that he had no model for his *Galatea* but, 'a certain idea', an abstraction derived from models he had considered beautiful. From this it was but a short step to the making of formulae for the creation of beauty in art as though this were an end in itself, as is shown in Carracci's altarpiece of *The Virgin Mourning Christ*. Clearly derived from Raphael is the triangular structure of the scene, and from the Venetians the technique of illumining Christ's body in a flood of light; the total effect is an idealised version of heroic beauty with not a hint of the agony or the horror of the Crucifixion. Painted as it was to be adored in the light of altar candles, it is unfair to expose it to the daylight but, lacking sincerity by its failure to recognise the truth of death, it is merely sentimental. The most prolific and the most talented of the Carracci school was Guido Reni (1575-1642). For many years he was extolled for his ability to recapture the mood of Raphael but his art, inspired by art itself rather than by life, was too self-conscious: what flowed freely in Raphael was contrived in him.

The pursuit of beauty by falsifying the truth, the sentimental evasion of ugliness and pain, angered Caravaggio (1569-1609) beyond measure, and led him to evolve a new style of painting. In place of emulating the successes of Raphael or Titian he determined to explore new country and to attempt new summits. Using the same technical skills evolved by his predecessors he deliberately chose to present the world as it was, neither bereft of beauty nor artificially redolent with it. This did not mean that he literally painted what he saw: Caravaggio's realism was expressed in a dark and vivid way, his pictures brilliantly composed, the gestures rehearsed and emphatic, and the models carefully selected. His characters, set against a background of shadows, were illumined by a harsh light which makes every gesture peculiarly significant, and in a manner which invites comparison with the Baroque; but, more revolutionary than the technique, was the choice of the characters themselves. Caravaggio shared the Jesuits' desire to give new life to the Bible stories and to impress the world with their immediacy. In his portraits of biblical scenes, therefore, he refused to idealise or ennoble the characters. The disciples were modelled as peasants, their features lined and their feet dirty, while Christ Himself in the *Christ at Emmaus* is a far cry from the idealised figure of the Carracci school. So accustomed, indeed, had people become to the latter tradition, that the portrayal of saints as earthly, earthy men aroused initial cries of horror and charges of blasphemy.

In France it was the classical tradition which triumphed, partly because of the French temperament which prefers form to feeling, and also because Richelieu, Colbert and Louis XIV regarded this tradition as the one most suited to a well-ordered monarchy.[59] There were significant exceptions. The Le Nain brothers pursued an independent course, wholly unaffected by the Italian schools, painting the French peasantry in a simple, sincere way which, by its frank confrontation of the spectator with the reality of peasant life, can be compared with the techniques of photography. A similar degree of social realism was also to be found in the work of Georges de La Tour (1593-1652), who learnt much from the school of Caravaggio, though his personality was too strong for his art to be wholly derivative. In *The Prisoner*, for example, the *chiaroscura*, the light from a candle illumining the two figures against the shadows, is wholly in the manner of Caravaggio, but the forms are uniquely his own since he has stylised and progressively simplified them, almost reducing them to abstract geometric shapes. The loss of individuality resulting from this elimination of superfluous detail lends a degree of ambiguity to his later work — *The Prisoner* has been variously entitled *St Peter delivered from Prison* and *Job taunted*

[59] For this point see above, p.99, and also p.290 for the French reception of Baroque architecture.

by his Wife — but it creates a mood of static calm far more akin to the French classical tradition than to the realist school. Against the work of these artists that of the official leaders of the classical tradition at court seems too consciously derivative to have any value of its own. Simon Vouet (1590-1649) and his pupil Eustache Le Sueur merely demonstrated that if uncontrolled romanticism degenerates into sentimentality, academic adherence to classical principles too easily results in lifeless pedantry. In such an arid environment it is not surprising that two great French artists in the classical tradition, Nicholas Poussin (1594-1665) and Claude (1600-82), should have chosen to spend their lives in Italy.

In Italy Poussin tried to absorb something of the Baroque manner, but found that he could not reconcile it with his need for formal coherence, a need only satisfied by the discipline of the classical tradition. Like the Carracci he tried to purge the visual world of its imperfections and oddities, and as this involved the adoption of a criterion Poussin deliberately chose that of classical antiquity, believing that the Greeks alone had arrived at a definition of ideal beauty. His method was formally adopted in France: 'When a painter has made a drawing from the living model', said one of the academicians in a discussion of Poussin's style, 'he should make another study of the same figure on a separate sheet and should try to give it the character of an ancient statue.' In 1640 Poussin visited Paris for eighteen months; he found the French Court uncongenial and his rivals incompetent, but he secured a list of patrons for whom he worked after his return to Italy, and whose intellectual temperament and Jansenist mentality accorded well with his own. For the rest of his life he produced work in which the moral content of the story is matched by the intellectual context of the composition. Since the formal essentials of drawing and design assumed prior place in his painting, he deliberately had to tone down his use of colour lest, by its sensuous appeal to the eye it might distract the intellect. His control of his own style was supreme: 'Je n'ai rien négligé', was his boast, and as a composer he had few equals. The logical discipline to which he freely subjected himself did not however result in frigidity or sterility. Though his followers in France violently criticised the *Rubénistes*, Poussin gave to his Bacchanals a sense of rhythm and movement which, for all the inherent classicism of his work, is closely akin to Rubens's *Rape of Proserpine*; and there is a moving sense of poignancy in his *Death of Narcissus* and his *Mourning over the Dead Christ.*

Poussin had been attracted by the portrayal of landscape, but with Claude it became an obsession. His purpose was not so much to capture nature's moods as to show that the landscape could in itself furnish material for a satisfying picture in the classical manner, and nature itself was generalised and idealised much as Raphael had treated humanity. This process of generalisation began with a series of sketches drawn from nature with no thought of the picture but simply to learn the secrets of the landscape. Back in the studio the scene was then arranged, often with one feature overlapping another, so that an illusion of infinite depth was achieved, the eye being led back into the heart of the landscape. It was from carefully proportioned scenes such as these, the classical portrayal of a romantic ideal, that men in the eighteenth century derived their view of natural beauty, and were led to re-create it for themselves in landscaping their estates: the beauty of English parkland thus owed much to the inspiration of Claude's works.

When Claude gave narrative titles of some complexity to his pictures, such as, *The Story of how Ascanius shot the Stag of Sylvia, Daughter of Tyrrhus, Virgil, Book 7*, he was to some extent seeking to protect himself against those who thought that landscapes alone were unworthy of consideration; and the rather inadequate figures in the foreground of his landscapes seem to have been hastily added for the same reason. But there was a deeper motive for both these things. The title set the mood of the picture, by invoking an ancient legend at a point of impending crisis, and in peopling the ancient landscape of the Campagna with these ghosts from the past he deliberately refrained from making them so robust as to recall the viewer to the present. For all his classicism, Claude revealed a romantic nostalgia, heightened by the powerful use of a gentle light to touch each part of the broad landscape with an air of mystery, creating a dreamlike vision of the past. These landscapes, it has been suggested, 'are pictures of something which one would have thought it impossible to put into visual form, of what Virgil calls *lacrimae rerum*, which nobody has succeeded in translating but which means something like that mood of poetic sadness which scenes of natural beauty evoke

by suggesting the passage of many centuries of human history.'[60]
Whatever the multiple and complex traditions of classicism, realism and romanticism, of portraiture and landscape, of pagan illustration and of Christian illumination, they were all absorbed and exploited by the universal zest and genius of Peter Paul Rubens. Born at Antwerp in 1577 he worked in the studios of several Flemish painters, acquiring the local tradition of Brueghel and Van Eyck with its intense love of detailed representation, until in 1600 he went to Italy. There he learnt the new techniques of colour and *chiaroscuro* and also the intellectual concepts which underlay contemporary controversy in art. After a term as court painter at Mantua, he returned home in 1608. Apart from occasional employment in diplomatic missions to Holland (1629), Spain (1628) and England (1629), which he used to become acquainted with other artists, notably Hals and Velazquez, his life was based upon Antwerp. Not only was he court painter to the Spanish Governor in the Netherlands but he established what can only be termed an 'artistic practice' which made him one of the wealthiest painters in history.

His studio closely resembled a factory, for not only did his assistants work at specialised tasks in each painting but a team of engravers made copies available for reproduction; yet without some formal division of labour Rubens could never have satisfied the demand for his work nor have successfully maintained his standards over the years. He himself would make sketches, freely painted or drawn in flowing lines, touching in the type of colour he required. These instructions given in a kind of painter's shorthand, were carried out by a staff of supremely talented assistants, some of whom, like Van Dyck, won fame in their own right. Their skill in execution, and that of Rubens's in planning, are exemplified in the *Return from Egypt*. The original drawing, recently identified in Moscow, was a rapidly executed pen and ink sketch, but so clear and implicit were its instructions that the design, the proportions and the movement are realised almost exactly in the finished work. The completed picture was always touched up by Rubens, supremely confident as he was that his own magic brushwork would bring the canvas swiftly to life and restore to it something of the unity of his first sketch. Indeed it was this technical brilliance, animated by the joyful exuberance

60 Ellis Waterhouse, from a BBC talk, published in *The Listener*, 18th February 1960.

and impassioned zest of his own nature, which gave him the power to transcend the mechanism of production. By imparting his own sincerity and vitality to the work, he ensured that it not only lived but lived as he had wished.

His style was never consciously eclectic, but so voracious were his interests and activities, so determined was he to turn his hand to everything, that he found no impediment to absorbing the dramatic sincerity of Caravaggio with the classically ordered composition of Carracci, or in blending Venetian colour with Flemish realism. What he absorbed he transmuted. In addition to buoyant energy and a sense of joy he possessed astonishing powers of invention and organisation in the grand manner: 'I confess', he wrote, 'that my natural inclination is to execute large works rather than little curiosities.' It was this which appealed to him in the commission to provide 39 ceiling paintings and 3 altarpieces for the Jesuit church of St Ignatius Loyola in Antwerp, since, in a manner essentially Baroque, he was to be intimately involved with the architect and also with the sculptor who made the external figures. The Baroque quality is to be found for example in his *Betrothal of St Catherine* in the sculptural, indeed architectural, treatment of space, in the light flooding in behind the Virgin, and in the throng of attendant saints and martyrs whose confused spiral pattern answers the stately counterpoint of the ascending staircase. Such a work also illustrates his capacity to introduce endless subsidiary elements without compromising or interfering with his main theme.

Rubens was gifted beyond all else with powers of observation and the ability to render what he saw in paint, an ability not confined to one genre alone. At first he paid little heed to landscapes; they scarcely lent themselves to allegory, and a painting without people offered nothing to interest him. In 1618 he referred to a painting from his studio as, 'by my hand, except for a most beautiful landscape done by the hand of a master skilful in that genre'. Nevertheless, increasingly his eye was engaged by the possibilities of landscape work. The result may be seen in the *Landscape near Moulins* in which he achieved a vivid image of an otherwise unspectacular stretch of countryside. This gift of observation explained his brilliance in portraying the nude, though his skill in the genre was not acquired without a long period of study. He began by drawing from antique models and by copying the work of other artists, of Michelangelo in particular, until from this intellectual discipline certain ideal forms emerged in his mind. With his mind thus informed he could then paint directly from nature itself, instinctively moulding nature to the patterns established in his imagination, without consciously checking the freedom of his brush. Thus 'he gave to his learned reminiscences so much of his own peculiar style and his own responsiveness to nature that we are seldom conscious of his sources'.[61] This 'peculiar style' was characterised as in all his work by a strong sense of movement, intensified in this case by rich modelling of the contours to convey a sense of solidity and weight, and thus of being truly alive. Above all else, he possessed a superb technique of rendering both the colour and the texture of flesh in which, save perhaps for Renoir, he surpassed all painters.

The ancient antithesis between flesh and spirit has led many critics to assume too readily that no artist could succeed equally with both; and Rubens's undoubted mastery of the flesh has prejudiced opinion against his spiritual subjects. Indeed his comfortable life, free from outstanding crises and sorrows, his lucrative studio techniques, and his exuberant acceptance of the world have appeared as faults to those who expect artists to sacrifice the world for their art, and who therefore hold that Rubens could never rise to the challenge of a religious theme. His *Visitation* has been described as a merely terrestrial encounter, his Madonnas 'strike appropriately noble gestures but they are none the less Flemish wenches who cannot fill those gestures with meaning',[62] and Sir Joshua Reynolds commented that, 'instead of something above humanity, the spectator finds little more than mere mortals such as he meets every day.' Nevertheless, to judge Rubens as a religious painter one must stand, not before the *Visitation* or the *Assumption of the Virgin* where too many of the strictures seem to apply, but before the *Three Crosses* in the Van Beuningen Collection or the *Descent from the Cross* in Antwerp Cathedral. Different though these works are from the spirituality of, for example, a Rembrandt, and though they belong to an iconography wholly different from that of Protestantism, they yet have a pathos and a sincerity of sentiment which mark them as classics of religious art.

[61] K. Clark, *The Nude*.　　　　[62] E. Newton, op.cit.

By way of contrast, no painter has been more wholly spiritual than El Greco (1541-1614). He eschewed the material world altogether and, after his retirement to Toledo in 1584, invoked a mood of increasingly mystic excitement, symbolised in the flame-like patterns, the elongated limbs and the shrill greens, blues and pinks, of his later works. He belonged, if indeed so individual an artist can be assigned to any category, to the Mannerist tradition of sixteenth-century Venice where he was trained, and to the tradition of Byzantine painting still preserved in his birthplace, Crete. Neither reflecting nor founding a national tradition in Spain, he remained wholly eccentric and inimitable.

Born half a century later than El Greco, it was Velazquez (1599-1660) who was to dominate Spanish art in the seventeenth century. In 1613 he became a student under a minor artist Pacheco, whose daughter he married, who taught him something of the techniques of Caravaggio. His early paintings showed this interest in the naturalistic representation of things seen in a strong light, and one of these, *The Water Carrier*, won him the attention of Olivares and appointment as court painter in 1623. His work was deliberate and sober, but at court he developed a greater degree of simplicity in handling detail, and began to infuse a touch of transparency into the dark shadows which silhouetted his figures. A visit to Spain in 1628 by Rubens gave him his first opportunity to talk with an artist of greater gifts than himself, and it aroused in him a desire to broaden his experience more fully by travel to Italy. Such a visit was essential to his development since at home he was unrivalled; Ribera, Zurbaran and Murillo, his only contemporaries worthy of mention, were not only unable to match his skills but were wholly derivative in their styles. Velazquez returned home in 1631 without having modified his basic realism but with a much enlarged range of colour: 'Raphael', he wrote, 'does not please me at all. In Venice are found the good and the beautiful; to their brush I give the first place; it is Titian that bears the banner'. For the next seventeen years he was occupied with commissions at court, but a royal embassy to Italy in 1648 gave him a second opportunity to visit Naples, Rome and Venice. On this occasion he painted a vividly impressive portrait of Innocent X and was so far influenced by the new environment as to share in its enthusiasm for the female nude — an art form discouraged in the Escurial — which resulted in the *Rokeby Venus*.

In many respects Velazquez resembled the genre painters of Holland in that his work was deliberate and sober, his view of life unimpassioned. Like the Dutch too he found interest in the familiar round of ordinary events, and it was by a series of *bodegones*, scenes of everyday life, that he first made his name. Of these the *Water'Carrier* was perhaps his greatest success. The action is suspended, as in a Vermeer, while attention is focused on a boy and two men, one barely visible in the shadow, the other the water carrier with his pots. The use of light is remarkable, falling on the crumpled collar of the boy and the carrier's sleeve, catching a drop of water, giving form to a glass, and revealing the texture of cloth, wood and earthenware. So satisfying is the total effect of light and texture, of balance and harmony, that the problem is less to analyse the work of art than to know exactly why it is so satisfying. Velazquez, in fact, seemed to have followed Pacheco's advice — 'I hold to the principle that Nature ought to be the chief master' — that to observe and to record is in itself art. This of course was not so. Though his pictures came to him through the eye rather than through the imagination, he did not simply copy nature. Velazquez, by instinct rather than by formal training, had a firm intellectual grasp of his work, and the *Water Carrier* is far from being a mere glimpse of everyday life. Its design is complex, the balance and counterpoint of masses contrived, and all insignificant detail has been simplified away to reveal only essentials.

This combination of the steady imperturbable eye with the unerring hand induced an element of impersonality in all but his final works, so that the subjects of his paintings are treated less as individuals to be loved or hated than as objects to be represented on his canvas. This does not make them less interesting since it was the problem of representing them which so clearly excited Velazquez, and which he solved by means of brilliant brush-work. The realism of his work is found upon analysis to be conveyed by a series of impressions so that the spectator is required to grasp his intention and to supplement it from his own imagination, a technique which was not to be fully exploited until the nineteenth century. As for the impersonality, Velazquez acquired from his second visit to Italy a much deeper interest in the problem of studying his sitters for what they were, rather than for what they seemed to be. His subsequent studies of the ageing king Philip IV, of the ladies-in-waiting, *Las Meninas*, and of the tapestry-weavers, *Las Hilanderas*, thus revealed a new dimension to his work, a greater sense of atmosphere and more sensitive appreciation of character.

II

THE THIRTY YEARS WAR

THE BACKGROUND TO THE WAR

Areas of Conflict throughout Europe

The Thirty Years used to be described as a German civil war in which other countries became involved. This interpretation is no longer tenable (see p. 128–9). Much of what happened in Germany was actually caused, or at least aggravated, by issues and conflicts in which other countries were independently engaged.

In the Baltic, for example, Sweden was engaged in bitter conflict with Denmark from whom the Swedes had declared their independence in 1523. Moreover the new Swedish king, Gustavus Adolphus, was also at war with his cousin, Sigismund, a Roman Catholic who had been elected king of Poland but still claimed the throne of Lutheran Sweden and both men had become entangled in the civil wars in Russia (see pp. 371–5). The struggle for Baltic supremacy, however, was of less immediate concern to other European governments than the long-standing conflict between France and Spain. Since 1494 these two great monarchies had fought for the control of Italy, with the victory going to Spain in the Treaty of Câteau-Cambrésis (1559). Indeed the treaty represented a high-water mark of Spain's power in Europe, recognising the rule of the Spanish Habsburg family in Naples and Milan, in Luxemburg and the Netherlands and in Franche Comté (the 'Free County' of Burgundy as distinct from the duchy which had been incorporated in France).

France on the other hand fell prey to the wars of religion which left her powerless to intervene in European affairs until the restoration of peace and the general recognition of Henry IV as

king in 1598. Even then, Henry's powers were limited and he was
cautious in his undertakings. These are described elsewhere (see
p. 198) but their underlying purpose was to break through the
encircling ring of Habsburg bases which, extending from
Flanders and Franche Comté to North Italy and the Pyrenees,
induced in France a sensation of isolation, indeed of claustropho-
bia. If the initial impulse was defensive, there was also an
aggressive element in French policy in as much as any
strengthening of the French frontier would correspondingly
weaken Spain and, in particular, endanger her lines of
communication across Europe (see p. 118). To that extent the
policy expressed later by cardinal Richelieu was also that of
Henry IV, 'to check the progress of Spain. Wherever that nation
aims at increasing its power and extending its territory, our one
object must be to fortify and dig ourselves in, whilst making open
doors into neighbouring states so that we can safeguard them
against Spanish oppression whenever occasion may arise'.

A state of hostility was not however automatic between the two
countries. There were many Catholics in France known as *les
dévots*, who believed it to be shameful that the two major Catholic
powers should be at odds with each other while Protestantism
established itself in Europe, and their influence was of profound
importance in the years 1610–24. In their eyes an alliance with
Spain would not only further the cause of the Counter-
Reformation but serve to make the Spanish troops based around
the French frontier seem less threatening. Such an attitude was
genuinely encouraged by the Spanish government in 1600. Philip
III had no wish to regard France as an enemy because Spain at
that date was concentrating all her forces on the defeat of the
Dutch, and he urged Henry IV to consider a marriage alliance
between their families.

The war between Spain and the United Provinces of the Union
of Utrecht had reached a critical phase. The rebellion of the
Spanish Netherlands against Philip II had become a war
between the northern provinces of the Union of Utrecht (1579),
dominated by the Calvinist-led states of Holland and Zeeland,
and the southern, Catholic provinces, fully restored to the
Spanish monarchy since the Union of Arras in 1578 (see
p. 224). The Dutch forces, commanded by Maurice of Nassau,
were secure behind the fortified line of the Rhine delta; the Army

of Flanders, comprising Spanish and Flemish regiments under the command of Spinola, was equally securely established below the river line. Neither could dislodge the other and since both governments were finding the cost of the war temporarily beyond their means, an armistice was arranged in 1607, leading in 1609 to the declaration of a Twelve Years Truce — a Truce during which both sides intended to strengthen their positions as much as possible for the renewal of war in 1621.

The conflict between Spain and the United Provinces was of more than local interest because it polarised many of the irreconcilable tensions in European politics. On the one hand a monarchy, autocratic with moribund representative institutions; on the other a republic whose Estates-General wholly depended upon the decisions of vigorous provincial Estates and town councils. Spain was Catholic, aristocratic, medieval in spirit, pastoral in its economy — a static society dominated by landowners, monks and soldiers. The United Provinces were a new creation, Calvinist, bourgeois and dynamic, brilliantly successful in commercial enterprises.

The contrasts are effective provided that the polarities are not exaggerated. It is of course true that most Dutchmen were still Roman Catholic, the north-eastern provinces of Friesland, Overijssel, Groningen and Gelderland remained aristocratic and pastoral, and the attachment of many citizens to the House of Orange demonstrated the strength of the princely connection within the republic. Yet the model of two rival, irreconcilable cultures is sufficiently valid to account for the fact that Spain and the United Provinces each represented what the other most hated, feared or suspected. Moreover, each was looked to and appealed to for aid by the enemies of the other. In consequence, many local disputes in other parts of Europe which might, at any other period, have gone unnoticed acquired an international significance because the governments in Madrid and The Hague were invited, or found it expedient, to intervene.

Spanish lines of communication and supply, (see Map 2, p. 118) upon which the outcome of the war in the Netherlands might depend, stretched across Europe like a web, whose delicate filaments were susceptible to disturbance by political, dynastic or religious changes in any one of a dozen minor states. Since Spain was perpetually concerned to protect her routes, and the Dutch

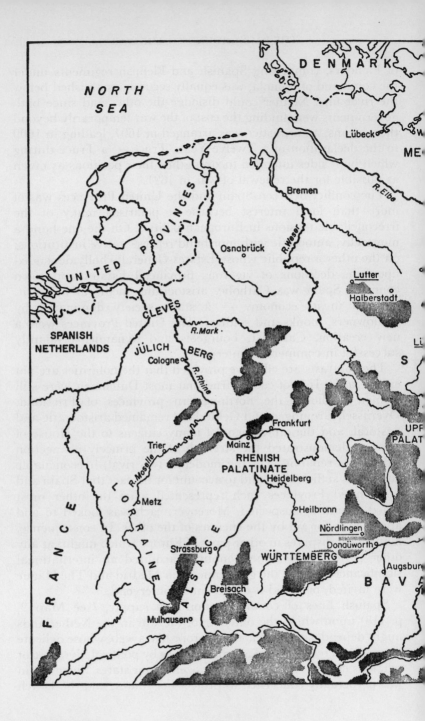

Map 1 The Thirty Years War

to disrupt them, incidents of apparently local significance could be transformed into crises of European magnitude.

A route vital to the outcome of the war was the so-called Spanish Road. Recruits from Castile, Sicily and Naples made their rendezvous in Genoa, a city whose fortunes were closely bound with those of Spain, and marched north into the Spanish possession of Lombardy. From there, the Road followed a variety of routes across Savoy into Franche Comté. Thereafter the dukes of Lorraine allowed free passage to the troops of all nations

Map 2   Spanish lines of communication to the Netherlands

provided that they spent no more than two nights in one place, and Spanish commanders had simply to avoid the French garrison in Metz, Toul and Verdun (established there by the Treaty of Câteau-Cambrésis, 1559) in order to bring their men safely to the Spanish duchy of Luxemburg. From there it was an easy march across the diocese of Liège, whose bishops relied upon Spain to protect them from the Dutch. In addition, the prince-archbishops of Münster, Cologne and Trier, who had good cause to fear the spread of heresy from the Dutch Republic, allowed the Spanish government both to recruit and to march through their territories, which were strategically of great importance in the lower Rhineland. Trier, moreover, lay conveniently adjacent to Luxemburg, and free passage from Münster and Cologne to Flanders was assured by a long-standing alliance between Spain and the Roman Catholic dukes of Jülich-Cleves.

The weakest stage of the Road lay through Savoy, because of the unreliability of its dukes. Accordingly, the Spanish viceroys in Milan tried to by-pass the duchy by an agreement with the Protestant Grisons (the Grey Lords) who controlled the Valtelline — giving access from Lake Como to the Alpine passes leading north to the Tyrol. Thereafter the route lay along the northern shore of Lake Constance, into the Breisgau and along the Rhine to Basel. On account of the implacable hostility of the elector Palatine, who controlled the middle Rhine (see p. 124), Spanish troops, instead of sailing downriver in barges, crossed the bridge at Breisach and reached Lorraine via Alsace which was largely under the control of the Austrian Habsburgs.

In order to safeguard her lines of communication it was vital to Spain's interest that the office of Holy Roman Emperor be denied to any one other than a member of the Austrian Habsburg family. In a memorandum widely circulated among European governments in 1617 the duke of Savoy wrote that the Spaniards 'will be in constant anxiety lest the transfer of the Empire from Austria may be the means of losing them Flanders', and the reasons were not hard to find. The emperor, for example, had the power to determine the succession to vacant or disputed fiefs, many of them adjacent to or an integral part of Spain's transcontinental routes. Indeed, as future events were to show, the decisions taken by emperors in the disputes over Jülich-

Cleves (1609), the Palatinate (1623, see p. 136) were to be of great importance to Spain.

Spain's interest in the Austrian Habsburgs was not confined to their exercise of Imperial authority but extended to the territories they governed in their own right — the 'hereditary lands' of Upper and Lower Austria; Alsace, the Breisgau and the Tyrol; Carinthia, Carniola and Styria; and the kingdoms of Hungary and Bohemia. Alsace, the Breisgau and the Tyrol for example, made up part of Spain's lines of communication with Flanders, and Austria and Bohemia together constituted a massive bulwark across Central Europe, abutting the important German states of Bavaria, Saxony and the Upper Palatinate. It was vital to Spain that these territories should not fall into the hands of any family other than the Austrian Habsburgs, and that the family's authority within its domains should not be weakened.

The Austrian Habsburgs in fact faced acute problems, some of which were to have important repercussions on events in Germany. Not all the 'hereditary lands' were ruled by the head of the family and not all were strictly speaking hereditary. Many, in terms of language, race and religion were different from each other and each was constitutionally self-regarding.

In Hungary the immediate challenge came from the Ottoman Turks, who had occupied more than two-thirds of the kingdom since their retreat from the siege of Vienna in 1529. To some extent the Ottoman lines of communication were too severely stretched to sustain a prolonged offensive into Austria and the Habsburgs had strengthened their frontier fortresses, constructed minor forts at river crossings and at the approaches to the main cities, and established Hungarian refugees and Germans in a defence system of marcher lordships stretching from the Adriatic to the upper reaches of the Sava and Drava rivers. Their strategy, though expensive in that it absorbed almost entirely the revenues of Carniola, Carinthia and Styria, was well conceived. Since it took ninety days to supply an Ottoman army by camel trains from the Balkans, the season for campaigning was reduced to a few months: the Habsburgs, therefore, relied on their new defence works to halt or at least to delay the invading army until the season was over. In the event, the line of effective Ottoman occupation lay midway between Vienna and Buda, allowing the Habsburgs a strip of Hungary varying in depth from 60 to 120 kilometres, for which they paid an annual tribute to the sultan. The emperor Rudolf II found this too humiliating to endure and declared war on the Turks in 1593. In the event he mismanaged affairs so badly, not least by an inopportune attempt to persecute the Hungarian Protestants who were powerfully entrenched among the nobility, that his brother Matthias was authorised by the other members of the family to placate the Protestants and make peace with the Turks. Fortunately for Matthias the Turks had problems of their own on their Persian border and the sultan agreed to negotiate peace at Zsitva-Torok in 1606. The treaty recognised the frontier of 1593 but required only one, final payment of tribute to establish Habsburg Hungary as independent of the Turks.

Matthias in effect became head of the family leaving Rudolf to govern Bohemia — though not its attendant provinces of Moravia, Silesia and Lusatia. Bohemia alone, however, was not easy to govern. Germans and Catholics were to be found in Prague and a few other cities but the population was predominantly Slav and generally non-Catholic. (In addition to the Lutherans and the Calvinists there were the Bohemian Brethren, an evangelical, apocalyptic sect, and the Utraquists, a group mainly Catholic in doctrine except for their custom at the Eucharist of administering both the bread and the wine to laymen.) As in Hungary the monarchy was elective, and the Habsburgs had to defer to local custom and privileges in order to keep the succession within the family. Indeed in 1609 Rudolf was compelled to appease his subjects further by granting to them the *Letter of Majesty* which guaranteed and extended the privileges to be enjoyed by Protestants and Catholics alike.

Rudolf's chancellor, Zdenec Lobkowitz, observed his action with alarm. As a German Catholic, devoted to the interests of the Austrian Habsburgs, Lobkowitz wanted to destroy the tradition-al liberties and franchises of Bohemia and the other territories by making them subordinate to an administration staffed in the main by German officials working in Vienna. The corollary of this would be the triumph of the Counter-Reformation. *The Letter of Majesty* in Lobkowitz's opinion strengthened the forces of separatism, nationalism and heresy. Significantly, he refused to add his own signature to it.

The issues of Protestantism and local autonomy were disputed with similar vigour in the duchies of Upper and Lower Austria, where the assemblies of the Estates tended to champion the Protestant cause and oppose the government's attempts to extend the authority of its Viennese-based councils and courts. George Tschernembl, a leader of the Austrian Protestants, kept in close touch with the Protestants of Hungary, Moravia and Bohemia, and also with those in the adjoining Palatinate. The signs were clear that any attempt to develop the policies associated with Lobkowitz in any one part of the 'hereditary lands' would have serious repercussions in the other parts, and might indeed involve the Palatinate and other German states at a time when the Holy Roman Empire was already on the brink of civil war.

Conflict within the Holy Roman Empire

The Peace of Augsburg (1555) was negotiated in the aftermath of the emperor Charles V's abdication. It recognised that the Lutheran Church was firmly established and that the German princes, Lutheran and Catholic alike, were too strong to be dictated to by the emperor. Accordingly, the Augsburg formula of *cuius regio eius religio* sanctioned what had already begun to happen in practice by affirming that the inhabitants of the Empire were to adopt the religious views not of their emperor but of their local ruler. It was a practical compromise, a successful response to the special circumstances prevailing in 1555: it was not however designed to cope with the rigorous and disruptive forces subsequently unleashed by the Catholic Counter-Reformation and the Calvinist Church in Geneva.

The Council of Trent, meeting at intervals between 1545 and 1563, reaffirmed the beliefs which Luther had challenged and ensured that every Catholic should be able to distinguish true doctrine from heresy. By rejecting compromise the council strengthened the will to resist Lutheranism and the missionary impulse to overcome it. Many German Catholic princes, who had been content in 1555 to compromise with their Lutheran neighbours, soon found that their confessors were urging them to become more active and aggressive in the Catholic cause.

Meanwhile the Calvinists, who had been denied formal recognition at Augsburg, were seizing the initiative from the

Lutherans. Strengthened by the coherence of their doctrine and secure in the assurance of predestined salvation, they were better fitted than the Lutherans to oppose the militancy of the Counter-Reformation. In defeat they withstood persecution, in victory they offered no toleration.

Under the pressure of these new forces the Augsburg settlement could offer no sure ground for future peace. Nor could it withstand the territorial expansion of Protestantism. The Diet of Augsburg had been silent on the matter but the emperor, of his own authority, forbade any further confiscation of the lands of the Catholic Church. The Lutherans, however, would not permit the rich enclaves of a rival religion to exist within their territories and they sought by one device or another to acquire them. The Catholics therefore became increasingly angry at their own apparent impotence as such wealthy and important bishoprics as Magdeburg, Bremen and Halberstadt fell into Lutheran hands. Indeed, by 1600 the Protestants controlled most of North Germany. Maximilian of Bavaria, a zealous champion of the Counter-Reformation who had inherited his duchy in 1597, was supported by many others in believing that only by a renewal of the war could the drift to Protestantism be halted and the territories and the subjects of the Protestant princes be restored to the Catholic Church.

Finally, the Peace of Augsburg so clearly reflected the impotence of the emperor that any subsequent revival of his authority would immediately threaten the settlement and prejudice its chance of survival. Such a contingency seemed unlikely in 1555 since the Catholic princes were as eager as the Lutherans to prevent any extension of imperial control; so much so that a triumph for their church was unwelcome to the Catholics if it also augmented the emperor's power.

Both the method of electing an emperor and the constitution of the Empire were enshrined in the Golden Bull of 1356. This entrusted the election to seven princes — the palatine of the Rhine, the margrave of Brandenburg, the duke of Saxony, the king of Bohemia and the archbishops of Mainz, Trier and Cologne. The constitutional assembly of the Empire was the *Reichstag* or Diet, which comprised the college of the seven electoral princes, the college of the other feudal and ecclesiastical princes and a college in which the so-called Free Cities were represented. As an institution it was rarely able to arrive at, let alone enforce, major decisions, and was little more than a convention of independent princes whose power to obstruct decisions they disliked denied the emperor the opportunity to impose his policies upon Germany.

The strength of an emperor's authority depended less upon the constitution than on his personality, the degree of unanimity he could achieve by persuasion and the extent of his personal territories, since what could not be done by an emperor might sometimes be brought about by the resolute action of a duke of Austria. The emperor since 1576 was Rudolf II, hereditary duke of Austria and elected monarch of Bohemia and Hungary. Although he had in the past revealed an ability to act swiftly and shrewdly he suffered increasingly from morbidity and occasional insanity, so that in the end he hid himself away in the Hradschin palace in Prague. If, however, one of his successors as head of the Austrian Habsburgs proved to be rigorous and resourceful he could, in alliance with his Spanish cousins, intervene in German affairs with considerable effect.

A minor foretaste of such a possibility was provided in 1606 by the events which arose over an incident at Donauwörth, a town of strategic importance on the upper Danube in which the Catholic monastery perpetually challenged the authority of the Protestant town council. After a riot in 1606, Rudolf in a rare demonstration of Imperial authority, invited Maximilian of Bavaria to intervene. Peace was restored, a Roman Catholic majority was created in the council, the town was transferred to the Bavarian Circle, of which Maximilian was the director, and Maximilian himself was authorised to occupy it until the emperor was able to repay him the costs of the operation.

The action taken by the emperor and Maximilian provoked a hostile reaction throughout much of Germany, not least in Calvinist Heidelberg, where Maximilian's cousin, Frederick IV ruled as the elector Palatine. The ally of the United Provinces and an implacable opponent of the Habsburgs, Frederick was well placed to be of service to the one and troublesome to the other: his Rhenish Palatinate controlled the traffic of the middle Rhine, while the Upper Palatinate shared a common frontier with Bohemia. Heidelberg, moreover, was the European centre of the Protestant printing industry. From its presses there poured a flood of pamphlets to alert the rest of Europe to the activities, real and imagined, of Rome, Madrid and Vienna.

The propaganda was supplemented by the diplomatic activity of Frederick's chancellor, Christian of Anhalt, whose ambition was to create a network of allies capable of thwarting the ambitions of the Habsburg families and of the Counter-Reformation. He was in touch with every government and individual whose services might be harnessed to this cause and, on hearing of the Catholic triumph at Donauwörth, he persuaded a number of German Protestants to defend their interests by forming an Evangelical Union under Frederick's leadership and the patronage of Henry IV of France.

The Union was almost exclusively Calvinist in character and therefore objectionable to most Lutherans, one of whom wrote picturesquely that 'the Calvinish dragon is pregnant with the horrors of Mohammedanism'. Many princes would have preferred to see the Lutheran Electors of Brandenburg and Saxony at their head, but both of them stood aloof from the conflict, perhaps lulled into a false sense of security by the importance of their own position. Christian II of Saxony refused to jeopardise the Peace of Augsburg on behalf of the Calvinists whom he hated and maintained that, whatever their inadequacies, it was only the time-honoured institutions of the Empire which stood between the Germans and anarchy. He mistrusted the motives of Henry IV and foresaw that the formation of a Protestant alliance would provoke the Catholics to mobilise their forces in similar fashion.

By July 1609 this had happened. The anxieties of the Spanish government over the security of its Rhineland routes prompted Balthasar de Zuñiga, the ambassador in Vienna, to negotiate the formation of a Catholic League with Maximilian, his immediate neighbours, the Rhineland bishoprics controlled by his family, and the city of Aachen. It did not include Austria, because Maximilian, though respectful of Imperial authority and on good terms with the Austrian Habsburgs, was aware that their interests were not always his own. The League none the less accepted the subsidies promised on behalf of Philip III of Spain, who made it a condition of his support that the League's policies be acceptable to the emperor.

The Jülich - Cleves Crisis 1609–14

The tensions between rival groups and rival states, not merely within the Holy Roman Empire but across Western Europe, were revealed in 1609 by the interest suddenly taken in the duchies of Jülich, Cleves, Mark, Berg and Ravensberg. The duchies, ruled by duke William, were of considerable strategic importance in the lower Rhineland. The Spaniards, in alliance with the duke, used them in 1605 and in 1606 as a base from which to attack the United Provinces through Overijssel: similarly, the Dutch, if ever they gained influence in that area, would be able to sever communications between Cologne and the Spanish Netherlands and to launch an invasion across the Maas against the undefended flank of the Army of Flanders.

Duke William (1539–92) had flirted with heresy in his youth and married his daughters to Lutheran princes, one to Philipp Ludwig of Neuburg and another to the duke of Prussia whose daughter subsequently married Johann Sigismund, the elector of Brandenburg. In the event William had remained Roman Catholic — and an ally of Spain — but when his son John died without children in 1609 the inheritance was disputed between Philipp Ludwig and Johann Sigismund. By the treaty of Dortmund they agreed to hold the duchies in common pending adjudication by the members of the Evangelical Union.

The German Catholics realised that no matter which candidate won, the fertile regions of the lower Rhine and the Ruhr would pass under Protestant control while Spain feared for the consequences this would have for her lines of communication. The Catholic League and its patron, Philip III, were therefore of one mind in regarding the situation as dangerous to their interests. The Evangelical Union and its patron, Henry IV, were equally unanimous in welcoming the advantages to be gained by freeing the duchies from the Catholics and by denying access to them to the armies of Spain.

At this stage the emperor Rudolf intervened. Angered by the Treaty of Dortmund which patently ignored his own rights as emperor in matters of disputed succession, he acted with uncharacteristic vigour by declaring the duchies to be 'fiefs escheated to the Empire in default of male heirs,' and, in the meantime, entrusted their administration to his younger brother

Leopold. As the representatives of Philipp Ludwig, Johann Sigismund and Rudolf faced each other in the disputed duchies, the Evangelical Union and the Catholic League mobilised their forces but made no overt move against each other. Their circumspection was largely due to the fact that neither Spain nor the United Provinces, though each was vitally concerned in the outcome of the crisis, was prepared to break the Twelve Years Truce which had just been negotiated between them (see p. 224). In the event it was Henry IV who brought matters to a head by declaring war on behalf of the Protestant candidates.

Henry's motives are discussed elsewhere (see p. 199). They are not easily discerned, since he had been actively pursuing the Spanish offer of a marriage alliance, but whatever it was he intended to do his plans were abruptly terminated by an assassin's dagger as he was leaving Paris at the head of his troops on 14 May 1610. Marie de Medici, his widow, became regent for the young king Louis XIII and to Spain's great relief agreed to withdraw from the war. In 1613 the rapprochement between Spain and France was celebrated by the marriage of the royal children.

Meanwhile the Evangelical Union and the Catholic League remained studiously aloof from each other on the borders of the duchies, while small forces of Spanish and Dutch troops operating under the flags of the emperor and of the Evangelical Union respectively, manoeuvred with caution. Spinola, the Spanish commander, forced the surrender of Wesel, a town of strategic importance at the junction of the Rhine and the Lippe. The Dutch had offered troops for its defence but as the offer had been rejected by the town council Spinola was free to attack without breaking the Twelve Year Truce.

The Dutch in return seized the opportunity to occupy Rees, another town of strategic value but, again, avoided direct confrontation with Spinola. The impasse was finally resolved in 1614 when Philipp Ludwig died and his son Wolfgang Wilhelm declared himself a Catholic and married a daughter of Maximilian of Bavaria. At Xanten in November 1614 the parties agreed to a compromise. Jülich and Berg were assigned to Wolfgang Wilhelm, and Cleves, Mark and Ravensberg to the elector of Brandenburg.

The crisis over Jülich-Cleves did not lead to a European war because Henry IV was murdered on his way to intervene. Moreover, both Spain and the United Provinces were anxious to preserve the Twelve Years Truce, especially when both Lerma and Oldenbarneveldt were beginning to find their positions of authority coming under serious challenge. (See pp. 214 and 250). In these circumstances neither the Catholic League nor the Evangelical Union was prepared to fight unaided by foreign allies, and a compromise settlement was made possible by Wolfgang Wilhelm's timely conversion. Nonetheless the events of 1609–14 demonstrated very clearly how easy it was for a dispute over the succession to a minor group of duchies to involve not only the rival German leagues and the emperor but also the governments of France, Spain and the United Provinces.

Recognition of this fact has raised serious problems for historians attempting to interpret the events which follow, events traditionally described as the Thirty Years War. The view adopted in the earlier version of this book, inspired by C.V. Wedgwood's classic work *The Thirty Years War*, was that the conflict of religions in Germany and the breakdown of the Peace of Augsburg led to a civil war in which the major foreign powers became involved. This view is no longer tenable, though it has yet to be convincingly replaced by anything quite so straightforward. Historians have disputed to what extent religious issues were genuinely valid during the war; some have maintained that economic and social forces were of greater importance — that there was indeed a socio-economic crisis affecting the whole of Europe, of which the Thirty Years War was only one among several manifestations — and others have discerned in the war the transition from Medieval to Modern Europe. (See in the Bibliography Rabb, T.K., ed. *The Thirty Years War*, Aston T., *Crisis in Europe 1560–1660* and Pagès G. *The Thirty Years War*.)

There is at present considerable agreement that the major European powers were not merely drawn into the German conflict but at critical moments actively thrust themselves into it, as Henry IV tried to do in 1610, thereby promoting conflict where conflict might not otherwise have taken place. Steinberg (Steinberg S.H., *The 'Thirty Years War' and the conflict for European Hegemony*) argues that in the last analysis the war was caused by the conflict between France and the Habsburg states of Spain and Austria, but others now see it is an adjunct of the Eighty

Years War between Spain and the United Provinces (see above pp. 114–20 and in the Bibliography Polisensky J.V. *The Thirty Years War*, Parker G. *The Army of Flanders and the Spanish Road, 1567–1659*, and Maland D. *Europe at War* 1600–1650). This latter view, given prominence in the account which follows, maintains that not only did Spain and the United Provinces represent, as Polisensky puts it, 'two civilisations in ideological conflict', but also that several of the events which are usually narrated with reference to the histories of Italy, France, Germany and the Baltic countries were actually caused by the Spanish and Dutch governments. In addition many other events were critically affected and their importance exaggerated because the two principal antagonists of the day intervened, directly or indirectly, to safeguard their own particular interests and to make of each specific event a microcosm of their own antagonism. Of all the complex and varied issues, therefore, which led to conflict in this period, the one which imparts a particular measure of coherence to the story was the war between Spain and the United Provinces.

THE PERIOD OF HABSBURG ASCENDANCY 1618–30

Bohemia and the Palatinate 1618–23

When Rudolf died in 1612 his brother Matthias was elected to succeed him as Holy Roman Emperor. Matthias had already shown his ability in administering all the 'hereditary lands' save Bohemia, and he shared with Lobkowitz (see p. 121) the ambition to establish one single authority in Vienna capable of imposing administrative unity and religious conformity throughout Austria, Hungary and Bohemia. On the other hand he believed that the perpetual threat of invasion by the Ottoman Turks made it prudent to refrain from interfering too directly with the traditions and privileges enjoyed by his subjects, and he accepted, albeit with bad grace, the terms imposed upon him in Bohemia by the *Letter of Majesty*. Matthias was already an old man, preoccupied with choosing a successor, but by his selection of Ferdinand of Styria he revealed his hopes for the future.

In private life a man of great good humour and kindness, Ferdinand was capable of ruthless cruelty in the defence of his authority and his faith. Where his father had made concessions to the Protestants of Styria, Ferdinand on his accession debarred them from public office, closed their churches and schools and gave all but those of noble birth three weeks in which to conform or leave the country. It was a calculated gamble which few other rulers in Ferdinand's position would have chosen to take but, although 10,000 of his subjects chose exile, his authority in Styria was established beyond doubt.

Zuñiga, in his days as Spanish ambassador to the Empire, was confident that Ferdinand would transform the Habsburg states into a more efficient and coherent empire. So too was Count Thurn, a Bohemian Calvinist who resolved that the Bohemian throne, being elective, should not go to so formidable a Catholic prince. Lobkowitz skilfully out-manoeuvred him. On the eve of the election he lobbied the most senior Protestant nobles, among whom Thurn was not included, and urged them to consider that

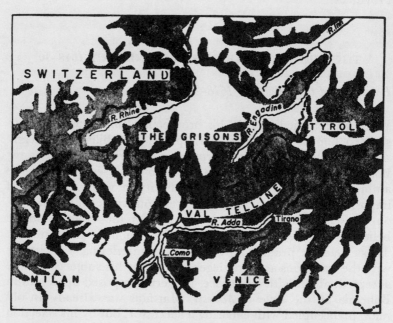

Map 3 The Valtelline

the election of anyone other than a Habsburg was out of the question, that as Ferdinand's election was a foregone conclusion it would be needlessly provocative to oppose it, and that Ferdinand in any case was willing to guarantee the *Letter of Majesty*. More to the point perhaps, the Protestant leaders could not agree on a suitable rival. When the Estates met on the following day Lobkowitz so arranged matters that the vote was given in order of seniority, beginning with those whose support had already been solicited. Thurn and his friends, who had been anticipating a lively debate, sat in horrified amazement as their senior colleagues declared their support for Ferdinand, so that when the moment came for them to vote there was nothing to do but tamely follow suit.

Once the election was over Thurn was deprived of his posts and when Matthias left Bohemia to supervise a similar election in Hungary, the Catholics were given a majority in the council of regents. They were led by Martinitz and Slavata, men of particular ability, eager to extend the authority of the government and to suppress heresy, and they wasted no time in questioning the legality of a number of Protestant churches which they claimed had been built, against the terms of the *Letter of Majesty*, on land belonging to the Catholic Church. If the Protestants had been disorganised and at a loss during Ferdinand's elections, this all too intelligible and specific attack on their religion provoked them to rebellion. In Thurn they found a leader, in the *Letter of Majesty* a cause. A series of public meetings demonstrated the unpopularity of the regents, and on 22 May 1618, a strongly supported deputation marched on the Hradcany Palace in Prague. Invigorated by the thrill of rebellion, and well aware of their most dangerous enemies, Thurn and his colleagues hurled both Martinitz and Slavata from the palace window. Their fall of over six metres was broken by a pile of rubbish and dirt, and astonishingly, neither was seriously hurt.

The significance of this celebrated defenestration was immediately apparent. It was planned and carried out in deliberate imitation of the event which precipitated the Hussite rebellion of the fifteenth century, and was intended by Thurn as an act of defiance, not necessarily against Matthias but against all who challenged the *Letter of Majesty*. The Protestants proceeded to elect thirty-six directors to replace Matthias' regents, and Thurn was appointed commander-in-chief.

Matthias was too old and too ill to act for himself and Ferdinand had yet no authority to act on his own. The day was saved by Oñiate, Zuñiga's successor as Spanish ambassador. In a series of remarkably high-handed and historically important acts he not only strengthened the will of the Austrian Habsburgs to fight back in Bohemia but also made that will effective by providing the necessary men, money and arms. He ordered troops to Vienna from north Italy and Flanders and raised a fortune on his own account so that by August 1618, when an army of 12,000 had been assembled, Oñate himself was in debt for 130,000 florins. His initiative alarmed the Spanish government but, prompted by Zuñiga's insistence that Spain could not allow Bohemia to fall into the hands of her enemies, Philip III declared his support: 'Germany simply cannot be lost'.

Matthias died in March 1619. 'Now we have in our hands the means of overturning the world,' proclaimed Christian of Anhalt. In his imagination the Dutch, the English and the Huguenots were to supply men and money for the cause; Savoy and Venice would block the Alpine routes while the Evangelical Union confined the Spanish army within Flanders; Bethlen Gabor, the prince of Transylvania, would rouse Hungary, Tschernembl in Austria would lead the Estates to unite with Bohemia against the Habsburgs, and the elector Palatine would not only become king of Bohemia but also ensure the election of a Protestant Emperor. Anhalt was very nearly proved right. In July 1619 by an Act of Confederation Bohemia, Moravia, Lusatia and Silesia adopted a. new constitution in which the chief offices of state were reserved to Protestants, and each state was to be independent of the other. It was clear that the Habsburg monarchy was to be repudiated, a monarchy damned twice over in Bohemian eyes since it threatened them with religious persecution and with subordination to the dictates of German officials from Vienna.

In one sense the revolt was a last desperate gamble to preserve for Bohemia an independent existence, but it had, as Anhalt had hoped it would have, repercussions more far-reaching than that. The Act of Confederation actually made provision for the incorporation of Austria and Hungary. Gabor led the Hungarian nobility in revolt, Tschernembl successfully urged the Estates of Upper Austria to repudiate Ferdinand and join the Bohemians, and, while Thurn marched swiftly on Vienna in the summer of 1619, Ferdinand's life was endangered by members of the Lower Austrian Estates who mobbed his palace. Only the chance arrival of troops recruited by Oñate dispersed the mob and drove off Thurn.

Since Ferdinand refused to accept the Act of Confederation the Bohemian Estates renounced their allegiance and took the first steps to offer the throne to the young Frederick V, the Elector Palatine who had married the daughter of James I of England. This was a matter of particular importance to Ferdinand since the king of Bohemia was one of the seven Electors who were about to choose a successor to Matthias as Holy Roman Emperor. Ferdinand was the strongest candidate, certain of support from the three archbishop-electors, but there were also the three Protestants of Saxony, Brandenburg and the Palatinate who had the right to vote. If they had exploited the occasion of the Bohemian revolt to put forward another candidate and denied Ferdinand's right to vote as king of Bohemia the long succession of Habsburg emperors might have been broken. John George of Saxony, however — like his father Christian (see p. 125) disliked anything to do with Calvinism or rebellion, and since he would not support Frederick, and since no other rival candidate could be agreed upon, Ferdinand was duly elected Holy Roman Emperor on 28 August, 1619.

On 26 August the Bohemian Estates formally offered the Bohemian throne to Frederick. Maximilian of Bavaria in a friendly note, as from one cousin to another, tried to reassure him that no Catholic conspiracy existed and pointed out that as king of Bohemia under its new constitution his powers were scarcely worth fighting for. James I and the Evangelical Union added their own advice to refuse the offer. Maurice of Nassau, however, anxious to see the Habsburgs challenged throughout Europe, urged him not to waste time, and with Anhalt seconding that opinion and with Bohemia temptingly on offer just across his frontier, Frederick accepted for himself and for the Protestant cause. 'It is a divine calling which I must not disobey ... my only end is to serve God and His Church.' Religious fervour and political ambition were so closely interrelated in the minds, not only of Frederick, but of Ferdinand, of Maximilian and of nearly all the great leaders in the conflict which followed, that it would be rash to accuse the Elector of self-deception. In the Thirty Years War, the cause of religion was something more than a mere rallying cry to the masses. Princes were often self-seeking but the defence of their faith was as much a matter of self-interest as the acquisition of territory, influence and power. There were few who could remain coolly dispassionate in the clash of confessions.

In October 1619 Frederick arrived in Prague, and the Bohemians, after an initial display of enthusiasm, began to examine him more critically. Timid and even fatalistic, he had none of the qualities required in a leader of rebels and he failed to inspire much affection. The Slav population became suspicious of the Germans who filled his court, the Lutherans were affronted by his extreme Calvinist views, and worst of all, he arrived without the allies it was expected he would bring in his train. James I had repudiated him for supporting rebels while the Dutch, who were desperately anxious that he should succeed, were in the midst of a bitter domestic crisis which had brought the United Provinces to the brink of civil war. (See p. 250). But for this Frederick's success might have been assured. The Estates of Upper and Lower Austria had both elected in September 1619 to join the Bohemian Confederation, and, in October, Bethlen Gabor advanced from Hungary towards Vienna. Fortunately for Ferdinand Gabor was in turn vulnerable to Cossack attacks on his own frontiers in Transylvania and it was these which compelled him to withdraw and make a separate peace in January 1620.

Spanish aid meanwhile continued to pour into Vienna. Between February 1619 and January 1620 Oñate received the equivalent of over two million florins from Madrid to maintain an army of 24,000 for the defence of Vienna and the invasion of Bohemia. In 1620 the Spanish government in Brussels ordered its commander-in-chief, Spinola, to invade Frederick's Rhineland Palatinate. At this the members of the Evangelical Union lost their nerve. But for the Arminian crisis in the United Provinces they would have been guaranteed massive financial and military support by the Dutch: without it they dared not face both Spinola and the Catholic League. By the Treaty of Ulm (July 1620) they declared their neutrality provided their territories were respected.

The Treaty of Ulm had the immediate result of allowing

Maximilian of Bavaria to march off into Austria and Bohemia with the Catholic League army. He had offered to resolve Ferdinand's authority in Upper and Lower Austria and then to defeat the Bohemian rebels. In return his expenses were to be paid and he was promised the Upper Palatinate together with Frederick's electoral title. The Lower Palatinate was provisionally reserved for Spain. Another ally to appear was John George of Saxony. He saw no sense in endangering the Lutheran cause on behalf of a Calvinist rebel, whose actions he condemned as rash and inexcusable, and he was happy to be rewarded with Lusatia which lay along his southern boundary.

The campaigns began in the late summer of 1620. Frederick was swiftly overwhelmed. Maximilian reduced the Estates of Upper and Lower Austria to abject obedience, removed Protestants from office and closed many of their churches. He then invaded Bohemia, joining forces with the army recruited by Oñate, while John George occupied Lusatia. On 8 November the Bohemians were defeated by Maximilian at the Battle of the White Mountain near Prague. It was the first great battle of the Thirty Years War and the most decisive. Frederick had had his fill: despite suggestions that he might with profit renew the struggle in Moravia he fled for refuge to the United Provinces.

The collapse of the Bohemian revolt owed something to Frederick's inept leadership and even more to the divided counsels and jealousies among the Bohemian nobility. The new administration, moreover, failed to establish any method of financing the war, other than by the confiscation of Catholic lands. The central fault was more serious. Thurn and his colleagues failed to persuade the mass of the people of the relevance and value of their cause. At the time of the confederation with Austria, Tschernembl proposed a more radical programme: 'Let the freedom of subjects be proclaimed in the land and villeinage be abolished'. The liberation of the peasantry would have released dynamic forces against which Ferdinand and his allies might have struggled in vain. Instead, as the armies closed in on Prague the rebel leaders, increasingly isolated from the people, had neither a policy to offer nor the means to carry one out.

In the last resort, however, it can be argued that the outcome was determined neither by Ferdinand nor Frederick, but by the governments of Spain, France and the United Provinces. It was Spanish support which alone saved Ferdinand in the desperate months when Thurn was able to mobilise his army unchallenged and when the Estates of Austria and Hungary declared their support for the rebels. Equally important was the inaction of the French and Dutch governments. The rapprochement between Spain and France (see p. 200) assured Spain of French neutrality during the crisis, while the coincidence of the Bohemian Revolt with the climax of the Arminian crisis was, from the Protestant point of view, one of the great tragedies of the period. But for that the Dutch, as the most active opponents of the Habsburgs, would have supplied massive support for the Bohemian rebels, stiffened the morale of the Evangelical Union and mobilised other allies in support of the Elector Palatinate and a Protestant crusade. Anhalt's vision (see p. 132) could have been realised.

After the defeat of the Bohemian rebels Maximilian advanced into the Upper Palatinate in 1621 while Spinola established control throughout most of the middle Rhineland. By the summer of 1621 the Evangelical Union recognised its inadequacies and disbanded itself. In the autumn, however, with the ending of the Twelve Years Truce (see p. 225) Spinola had to withdraw most of his forces to face the Dutch once again across the Rhine delta, but the main business of his campaign had been achieved. Tilly, Maximilian's commander-in-chief, completed it by receiving the surrender of Heidelberg, the capital of the Palatinate, in September 1622.

It was clear that Ferdinand's success had enhanced his authority, both as ruler of the Habsburg kingdoms and as Holy Roman Emperor, and a reaction of some sort was to be expected. For the moment it was only a mild one. The Imperial Diet, meeting at Regensburg in 1623, opposed his action in transferring the Electoral title from Frederick to Maximilian. The Protestants, of course, objected to the clear majority created for the Catholics in the Electoral College, but the Catholic princes also had reason to protest. Any extension of Ferdinand's power was a threat to their own, and so drastic a use of imperial authority was alarming. A compromise was arrived at by which Maximilian was to retain the title for his own lifetime, but when he died the Diet, not the emperor, should determine the succession.

Meanwhile the emperor's triumph within his own hereditary lands was assured. After the brutal treatment meted out by Maximilian and his army of occupation the Estates of Upper and Lower Austria were to be entirely obedient to Ferdinand's authority in the future (see below p. 418) and the cause of the Counter-Reformation was assured. In Hungary where Habsburg influence had always been tenuous in the extreme Bethlen Gabor once again led a rebellion but, when checked by Imperial troops, agreed to negotiate. The Treaty of Nikolsburg (January 1622) while it granted the Estates' demands for virtual autonomy nonetheless surrendered the Hungarian crown to Ferdinand and secured peace along the Danube.

In Bohemia the Habsburg triumph was unqualified, and in the years which followed the battle of the White Mountain the kingdom was transformed into an obedient province of the Austrian empire. No mercy was shown to the rebel leaders, most of whom were executed. As for the Protestants, their clergy were outlawed, their chapels destroyed and their schools and universities taken over by the Jesuits. The progressive debasement of the coinage destroyed the wealth of the cities, and over half the land was confiscated and sold. In this it was the speculator rather than the emperor who reaped the immediate profit, but in the long run Ferdinand's own ends were also served. With the nobility deprived of its estates, the townsmen ruined by the currency changes, and the peasants burdened with the troops of the victorious army, the kingdom might be worth little as a source of revenue, but its inhabitants were in no condition to oppose their sovereign, especially as the new landowning class was predominantly Catholic and German in its outlook. In 1627, when a new constitution was drawn up, Ferdinand's triumph was complete: the *Letter of Majesty* was annulled, the succession to the throne vested in Ferdinand's heirs, the power of the Estates curtailed, and the combination of Germanic custom and Roman law as practised in Austria was applied to Bohemia. As a final blow to local patriotism, the Chancellor was to travel with the king; in other words, Vienna was to be the effective centre of Bohemia's administration. It remained so for nearly three centuries.

The Conflict Extended Across Europe 1623–28

The Habsburg successes in Bohemia and the Rhineland owed a great deal to the friendly neutrality of France during the minority of Louis XIII, and when Louis himself came to power there was no immediate change of policy until Spanish troops occupied the Valtelline in 1621.

The Valtelline, which afforded Spanish troops a convenient route from Lake Como to the Alpine passes leading to the Tyrol (see Map 3), was a region torn by faction. The Italian population of the valley was predominantly Catholic and at odds with a minority of Protestant families: these, however, were supported by an association of Swiss Protestant landlords, the Grisons or Grey Lords, who exercised jurisdiction over the Valtelline and the Alpine valleys south-east of Switzerland. In 1621, after a succession of riots and massacres by both sides had endangered the security of their lines of communication through the valley the Habsburgs decided to intervene. The Austrians secured the passes on the Tyrolean side while the Spanish governor in Milan repudiated the sovereignty of the Grisons and constructed a chain of fortresses along the Valtelline itself. Spanish military intervention on such a scale angered the French government which, in alliance with Venice and Savoy, pledged its assistance to the Grisons by the Treaty of Paris (1623). Thereupon the Spaniards, anxious to avoid a conflict with France while the war continued in the Netherlands, persuaded the Pope to undertake the protection of the Catholic population of the valley and replace the Spanish garrisons with his own troops.

This was a shrewd move which not only safeguarded Spain's access to the valley but also embarrassed Louis XIII who was unwilling to provoke a storm of protest from the extreme Catholics, the *dévots*, by ordering his army to make war on the Pope. Nothing was done therefore for several months until the appointment of cardinal Richelieu, a minister whose views on foreign policy were very much in line with those of Henry IV, and who encouraged Louis to invade the Valtelline at the end of 1624.

The operation was very successful. The Papal garrisons were handled with considerable tact and eventually agreed to withdraw, but the French found themselves in difficulties when their allies, the Grisons, required them to suppress the liberties of the Catholic population. To make matters more difficult for Louis XIII, a Huguenot rebellion at home made it impossible to maintain an army abroad (see p. 182). A compromise was reached with Spain in the Treaty of Monzon (1626) by which the forts were to be demolished and the sovereignty of the Grisons upheld. This implied a defeat for Spain but as the only troops capable of checking the progress of her own were now to be withdrawn to France she was satisfied with the treaty — and continued to make use of the route for many years to come.

The Valtelline affair proved to be a damp squib, and it is possible to suggest that apart from this minor episode in the Alps Western Europe might well have enjoyed an era of peace and stability following upon the Habsburg successes in Bohemia and the Rhineland. There remained problems to be resolved, such as the fate of the exiled Frederick V, but the Bohemian Revolt was unquestionably over, Ferdinand's authority was greater than his predecessors' throughout his 'hereditary lands', Bavaria and Saxony, the two most powerful German princes, were content with the results of their alliance with the emperor, the Evangelical Union had been disbanded, and France, plagued by Huguenot rebellions and the excesses of some of the great nobles, was generally anxious to support a peaceful settlement of international affairs. The peace of Europe therefore depended not upon a resolution of the old rivalry of Habsburg and Bourbon, nor upon the reduction of tensions within the Holy Roman Empire, but upon the decision of Spain and the United Provinces whether or not to renew the Twelve Years Truce when it expired in 1621.

In the bitter struggle between Spain and the United Provinces, however, both sides were intransigent (see pp. 225 and 251), and the renewal of what the Dutch were to call their Eighty Years War (1568–1648) accounts for the continuation of the conflict in Germany which was eventually to be known as the Thirty Years War. The main area of operations was initially confined to the Netherlands. Maurice of Nassau in his old age achieved none of the victories he had dreamed of throughout the Truce, and it was Spinola who seized the initiative for Spain by his capture of Breda in 1625 (see p. 252). Both sides nonetheless had a truly continental grasp of strategy which became evident as each formulated its plans for the destruction of the other.

The Dutch for example discussed an alliance with Gustavus Adolphus, the young king of Sweden who, since his accession in 1610, had rapidly extended his empire along the coastline of Lithuania and Poland (see p. 376). Gustavus offered to assist the Protestant cause by leading 55,000 troops into Bohemia and Austria, but he asked for two-thirds of his costs to be paid and the Dutch suspected that he would in the event be more interested in Poland than in Austria. In his place they decided to give subsidies to his rival, Christian IV of Denmark, who was ambitious to extend his influence in north Germany under the pretence of helping to restore the exiled elector Palatine. Christian already possessed the duchy of Holstein, and the former Catholic bishoprics of Verden and Halberstadt. With Dutch support he was elected Director of the Lower Saxon Circle of the empire and he hoped to acquire Osnabrück and Minden. In the summer of 1625 his army advanced towards that of the Catholic League in Lower Saxony but the campaign ended without a battle when Christian was thrown from his horse down a 24 metre drop and was so badly stunned that for several days he was paralysed and taken for dead.

Another soldier about to take the field was Albrecht von Waldstein, more generally known as Wallenstein. Born into a family of the Bohemian Brethren, he had been educated by the Jesuits when his parents died, became a Catholic, and entered the emperor's service when Ferdinand was archduke of Styria. The suppression of Bohemia made his future. He became the military governor of Prague, profited from the debasement of the coinage and speculated in the sale of confiscated estates. Within a short time he had become prince of Friedland, owning over 2,000 square miles between the Elbe and the Sudeten mountains. Here he created a self-sufficient military supply base, directing the activity of the peasants so that a surplus of cereals was produced and recruiting armourers, smiths and weavers to fill his warehouses with weapons and uniforms. He planned to raise an army of 50,000 for the emperor's service and to make warfare profitable, not by the indiscriminate looting which characterised most armies of the period, but by compelling the towns where he operated to pay heavily for protection from his troops. With the money thus raised he would then supply his army from his base in Bohemia and his troops, well paid and well supplied, would therefore be better disciplined than others.

By this means Wallenstein planned to establish the emperor's authority beyond question throughout north Germany, and win for himself further rewards of land and titles. Ferdinand recognised that he had been dependent for his success upon the troops of Spain, Saxony and the Catholic League, and that without an army of his own his authority as emperor would be insufficient for him to undertake the plans he had in mind for the recovery of Catholic lands. Nonetheless he was a little taken aback by the scale of Wallenstein's proposals and cautiously limited his commission to 21,000 troops until Christian IV's invasion of Lower Saxony prompted the emperor to increase the number. In the winter of 1625 Wallenstein moved north into Saxony and took up his position alongside Tilly and the Catholic League army in readiness for the next Danish campaign.

The Danish Campaign of 1626 was in fact part of a carefully planned operation worked out at The Hague in the previous December. With the Dutch as paymasters the Treaty of the Hague laid down that Christian of Denmark was to engage the forces of the Catholic League and thus create an opportunity for two smaller armies to slip by Tilly — one, on the western flank, to enter the Rhineland and restore the exiled Frederick to his Palatinate; the other, on the eastern flank, to evade Wallenstein, enter Bohemia, raise the persecuted Protestants against the Habsburgs and march on Vienna.

The strategy conceived by the Dutch was sound and far-reaching; equally sound and far-reaching was the strategy conceived by Spain and her allies at a conference held in Brussels in May 1626. The Spanish minister Olivares recognised that the Dutch economy depended to a large extent on the trade with the Baltic. Accordingly he proposed to offer the Baltic ports of the Hanseatic League (see p. 16) the monopoly of Spanish trade with Europe provided that they denied Dutch merchants access to their ports.

Since the Hanseatic ports were afraid of Dutch naval power in the Baltic such an offer was unlikely to be accepted. For this reason Olivares conceived his plan of campaign for 1626. The Catholic League was to contain Christian of Denmark and thus protect its own interests by keeping Frederick out of the

Rhineland Palatinate and by creating the opportunity to recover
the secularised bishoprics of north Germany for the Catholic
church. Wallenstein meanwhile was to advance to the Baltic
coast and, by making himself master of it and by launching a fleet
in due course, to reassure the members of Hanseatic League that
they could count upon Habsburg protection if they closed their
ports to the Dutch. A Spanish fleet meanwhile was to assemble in
the Channel and enter the Baltic in support of Wallenstein. The
plan threatened the economy of the United Provinces at its most
vulnerable point and would certainly have assisted the Army of
Flanders to re-establish Spanish control north of the Rhine delta.
Wallenstein, though not especially concerned to witness the
defeat of the Dutch, nonetheless welcomed the plan as an
opportunity to make himself, and his emperor, supreme in north
Germany.

The wide-ranging and ambitious schemes debated by the
Dutch and their allies at the Hague, and by Spain and her allies
in Brussels, affected an area stretching from the Atlantic to the
Balkans, from the Baltic to the Danube. In 1626 they were put to
the test when Christian IV advanced against Tilly and the
Catholic League army. The Rhineland venture was entrusted to
Christian of Brunswick, the Bohemian campaign to Mansfeld,
but as both men had proved to be largely ineffectual against
Spanish and League troops in the campaign of 1620–21 it was not
surprising that they failed yet again. Tilly fell back to cover
Christian of Brunswick, whose death in June removed any threat
to the Rhineland, while Wallenstein held the Elbe crossing at
Dessau against Mansfeld. Mansfeld however was reinforced with
Danish infantry and set off in August on a route-march curving
east and south to reach Moravia. Wallenstein followed, carefully
holding the inside of the curve to prevent any sudden break
through into Bohemia, when he learned that Christian IV had
moved into the ever-widening gap between himself and Tilly. He
detached 8,000 men to turn Christian's advance, and, when the
Danes retreated, Tilly caught them and defeated them utterly at
Lutter. Christian lost half his army and the strategy conceived at
The Hague was in ruins.

Wallenstein shadowed Mansfeld as far as the Hungarian
border until Mansfeld's death in November allowed him to
return north in the winter to join Tilly for the offensive of 1627.

Tilly and Wallenstein were uneasy allies, with different long-term aims, but when they combined to invade Denmark Tilly was badly wounded leaving Wallenstein free to act on his own. No time was wasted. He overran the Danish mainland and then turned eastwards to Pomerania, seizing for himself the duchy of Mecklenburg. All this time he recruited more troops until by 1628 he commanded at least 125,000 men. With such a force, maintained by contributions ruthlessly levied on all the north German states, save Mecklenburg of course, there seemed no power to equal him. The Genoese envoy reported that the Hanseatic towns 'though they may sympathise with their Protestant brethren, are trembling at the emperor's good fortune and so will probably bow before his commands'. To convince them of the necessity of doing so Wallenstein in July 1628 set about the siege of Stralsund, the one Baltic port not yet under his control.

The city authorities agreed to surrender but the citizens rebelled against the decision, encouraged by the news that support was on its way. Despite the bitter enmity between Sweden and Denmark Gustavus had invited Christian to join

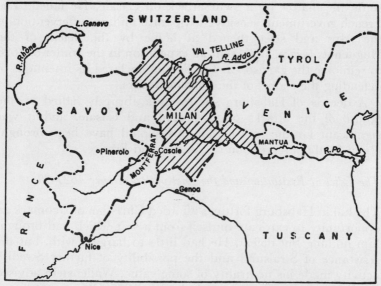

Map 4 The Mantuan Succession and North Italy, 1630

him in saving Stralsund: 'I now see with little difficulty that the projects of the House of Habsburg are directed against the Baltic; and that by a mixture of force and favour the United Provinces, my own power and finally yours are to be driven from it'. Christian agreed. Since Stralsund stood on a triangular promontory connected by a causeway with the mainland, Danish and Swedish ships supplied the city without difficulty and Wallenstein, who did not wish to damage the city by taking it by storm but only to coerce its surrender, abandoned the siege after a few weeks.

Meanwhile the Habsburgs had become involved with another siege, many miles from the Baltic coastline. In North Italy the duke of Mantua had died. Mantua itself had little international importance but its dukes controlled Montferrat and the fortress of Casale on the borders of Milan and Savoy (see map 4). When the duchy passed to a French prince, the duke of Nevers, the danger to Spain's transalpine route was evident. Spain put forward a rival candidate and the emperor, since the duchy was an imperial fief, ordered its occupation by his own troops pending his verdict on the succession. Acting on his own authority, however, the Spanish commander in Milan decided to settle the matter by a swift attack on Casale. He failed. The French government, sensitive to Spanish military intervention in the Alps and strengthened at home by the defeat of the Huguenots (see p. 182), sent an expedition in the winter of 1628 to reinforce the garrison at Casale and declared its intentions of defending the claims of the duke of Nevers.

A decade of Habsburg success was abruptly halted by the failure of the attacks on Stralsund and Casale, and it was significant for the future that this should have been brought about by the intervention of Sweden and France.

The Edict of Restitution and the Diet of Regensburg 1629–30

The lull in Habsburg fortunes afforded Christian of Denmark an opportunity to extricate himself from a war which had brought him nothing but defeat. He had little to bargain with, but the resistance of Stralsund and the possibility of further Swedish activity made his neutrality of some value. Wallenstein advised the emperor to make peace at Lübeck in 1629. Christian forfeited his claims to the north German bishoprics and resigned his position as director of the Lower Saxon Circle. In return he was restored to all his Danish possessions and released from the payment of any indemnity.

The settlement was timely from the emperor's point of view because Wallenstein's deliberate and methodical exactions from the north German princes had caused widespread protest, and the Catholic princes were as alarmed by his successes as were the Protestants. In October 1627 Maximilian had summoned a special meeting of the Electors at Mülhausen to protest against Wallenstein's conduct of the war. The Electors realised only too well that these same troops might one day be directed against themselves. Ferdinand himself began to wonder how far he could control his own agent; in the face of so much opposition it might be politic to disown him, particularly after the failure at Stralsund. On the other hand, he was heavily in debt to Wallenstein and he needed his army to carry off what was to be the greatest gamble of Ferdinand's career.

Ferdinand's plan was nothing less than the wholesale enforcement of the Augsburg settlement: revolutionary in its implications, this involved the outlawry of Calvinism and the surrender of all land seized from the Church since 1555. At one stroke the boundaries of Germany were to be redrawn. The princes whose power depended on the secularised territories would be condemned to insignificance, their subjects to Catholicism. But this was not all, for otherwise the Catholic League would have applauded the emperor's zeal. When Ferdinand issued the Edict of Restitution in March 1629 he did so without reference to the Diet, and in terms which exalted the theory of imperial absolutism. The archbishoprics of Magdeburg and Bremen, twelve other dioceses and over fifty large monastic estates were to be surrendered to the imperial commissioners on no greater authority than the emperor's own writ. It was neither the writ nor the commissioners, however, which perturbed the princes; behind both they saw the sword in the hands of Wallenstein. In private he opposed the emperor's policy, believing it to be an unnecessary distraction from the Baltic campaign and one that might provoke the Protestant princes to rebellion, but, cynical and critical though he might be of his master's policy, Wallenstein nevertheless enforced it with

characteristic efficiency and speed. Magdeburg, Halberstadt and
Bremen were occupied; the duke of Wolfenbüttel was deprived of
a third of his territory, and the proud city of Augsburg submitted
to the rule of a Catholic bishop.

If the edict threatened the Protestants with disaster, the
manner of its enforcement was equally alarming to the Catholics:
the long-awaited triumph of their Church was not to be
celebrated when it represented an even greater triumph of the
imperial prerogative. The time-honoured bonds which condemned an emperor to impotence had been burst open by
Ferdinand, at the very moment when his army threatened to
control the Baltic coastline. The relation between these two
events was even more apparent when the archdiocese of
Magdeburg, the strategic key to north Germany, was assigned by
the emperor to Leopold William, his younger son.

The emperor seemed to be at the peak of his career. The
Bohemian rebels, the Elector Palatine and the king of Denmark
had all been defeated in battle, while the suppression of the
Protestants in Austria and Bohemia and the enforcement of the
Edict of Restitution had advanced the Catholic cause further in
ten years than the policies of his predecessors had done in sixty.
But the price of success was the hostility of all the German
princes, Catholic and Protestant alike. It was ironical perhaps
that it should have been Maximilian of Bavaria who, despite the
manner of his appointment to the electoral title, began to invoke
the liberties of the Empire against the emperor: 'Today', he wrote
to his son, 'it is not only the prosperity and liberty of the whole
empire which is at stake but also the dignity and the prerogatives
of the Electors.' The struggle for power in Germany transcended
the conflict between Protestant and Catholic, and in this struggle
Ferdinand's long series of successes had left him in a dangerously
isolated position.

This became clear when Ferdinand summoned the Diet to
Regensburg in 1630 to secure its assent to three proposals. He
wanted his son recognised as King of the Romans, a title which
would have ensured his succession without further election to the
imperial throne. In addition he wanted support for his policies in
Mantua and an agreement to support Spain against the Dutch
who had suddenly burst through into Brabant (see p. 253). In
the circumstances the emperor was unlikely to be successful

despite his willingness to sacrifice Wallenstein — who had flatly refused to divert his own troops from north Germany for the occupation of Mantua, and whose power had aroused the emperor's suspicions. To add to the problem French agents at the Diet made great play of all the emperor's successes and encouraged the princes, who in fact needed little prompting from anyone, to withhold their co-operation.

In the event Wallenstein was abandoned, accepting his dismissal with apparent equanimity, but the Diet was not mollified. It disclaimed any interest in Mantua, refused to consider action against the Dutch and postponed discussions about the election of a King of the Romans.

In Mantua meanwhile the emperor's position seemed to have improved. Although Wallenstein had refused to co-operate, other troops had been found to march through the Valtelline in September 1629 and take possession of the duchy of Mantua. The French had tried to strengthen their position against the Spaniards at Casale by occupying Pinerolo, a nearby Savoyard fortress, but their lines of communication across the Alps put them at a disadvantage against a Spanish army operating from Milan. When the emperor's forces occupied the duchy of Mantua the French agreed to a truce pending a settlement at Regensburg. The Diet refused to consider the matter but Ferdinand adroitly offered to award the inheritance to the duke of Nevers provided Spanish troops were allowed into Casale and Pinerolo and that the French government agreed to withhold support from the emperor's enemies. The extreme Catholic party at the French court urged Louis XIII to abandon Richelieu's alliances with the German, Dutch and Swedish Protestants and thereby secure the Mantuan duchy for Nevers, but Richelieu's personal triumphs on the Day of Dupes, November 1630 (see pp. 183–4) allowed him to ignore the offer and resume the war. At this moment the Swedish invasion of Germany became evident and the emperor, afraid to fight on two fronts, capitulated in Italy. By the Treaty of Cherasco in June 1631 Nevers was granted Mantua, Montferrat and Casale without conditions, and subsequently, in a secret deal with the duke of Savoy, Richelieu purchased Pinerolo for France.

THE PERIOD OF HABSBURG DECLINE 1630–48

The Intervention of Sweden 1630–34

Gustavus Adolphus landed at Peenemünde in Pomerania on 16 July 1630. The reasons for this historic intervention in the affairs of central Europe have been much debated, and are described more fully in Chapter VIII (see p. 378). Briefly, there is broad agreement that the issues uppermost in Gustavus' mind were those which had prompted him to help Stralsund — his anxiety at the Habsburgs' advance upon the Baltic and a deep concern to defend the Protestant cause. His chancellor, Oxenstierna, opposed the venture, reminding Gustavus that he was already at war with Sigismund of Poland, a Roman Catholic claimant to the Swedish throne. Gustavus brushed this aside. The emperor, he claimed, was the more serious danger in the long run both to Sweden and to Protestantism. Moreover, by denying him access to the Baltic Gustavus intended to provide himself with a secure base in Germany from which to direct operations, as circumstances required, not only against the Habsburgs but also against Sweden's ancient enemies, Poland and Denmark.

The first thing to be done was to negotiate a truce with Poland. The Dutch offered valuable diplomatic assistance. They were anxious to see an end to the war which disrupted their vital trade in Polish grain, and they were more than anxious to launch Sweden's troops against the Habsburgs in central Europe. So too were the French, whose agents helped to persuade Sigismund that he could not for the time being hope to defeat Sweden. In the event a truce was signed at Altmark in September 1629 which allowed Sweden, for a period of six years, to occupy Livonia and collect the customs duties in the Prussian ports, a privilege worth 600,000 *talers* in a good year.

As soon as Gustavus landed in Pomerania the French followed up their diplomatic offensive. A few months earlier, Richelieu had hoped to stir up Maximilian of Bavaria against the emperor at the Diet of Regensburg, but the dismissal of Wallenstein had eased relations between them, and it was to Gustavus that Richelieu now turned. By the treaty of Bärwalde, signed in January 1631 he promised a subsidy of 200,000 *talers* every six months if Gustavus agreed to lead 30,000 troops against the

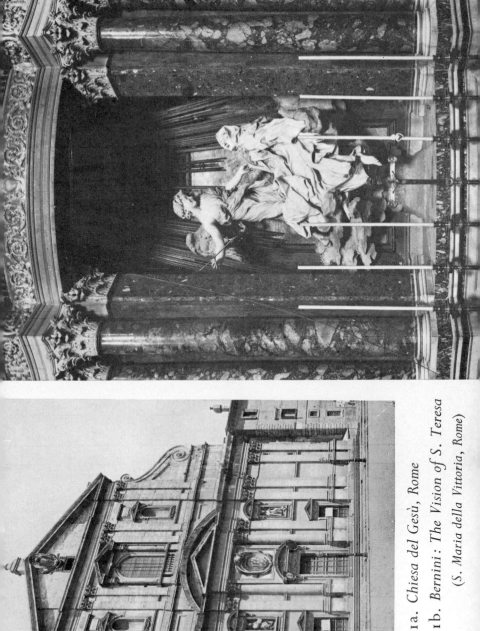

1a. *Chiesa del Gesù, Rome*
1b. *Bernini: The Vision of S. Teresa*
   (S. Maria della Vittoria, Rome)

2. *The Worship of the Holy Name of Jesus*
(Ceiling of Il Gesù, Rome, by Gaulli)

3. *Sant' Agnese, on the Piazza Navona, Rome*

4a.
San Carlino
alle Quattro
Fontane,
Rome

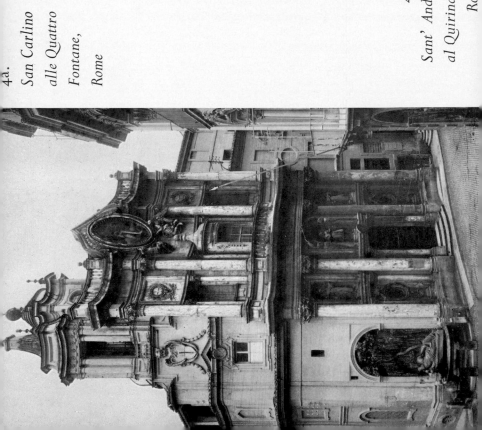

4b.
Sant' Andrea
al Quirinale,
Rome

emperor and to leave unharmed all Roman Catholic churches in regions where the Catholic religion was established by the Peace of Augsburg.

In retrospect it is clear that Richelieu was too optimistic in hoping to harness so vigorous a warhorse to the Bourbon chariot. Gustavus was a man of independent spirit and although the subsidies were of value they were not entirely indispensable. The price of copper, a valuable commodity in the Swedish budget, had fallen on the Amsterdam market but there was now the revenue of the Prussian ports. Russia, moreover, Sweden's ally against Poland, had granted Gustavus the right to export Russian corn at a low price, which had just gained him a profit in Amsterdam of 400,000 *talers*.

Anxious to make the outcome as secure as possible Richelieu proposed an alliance between Gustavus and the German Protestants. 'The King of Sweden', he wrote, 'is a sun which has just risen: he is young but of vast renown. The ill-treated or banished princes of Germany have turned to him in their misfortune as the mariner turns to the Pole Star.' John George of Saxony did not agree. Gustavus might talk of the defence of the Reformation but he was nonetheless a foreigner intent on acquiring territory in north Germany. Moreover his invasion would only serve to prolong the war. John George therefore recruited whatever troops were available in north Germany in order to deny their use to Gustavus, and summoned his fellow Lutherans to a conference at Leipzig where it was agreed to ally with the emperor provided that he revoke the Edict of Restitution. It was an offer of historic importance, and a tragedy for Germany that it failed. Ferdinand, however, underrated Gustavus' strength and saw no need to purchase help by compromising over Church property.

Maximilian, too, misread the situation. Anxious above all to safeguard his electoral title and his acquisition of the Palatinate, he was persuaded by Richelieu that the Habsburgs were not to be trusted in this matter while Spanish troops still occupied the Rhineland. In May 1631, therefore, by the Treaty of Fontainebleau Louis XIII undertook to defend the elector's titles and territories provided he did not assist the enemies of France and Sweden. It apparently went unnoticed that although Gustavus agreed in consequence to respect the neutrality of Bavaria and the Catholic League, he had already published his intent of restoring the former elector to the Palatinate.

The Lutheran camp was left in a state of fearful neutrality. If the princes could not support their persecutor, they dared not join their self-appointed saviour — who meanwhile overran Mecklenburg and Pomerania, thereby establishing Swedish control of the Baltic coastline, from Finland to the Danish peninsula. Gustavus had thus achieved one of his principal war aims. What he needed was a settlement to guarantee it, but no one was prepared to deal with him.

Matters were suddenly brought to a head by the sack of Magdeburg in May 1631. One of the most appalling incidents of a war rich in atrocities, the sack resulted indirectly from Wallenstein's dismissal. His army had passed into Tilly's hands, but not the granaries and storehouses which supplied it. These remained safe in Wallenstein's own keeping and, with every justification, he refused to provision Tilly without advance payment. Tilly was in despair. The emperor had no money to send him, the men deserted daily to enlist in Saxony's new army, and the only remedy seemed to be the seizure of Magdeburg. The city was one of the few to have declared for Gustavus and it enjoyed a position of strategic importance on the Elbe, but its chief interest for Tilly was that it was well stocked with provisions. The marauding army began the siege in April, and four weeks later Magdeburg fell. Fire, famine and disease destroyed those who survived the sack, leaving a mere five thousand of the thirty thousand inhabitants. Unfortunately for Tilly, the all-essential provisions had also been destroyed.

The news of the sack passed like a shock wave through the Protestant states, doubling and redoubling its effect with every repetition. In the midst of all the uncertainty and dismay, one thing was clear: Tilly's army was in full cry after provisions, and when it occupied Leipzig even John George had to follow the elector of Brandenburg into the Swedish camp. By the end of the summer Gustavus was assured of the alliance of all the north German princes. The way was clear for his advance. At Breitenfeld, in the broad Saxon plain outside Leipzig, he fought his first battle in Germany. His allies were driven from the field, exposing his flank, but his own men stood firm in solid squares, supported by light artillery and small groups of fast moving cavalry. By this combination of strength with manoeuvrability he won the day.

If Gustavus had been nothing more than Richelieu's mercenary he would have marched south into the Habsburg homeland, but the sequel to Breitenfeld proved as alarming to the French as the victory itself had been to the Habsburgs. Gustavus refused to take the risk that John George, whose motives he understood only too well, might betray him in his absence and cut his lines of communication with Pomerania. Instead, and also with a view to committing John George more deeply against the emperor, he compelled the Saxons to invade Bohemia, where they liberated Prague and inspired the return of exiles from all over Europe. Meanwhile the Swedish army marched westwards to the wealthy Catholic lands of Franconia and the Rhineland, the celebrated 'Priests' alley'. With Catholic loot in abundance to pay his troops Gustavus could afford to forfeit the French subsidies: at the same time he was well placed to control the north German waterways and his lines of communication.

Frankfurt, captured in November 1631, was the constitutional centre of the Holy Roman Empire and it was here that Gustavus held court throughout the winter and pondered upon his purposes. In invading Germany he had summarised his policy in two key words : *assecuratio*, the need for a secure base in north Germany, and *satisfactio*, the payment he required from the Protestants to recompense him for saving them from the Edict of Restitution and the Counter-Reformation. These were now to be achieved by his proposal that the German Protestant princes dissolve their connection with the emperor and unite with Sweden. It was not received with any enthusiasm. The Protestants as Gustavus' allies, had already experienced his heavy hand; they had no wish to become his vassals. They could merely play for time and await the outcome of the next campaign.

Gustavus' occupation of the Rhineland was a disaster for Spain since the garrisons protecting the vital lines of communication to the Netherlands were scattered. Worse still, from Spain's point of view, was the action of the French government which, in order to contain the Swedish advance, moved its own troops into Alsace and Lorraine and offered treaties of protection to the

Rhineland princes. As a result the archbishop-elector of Trier
agreed that the great fortresses of Ehrenbreitstein and Philippsburg (formerly garrisoned by Spain) would be assigned for
French use once they had been cleared of Swedish troops.

The emperor meanwhile, with Maximilian's agreement,
recalled Wallenstein to take command of his army. Wallenstein
had accepted disgrace in 1630 with characteristic fatalism, taking
comfort from his horoscope and awaiting a more favourable
conjunction of the stars. The terms on which he accepted
command have never been known but there is little doubt that he
demanded and secured a free hand in the conduct of the war: his
first action was to drive John George from Bohemia and recover
control of Prague. He then moved south-west towards the upper
Danube to meet the Swedish army which had taken the field in
the spring of 1632. Gustavus had restored the exiled elector
Frederick to the Palatinate, driven Maximilian from Bavaria
and, by the summer, was poised to advance down the Danube
towards Vienna.

Wallenstein handled the crisis with considerable finesse. He
occupied a strong position along a ridge of high ground
overlooking the Swedish camp at Nuremberg. Gustavus was
reluctant to attack but dared not continue his advance with
Wallenstein at his heels. In the event he chose to sit things out,
but whereas Wallenstein, with Bohemia at his back, could supply
his men for months on end, the Swedish army began to run short
of provisions. Finally, when Gustavus in some desperation
seemed about to advance down the Danube regardless,
Wallenstein moved north to threaten the Swedish bases in
Pomerania. Gustavus felt obliged to follow and the armies met at
Lützen in November 1632. The Swedes drove Wallenstein's
army from the field but in victory suffered a blow more serious
than any defeat. Gustavus was killed.

Fortunately for Sweden the chancellor, Oxenstierna, was in
Frankfurt at the time and was able to take command of the
situation. He summoned the Protestant princes to meet him at
Heilbronn in order to safeguard the fruits of Gustavus' victories
— not least the Swedish occupation of Pomerania — by forming
a new Protestant league. John George of Saxony remained aloof
but the others accepted Sweden's leadership. So swiftly was the
Heilbronn League created that the French ambassador arrived

too late to reduce the princes' dependence upon Sweden but nonetheless committed his government to provide the appropriate subsidies.

Meanwhile, in the Catholic camp, the old quarrel between Maximilian and Wallenstein had broken out afresh, especially because Wallenstein failed to attack the Swedish army in possession of Bavaria. This time, however, Ferdinand was not prepared to defend his servant. While Gustavus lived, Wallenstein could dictate his own terms to the emperor, but from the moment of Gustavus's death he was no longer indispensable. Maximilian's enmity and Ferdinand's obvious mistrust drove him to consider desperate measures to safeguard his own position. Controversy surrounds his plans. Certainly he negotiated in secret and separately with Sweden, Saxony and France. This might have been done to divide his enemies: equally, he may have been planning to capitalise his one asset, the army, and sell out to the Heilbronn League, his price being the kingdom of Bohemia.

Ferdinand for his part had no notion what his servant might be up to and in January 1634 he ordered Wallenstein to resign his command. No one knew whether the dismissal would carry any weight with the army. Wallenstein himself never doubted the loyalty of his own officers, and he failed to perceive that some of them were genuinely attached to the emperor and to Catholicism; others were simply ambitious, seeking the promotion which might result from effective service in the emperor's cause. Despite the need for haste, the mutiny was well planned and in February Wallenstein was murdered.

Wallenstein's death gave new life to the emperor. During the past three years he had lost his resilience, prayer and fasting being his only response to the disasters which befell his cause. Now, with Gustavus and Wallenstein dead, he regained his spirits and renewed his efforts to forward the cause of his family and his religion. His son Ferdinand, king of Hungary, was appointed commander in Wallenstein's place, and soon justified himself as a soldier by defending both Bohemia and Bavaria from attacks by the Heilbronn League. Better still, help from Spain was on its way as Olivares mobilised all the resources of Castile for yet one more major campaign against the Dutch and their allies (see p. 226).

Twenty thousand men, under the command of the Cardinal-Infante Ferdinand landed at Genoa, marched through the Valtelline and joined forces with those of Ferdinand of Hungary in the Tyrol. Together they marched against the Heilbronn League and, at Nördlingen in September 1634 they won one of the most decisive battles of the war. Fifteen desperate charges were made against the impregnable lines of Spanish infantry, but the armies of the League were outnumbered and, in the event, outmanoeuvred. When finally they began to withdraw from the field, the Catholic armies seized the opportunity and launched their own attack. The exhausted Protestants could make no effective resistance, and their retreat became a rout.

The Treaty of Prague and the German War 1635–48

The immediate results of the battle of Nördlingen were startling. The Habsburgs broke the power of the Heilbronn League, recovered control of the Rhineland and strengthened their position in the Netherlands. So great indeed was the triumph that the French government, after years of underhand conflict with Spain, felt itself obliged to intervene more directly by declaring war openly. It was a decision which proved to be disastrous for Spain, and whatever it did for France, assured the triumph of the United Provinces. (See pp. 201–4, 252–8 and 382–5 for an account of warfare outside Germany, in particular in the Netherlands, in the Baltic and between France and Spain.)

These, however, were the long-term consequences, not evident in 1635. Within the empire the victory left Ferdinand II in a commanding position from which he wisely chose to seek an accommodation with the defeated Protestants. He was persuaded by his son that the Edict of Restitution should be abandoned on the grounds that the 'hereditary lands' of Austria and Bohemia could never be secure while the protestant princes of the north remained hostile to the house of Habsburg. This therefore eased the way to settlement, and John George of Saxony was the first to accept the emperor's terms, confirmed in the Treaty of Prague, May 1635. He was allowed to retain all lands secularised by his family since 1626 and confirmed in his title to Lusatia. In return, however, he was required to make no alliance with the emperor's enemies. This, the elector hoped, was merely a negative undertaking, but he discovered that its effect was to make him the ally of the emperor against Sweden and thus to exchange one enemy for another.

The other princes, after considering rival proposals by Sweden and France, eventually followed suit by signing agreements similar to that of Prague. The remarkable consequence of this was to unite nearly all the Catholic and Protestant princes of Germany in one army under the leadership of the emperor's son, a position wholly unimaginable before 1635 and one which very nearly led to the destruction of the Swedish power in north Germany. Sweden's troops were unpaid and mutinous; the treaty of Prague removed from her all hope of assistance from the German princes; the expiry of the truce of Altmark (see p. 155) deprived her of the revenues of the Prussian ports and condemned her to renew the war with Poland; and the subsidies offered by France could not be accepted without an undertaking, unacceptable to Oxenstierna, that Sweden abandon her claim to territory in the Rhineland. Baner, the commander of the mutinous garrisons, was at his wits' end to prevent them deserting to Saxony or Denmark and it was not until his government had purchased peace with Poland (Treaty of Stuhmsdorf 1635, see p. 382) that 10,000 men were released from the Polish war to join him in Pomerania. With their support he restored a measure of morale by defeating a Saxon army at Wittstock in 1636 but the emperor's troops drove him back into Pomerania the following year.

Ferdinand II had already died (1636) having successfully ensured the election of his son as Ferdinand III. He had indeed fulfilled the expectations of the emperor Matthias in 1618. Bohemia and Austria had never been so obedient to the government in Vienna, and, both by persecution and by gentler methods, the influence of Protestantism within the 'hereditary lands' had been substantially reduced. Within the empire, no emperor had so dominated events since the reign of Charles V, early in the sixteenth century, and the Edict of Restitution was in many respects the high-water mark of imperial authority. It could not, however, be sustained without the army of Wallenstein, whereas the treaties negotiated after the treaty of Prague left the emperor, having abandoned the edict, in a much stronger position both politically and militarily.

At this juncture Oxenstierna decided to abandon the
Rhineland to France and, by the treaty of Hamburg (1638)
received an annual subsidy of 400,000 *talers*. Thus reinforced,
Baner took the field with great success. In 1639 he led his army to
the gates of Prague, in 1640 to Regensburg where Ferdinand III
was addressing the Diet, but on each occasion when it was in his
power to deliver a crushing blow to the Habsburgs, he withdrew
to allow secret negotiations to take place, the object of which was
to provide him with the title to a German principality. Before
anything had been resolved he died in the spring of 1641, to be
replaced by a tougher, less self-seeking, commander in
Torstensson. Within two years he had defeated the Imperialists
in the second battle of Breitenfeld (November 1642) and
established Swedish outposts in Bohemia and Moravia.

For the next two years Torstensson was recalled to the Baltic
coast line to conduct Sweden's campaign against Denmark (see
pp. 383–4), but when victory had been secured in the Peace of
Brömsebro in 1645 he returned in strength against the emperor's
forces. Meanwhile French troops, in alliance with those formerly
raised by Bernard of Saxe-Weimar (see p. 202), established
mastery of the Upper Rhineland, and began to overrun parts of
Bavaria.

Every advantage the emperor had hoped to derive from the
Treaty of Prague was now denied him. The 'hereditary lands'
were invaded every year and his enemies quartered their troops
each winter on the territories of his allies. One such ally had
indeed already deserted him. The new elector of Brandenburg, a
more resolute and imaginative prince than his father, had
succeeded him in 1640, determined to take the risk of repudiating
the Treaty of Prague and seek instead the support of Sweden,
France and the United Provinces (see p. 401). His example was
eventually followed by Saxony, Bavaria and others, not least in
defying the emperor's ban by accepting separate invitations to
the peace conferences assembling in Westphalia.

By 1648 the emperor's position resembled that of his father in
the worst months of 1631–32, with Bavaria under French
invasion and a Swedish army at the gates of Prague.

The Peace of Westphalia 1648

For many years before this critical position had been reached in 1648 negotiations to end the war had been intermittently in progress in Westphalia. As early as 1641 the emperor agreed to meet representatives of the French and Swedish governments — separately at Münster and Osnabrück respectively — but it was many months before serious discussion took place. Each government awaited the outcome of a campaign before deciding whether to raise or lower its terms and the second battle of Breitenfeld (1642), for example, while it increased the anxieties of the emperor to achieve a settlement, correspondingly reduced those of Sweden. A new turn was given to events in 1643 by the decision of Brandenburg, Bavaria and others to insist upon sending their own representatives to Westphalia, so that the emperor's freedom of action was substantially restricted. Even more humiliating from the emperor's point of view was the French demand that Spain be excluded from the negotiations. Mazarin (see p. 203) was resolutely determined to deny Spain any opportunity to restore her influence in the Rhineland and, by concluding a peace settlement with the other European powers, to leave Spain the more vulnerable to a French offensive thereafter. It was a measure of the emperor's rapidly worsening position in Germany that, despite the invaluable help given to his father by Spain in 1619 and 1634, he should find himself unable to protect Spain's interests in Westphalia.

In December 1645 the emperor recognised the danger of his position and sent his closest adviser, Trautmannsdorf, with full powers to bring about a settlement. A detailed examination of the policies and proposals of the governments of France, Sweden, Brandenburg, Spain and the United Provinces, and of the problems they faced in determining these policies, is provided in the chapters appropriate to these countries (see pp. 203, 226, 258, 384 and 401). The most important issues affecting the outcome of the negotiations and with which Trautmannsdorf himself had to deal were, in general, as follows:

1. Christina of Sweden was determined to bring peace to her country, partly because the continuation of the war prolonged the period in office of her father's advisers. On the other hand she recognised the military strength of

Sweden 1645–1648 and was not prepared to forfeit the fruits of her father's victories.

2. The elector of Brandenburg, recognising that Sweden was determined to retain Pomerania showed unusual diplomatic skill in soliciting the support of France in particular to secure compensation quite out of proportion to the territory lost to Sweden.

3. The French government, having successfully excluded Spain from the negotiations, was resolved to make gains on its eastern frontier, to support the German states against the emperor and, when civil unrest became serious at home in 1648, to secure a settlement without delay.

4. The Dutch government recognised that although it had little to fear from Spain, the conquest of the Spanish provinces was out of the question. It determined therefore to secure the best possible terms to conclude its Eighty Years with Spain.

In the event it was the Dutch who settled matters by private negotiation with the Spanish representatives. In January 1648, in a separate treaty of Münster, Spain granted full independence to the United Provinces, partly because the Dutch could not be defeated, partly because this would deprive the French of a powerful ally in their continuing war with Spain. The possibility of other bilateral agreements so alarmed the other governments that their agents in Westphalia were ordered to conclude the negotiations as swiftly as possible.

All the agreements and compromises negotiated by Trautmannsdorf were finally put together in the two treaties of Münster and Osnabrück. These treaties, along with the separate Treaty of Münster between Spain and the United Provinces, and the Treaty of Brömsebro (1645), provided or confirmed the solutions to nearly every international crisis which had occurred in the first half of the seventeenth century.

The main points of what was collectively to be known as the Peace of Westphalia may be summarised as follows:

1. To all intents and purposes the separate states of the Holy Roman Empire were recognised as sovereign members of the Diet, free to control their own affairs independently of each other and of the emperor.

2. The principle of *cuius regio, eius religio* was reaffirmed, but

construed to relate only to public life, so that attendance at the established church was no longer compulsory and freedom of private worship was permitted. Moreover, any subsequent change of religion by the ruler was not to affect that of his subjects.

3. Calvinism was recognised within the Confession of Augsburg and was thus protected by the Augsburg settlement of 1555. The Edict of Restitution, shelved in 1635, was abandoned and, except within the Bavarian and Austrian lands, the retention of all land secularised before 1624 was allowed.

4. In matters of religion there were to be no majority decisions taken by the Diet. Instead both sides were to meet separately to prepare their cases and disputes were to be settled only by compromise.

5. Maximilian retained his electoral title and the Upper Palatinate.

6. A new electoral title was created for Charles Louis, the son of the former Elector Palatine, on his restoration to the Lower Palatinate.

7. John George of Saxony was confirmed in his acquisition of Lusatia.

8. The terms of the Treaty of Xanten (1614), assigning Cleves, Mark and Ravensburg to the elector of Branden-burg, were confirmed. In addition, Frederick William acquired eastern Pomerania and the bishoprics of Cammin, Minden and Halberstadt, along with the succession to Magdeburg.

9. The emperor's claim to hereditary rights in Bohemia, Moravia and Silesia was established. The Sundgau was surrendered to France.

10. The duke of Nevers was confirmed in his inheritance of Mantua, Montferrat and Casale (Treaty of Cherasco 1631).

11. Sweden had acquired her mainland provinces of Jemte-land, Herjedalen and Halland, with the islands of Gotland and Osel by the Treaty of Brömsebro (1645). The Peace of Westphalia confirmed her control of the river-mouths of the Oder, the Elbe and Weser — virtually the entire German coastline — by the occupation of western

Pomerania, Stettin, Stralsund, Wismar, the dioceses of Bremen and Verden and the islands of Rügen, Usedom and Wollin. She was paid an indemnity of 5 million *talers*.

12. France acquired the Sundgau and, in effect, Lower Alsace, though the six free cities along with the city and bishopric of Strassburg retained their membership of the Diet. In Lorraine, her occupation of the bishoprics of Metz, Toul and Verdun (Treaty of Câteau-Cambrésis 1559) was confirmed, along with her more recent gains of Moyenvic, Baccarat and Rambervillers. Other acquisitions included Pinerolo in Savoy, and Breisach and Philippsburg on the right bank of the Rhine.

13. The United Provinces were declared independent of Spain and also of the Holy Roman Empire.

14. Spain was excluded from the Westphalian settlement. Having been forced to give way on all points to the Dutch, her position in the Rhineland was substantially weakened by the French acquisitions and by the restoration of the elector Palatine. The apportioning of Lorraine was determined without reference to Spain or to her ally the duke. Left alone in her war with France, no prince of the Empire, not even the emperor himself might come to her aid, unless Imperial territory was involved — and for this purpose Franche Comté, despite its membership of the Diet, was specifically excluded.

Earlier historians have tended to exaggerate the significance of the Thirty Years War. The war and the peace treaty, they claimed, marked the end of an epoch, paved the way for the greatness of France, discredited the emperor's authority in Germany, replaced religious standards in public life by those of secular self-interest, ruined the economy of the German states, and brutalised the German peoples so totally that they could never again become a civilised race. All these claims, save the last which is nonsense, did contain some element of truth, but it would be wrong to suppose that these developments were necessary consequences of the war. Some of them would have occurred in any case; others had already taken place before 1618. France did not owe her ascendancy in Europe solely to the disintegration of the empire, nor was Ferdinand III's power any more negligible than that of Ferdinand I, Rudolf or Matthias. It was only in contrast with the temporary, and unexpected, triumphs enjoyed by his father in 1629 and 1635 that his own authority appeared to have been discredited.

It is true that religious zeal, as a dominant factor in political behaviour, became less evident in Europe after 1648, and, with some hesitation, this process may be described as the secularisation of public life, or the triumph of *raison d'état*. Men were as devout or as pagan as they had always been, but their public utterances, their justification of their actions to the world, were being phrased in different terms. Warfare after 1648 was more frequently waged for reasons of national security, commercial ambition or dynastic pride. It would, however, be wrong to assume this to be a consequence of the Thirty Years War.

Nonetheless the negotiators at Westphalia were justifiably criticised for betraying the religious principles which had been so vital an ingredient in the conflict of the past thirty years. Pope Innocent X uttered his formal condemnation of it as 'null, void, invalid, iniquitous, unjust, damnable, reprobate, inane, empty of meaning and effect for all time'. More poignantly, the Bohemian scholar Comenius gave vent to the cry of the Calvinist exile: 'They have sacrificed us at the treaties of Osnabrück...I conjure you by the wounds of Christ that you do not forsake us who are persecuted for the sake of Christ.' But the truth of the matter was expressed by an anonymous writer: 'This war has lasted so long that they [the German princes] have left it more out of exhaustion than from a sense of right behaviour.'

What, then, had been achieved? The remarkable thing was that within the Empire so little had been changed. Alsace and western Pomerania were now in foreign hands; Saxony, Brandenburg and Bavaria had increased their territory, the elector Palatine had lost much of his, and Bohemia had been brought entirely under the control of Austria. Apart from this, the situation established in 1648 was fundamentally that of 1618. The Catholic powers had hoped to recover the land secularised since 1559, the emperor to revive Imperial authority, and Sweden to control the destinies of the German Protestants; but none of these ambitions was achieved. The Empire remained, as it had been since 1559, an untidy collection of autonomous states, some Catholic, some Protestant. If the fighting had stopped in 1621, in 1629, or even in 1635, there might have been many changes to record, but its wearisome prolongation had finally brought Germany full circle, to perpetuate for another hundred years the political fragmentation of the past hundred.

Yet there were some significant differences of emphasis and direction. The Palatinate was not again to be the hub of international Calvinist politics; and, if Saxony was a spent force, Brandenburg was a potent new one. The efforts of Ferdinand II to impose Imperial authority, of a kind which no emperor had exercised for centuries, came near to success in 1629 and 1635, but the oligarchic, federalist, centrifugal forces within the Empire, assisted by the armies of Sweden and France, had rendered vain his unifying, authoritarian and monarchic aspirations, and, in so doing, had ensured the survival of religious diversity within the Empire.

Ferdinand III accepted this because his ambitions lay in a different direction. As head of the House of Austria, his power had been strengthened by the years of war. Hungary was a problem that had yet to be solved, but the other 'hereditary lands' had been reduced to order. In Bohemia and, no less important, in Upper and Lower Austria, the Estates had been deprived of their powers, the administration was centralised on Vienna and religious uniformity was established. In addition, Ferdinand was recognised as the hereditary sovereign of Bohemia, Moravia and Silesia. The contrast between the overall position of Ferdinand III and that of Rudolf or Matthias indicates the full measure of the revolution which had taken place. The price, in territorial terms, had not been high — Lusatia, sold to Saxony for support against the Bohemian rebels, and the Sundgau; Trautmannsdorf had brilliantly contrived that the gains of Sweden and France were made at the expense of powers other than Austria. Consequently, the Austrian house of Habsburg was left free to fulfil its dynastic ambition outside the Empire, to make Austria once again the Eastern March against the Ottoman Turks, and, in pursuit of its mission to liberate Hungary, to create the Danubian monarchy.

Economic trends and differences of emphasis are less easy to discern than shifts in political power and are the subject of considerable debate. That there was misery endured throughout the hideous progression of campaigns and sieges, with the slaughter, plague and famine which attended them, cannot be questioned. It was not, however, so widespread or devastating as was sometimes put about later by propagandists to heighten the achievement of their princes in creating prosperity out of adversity. Not only is it impossible to assume a uniform condition, whether of improvement or of decline, before or after the wars; but there is also disagreement about the nature of the evidence and how to interpret it (see *The Thirty Years War* ed. T.K. Rabb). Population figures for example, even when reliable, are not always interpreted in the same way. A fall in numbers, evidence of deaths or permanent migration to one historian, is taken by another to indicate merely a temporary evacuation or a failure to investigate correctly the compensatory number of births.

Much of the decline, where evidence of decline can be established, is often attributed to events preceding the outbreak of war; most regional studies, however, leave little doubt that in the areas selected for scrutiny the consequences of the war itself were disastrous. 'The death and destruction was extensive: even worse, it was prolonged. When all allowance is made for the exaggeration and propaganda of stories about the horrors of war, there is still no reason to discount the reality of devastation, plague, famine and the sheer barbarism of the soldiery.' (Kamen *The Iron Century*).

Though the warfare was destructive it was not universal. The areas worst affected were those of the greatest strategic importance — the Saxon plain, the Rhine crossings, the roads across the Black Forest and those leading to Vienna and Prague. Hamburg, Bremen, Lübeck and Danzig, on the other hand, grew rich from the war and were spared the presence of enemy troops within their gates.

Whatever the precise nature and extent of the economic consequences of the German wars, the conclusion of the conflict was the prerequisite of recovery, and recovery could be surprisingly rapid. A good harvest safely gathered in made all the difference: wooden houses were rebuilt, traders moved freely across the land and births began to outnumber deaths. For most Germans it was the harvest of 1650 which was celebrated as the first fruits of the peace.

On 22 August 1650, in the city of Ulm and throughout its neighbouring villages, thanksgiving feasts and services were held, when the memories of past sufferings and the hope of a peaceful future were alike commemorated in a prayer written specially to be said in every pulpit:

'We thank you, Dear Lord, that you have given us peace after years of suffering, turmoil and war, and that you have granted our pleas. We thank you for pulling us like a brand out of the fire, allowing us to rescue our life almost as if it were itself war booty...Oh Lord, you have indeed treated us with mercy that our city and lands, which had previously been full of fear and horror, are now full of joy and happiness. We beseech you, who has saved us from the sword, mercifully to let our corn grow again, that we may multiply and prosper once more...Oh God, the lover of peace, grant us henceforth permanent peace and leave our boundaries and houses in calm and peace that the voice of the war messenger shall not frighten us and the man of war touch us not.'

As for the powers outside the Empire, it was not yet time to apportion the laurels of victory. Sweden was well on the way towards her goal of Baltic supremacy, Spain had suffered serious losses in north Italy and the Netherlands, and France had extended her hold over the Rhineland; but it was not until 1660, when the treaties of the Pyrenees and Oliva had been signed, that we can think in terms of one period ending and another beginning. The Thirty Years War, in fact, continued without any appreciable break for another twelve years.

III

THE REVIVAL OF FRANCE
1598–1660

THE REIGN OF HENRY IV 1598–1610

Introduction to 1598

The struggle for power between the crown and its overmighty subjects had been the central theme of French history in the sixteenth century, and one to be repeated with variations for another hundred years. The French wars of religion which took place before the reign of Henry IV had not been the cause of the crown's weakness but a symptom of it, and the factious rivalry of the great families had demonstrated that France would continue a prey to civil war until the crown was able to assert once more its authority.

When Henry III died in 1589, Henry of Navarre was little more than the leader of one among many armies, a Huguenot in a country where Catholicism was predominant, and opposed by the city of Paris, the formidable league of the Catholic nobles and the armies of Spain.[1] His assets were an impeccable claim to the throne and an ability to handle men. For four years he waited, strengthening his position when opportunity occurred by skilful military action, while his enemies fell out among themselves and forfeited their popularity by appearing to be the puppets of Spain. When Henry declared his conversion to Rome in 1593 it was a brilliantly-timed stroke which removed the principal bar to his accession and opened to him the gates of Paris. From there he was able to make a fervent appeal to the patriotic sentiment of his subjects, urging them to drive the Spanish troops from the country.

[1] By the Treaty of Joinville, 1585, Philip II had allied with the Catholic League to safeguard the Catholic cause in France.

Within four years this was done. Philip II of Spain had no other candidate to put forward for the French throne apart from himself, and a war of conquest was out of the question. His best general, Parma, had died of wounds, and Philip himself was an old man, his finances utterly ruined. Once Henry had succeeded in driving the Spanish from Amiens, Philip recognised that he could not pursue the war any further. The Treaty of Vervins was signed in 1598, both sides agreeing to respect the frontiers decided upon at the last peace settlement in 1559.[2] Despite the long years of civil warfare, France had not lost any territory.

Meanwhile, the nobles of the Catholic League were handled with care. Like Philip, they were unable to find any alternative ruler to Henry, whose conversion to Catholicism had undermined the whole basis of their opposition. Henry exploited their predicament by dealing with them individually, promising them indemnity, pensions and titles. This skilful, if undramatic, policy served the best interests of the king and of France by bringing an end to the civil war, and the last of Henry's opponents, the Duc de Mercoeur, came to terms in 1598 for the sum of 4,000,000 *livres* and the governorship of Brittany.

In winning over his enemies, however, Henry forfeited the affection, and very nearly the loyalty, of his original supporters, the Huguenots. His conversion outraged those who had genuinely fought for religious principles, and the remainder were jealous of the generous pensions awarded to the Catholic nobles. Unless substantial concessions were made to them, the Huguenots were prepared to renew the civil war. The measure of their strength may be judged from the terms they secured by the Edict of Nantes in 1598, summarised here:

(i) The Huguenots were allowed full liberty of worship in all places outside Paris where their faith was already established.

(ii) The Huguenots were accorded the same civil rights enjoyed by Catholics, and provision was made for the establishment and protection of their schools and colleges.

(iii) Over one hundred fortified towns, many of them of great strategic importance[3] were leased to the Huguenots for

[2] See below, p.197, for a more detailed account.

[3] e.g. Saumur, La Rochelle, Montauban and Montpellier. This lease was subsequently renewed in 1603.

eight years, to be garrisoned by them at the royal expense.

(iv) The provincial synods of Huguenot clergy and laymen were to meet freely, and even a national assembly could be summoned with royal permission.

(v) Special courts were established in every *parlement* of France, made up of equal numbers of Catholics and Huguenots to whom all breaches of the Edict were to be referred for adjudication.

Not one of these concessions was made as an act of grace to former colleagues and comrades; still less was Henry giving currency to any theory of toleration. Each article represented a serious limitation of royal authority, and the Edict as a whole established the Huguenots as over-mighty subjects, whose political and military privileges gave them the power to defy the crown if they chose. Spain had gained nothing from the wars, the Catholic nobles had to rest content with royal favours and pensions, but the Huguenots had driven one of the hardest bargains that a king of France had ever been forced to accept. For the moment it was worth it. By the end of 1598 the wars were ended and Henry was recognised by all parties as the rightful king. This was the all-important issue, for, as Henry remarked, 'La France et moi, nous avons besoin de haleine.'[4]

The Restoration of Royal Authority

It was not enough for Henry IV to secure the title of king if his authority could not be exercised throughout the kingdom. His Valois predecessors over the past century and a half had extended the power of the crown in a variety of ways which had made them the envy of other rulers, but France was by no means an administrative unit. The Valois ruled over a complex of provinces, districts and cities which had been acquired at different dates in the past and on different terms. Despite their efforts the kingdom still resembled a patchwork of separate jurisdictions, each with its own traditions, privileges and customs.

The Estates-General — the national assembly of representa-

---

[4] i.e. 'France and I both need a breather.'

tives of the three Estates (nobility, clergy and *bourgeoisie*) which potentially could have rivalled or restrained the authority of the crown — was rarely allowed to meet and the king could impose taxes without its consent. On the other hand it was only in the *pays d' élections*, the central provinces which had been brought most closely under royal control, that the principal tax, the *taille*, could be levied at will. In the *pays d' états*, the provinces of more recent acquisition and lying mainly along the frontiers, there were regular and lively sessions of the local Estates with whom the central government had to negotiate the value of the *taille* to be collected.

Whatever the Valois succeeded in creating of a centralised administration was swept away in the anarchy created by the wars of Religion. In every province of France effective power was exercised by the dominant noble family. Henry of Guise had, with some justification, claimed to be king of Paris in 1590, and there were many other nobles who enjoyed similar powers in the provincial capitals: the Catholic Mercoeur, the Huguenot Condé and the *Politique* Damville, for example, were able to assert an almost independent authority within their respective provinces of Brittany, Berry and Languedoc. Moreover, every great lord had his clientèle of followers, bound to him by ties of close allegiance and prepared to champion his cause in any way, while he in return afforded them protection and helped them on in the world. It was an extremely personal relationship, and the reciprocal duties of lord and vassal took precedence over all others, even, if need be, over obedience to the king.

The kingdom of France, therefore, was becoming nothing more than a federal union of virtually autonomous states. In order to destroy this legacy of the Wars of Religion one thing was critical — the ability of Henry IV to secure the loyalty and respect of his subjects. The long face with its incredible nose, curling moustache and aggressive beard, attracted attention and respect, and his lively tongue and quick wit could charm or rebuke without offence. The role of a swaggering Gascon soldier, deliberately assumed during the wars, had made him a popular figure, and his bravery and enjoyment of war added to his reputation. He was also known to be concerned for the welfare of the peasants, the greatest victims of the wars, and there was genuine feeling as

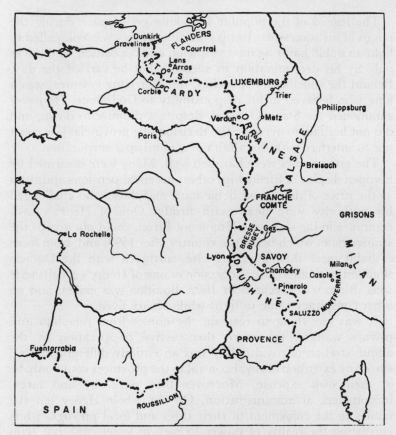

Map 5 The Frontiers of France, 1598–1643

well as astute propaganda behind the legend of the king who
wanted all his subjects to be able to afford 'a chicken in the pot' -
le roi de la poule au pot. Here indeed was a man to capture the
imagination of his subjects, in sharp contrast to the sickly youths,
neurotic invalids and effeminate playboys who had ruled since
1559. Henry's virtues commanded respect; his vices, too, his
tempestuous love affairs, were regarded with a measure of
indulgence. He was, as Madame de Staël once commented, 'the
most French king that France ever had'.

The legend of the popular hero-king grew apace during the reigns of his successors. In his own time Henry was compelled to fight an uphill battle against suspicion and opposition, and it was only by his determination to succeed that he carried the day. Behind the conciliatory speeches, the disarming gestures, was a king who believed in his responsibility to God alone. He never summoned the States-General, despite a promise to do so, and did not hesitate to override the decision of a provincial law court nor to interfere with the affairs of a municipal corporation.

The great nobles were handled well. Many were disarmed by his open display of friendship, others accepted pensions and titles as the price of their good behaviour, and those who challenged his authority were dealt with firmly. One of Henry's own comrades in the wars, the Huguenot Biron, could not accept the strange quiet which befell the country after 1598, and, from force of habit more than anything else, intrigued with the Duc de Bouillon to promote the succession of one of Henry's illegitimate sons. Biron was executed in 1602, Bouillon was exiled, and no other conspiracy came to light while Henry lived.

It was one thing to restrain the nobles from rebellion and private warfare; to secure their active co-operation in the administration of royal policy was an entirely different matter, since any extension of royal control in the provinces could only be at their own expense. Moreover they were, by and large, incompetent at administration. On the whole Henry left the nobles to the enjoyment of their titles and local prestige, while entrusting the reality of power to men of lesser rank but with greater experience of government.

The Valois kings had built up a rudimentary form of civil service more efficient and more extensive than in any other country. It was staffed by men from the professional middle-class, trained in the principles of Roman Law which tended to exalt the status of the prince,[5] and jealous of the privileged status enjoyed by the nobility. Through these *officiers* the crown could extend its jurisdiction at the expense of the seigneurial, or feudal, courts, and secure greater obedience to its edicts.

Unfortunately for the French monarchy, its foresight in creating this nascent bureaucracy had been undermined by its financial indebtedness, which had forced it to raise money by selling the

[5] See Chapter 1, p.19.

offices in the administration to their holders. As a result, the *officier*, no matter how incompetent or obstructionist, could not be dismissed unless the purchase price of his office was repaid. The evils of this system, by no means uncommon in other European states, were made worse in 1604 when the *officier*, for an annual payment,[6] could not only insure against dismissal but also secure the right to pass on his office to his heir or sell it to the highest bidder. In this way, the poverty of the crown created a situation in which the administration tended to pass out of royal control into the hands of those who had purchased their offices. While Henry lived, however, this tendency was not immediately obvious. The *officiers* were eager to assist the crown by encroaching upon the powers and jurisdictions of the nobility since the value of an office was in direct proportion to the extent of its authority, and the greater the extent of the royal administration, the greater the profit for the office holders. It was not until later in the century that the interests of the *officiers* as a class began to diverge from those of the crown.

The conflict between the *officiers* and the nobility must not be exaggerated. The senior officials made considerable fortunes out of government service, purchased estates in the country and were granted the privileges of nobility. The old nobility, *la noblesse de l'épee*, was scornful of the pretensions of *la noblesse de la robe* but there was intermarriage between them. Moreover the old nobility itself sometimes found office-holding a useful source of wealth, and the rigid divisions between the two kinds of noble were beginning to become blurred.

It was from the *noblesse de la robe* that Henry recruited his principal advisers, with the exception of Sully (see below) who, as an ex-soldier and a Huguenot noble, found it difficult to conceal his contempt for *officiers*. Bellièvre, the chancellor, and Villeroy, who supervised foreign affairs, had served their apprenticeship to government service in the reign of Henry III. They provided the necessary expertise in the handling of affairs, in organising the business of the council and in directing its subordinate committees and officials. In the provinces the *officiers* resumed their task of enforcing the council's edicts and of

---

[6] The *droit annuel*. A payment of one-sixtieth of the estimated value of the office. A newcomer to the office paid an initial fee of one-third its value. The tax was known as the *Paulette* after Charles Paulet, to whom it was first farmed out.

challenging when necessary the rival jurisdictions of the provincial law courts and town councils. The great provincial governors remained a law unto themselves, provided they remained loyal and kept the peace, but in the *pays d' élections* at least some of their administrative responsibilities were transferred to the senior tax officials operating in the province, the *trésoriers* and *élus* — the latter being strangely misnamed since there was no elective principle in their appointment. In addition, but only occasionally, commissaries, later to be known as intendants, were despatched by the council to investigate a particular local matter or to settle a particular problem.

One area of provincial life enjoyed a special degree of immunity from royal interference. The Huguenots, in addition to the hundred garrison towns allowed them under the Edict of Nantes, dominated the provinces of the Midi. A considerable number were rewarded by Henry with appointments at court but their colleagues in the provinces regarded them, as Henry himself, as time-servers whose loyalty could not be relied on. But conversion to Roman Catholicism was not confined to court circles. The renewed vigour and spiritual revival of the Catholic Church in France was one of the most remarkable developments to follow the Wars of Religion (see Chapter 1, p. 82) and its missionary efforts began to take effect before the end of Henry's reign. Henry himself, by his own conversion, had damaged Huguenot morale but his action went beyond that. He assiduously cultivated the alliance of the Papacy, for reasons of foreign policy and also to secure the dynasty by arranging the annulment of his first marriage, and was instrumental in recalling the Jesuits to France by the Edict of Rouen in 1603. Indeed, he endowed a Jesuit college at La Flèche in Anjou — where the heart of this former Huguenot was preserved after his death.

There was nothing essentially novel in Henry's style of government. Having once established his title to the throne he exercised his authority with firmness but without provocation. It was not a time for experiment and innovation: there were too many serious limitations on his freedom of action. Interference by the king and his council in their affairs was only grudgingly accepted by the great families, the provincial courts, the municipal corporations and the Estates of the *pays d' états*, and could not be pressed too far. The Huguenots, now a dangerously powerful state within the state, became increasingly suspicious of every move made by their former leader. To appreciate Henry's work the good order of his reign must be compared with the anarchy of the Wars of Religion. For the first time in fifty years France was governed as a unit, and the directing force behind this government was the king himself. Henry IV was universally recognised as the head of the state, and France remained obedient and peaceful throughout his reign.

Sully

Whatever Henry's personal achievements in securing the throne and extending his authority throughout the kingdom, the effort would have been fruitless if the perennial bankruptcy of the crown during the years of civil warfare were to be prolonged. In 1598, for example, the administration was spending nearly twice as much as it received and debts of over 300,000,000 *livres* had been incurred. The first step in remedying this dangerous situation was taken by Henry himself in putting an end to warfare, for not only was the crown able to cut its military expenditure, but the provision of internal peace and security encouraged a revival of trade and agriculture, which in its turn created a greater amount of wealth in the country to be tapped by the tax collector. The remaining steps were the responsibility of Sully, the *surintendant des finances*.

Maximilien de Béthune, Duc de Sully, had served the king as paymaster of the army in the difficult years before 1598, and it was his reward to be given charge, not only of the royal finances, but also of the French economy as a whole. A devout Huguenot, cautious, thrifty, tactless and conceited, he lacked the engaging virtues and vices by which Henry captured the imagination of the French people. No one with a sense of humour could have spent his evenings, as Sully did, solemnly dancing to the lute in front of sycophantic admirers, and the great opinion which he held of himself is one of the few reliable facts to be drawn from his *Mémoires*. Two qualities, however, he did possess which made his services invaluable to Henry IV. He was utterly devoted to his work and, by the standards of his time, singularly honest. It can be said of him that he looked after the king's finances with the same attention to detail which he lavished on his own. In no sense was he a financial expert any more than he was an innovator; and in the circumstances this too was of value. The outdated and hopelessly entangled system of French taxation could not be reformed nor put on a more rational footing without destroying the privileges of the nobility, the clergy and the middle classes; and this would have provoked rebellion.[7] Instead, Sully exerted his administrative talents in securing the best possible results from a system which remained essentially incurable.

The principal direct tax, the *taille*, varied in its incidence between the *pays d' élections* and the *pays d' états* (see above p.168), but in each case the chief contributor was the peasant, for it was one of the anomalies of the fiscal system that all the classes best able to support the state, the nobility, the clergy and the *officiers*, were exempt from direct taxation. All that Sully could do was to keep the closest possible control over his tax-collectors so that the little which was collected did not disappear into their pockets, and to examine more closely the cases where exemption was claimed. Henry III, for example, had sold over a thousand patents of nobility in Normandy alone, in a desperate bid to raise money: these and all similar patents dating back to 1578, were annulled by Sully.

The other taxes were even more difficult to control since they were farmed out to speculators, *fermiers*, who then undertook the business of collection and usually made a handsome profit. Once again, Sully accepted a situation which he could not hope to reform, but made certain that all future bargains with the *fermiers* were more advantageous to the crown. By combining certain taxes together, thus making their collection more economical, he could sell them at a higher price; all the feudal aids, for example, were treated in this way and were auctioned for a period of five years at a time. The *gabelle*, the compulsory purchase of salt at a price determined by the government, was increased until it produced nearly one-fifth of the total revenue; some of the crown lands which had been sold or abandoned during the civil wars were recovered, and the clergy were prevailed upon to revive the payment of an annual *don gratuit* to the king. Henry himself was

---

[7] It should be noted that even when Louis XIV had made the monarchy far more powerful than in Henry's reign, his financial advisers dared not introduce any radical reforms for the very same reason: see Chapter VI, pp.313–17.

subjected to Sully's control. His generous impulses to donate monopolies and tax-farms to his favourites were quickly stifled by the *surintendant*, whose Huguenot austerity made him view the expenses of the court with a particularly disapproving eye.

The sole innovation of importance was the *Paulette*,[8] and this, in effect, did nothing more than exploit the well-established practice of selling offices in the royal administration. With this slight exception, Sully broke no new ground and the only novel aspect of his administration was its success. His concern was to husband the existing sources of revenue, not to devise new ones, and the total effect was one of piecemeal gains within a highly traditional and conservative system. If Sully could not reform the fiscal system, at least he became one of the few men who ever understood its workings; and by this constant supervision and efficient book-keeping he restored the crown to solvency. By 1610 he had not only reduced the royal debt and covered all current expenses, but had secured the astonishing surplus of 15,000,000 *livres*.

Sully's work was not confined to the treasury alone, since he was also in charge of the economic recovery of France as a whole, a task no less valuable to Henry than the increased yield from taxation. State direction of the country's resources and a paternal interest in the welfare of the people were characteristic features of the type of absolute monarchy represented by Henry IV,[9] but the encouragement given to Sully's work of reconstruction was prompted by other, more personal, reasons. Henry welcomed the name of *le roi de la poule au pot*, and was genuinely eager to improve the condition of his subjects. The devastation of the fields, the destruction or seizure of the peasants' possessions, the decline of industry, the dislocation of trade, were the results of the civil wars, and the greatest single benefit which Henry afforded his people was the establishment of peace. Free from the threat of a marauding soldiery, the peasant could once again till his fields in the expectation of reaping the harvest, and the merchant was safe to travel the country with his goods.

Barthelemy Laffemas, the king's valet, attracted Henry's attention by his enthusiastic advocacy of mercantilist policies (see Chapter 1 p. 24) and, in particular, by his proposals to promote the expansion of the textile industry. In 1600 he was

---

[8] See footnote on p.171.   [9] See Chapter 1, p.26.

appointed *controlleur-général de commerce*. He forbade the export of raw materials used in the textile trade and the import of manufactured textiles and, in order to make the direction of labour more efficient, compelled craftsmen to register in their appropriate guilds. In addition he established over two hundred companies for specialist production with monopolistic rights and state capital, and attempts were made to cultivate mulberry bushes on a vast scale for the production of silk. His schemes failed dismally. Henry had to cancel the trade restrictions within a matter of months, the mulberry scheme collapsed as did most of the *manufactories royales*, and the registration of workers was of benefit only to the Treasury which received the registration fees.

Sully has often been blamed for these failures. It is true that he showed little interest in industry, and he even opposed the manufacture of luxury goods on moral grounds, but the real cause of failure lay in the nature of French society. No new industry could develop without capital investment, but the middle classes, in strange contrast to those of England and the Netherlands, had no interest in commerce for its own sake: for them it was merely a means to acquire sufficient wealth to invest in a government post or to purchase a title. Once this was achieved, they severed their connection with business and attempted to conceal the lowly origin of their wealth by aping noble pursuits. Capital which might otherwise have been directed to the expansion of industry was thus diverted to the pursuit of social status. Nor could any great advances be expected of agriculture while the peasant continued to bear the whole burden of taxation and the nobles showed no interest in the management of their estates. They preferred to direct their efforts to hunting, warfare, politics and intrigue, an attitude epitomised by Biron: when his son had expressed some hope that the civil war might end, he had retorted in amazement, 'Do you want to pack us off to Biron to grow cabbages?' De Serres's classic textbook on farming methods, *Théâtre d'agriculture et Mesnage de Champs*, which analysed the qualities of different soils and the methods of cultivating cereals, vines and mulberry bushes was read at mealtimes to an enthusiastic king and issued free to every parish. It was, however, given scant attention by the nobles, and it is significant that Sully failed in his attempt to forbid the practice of hunting over the crops.

Sully's work was designed to ease the process of recovery rather than to stimulate new ventures. To this end he gave priority to the problem of communications. Local authorities were constantly reminded of their duty to repair roads and bridges, the postal services were improved, and a start was made on a great scheme of canal construction. The Briare canal was built to connect the Seine and Loire valleys, but its extension to the Saône, which would thus have created an inland waterway from the Channel to the Mediterranean, was not completed in Henry's reign. For the rest, Sully preferred to leave the development of the economy to the individual efforts of those who were prepared to exploit the advantages of a period of internal peace.

THE REIGN OF LOUIS XIII 1610–43

The Regency Crisis and Richelieu's Rise to Power 1610–24

Although Henry IV had succeeded in providing France with a period of freedom from internal disorder, this did not prevent a return to civil war and anarchy after his death.[10] His achievements were the result of day-to-day improvisation, and in essence were similar to those of Francis 1 and Henry II in the early sixteenth century. In each case, everything depended upon the strength of the ruler's personality. Without a powerful king to restrain them, the over-mighty subjects were free to revive old feuds and, above all, to exact reprisals from the crown for the loss of power they had suffered. Sully, at least, realised this and when Henry died he remarked shrewdly, 'France will fall into strange hands.'

Henry's widow, Marie de Medici, became regent on behalf of Louis XIII, who was only nine years old. Her accession was the signal for the great nobles to flock to court, demanding pensions, titles and positions of authority. Marie could do nothing but purchase their assent to her title and her nickname of *la grosse banquière* aptly combined a description of her enforced liberality

[10] He was assassinated in 1610, at the moment of going to war in Germany. For this, and for Henry's foreign policy, see below p.197–9.

with a scornful reference to her descent from the Florentine bankers. The little power she retained was squandered on the promotion of her Italian foster sister, whose husband, Concini, became the principal figure at court.

As had happened in the previous century, royal authority when exercised by a regent was not respected, and the administration of France fell into the hands of those strong enough to seize it. The Duc de Bouillon, exiled after Biron's conspiracy, returned to flaunt his immunity at court; the Huguenots secured exemption from the *taille* for their clergy, and the great nobles made themselves masters of their provinces. Condé, the greatest of them all, compelled Marie to summon the States-General in 1614, in an attempt to strengthen his own position and that of his class. The nobles, however, had no need to seek constitutional restraints upon the crown; it was they, not the Queen Mother, who had inherited the throne of Henry IV. The meeting of the States-General revealed both Henry's wisdom in dispensing with it, and its own inadequacy as a representative institution. It existed solely as a platform for the causes of class interest and provincial separation, all of which cancelled each other out, leaving a political vacuum which only a strong king might fill. It did not meet again until 1789.

It was at the States-General, however, that Armand de Richelieu made his first important appearance. As the third son of a minor noble family he had intended to serve in the army, when his plans were suddenly altered by his elder brother Alphonse leaving the secular clergy to become a monk. The family had long controlled appointments to the bishopric of Luçon, and as Alphonse was no longer eligible, Armand had to be hastily ordained and installed in his place. Richelieu accepted his new career with good grace, and for six years he proved to be an efficient bishop. It was a period when the Catholic Church in France showed signs of a new fervour. Among the leaders of this spiritual revival were Father Joseph and Pierre de Bérulle,[11] who became friendly with Richelieu and looked upon him as their protégé in the cause of the Counter-Reformation. Although Richelieu was active in attacking the Huguenots within his diocese, he was not prepared to live his life entirely as a minor

[11] See Chapter 1, p.82.

champion of the church; and when he was chosen to compose the address to the crown on behalf of the clergy in the States-General, he made use of the occasion to promote his more secular ambitions. Catching the Queen Mother's ear by simple flattery, he emphasised the peculiar fitness of the clergy for positions of trust in the state. Marie took him at his word and gave him a minor post in the royal council.

Marie's patronage, however, nearly proved fatal to his public career. While she and Concini were able to satisfy the great nobles by sharing their power with them, they could not prevent the young Louis XIII from growing up and becoming resentful of the misgovernment which disgraced his name. Concini tried to distract the king by handing him over to the care of Luynes, a swaggering Provençal with no apparent interests beyond hunting; but the device failed. In 1617 Louis and Luynes organised a palace revolution in which Concini was murdered, and Marie was forced into retirement. Fortunately for Richelieu his comparative unimportance ensured a safe retirement to Luçon.

Louis and Luynes undertook a series of campaigns to restore royal authority in the provinces. In the event the appearance of the king himself was enough to secure obedience to his wishes but many of the Huguenots, alarmed by the growing influence of the Catholic zealots (the dévots) at court, maintained a stiff resistance. Luynes died in 1621 at the siege of Montauban but Louis persisted and was able to impose a peace settlement in October 1622. By the Treaty of Montpellier the Huguenots forfeited a number of their strongholds.

Richelieu meanwhile was preparing for the next stage of his career. In 1619 he had acted as an unofficial mediator between the king and his mother, securing Marie's return to the court. It was an important service, for the rivalry between the two had only served to stimulate intrigue and faction, and Richelieu was rewarded with a cardinal's hat. When Luynes's successors proved ineffectual Louis was persuaded by Marie and Father Joseph to appoint Richelieu to the council in 1624. This was his opportunity and within a few months he had made himself the king's chief minister.

Richelieu's Struggle for Survival 1624-30

Marie de Medici had expected that Richelieu would act as her agent, but from the moment of his appointment an alliance was created between the cardinal and his king which endured for the rest of their lives.

There were many who believed that Louis himself was reduced to impotence, that the servant had become the master, but they misjudged both the king and his minister. Louis, as was natural for a son of Henry IV, had a strong will of his own and the intelligence to know what France needed, but for all his intelligence and determination he needed men to take some of the burden from his shoulders. His lonely and neglected childhood had made him particularly dependent upon the affection and support of others, and in maturity he remained to some extent neurotic, ill-equipped to endure the violent clash of temperaments and personalities which court life produced. He disapproved of his mother's policies, but so great was her emotional hold over him that he needed the support of stronger men before he could oppose her openly.

Curiously enough, Richelieu was physically his inferior. He was frequently ill, especially subject to nervous disorders and migraines, but the strength of his resolution and the overriding power of his intellect defeated the weaknesses of his body. A thin, slight figure, he could silence with his glance the noisy bluster of men who towered above him, and he proved to be an ideal servant for the king. He loved the directions of affairs and was utterly loyal. Above all he recognised his total dependence upon the king. 'The three square metres of the king's cabinet', he said, 'are more difficult for me to conquer than all the battlefields of Europe.'

In the first instance Richelieu knew that he had been virtually forced upon the king, and that he too might shortly go the way of the others who had failed to meet the king's requirements after the death of Luynes. He was not a chosen favourite and his tenure of office was insecure. Moreover, he was threatened by every other member of the royal family; by Gaston d'Orléans, Louis's effeminate and treacherous brother, whose whole life was shamelessly devoted to intrigue; by Anne of Austria, Louis's wife, who resented Richelieu's influence at court; and by Marie de

Medici, outraged beyond measure by the Cardinal's defection from her and his devotion to her son. Of all these, Gaston was the most dangerous, not in ability but by his position. Louis's hold on life was uncertain, and should he die without children of his own Gaston would inherit the throne. The threat of this remained like a shadow at Richelieu's back for fourteen years, to be dispelled only by the birth of a dauphin in 1638.

The very first plot to challenge Richelieu's position arose from Gaston's refusal to marry Mademoiselle de Montpensier, the wealthiest heiress in France. The match was strongly urged by Louis, but Gaston disliked the lady and hoped to free himself by conspiring to destroy Richelieu. He was abetted by the Duchesse de Chevreuse, the queen's *confidante*, and by one of her lovers, the young Comte de Chalais. Chalais, perhaps, was never fully implicated but he talked too freely of the intrigues afoot, and Gaston immediately confessed everything to the king. Louis was not easily appeased. Chevreuse was exiled, her foolish accomplice was executed, and Gaston was required to proceed with the marriage. The king's severity pointed two morals. It reaffirmed his growing commitment to Richelieu and made it clear that while his own brother might enjoy a degree of immunity, those who dared to intrigue with him did so at their peril.

Encouraged by Bérulle and the *dévots* at court, Louis decided to revive the laws against duelling. Richelieu was less anxious than his master to strike so directly at one of the nobles' most cherished traditions, but his own brother had died in a duel and he carried out the king's wishes. The sequel was unexpected. Montmorency-Bouteville, a young braggart with twenty-two duels to his name, had already been exiled for duelling, but in 1627 he returned to France to fight yet again, choosing his ground under Richelieu's window in the Palais-Royal. Despite the pleas of most of the court Louis insisted that the affront to his authority be punished by death, and even though duelling was never suppressed the incident impressed the nobility with the king's determination to uphold his royal dignity.

The Treaty of Montpellier (1622) had not materially weakened the position of the Huguenots. 'So long as they have a foothold in France', wrote Richelieu, 'the king will not be master in his own house, and will be unable to undertake any great enterprise abroad.' This was confirmed when, at the height of the

Chalais conspiracy in 1625, which coincided with a critical moment in the Valtelline crisis[12], the Huguenot leader Rohan organised a revolt in Languedoc while his colleague Soubise raised a naval squadron which destroyed all there was of a royal fleet off the Normandy coast. It was in fact a desperate gamble by the Huguenots to demonstrate their strength in the hope that they would then be left alone in the enjoyment of their privileged position since they were alarmed by the influence at court of the *dévots* and by the appointment of a cardinal as Louis' chief minister.

Preoccupied with his other crises, Richelieu was unable to take any measures against the Huguenots until, in 1627, the revolt flared up again, principally at La Rochelle where the citizens had been promised the support of the English fleet led by the duke of Buckingham. When Buckingham's expedition proved a failure, Richelieu was free to begin the siege of the city. It was not an easy task, since there was no royal navy to blockade the port and prevent the entry of another English fleet, but the cardinal was not to be beaten. With a bold sweep of the finger he isolated La Rochelle from the sea, his engineers constructing a mole which enclosed the harbour, leaving a small gap for the movement of the tides. It was an imaginative stroke, brilliantly executed despite all difficulties; and when two successive attempts by the English had failed to break through the artificial barrier, La Rochelle was compelled to surrender in 1628.[13]

Richelieu was prepared to offer reasonable terms to the Huguenots, being eager to intervene again in north Italy, but Rohan remained defiant in the south and had been promised aid from Philip IV of Spain. This threat of Spanish intervention on the soil of France was too sharp a reminder of the old wars of religion, and Louis reacted swiftly. The royal army swept down the Rhône valley, seizing one Huguenot stronghold after another. Rohan could not halt its advance, and the surrender of his last fortress, Montauban, in 1629 compelled him to sign one of the more momentous of the many treaties ending civil war in France. The Grace of Alais, as it was termed, allowed the Huguenots complete freedom of worship in those areas where they were already established, and protected them from discrimination in

12 See below, p.139 and 200.

13 The sea wall was destroyed by a storm one week after the city had surrendered.

their careers. Their political and military privileges, however, were destroyed by the abolition of all their separate law courts, assemblies and fortresses. In this Richelieu acted as a statesman rather than as champion of the Counter-Reformation, since he made no move to compel the conversion of the Huguenots. It was not their unorthodoxy but their fortresses which had caused him alarm, and the Grace of Alais provided the solution to one of his major problems. Never again did the Huguenots challenge the authority of the state.

The Grace of Alais left Richelieu dangerously exposed in the council, since those of the *dévots* who had supported him in the past were outraged by his apparent leniency in dealing with heretics. Chief among these was Marillac, the keeper of the seals (*garde des sceaux*). Marillac, despite his close link with Marie de Medici, had co-operated well with Richelieu in the council, but by 1630 they found themselves ranged against each other on a variety of issues.

It was not simply a matter of the Huguenots. Marillac disliked Richelieu's policy of undermining the power of Spain by alliances with Protestant states and princes, and in particular was very critical of Richelieu's intervention in the Mantuan affair.[14] Marillac argued moreover that any extension of the conflict would result in a degree of taxation wholly beyond the resources of the inadequate fiscal machinery of France. Instead, he advised the king to settle for peace, reduce taxation and to exploit the opportunity to achieve radical reforms in the administration. Marillac's proposals had been embodied in a set of ordinances published in 1629, nicknamed the Code Michaud, which would, if rigorously enforced, have reduced the fiscal privileges of the *pays d' états*, abolished *La Paulette*, reduced the sale of offices in the army and in the royal household, and restricted the power of the *parlements* to modify the terms of royal edicts.

Richelieu endorsed all Marillac's proposals: he argued simply that the time was not yet ripe for their full enforcement and that they should give way to the demands of his foreign policy. The crisis broke in 1630 when Louis was seriously ill, and the court was immediately filled with envious rivals, slighted place-hunters and discontented nobles, eagerly anticipating Louis's death and Richelieu's destruction. Louis in fact recovered, but his illness

[14] See below p.200.

had left him weak and irresolute; above all it left him in the care of Marie de Medici, who used each moment and exploited every maternal art to persuade her son to dismiss his minister. The struggle centred on the appointment of a new commander for the army in north Italy. After a violent and emotional scene, such as the king always dreaded, in which the cardinal and the Queen Mother confronted each other in his presence, it seemed that Richelieu had fallen. Louis appointed Marillac's brother to the army and retired to his hunting lodge at Versailles, leaving the Queen Mother and her delighted followers to celebrate their triumph. But they deceived themselves. Louis had left Paris in a desperate bid to escape his mother's hysterical outbursts, and that night he ordered Marillac's arrest.

The Day of Dupes, as it was called, not only emancipated the king from Marie's emotional tyranny but confirmed, once and for all, his intention to employ Richelieu as his chief minister and to support his foreign policy. Richelieu himself was so overcome by the unexpected outcome of the day's events that he could not restrain the fervour of his gratitude to the king: 'I shall have no greater happiness in this world than in making known to Your Majesty by ever-increasing proofs that I am the most devoted subject and the most zealous servant that ever king or master had in this world. I shall live and die in this condition, being a hundred times more Your Majesty's than I am my own.'

The Consolidation and Extension of Royal Authority 1630–43

The royal conspirators never recovered from the humiliation they suffered on the Day of Dupes. Gaston fled to Lorraine, and Marie took refuge with the Spanish viceroy at Brussels. Richelieu found them less dangerous abroad than at court, and his only precaution was to dismiss their supporters from positions of influence in the administration. Marillac was imprisoned, his brother was executed on a trumped-up charge, and an edict declared that all who offered support to Gaston were guilty of treason.

The Day of Dupes confirmed Richelieu's standing with the king and endorsed his foreign policy — the treaty of Barwälde being signed two months later (see p. 201). It did not mean however that he was indifferent to Marillac's measures for strengthening royal authority. Indeed the consequences of the crisis precipitated a conflict with the Paris *Parlement*, which had begun to claim that its rights to register all edicts allowed it to reject those it disliked. This was to transform a judicial privilege, accorded to it as a sovereign court, into a political weapon, although the members' concern was not to propound a new constitutional theory but simply to safeguard their own interests as a class. As the administrators and officers of the law they had benefited greatly from their alliance with the crown against the nobility, but their privileges as *officiers* were threatened by the Code Michaud and their jurisdiction impaired by Richelieu's creation of special courts and tribunals to enforce his policies: the Marillac brothers, for example, had been tried in the *Chambre de l'Arsenal*, an offshoot of the royal council and the *parlement* was determined to remind Richelieu of its own importance and power.

By refusing to ratify the edict against Gaston's supporters, however, it chose to fight on dangerous ground, since Gaston's guilt was self-evident. Moreover, the *parlement* had no allies, and no means of enforcing sanctions against the crown. It was not a representative assembly but one of the king's own courts; and it was enough for the king to appear before it in person, in a ceremony known as a *lit de justice*, for all opposition to be silenced. When Louis XIII secured the registration of his edict against Gaston in this manner, he was prompted by Richelieu to remind the members of their limited jurisdiction: 'You exist only for judging disputes betwen Master Peter and Master Paul, and if you try to exceed your commission I will cut your nails to the quick.'

Richelieu was not entirely satisfied by the sullen acquiescence enforced by the *lit de justice*, and he looked for other means to weaken the *Parlement's* authority. Its members could not be dismissed from the positions they had purchased, but the offices of the greatest importance and profit could be effectively disparaged by increasing their number and auctioning them off. These measures did not prevent there being considerable resistance over the next ten years to the flood of expedients by which the war was financed, and several outspoken members were arrested and exiled. Finally, in 1641, the chastened *Parlement* registered an edict which forbade it to discuss affairs of state without the king's permission.

The enforcement of the Code Michaud was not undertaken by Richelieu. It was bound to arouse the opposition of too many vested interests at a time when the government was preoccupied with conducting and paying for the war. Yet one step had already been taken before the Day of Dupes to attack the privileged position of the *pays d'états* (see p. 168). It was no accident that the *pays d' états*, representing one-third of the kingdom, contributed only one-tenth of the revenue, and it was to remedy this that *élus* (the senior tax officials of the *pays d' élections*) were appointed in 1628 for the provinces of Burgundy, Dauphiné, Languedoc and Provence. Dauphiné capitulated for the special reason that, because of long-standing rivalries between them, the Estates were unable to agree on anything. They ceased to meet in the future. In Burgundy and Provence there were risings, assisted by the *officiers* of Dijon and Aix respectively who were angry at the threat to abolish the *Paulette*, but it was in Languedoc, where the Estates met the most frequently and for the longest periods, that rebellion broke out on a large scale.

Like the Paris *Parlement*, Languedoc weakened its cause by associating with Gaston d' Orléans, with whom its governor, Henri de Montmorenci, was in correspondence. The appointment of the *élus* was swiftly followed by Gaston's arrival from Lorraine, and in 1632 rebellion broke out. The powerful pressure groups within the province, however, were at odds with each other. The Huguenots were afraid to risk the forfeiture of their remaining privileges, and chose to remain inactive: the *officiers*, like those elsewhere, anxious about the *Paulette*, championed the cause of the Estates; the nobility, enrolled beneath the feudal banner of the Montmorencis, fought for Gaston and a return to the 'good old days'. Against this array of divided interests the royal army stood firm. At the first setback, Gaston forsook the rebels and rushed to make his peace with the king. His followers lost heart, the revolt was broken and Montmorenci was executed. Richelieu wisely negotiated a moderate settlement in order to prevent further outbursts and the *élus* were withdrawn along with those of Burgundy and Provence.

In both *pays d' états* and *pays d' élections* the powers of the governors remained considerable, not only as the heads of the military administration but also as the principal sources of patronage throughout their provinces. It is not surprising therefore that a remarkable number (R. Bonney, *Political Change in France under Richelieu and Mazarin*) were disgraced, exiled or imprisoned by the royal council, or that many others found their term of office limited to three years. The new governors were no less noble than their predecessors but were often men like Henri de Sourdis, archbishop of Bordeaux, who had made their careers in royal service and whose loyalty was assured.

Within the provinces, too, the royal council made increasing use of its own agents who, unlike the provincial *officiers*, could not purchase their appointment and could be dismissed for failure or incompetence. Variously referred to as *commissaires* and intendants they were often to be found for short periods in the provinces before 1630, appointed to deal with an immediate problem. After 1630 they appear to have become resident in every *generalité* of France, becoming an important and regular feature in the supervision of provincial affairs.

In this respect the crux of the matter proved to be the ever-increasing cost of the war. In 1630 the French government spent 41 million *livres* to carry out its policies at home and abroad. In 1636, the year of the Spanish invasion, it spent 108 million *livres*, in 1642, 88 million *livres* and in 1643 120 million *livres* (see R. Bonney, op. cit.). In order to finance the loans by which France waged war between 1630 and 1648, taxation was increased threefold, the most remarkable rate of increase in the history of the *ancien régime*. As taxes mounted so did the arrears of payment, and troops had to be used more widely than in the past to assist the collectors to confiscate goods and chattels. This led to a series of revolts in many regions, principally but not exclusively in the south and west, which continued throughout the war years. The pattern was similar in most cases: disturbances in the spring, declarations of loyalty to the king and complaints against his ministers who burdened the poor with extra taxes, confrontation with royal troops and dispersal when harvest time came round.

The revolts had an unlooked-for consequence. Although they threatened to destroy the government, they ended by compelling it to make itself more powerful, spurred on by the inexorable pressure of financing the war. Richelieu, in short, began to employ intendants in place of the *élus*. Wielding the exceptional powers assigned them by the council they assumed control of tax assessment and collection, and raised their own regiments of *fusiliers* to suppress resistance. In 1638 intendants were also sent into the *pays d' états* to levy *subsistances* for the troops billeted there for the winter — even in Languedoc — and continued to do so for the rest of the war.

In this unexpected administrative revolution, able and ambitious men were established in parallel with the existing bureaucracy but with the authority to override it. Their concern lay with the two most critical areas of government — taxation and order — and in all things they answered directly to the king's ministers. The measures taken to finance the war thus paved the way for the absolutism of the reign of Louis XIV.

In an entirely different field, Richelieu broke new ground by creating a French navy. A fleet, a mere handful of ships in 1624, was destroyed by Soubise's Huguenot squadron off the Normandy coast. The siege of La Rochelle brought home to Richelieu the need for a navy, and he appointed himself to the newly-created office of *Surintendant Général de la Navigation et Commerce*, having abolished the post of admiral lest its occupant should attempt to contest his authority. Brouage, Le Havre and Harfleur were selected as bases for the royal navy, and Richelieu launched a naval programme designed to create fifty ships of the line and the necessary ancillary craft. Every port in the kingdom with its own shipyard was invited to construct one ship, resistance to central direction being thus overcome by a calculated appeal to local pride and rivalry. New foundries and arsenals were also established, as at Brest and La Rochelle, though it still remained necessary to purchase naval supplies from the Dutch.

By 1636, the Atlantic fleet boasted thirty-eight new ships. Twelve of these were over 500 tonnes; and *La Couronne*, displacing 2000 tonnes, had seventy-two guns and required a crew of 600 men. Once the navy was established Richelieu revived the office of admiral and appointed Henri de Sourdis, Archbishop of Bordeaux: a strange choice, perhaps, but as a provincial governor he had proved both his loyalty to the crown and his ability to administer large organisations. He sailed out to attack the Spaniards off Fuentarrabia in 1638,[15] destroying fourteen

---

[15] See below, p.202.

capital ships and three frigates, a triumph which sealed Richelieu's efforts to establish France as a naval power. Richelieu was less successful in reviving the mercantile marine. Along the well-established routes to West Africa, the Levant and the East Indies, French merchants were able to hold their ground, but the attempts to open up new routes and markets all failed. English and Dutch merchants were ready to finance their own undertakings in overseas trade, but in France the burden of investment was left to the government,[16] whose financial resources were limited. Moreover, the government officials who thus directed the new companies, were unable to understand that mercantile expansion depended upon the initiative of opportunists; instead of encouraging trade, their well-intentioned efforts only served to stifle it. Under-subscribed and over-regulated, none of Richelieu's ventures had any chance of success. The *Compagnie du Morbihan* was founded to trade in Canada, the West Indies, Russia and the North. It lasted twelve months, to be followed by the *Compagnie des Cents Associés*, which limited its aims to Canada alone. This again failed, as did its successor, the *Compagnie des Îles d' Amerique*, and not even its imposing title could save the *Compagnie de la Nacelle de St. Pierre Fleurdelysée*, which in an outburst of enthusiasm claimed the whole world as its market.

By the last year of the reign the crown's authority had been strengthened, and Richelieu's own position seemed to be well assured. Since the Day of Dupes he had had to face no major rival in the royal council. Instead he had succeeded in introducing a number of ministers dependent upon his patronage, who worked closely with him and with each other. Among these *créatures* were Father Joseph, Bullion, the *surintendant des finances*, and the brothers Claude and Léon Bouthillier. Latterly they were joined by the Italian Jules Mazarin. In addition Richelieu had extended his properties, enjoyed an annual income of three million *livres*, created a new town named after him, married his nephews and nieces into the best families and had himself become one of the king's most powerful subjects.

His old enemy Gaston had made his peace with Louis after the Languedoc rising, and although he remained a centre of intrigue and disaffection his position was weakened by the unexpected birth of an heir to the throne in 1638. A more serious threat

16 See above, p.176.

resulted from the rise to favour of a lively young noble, Cinq Mars, whom Richelieu had encouraged as his presence served to enliven the king in his old age. Unfortunately his head was turned by Louis's affection, and by the attention it brought him from the rest of the court. The cardinal's enemies assiduously encouraged Cinq Mars to believe that he might supplant Richelieu in the king's favour, and the nobles in exile at Brussels looked hopefully for a speedy return to France. Thus, in the last year of his life, Richelieu discovered a plot as dangerous as any that had occurred in the past.

Cinq Mars was executed, but his conspiracy demonstrated that the problem of the unruly nobility had not been solved. When Louis died, a few weeks after his minister, he left a five-year-old boy to succeed him; and the nobles, the provincial Estates and the *parlements*, seized with delight the opportunities afforded them by yet another regency administration.

Towards the end of his life, Richelieu recorded in his *Mémoires* an idealised version of the aims he had proposed to achieve in 1624. 'I promised the king to use all the industry and all the authority which it pleased him to grant me, to ruin the Huguenot faction, humble the pride of the great nobles, reduce all his subjects to their proper duty and to raise his name amongst foreign nations to the pinnacle where it ought to be.' None of these achievements, however, save perhaps the first, solved the long-term evils and weaknesses inherent in the French political system. Richelieu suppressed each rebellion and each conspiracy against the crown; he could not destroy the habit of irresponsible intrigue and factious opposition which remained endemic in France.

THE MINORITY OF LOUIS XIV 1643–60

The Regency Government and the Fronde Parlementaire

Louis XIII knew only too well the dangers that attended a royal minority, and he wanted to save France from the anarchy of his own childhood. Unhappily there was no member of the royal family whom he could trust to act as regent. His wife Anne and his brother Gaston had been perennially involved in intrigues against his government, and the young prince of Condé was already proving himself as irresponsible in politics as he was brilliant at war. Louis therefore appointed a council of regency in which they were to be outnumbered by Cardinal Mazarin and three other officials, all trained by Richelieu. On Louis's death, however, Anne, Gaston and Condé immediately tried to remove the official members from the council, with the support of the nobles, who dreaded a continuation of Richelieu's stern policies. At the same time they intrigued bitterly amongst themselves since none would accord precedence to the others. In the end it was Anne who triumphed. She deftly succeeded in setting Condé and Gaston against each other, while she herself appealed to the Paris *Parlement* to accord her full powers as regent. The members were so gratified by her invitation to discuss an affair of state, and so mindful of her position as the king's mother, that they rescinded Louis's will without demur.

With full authority to do as she wished, Anne then appointed Mazarin to be her minister to the fury and amazement of all those who had been intriguing for power and a share in the spoils. Anne's relationship with Mazarin has been variously interpreted. The possibility of a secret marriage cannot be discounted and would help to explain the extraordinary influence Mazarin exerted over Anne in the critical years which followed. Alternatively it is suggested that Anne selected Mazarin as the only man capable of maintaining the policies of Richelieu — an unlikely course of action for the widow of Louis XIII, perhaps, but one wholly intelligible in the mother of the infant Louis XIV, anxious above all to protect her young son's patrimony.

Richelieu respected Mazarin's abilities, but to the nobles he appeared effete and contemptible. He surrounded himself with elegant tapestries, works of art and carefully perfumed pets; he paraded in company with his astonishingly beautiful nieces whose arrival took the court by storm; and, after 1643, his influence with the regent smacked of petticoat government and backstairs intrigue. Richelieu had cultivated an icy austerity which made him aloof and unapproachable, while his commanding features instilled fear among his enemies: Mazarin, cheerful and pleasure-loving, could even be obsequious. 'On the steps of that throne from which the fierce and terrible Richelieu had crushed rather than governed mankind we saw a gentle and kindly successor ... who was exceedingly sorry that his dignity as cardinal prevented himself from humiliating himself before you as much as he could have liked.' (de Retz) For all its irony, the contrast was well drawn, but de Retz failed to notice that Mazarin could be as resolute as Richelieu when need arose.

His abilities were immediately put to the test. The nobles who had already imagined themselves in positions of power resented the destruction of their ambitions, and were furious at the way Anne had tricked them. Among the conspirators were Vendôme, Henry IV's illegitimate son; Vendôme's son Beaufort, idolised by the Paris fishwives for his braggart manliness; and the irrepressible Duchesse de Chevreuse, only just returned from sixteen years of exile. The *Importants*, as they were called, were no match for Mazarin, however, who arrested and exiled them before their plans were complete.

If a discontented and factious nobility had been the only source of trouble, then the Regency might well have been a model of efficient government; but there were other, more serious, problems to be faced. The war was still in progress, and under Mazarin had become more expensive than ever. In a desperate gamble to bring Spain to her knees, Mazarin mobilised all the troops at his disposal and government expenditure soared to record heights — to 120 million *livres* in 1643, to 136 million *livres* in 1645. This was made possible only by borrowing more extensively than ever and by pledging future revenues until the end of 1647. As a result, since he could not increase the revenue from taxation to service these loans, further loans were denied him. He was forced to sell more offices, withhold the salaries of the *officiers* and invent new taxes — expedients which did little to ward off bankruptcy but a great deal to bring dissatisfaction to a head.

The members of the Paris *Parlement* combined their anxiety about the conduct of the war with their fears that the government, under the pressure of financing its campaigns, was eroding the privileges of the *officiers*. In these circumstances it was unwise of Mazarin to threaten to withhold the renewal of *La Paulette* unless it was renegotiated on terms more favourable to the government. When the *parlement* therefore was asked to register a further list of expedients in May 1648 its members, in a manner without precedent, united with those of the other sovereign courts (the *chambre des comptes*, the *cour des aides* and the *grand conseil*) to prepare a manifesto of their grievances. They referred to the suffering of the peasantry and the tax rebellions in the provinces but concentrated at greater length on the non-payment of their own salaries, the reduplication of offices and the threat to *La Paulette*. More significantly, they condemned the employment of intendants to take over so many of their administrative duties.

Faced with the united opposition of his senior civil servants, judges and officials, and aware that their manifesto was acclaimed everywhere as the true voice of the people, Mazarin hastily withdrew the offending edicts and recalled his intendants. By the end of the summer the government was virtually bankrupt.

1648 was indeed a year of revolution in Europe. In Portugal, England, Naples and Catalonia there was rebellion against the crown, but it is misleading to make an analogy between these events and the resistance of the Paris *Parlement*. With the States-General in abeyance, it is true that it had become the sole outlet for public opinion and therefore enjoyed a more than local prominence. Nevertheless, it remained essentially representative of its own class, a privileged body concerned with the individual privileges of its members, and the articles drawn up in their manifesto reflected this limited outlook.

Mazarin pretended to consider the demands of the *officiers* while he waited anxiously for news of the armies in the field against Spain. A timely French victory at Lens revived the government's prestige at home, and he ordered the arrest of three members of the *parlement*. The arrests were bungled. One man escaped. Broussel, who had attracted some attention by an outspoken attack on taxes in general, was seized in full view of the mob, and a riot broke out immediately, from which the Fronde derived its name.[17] At first it was nothing more than a spontaneous and violent demonstration, but soon the hand of an organiser became apparent, that of Paul de Gondi, better known by his later title, de Retz. Gondi's ambitions were well defined: he wanted the archbishopric of Paris, a cardinal's hat, and control of the administration; his strategy was to exploit the crown's weakness and difficulties until these ends were achieved.

---

[17] A *fronde* was a sling. It was de Retz, in his *Memoires*, who contemptuously likened his supporters to 'schoolboys who sling mud (*qui frondent*) in the gutters of Paris.'

His close liaison with the disaffected nobility, and with the mob, made him a figure of particular importance, for it was he who transformed the riot into an act of rebellion, inspired the creation of barricades in the streets, and organised a march on the Palais Royal to demand Broussel's release.

Powerless for the moment, Mazarin released Broussel and accepted all the demands of the sovereign courts. His one hope lay in the speedy conclusion of the peace settlement at Westphalia, and the return of the army. Until then, he advised Anne to take her son away from Paris to Rueil, where the family endured a miserable winter without even the means to purchase furniture and firewood. The arrival of Charles I's widow from England in January 1649 was an ominous indication of their own predicament.

The Peace of Westphalia left Spain as the only power still at war with France, and the recall of part of the army in 1649 was therefore possible, although the noble leaders of the army were so hostile to Mazarin that they refused to march against Paris. Condé, formerly the duke of Enghien, alone remained loyal, being more contemptuous of the mob than of the minister, but his brother, Conti, and most of the other princes, the *Importants* and their hangers-on, joined the Frondeurs and appealed to Spain for assistance. The *parlement* anxiously declared that, 'while we order the levying of troops, we must also indicate that it is against the minister that we fight and not the King, for we must not fall into rebellion'. The distinction was of vital importance for the men who administered royal justice, but, by the end of March 1649, they found it was no longer valid. Embarrassed by their noble allies, and terrified of the mob, the *officiers* made a separate peace with the court at Rueil, by which the demands of the sovereign courts were again confirmed.

The Fronde of the Nobles and its Aftermath 1649–60

The treaty of Rueil did not settle anything, since the nobles who had joined in the Fronde did not want to be pacified and refused to accept its terms. For the next three years they treated France as a private battleground, settling all disputes and jealousies by a resort to arms.

Condé fought to assuage the slightest affront to his vanity, which had become intolerably sensitive by reason of his spectacular victories at Rocroi and Lens. In his conceit he wanted nothing less than control of the kingdom, an ambition rivalled only by that of Gaston of Orléans, the veteran of a score of intrigues against Richelieu and Louis XIII. The remainder took arms to avenge an insult, settle an old score, or because they had nothing better to do. The count of Alais marched against the *Parlement* of Alais because it had denied his claim in a land suit, Gaston's daughter raised her own army to bargain for her cousin the king's hand in marriage, and Madame de Longueville, a restless beauty married to a dullard, relieved the tedium of her life by inciting lovers to deeds of martial valour. Gaston, of all men, confessed himself baffled: 'I remember every intrigue of the League, every faction of the Huguenots, but I have never found anything so difficult to comprehend as the present situation.' For the nobles and their ladies the Fronde became an exciting game in which foreigners of their own class were welcome to join, exiled cavaliers from England and princes of the Empire bored by the return of peace to their territories.

Anne of Austria rode out the storm with great courage and determination, enduring danger and indignity to protect her two sons while Mazarin bobbed and weaved his way through the tangle of intrigues. When Mazarin left France in 1651 the Paris mob invaded the palace to make certain that the young king had not left with him; throughout the night Louis XIV feigned sleep to reassure the noisome throng which passed his bedside. Anne, too, was in danger since the Frondeurs planned to remove her to a convent. With great courage, however, she remained in close touch with Mazarin and played a skilful part in encouraging signs of dissension among her enemies. Once Mazarin had left, in fact, the coalition against him began to collapse under the strain of irreconcilable interests.

Condé was the first to be isolated, since no one could withstand his disdain, and he took his revenge by entering the service of Philip IV. At this, his rival Turenne returned to his allegiance, and there ensued a dramatic struggle between them for the mastery of Paris, in the course of which Gaston's daughter forfeited her chance of marrying Louis XIV by training the Bastille's artillery on his army. Condé ruled for a while in Paris, the hero of the mob, but he was driven out by 1652 and the nobles began to tire of a conflict which had become so confused as to be unprofitable. When Louis XIV, still in his teens, proclaimed his majority, he provided the occasion for most to make their peace. The end of the regency signalised the end of the Fronde and, though Condé remained defiant at the head of a Spanish army, Mazarin was back in control of the administration by the end of 1653.

The Fronde had failed because none of the Frondeurs had been able to provide the sustained direction and leadership so necessary in an enterprise against the crown. The *parlement* had evolved a policy of sorts, but lacked the capacity to enforce its demands. The nobility, with its excess of military talent, was barren of any policy save that of individual self-interest. Moreover, the fact that so many of the nobles so freely entered the Spanish service during a time of war identified the Fronde with the stigma of treason.

The end of the regency signalised the end of the Fronde and as the Frondeurs made their submission, Mazarin began again the work of restoring royal authority. The government still faced the most serious financial problems and disorder in the provinces kept breaking out afresh, like a bush fire, over the next five years, but the intendants were soon back at work. By 1658 there were as many in the provinces as in the years before the Fronde, and their role both in suppressing disorder and in collecting taxes gave France the advantage in the final years of the war with Spain. Condé remained defiant in exile until 1659, but most of the nobles followed Gaston's example and retired to their estates. A few, such as Conti and Madame de Longueville, made a suprising renunciation of worldly vanities by associating with the Jansenist community at Port-Royal.[19] De Retz did not enjoy his new title for long. Imprisoned by Mazarin, he eventually escaped to spend the rest of his life in exile, committing to his *Mémoires* a mordant and satiric account of the events in which he had played so prominent a part.

The Paris *Parlement* was deprived of the privileges gained by the Treaty of Rueil and, as an important postscript to the story, Louis XIV proclaimed in 1661 the supreme authority of the Council over the sovereign courts. As a consequence of the

[19] See Chapter VI, p.311.

policies maintained by Richelieu and Mazarin, the administration of public law had become almost exclusively the council's preserve, leaving the sovereign courts to deal with private litigation in which the crown's interests were not involved.

The achievements of Louis XIII and Richelieu were thus salvaged by their successors, and royal authority was more firmly based than ever when Mazarin died in 1660. Nonetheless it is not true that the Fronde taught Louis XIV the need to be absolute. On the contrary it now appears that he learned that he could not afford to challenge head-on the nobility, the *parlementaires* and the other privileged groups within French society, no matter how much they had been discredited by the Fronde. Indeed, the absolutism of Louis XIV was to be exercised with considerable caution, and his reign witnessed a surprising degree of compromise in his handling of those particular groups which had, from 1648 to 1653, so dangerously challenged his authority.

THE CONTINUITY OF FRENCH FOREIGN POLICY 1598–1660

Henry IV

The Treaty of Cateau-Cambrésis in 1559 represented the climax of fifty years of Spanish supremacy in Europe. It recognised Spain as the ruler of Naples and Milan, Franche Comté, Luxemburg and the Netherlands; France on the other hand, isolated and encircled by her enemy, fell prey to the evils of prolonged civil war. The Treaty of the Pyrenees in 1659 inaugurated fifty years of French supremacy and recorded the collapse of Spain.

This dramatic reversal of roles was explained in part by the decline of Spain,[20] but it was a decline accelerated and exploited by the three great figures of Henry IV, Richelieu and Mazarin. For sixty years their policies were identical: their aim, as Richelieu once expressed it, was 'to check the progress of Spain. Wherever that nation aims at increasing its power and extending its territory, our one object must be to fortify and dig ourselves in, whilst making open doors into neighbouring states so that we can

20 See Chapter IV.

safeguard them against Spanish oppression whenever occasion may arise.' To this end they directed their principal efforts; to this end they subordinated their internal policies, which were essentially designed to put France on a more effective footing for the successful prosecution of their foreign policy.

Sully's *Mémoires* contain many references to Le Grand Dessein, a supposed declaration of Henry's policies which outlined the formation of a European confederation to destroy Habsburg supremacy, and to drive the Turks and the Russians out of Europe, and finally to safeguard universal peace. This grandiose scheme existed, however, only in Sully's imagination. Henry himself was more practical and more limited in his aims. In 1598 he had made peace with Spain by the Treaty of Vervins, which virtually repeated the terms of Cateau-Cambrésis. He knew that France was not strong enough to wage open war against her enemy, and he planned to encroach upon the Spanish empire piecemeal, by cautious attacks at its weakest point, its lines of communication. From Milan to Brussels there existed a tenuous line of provinces which served a dual purpose: through them the Spanish armies could march at will, from them the French frontier could be invaded at any point.

Henry's first enterprise was directed against Savoy. This duchy, an important link between Spanish Milan and Franche Comté, had been for some time an ally of Spain, and its dukes had tried to expand their territory into France during the anarchy of the wars of religion. In 1600 Charles Emmanuel of Savoy had agreed to restore to Henry the marquisate of Saluzzo, across the frontier from Dauphiné, but he hoped that the conspiracies of Biron and Bouillon would make it unnecessary for him to keep his promise. Henry did not wait upon events. Seizing Chambéry, the capital of Savoy, he compelled the duke to offer him, not Saluzzo, but the more valuable provinces of Bresse, Bugey and Gex, which lay along the east bank of the Rhône between Lyon and Franche Comté. This acquisition considerably strengthened the French frontier at a dangerous point, and reduced the 'Spanish Road' (see p. 119) between Savoy and Franch Comté to a narrow corridor which could be easily occupied in time of war.

Henry wisely sought the alliance of other states who feared the extent of Spanish power. He made treaties with Venice, Switzerland, Tuscany and Mantua in order to isolate the Spanish base in Milan, and began negotiations with the Protestants of the Grisons, whose canton converged on the Valtelline through which the Spaniards communicated with the Tyrol and Austria. Even the Duke of Savoy was eventually seduced from the Habsburg camp; but none of these alliances was put to the test of war, for Henry was merely reconnoitring the ground and strengthening his position.

Further north his action was more positive and more dangerous. He allied with the Dutch in their revolt against Spain, and helped to bring about the Truce of 1609 which recognised their independence for the time being. He also became patron of the Evangelical Union in Germany,[21] believing it to be a useful weapon with which to embarrass the Habsburgs. Because of these alliances he prepared to fight in 1610 over the disputed territories of Jülich-Cleves. These duchies occupied an area of considerable strategic importance in the lower Rhineland: it was also a matter of considerable strategic importance to deny Spain access to them (see p. 126). Nevertheless Henry's motives were not entirely straightforward. He began to mobilise while still negotiating a marriage treaty with Spain. Suddenly he became more belligerent, indeed bellicose and the explanation may well lie in the fact that the young princess of Condé, which whom he was temporarily infatuated, had been rushed off to the safety of the Spanish court in Brussels by her aggrieved husband.

Whatever his prime motive Henry was undertaking a dangerous venture, since he faced the formidable might of Spain, the emperor and the Catholic League. The gamble was never made. As Henry left Paris in 1610 to join the army, he was stabbed to death by Ravaillac, a Catholic fanatic who believed himself divinely appointed to destroy the apostate and friend of heretics. In one sense Henry's reputation was saved by his assassination, since it invested him with the halo of martyrdom, and prevented a war which might have proved disastrous for France. As Richelieu was to realise, Spain could not yet be challenged in open war: the attack 'must be done with great caution, tact and secrecy'.

Richelieu

After Henry's death, Marie de Medici withdrew cautiously

[21] For a discussion of this, and of the Jülich-Cleves crises, see Chapter II, p.126.

from the Jülich affair and revived the marriage negotiations with Spain, supported strongly by the Catholic party, the *dévots*, at court. In 1613 Louis XIII was married to the Infanta, Anne of Austria, and his sister to Philip IV. For several years the *rapprochement* held firm, allowing the Habsburgs to deal with the Bohemian rebellion and to occupy the Palatinate without protest from France. When, however, Spain occupied the Valtelline in 1621 (see p. 138) Louis decided that this was interference in an area important to France. By the Treaty of Paris, 1623, he allied with the Grisons, Venice and Savoy to drive the Spaniards from the valley. Spain riposted by withdrawing her troops, leaving papal garrisons in their place to protect the Catholic inhabitants of the valley, a move which caused the *dévots* considerable embarrassment.

This was the difficult situation which Richelieu took over in 1624. He successfully persuaded the papal garrisons to leave peacefully but when the Grisons insisted that the French assist them against the Catholic population he looked for an excuse to extricate himself. To some extent he was saved by the Huguenot rebellion (see p. 182) of 1625 which allowed him to recall the army from the Valtelline and negotiate a face-saving peace treaty at Monzon in 1626.

Three years later Richelieu was in a stronger position. La Rochelle had fallen and the Huguenots had surrendered at Alais. He was free, therefore, to intervene in a dispute which had arisen over the duchy of Mantua (see p. 144). Mantua itself was of minor importance, but its dukes also controlled Casale and Montferrat, two powerful frontier towns between Milan and Savoy. When the duchy was claimed by the duke of Nevers, a French prince, the danger to Spain's transalpine route was evident. The emperor ordered the occupation of the duchy, pending a settlement favourable to Spain, and Spanish troops besieged Casale. Richelieu marched through Savoy, relieved Casale and occupied Pinerolo, another valuable frontier base.

The Mantuan affair became entangled in the struggle for power at the French court (see p. 184). When the emperor offered the succession to Nevers if France withheld her support from his Protestant enemies, the *dévots*, represented principally by Marie de Medici and Marillac, urged Louis XIII to agree. Richelieu, however, opposed any settlement which prevented him from allying with the Dutch or with Gustavus Adolphus of Sweden. Matters came to a head over the appointment of a commander for the army in Italy and Richelieu's triumph on the Day of Dupes determined the direction of French foreign policy. Within two months the treaty of Barwälde was signed with Sweden, and the Swedish invasion of Germany compelled the emperor to give way over Mantua. The treaty of Cherasco in 1631 secured Mantua for the French candidate, and Savoy agreed to sell Pinerolo to France.

In the event the Swedish alliance did not turn out as Richelieu had intended since Gustavus proved to be too independent, too powerful and too Protestant. His campaigns in the Rhineland and in Bavaria destroyed Richelieu's plan to unite the German princes against the emperor, and gave point to Father Joseph's remark that Sweden was like a poison — useful up to a point as an antidote to Habsburg supremacy, but fatal when taken to excess. Only one good result emerged. When the Archbishop of Trier was threatened by Gustavus's army, he turned to France for protection and granted her the right to garrison Philippsburg and Ehrenbreitstein. Significantly enough, these fortresses lay along the Spanish route from Franche Comté to the Netherlands.

When Gustavus was killed at Lützen in 1632, Richelieu recovered some measure of influence over the German Protestants by joining with Sweden in the formation of the Heilbronn League. Its members, however, could not withstand the combined armies of Spain and the emperor. At Nördlingen, in 1634, its forces were destroyed and the balance of power in Europe was upset: Sweden was eclipsed for the moment as a military power, the Protestant princes submitted to the emperor, and the Spaniards seized control of all French bases in the Rhineland. One course only lay open to Richelieu if his policies were to be achieved, a declaration of war against Spain. The danger was great, since the French frontier was vulnerable at every point, and the French army had not yet been tested in any major battle. Nevertheless, the assault on Spain by sap and mine had failed: it was time to advance in the open.

Within four months Richelieu had marshalled his forces; Sweden promised to harry the imperialists in Germany; Bernard of Saxe-Weimar was commissioned to invade the Rhineland and establish bases in Alsace; the United Provinces agreed to join forces with France in the Netherlands; while Savoy, Mantua, Modena and Parma were enrolled against Spain in north Italy. The Habsburgs, in short, were to be attacked at three vital points, Milan, the Rhineland and the Netherlands. The scheme was brilliantly conceived, but the allies lacked the strength to carry it out. All their attacks failed, and the Habsburgs counter-attacked with disastrous effect in 1636.

Richelieu tried to conceal the danger in which France stood by celebrating every minor triumph with a *Te Deum* in Notre-Dame and banner headlines in the *Gazette*, but his own nerve broke when the Spaniards from the Netherlands and the imperialists from Lorraine joined forces to overrun Picardy. They passed Amiens, seized Corbie, and their outriders approached the suburbs of Paris. While the Cardinal lay sick from nervous exhaustion, it was Louis XIII who saved France and showed himself a true son of Henry IV. He calmed the frightened citizens, rallied the dispirited troops, and rode out to Señlis, midway between the capital and Corbie, to await the final assault. His stand was decisive, for Bernard of Saxe-Weimar had recovered sufficiently to move up on the imperialist flank, and the enemy refused to risk a major engagement in these circumstances. As winter approached, the invaders left France.

The 'year of Corbie' was the most critical of Louis XIII's reign, and if Richelieu's self-confidence was soon restored, the recovery of France was necessarily slow. An invasion of Spain, and the seige of Fuentarrabia in 1638, were the first indications of a turn in the tide. The navy won its first victory by defeating a Spanish fleet which had sailed to relieve the city, and Spain had barely recovered from this before she was again defeated, by the Dutch, in the Battle of the Downs.[22] Nevertheless, Fuentarrabia was not taken by the French, and Richelieu's disgust at the incompetence of his army commanders was only allayed by news of the fall of Breisach. Bernard of Saxe-Weimar had at last proved victorious, and his death in 1639 gave Richelieu the chance not only to enrol his men in the French army, but to use Breisach as a base for further operations in the Rhineland.

The initiative at last lay with France. Harcourt defeated a Spanish army in north Italy, and occupied Turin in 1640. In the following year, he was sent to Spain to assist the Catalans in their

22 See p.256.

rebellion against Philip IV.[23] Portugal too was in revolt, the Spanish Netherlands were threatened by Dutch and French armies, and the emperor was unable to prevent Swedish raids into Austria. The Habsburgs were no longer a match for the resurgent power of France and her allies. As Richelieu lay dying, in 1642, he learned that French troops had recovered the provinces of Perpignan and Roussillon in the Pyrenees, lost to Spain in 1494. Despite the disasters of the 'year of Corbie', despite the chronic shortage of money and the lack of an efficient army, he had laid the foundations of French power in Europe.

Mazarin

At last France had men of military genius, in Harcourt, Condé and Turenne, and at Rocroi in 1643 Condé destroyed not only a Spanish army but the legend of Spanish invincibility. Along the Rhineland French armies took Philippsburg, Mainz and Worms; further victories were won in 1646 at Courtrai and at Lens in 1648, whilst Turenne ventured into Bavaria in alliance with a Swedish force. Mazarin, distracted though he was by the growing unrest at home, was resourceful enough to ensure that these victories were not forfeited by his diplomats in Westphalia.

The bridgeheads, the forward bases athwart the Spanish lines of encirclement and communication, which Richelieu had striven so resolutely to establish, were finally assured in the Peace of Westphalia.

(i) Metz, Toul and Verdun, the bishoprics of Lorraine which had first been granted to Henry II in 1559, were officially confirmed as French possessions;

(ii) Moyenvic, Baccarat and Rambervillers, also in Lorraine, were ceded to France, along with Breisach and the right to garrison Philippsburg;

(iii) The Treaty of Cherasco (1631) and the sale of Pinerolo to France were confirmed;

(iv) In Alsace, save for the city of Strassburg, France obtained virtual control, although there was some doubt over the legal status of the Alsatian towns. Either they were ceded in full sovereignty or else they retained their status as

[23] See Chapter IV, p.218–23, for an account of revolts within the Spanish empire.

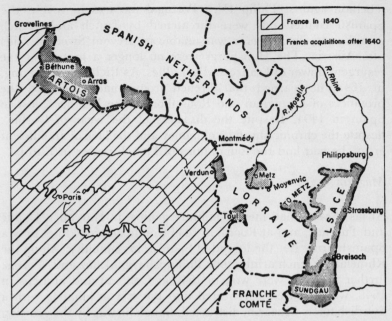

Map 6   French Gains on North-Eastern Frontier, 1643–59

imperial fiefs, with membership of the Diet. Mazarin was so eager to conclude the negotiations, on account of the Fronde, that he accepted a final draft riddled with ambiguity. This in no way perturbed him; rather, as a skilled diplomat, he even hoped to derive some advantage from this in the future.

The settlement negotiated at Westphalia did not end the war between Spain and France since neither side was prepared as yet to concede victory to the other. Philip IV was handicapped by revolts in Portugal, Catalonia and Naples, but Mazarin was equally at a disadvantage because of the Fronde. Although Condé deserted to the Spanish army in 1652, Turenne remained loyal, and the two rivals manœuvred endlessly against each other in the Netherlands, with great caution and to little effect. In order to break the deadlock, Mazarin determined to prevent Austria from coming to the aid of Spain, and at the same time win the support of England.

He began by an attempt to secure the imperial throne for Louis XIV when Ferdinand III died in 1657. Although his agents won promises of support from the Elector of Bavaria and the Elector Palatine, the money spent on bribery was of no avail against the general suspicion of France which prevailed within the Empire. Leopold of Austria was elected unanimously, and the Habsburgs retained the title which had been held by their family since the fifteenth century. But Mazarin was not disappointed. The chief object of his negotiations had been to prevent an alliance between Austria and Spain, and the German Electors who accepted French money insisted that Leopold should remain neutral after his election, provided imperial territory was not involved. Moreover, the election did not terminate Mazarin's interest in Germany, for in 1658 was founded a League of Rhine Princes, whom he persuaded to accept France as its protector. Led by the three ecclesiastical Electors of Mainz, Cologne and Trier, its aims were unexceptionable, unity and peace, and it proved to be a useful instrument of Mazarin's policy since it helped to ensure the neutrality of the German princes in the war between France and Spain, and provided him with a private pressure group in the Imperial Diet. One day Leopold would die, and another attempt to secure Louis's election could be made.

At first sight, an alliance with England seemed out of the question, since Louis XIV was a Catholic monarch and Oliver Cromwell a Puritan regicide. Cromwell, however, believed that war with Spain might lead to valuable acquisitions in the West Indies, and the Catholicism of France paled into insignificance when set against the Spanish Inquisition. Mazarin approached him cautiously in 1655, and he understood the English well enough to offer them first of all a commercial treaty. He also drew attention to the presence of leading cavaliers in Condé's army, and offered the tempting prize of Dunkirk if Spain were defeated. In 1657, Cromwell agreed to join France.

Mazarin's careful diplomacy secured its end, the defeat of Spain. Deprived of allies, her finances ruined and her provinces of Catalonia and Portugal still in revolt, she could not hope to survive against both France and England. When an English fleet appeared in the West Indies, and an army of 6,000 Ironsides joined with the French to seize Dunkirk and Gravelines, she gave up the struggle and sued for peace. This was the greatest moment in French history over the past hundred years, and Mazarin was determined to exploit his advantage to the very limit. The Treaty of the Pyrenees, signed in 1659, represented the full achievement of the ambitions of Henry IV and Richelieu.

(i) France agreed to deny further aid to the rebels within the peninsula, and Condé was pardoned for his treason. This was all that Mazarin would concede to Spain.

(ii) Roussillon and Perpignan; Montmédy in Luxemburg; Artois, and the Netherland towns of Arras, Béthune, Gravelines and Thionville were ceded to France.

(iii) England was given Dunkirk.

(iv) Spain recognised all French acquisitions in the Peace of Westphalia.

(v) Louis XIV was married to Maria Theresa, the Spanish Infanta.

The marriage alliance was the most important clause in the treaty, since Philip IV had no sons at that date and Maria Theresa was heiress to the entire Spanish empire. Mazarin's diplomacy, therefore, paved the way for a dramatic extension of the policies of his predecessors. France was content no longer to think in terms merely of limiting the power of Spain but rather of absorbing it altogether within a new French empire which would bestride the world. Philip IV understood Mazarin's purpose only too well, and he insisted that his daughter renounce her claim to the Spanish throne. At this juncture, however, Mazarin's able negotiator, Hugues de Lionne, demonstrated the talents which were to make him the greatest diplomat of the seventeenth century. He secured the inclusion of a clause by which Maria Theresa's renunciation was made dependent upon the payment of her dowry. Spain was bankrupt but, as Lionne realised, her rulers were too proud to admit that the dowry might never be paid; they could not, therefore, object to Lionne's proviso.

Soon after this crowning achievement of his life's work, Mazarin died in 1661. France owed him much, and it was from him that Louis XIV inherited, not only a firmly established throne, but a vision of two empires, the Imperial and the Spanish, which might conceivably lie within his grasp.

IV

THE DECLINE OF SPAIN

THE AFTERMATH OF A GOLDEN AGE 1598–1665

Castile, the burden of empire and the economy

The failure of the Spanish Armada and the success of the Dutch rebels have been so prominently displayed in the image which English historians have created of Philip II that it is difficult to envisage the king as his own subjects remembered him in 1598. They, indeed, honoured him as *El Prudente* and proudly rehearsed his successful exploits as the champion of Spain and the Catholic Church. The Turks, defeated at Lepanto (1571), had been forced to relax their hold upon the western Mediterranean, and a crushing blow had been dealt at the legend of Ottoman invincibility; a heretic had been denied the throne of France until his conversion, and heresy expunged within the borders of Spain; royal authority had been strengthened throughout the separate kingdoms of the peninsula and dramatically extended in 1580 by the inclusion of Portugal and her overseas empire. The Dutch Revolt had been a serious blow yet Philip's control of the southern Netherlands had been intensified, and the vital lines of communication between Brussels and Milan enabled the Spaniards to harass the vulnerable frontier of France at a dozen different points from Amiens to Lyon.

Entrusted by God with pre-eminence in Europe and with an empire encircling the globe, furnished by His munificence with the dazzling riches of the Americas, sustained by the witness of His saints, Theresa and Ignatius Loyola, and endowed with such a king as Philip II, for the Spaniard it had indeed been a Golden Age.

It is misleading, however, to refer to Spain as if it were a unified nation-state. Philip II had ruled a variety of separate kingdoms within the Iberian peninsula — Castile, Aragon, Granada and Portugal — and it was Castile which had been most closely associated with the empire, which had indeed jealously excluded the other kingdoms from its management and which was now left to furnish the means for its defence. She had acquired the American mines as her reward but this had proved to be a mixed blessing. The government had amassed such enormous debts on the security of these mines that the payment of interest on the public debt had become the largest item of expenditure. Periodically, when too many ventures coincided, when too many bankers simultaneously demanded satisfaction, the government failed to meet its obligations. There were in all six such crises — in 1567, 1596, 1607, 1627, 1647 and 1653 — when undertakings of great moment had to be abandoned or postponed until new creditors, demanding higher rates of interest by way of insurance, had been discovered.

The government's failure to balance its books, not least because it refused to reduce the range of its overseas commitments, did not necessarily mean that the Castilian economy was equally bankrupt. Nonetheless, the heavy taxes imposed by the government, in order to finance its international activities, considerably weakened the economy of Castile. Whereas the other kingdoms of the peninsula, protected by their constitutional conventions and institutions (see below p. 217–18), went more or less scotfree, the burden of taxation fell almost entirely on Castile alone. Indeed, assessments for the basic tax, the *servicio*, were increased despite clear evidence of a significant fall in the population (see below, p. 209). In Villatoro, for example, the number of recorded households fell from 300 to 80, but the assessment of 135,000 *maravedis* was not reduced below 120,000 and only then as a temporary concession. In addition to the effects of the *servicio*, a ten per cent tax on all sales (the *alcabala*) and taxes on essential articles of consumption (the *millones*) combined to push up prices and depress the living standards of the poor.

Even more damaging to the Castilian economy was the government's tampering with the *vellon*, a bulky coinage containing silver and copper. Finding his revenues for 1599 and 1600 pledged in advance, Philip III removed the silver; in 1602 the weight of the copper was reduced by half; in the following year the debased coinage was called in to be stamped at double its value, a device repeated in 1618 and again in 1640. Since the new coins were immediately discounted by the public, each debasement resulted in a sharp increase in prices. To counter this in 1642 the coinage was recalled to be reissued at half its value. In 1651, however, there was a further debasement, by increasing the face value of the coins fourfold, and, after prices had soared, yet another reissue at half the value. Instead of the steady price-rise of the previous century which had stimulated investment and production, these sudden and varied fluctuations in the value of money produced similar variations in the price of goods — with disastrous effect. The capitalist was unable to estimate the costs of future production, the worker could never tell from one year to another the true purchasing power of his wages.

Castile's predominance, not only within the peninsula but throughout Europe and the world, had depended upon fiscal resources which were more easily exploited than in the other Iberian kingdoms, upon the vitality of a population in excess of the other kingdoms and upon a monopoly of the trade and wealth of the New World. In the early seventeenth century there was clear evidence that all three assets were wasting away.

The first of these, the fiscal resources, had been exploited to the extent that the economy had been damaged (see above). In 1597 the Castilian Cortes reported to Philip II on the economic situation: 'No one has either money or credit, and the country is completely desolated. Any money that is made is hidden away and the owner lives poorly upon it until it is gone. Trade is killed by taxation. In the principal cities most of the houses are closed and deserted.' Every allowance must be made for the exaggerated sentiments of a body which sought to avoid further taxes by a plea of poverty, but the situation which was so gloomily exaggerated in 1597 became true within the next four decades.

The fall in population was clear to all observers and was variously attributed to emigration, to the entry of thousands of young men into the monasteries and to the expulsion of the Moriscos (see below p. 214). The root cause, however, was the plague which swept the peninsula in 1599–1600, in 1629–31 and again in 1647–52. Castile suffered more than the other kingdoms, and the fall in Spain's population, from eight millions to just over six, was more or less accounted for by the fall in Castile's population alone. In Burgos, the old *entrepôt* of Castilian trade, the number of households fell from 2247 (1587–94) to 800 (1640–50), in Toledo from 10,933 to 5000. This was a grievous blow. The fall in numbers created a labour shortage which sent up wages but reduced the demand for goods, and with fewer households to sustain the increasing burden of taxation there was even less money than before to spend on goods and thus to stimulate the economy. The decline was self-perpetuating in that poverty militated against marriage: 'people no longer get married', wrote a friar of Toledo, 'because they have no money to buy food and set up house together'.

The countryside was the worst-affected area. Castilian agriculture had always been inadequate to feed the population: the soil was infertile and its use was controlled by conservative landowners indifferent to methods of production. The absentee landlords of the vast estates, the *latifundia*, looked upon land to confer social status not to produce food. The depopulation of the villages made matters worse. Even the wealthy institution of the *Mesta* went into decline. This was an association of migrant sheep farmers which controlled the six-monthly movement of their flocks along special routes, *canadas*, between the mountains and the plains. In return for the right to impose tolls on the *canadas* the crown had allowed the *Mesta* extraordinary powers to protect its members, its sheep and its pasture grounds. In the seventeenth century, however, its jurisdiction was challenged by local authorities and much of its fortune was exhausted in litigation. Its flock, once estimated at four million sheep, were more than halved, and the decline of the *Mesta* was not signalised by any revival of arable farming.

It was equally evident that the flow of bullion into Castile was rapidly dwindling, from approximately £4,000,000 in value in 1600 to £1,500,000 in 1650 (see C.H. Haring, *Trade and Navigation between Spain and the Indies. NB* The valuation in sterling was made before 1939.) Outside Spain there were many who liked to believe that this was the result of daring raids by their sea-dogs — French, Dutch or English — but this accounted for only a small proportion of the loss. Much more serious was the exhaustion of the best mines, the shortage of native labour to work the remainder and the growing population of colonists. As these increased in number more of the bullion was retained by the colonial government to cover the costs of administration and defence, and vast amounts were traded elsewhere to purchase European goods. In the sixteenth century the colonists had wanted the cereals, oil, wine and cloth which Castile had to offer, but as Mexico developed its textile industry, and Peru its agriculture, the goods required by the colonists were the manufactured products and luxuries which Castile could not supply — but which English, French and Dutch merchants were only too happy to make available. The greatest single drain on the colonists' reserves of bullion, however, was the trade with China and the Philippines which, in the years 1618–21, resulted in the export of 1,650,000 *pesos* to the Orient while only 1,500,000 went to Castile.

The real tragedy of Castilian history was that she had never learned the proper use of her bullion imports, great or small: as the Cortes complained to Philip III, 'the treasure immediately goes to foreign kingdoms leaving this one in extreme poverty'. One reason for this was the government's chronic indebtedness to foreign bankers which accounted for most of the royal share of the bullion. More than half the bullion imports, however, passed into private hands but this too failed to enrich the economy because industry produced so little to sell. Even the great cloth centres of Toledo and Segovia fell into decay, because the rate of inflation in Castile in the sixteenth century had exceeded that of the rest of Europe, leaving Castile's products overpriced in the European markets. There was also a shift in European taste from the heavy Castilian cloth to a lighter product, so that instead of producing her own Castile had to export her raw wool to the 'new draperies' of England and the Netherlands, and purchase back the finished products. In addition, the problem was aggravated by the growing labour shortage, by the fluctuations in the value of money and by the restrictive practices of the gilds. As a result, not only in textiles but in the production of iron and steel Castile was unable to withstand European competition; instead of selling her goods abroad she became 'the distributor of precious metals to Europe' (Haring op. cit).

A contributory cause of the decline of the Castilian economy was the decline of Antwerp. The Venetian ambassador in 1552,

recognising that the true sources of a nation's prosperity lay not
in its bullion imports but in its industry and trade, remarked of
the Spanish Netherlands: 'These are the treasures of the King of
Spain, these are the mines, the Indies which have sustained
Imperial ventures for so many years.' Antwerp, a clearing house
for European finance and the centre of international trade, had
become the market for American bullion and Castilian wool. In
Antwerp, too, were purchased the Baltic naval stores for the
shipbuilders of Barcelona and the Basque provinces, along with
the weapons and manufactured goods which Castile could no
longer produce herself. The sack of Antwerp in 1576 and its
subsequent blockage were therefore of great significance in the
history of Castile.

Deprived of her vital entrepôt, there still remained her
commerce with America, a jealously guarded perquisite of the
Castilian crown which had controlled it with painstaking
thoroughness through the office of the *Consulado*. Like most such
perquisites, however, it had been pawned to finance the great
undertakings of the sixteenth century, and the monopoly of
American trade thus passed to a small group of merchants in
Seville. The massive regulations of the *Consulado* forestalled both
initiative and innovation but the fact that they also prevented
competition made them invaluable to the monopolists. For them
it was of little concern that by 1640 three-quarters of the goods in
Spanish ports were delivered in Dutch ships and that the volume
of trade declined with each decade: the fewer the goods the
greater the price, a trend which the crown did not actively
contest since it benefited from the sales tax of 10 per cent.

One basic reason for Castile's failure to meet the challenges of
the seventeenth century was the dominance throughout society of
noble values, of the *hidalgo* mentality. The nobility, which
comprised a tenth of the population, dominated the towns and
the countryside and devoted its wealth to the pursuit of
government office, to investments in government bonds and to
ostentatious display. There was no indigenous middle class to
practice the capitalist virtues of thrift and investment in trade
and industry, and the few merchants who did so were the first to
re-invest their profits in land and government offices. All classes,
therefore, reflected the *hidalgo* disdain for business as fit only for
Jews, Arabs and other foreigners.

The pernicious effect of the *hidalgo* mentality was noted by many of the commentators and critics, known as the *arbitristas*, who jockeyed with each other in the press and at court to propose remedies for the ailing economy. 'Our republic has come to be an extreme contrast of rich and poor,' wrote Gonzales de Cellorigo in 1600. 'Our condition is one in which there are rich who loll at ease or poor who beg, and we lack people of the middle sort, whom neither wealth nor poverty prevents from pursuing the rightful kind of business enjoined by Natural Law.'

The *arbitristas* also bemoaned the loss of silver to other countries, the adverse balance of trade, the ostentatious expenditure on imported luxuries by the rich, and the domination of Castile's economy by foreign merchants and foreign merchandise. Above all they perceived that the government itself was a cause of Castile's ills by its expensive court, its ever-expanding bureaucracy, its heavy burden of taxation and its failure to reduce its overseas commitments. This of course proved to be vain criticism since it was the court and the bureaucracy which monopolised power: only on occasion did a particular member of the government, in a short-lived flurry of activity, attempt to pay heed to the *arbitristas'* advice.

Lerma and Olivares

'God', wrote Philip II, 'who has given me so many kingdoms to govern has not given me a son fit to govern them.' Philip III (1598–1621), who so closely resembled his father in appearance, was wholly incompetent to succeed him. The progressive deterioration of mind and body, the result of generations of Habsburg inbreeding, was already apparent in him. Spectacularly prodigal of money, he exhausted his emotions too by intermittent bouts of frenzied gaiety and fits of religious melancholia. Ultimately honoured as an example of piety, he performed his daily devotions with an automatic regularity that dispensed him from the necessity of thought. Unfortunately, he could not so easily fulfil his political duties. The arduous task of exercising the highly centralised powers of the Spanish monarchy was far beyond his capabilities, and he immediately abdicated his authority into the hands of his court favourite, the Duke of Lerma.

Lerma was not chief minister (there was no such official), nor was he always in attendance at the principal councils, but as the king's favourite he was able to interfere wherever he chose. His influence was disastrous. The years of peace following the Truce with the Dutch in 1609 presented a remarkable opportunity for reform and retrenchment, but Lerma was incompetent to recognise either the opportunity or the measures by which it might be exploited. Because of his inadequacy and preoccupation with his own interests, the years of the Truce were squandered.

Since he did not come from the top rank of noble families, the *grandees*, Lerma set out to ingratiate himself with them, to purchase by the favours he was able to confer the recognition of those before whom he stood in awe. To strengthen his own position he devoted his efforts to exploiting his opportunity to acquire wealth and to the creation of an extensive clientele, dependent upon his support. As Lerma stood to Philip III, so Rodrigo Calderon stood to him, and the succession of parasites, each with its own family of relatives to cater for, grew to an almost infinite extent and battened upon the offices of the state.

An unfortunate consequence of Lerma's period of influence was that he set an example of extravagance and speculation which emptied the Treasury and aggravated the collapse of the economy. Occasions for ostentatious display were exploited to the full, and the court became three times as expensive to maintain as in Philip II's day. Offices and titles were created by the king and sold to fill the pockets of his favourite, the currency was debased to procure a quick profit and the resources of the state were ransacked in an attempt to satisfy insatiable appetites.

When public protest at the unbridled corruption of the administration mounted so high that even the court took cognizance of it, Lerma jettisoned the more unpopular of his hangers-on in order to safeguard his own position. Subsequently, in 1618 he found it politic to retire from court to assume the dignity of a cardinal and to enjoy a fortune rumoured to be 44,000,000 *ducats*.

The unhappiest incident of Lerma's administration was the expulsion of the Moriscos, the baptised descendants of the Moors who had been overrun in the fifteenth century. Since 1492 the government had tried in vain to assimilate them into the Spanish population. Christian to all appearance, many were suspected of performing Moorish rites and ceremonies within their houses, and despite all the laws they clung obstinately to their traditional dress and language. Denied civil equality with the Spaniards, barred from the professions and forbidden to own land, the 500,000 Moriscos, living mainly in Valencia, formed a separate, under-privileged and unpopular community amidst the seven or eight million inhabitants of Spain. The Valencian landowners, from whose class came Lerma, regarded them with jealousy and hatred. Whatever they did was criticised: their tradition of early marriages and large families betrayed improvidence, their frugality a device to cheat the government of its purchase taxes, and their capacity for unremitting toil the fruit of avarice. Not even the high rents which the Moriscos were compelled to pay for their lands could reconcile the Spaniards to so nonconformist a group. In an age which set such store by uniformity they were hated simply for being different.

It was not Valencian prejudice alone which prompted Lerma's decision to expel the Moriscos. More than anything else the government was so embarrassed by its coming to terms with the Dutch Calvinists that it felt obliged to demonstrate its Catholic credentials and avenge its shame by persecuting the Moriscos. Those of Valencia were deported in 1609, the remainder from other kingdoms followed in 1610. For these last the expulsion was particularly cruel. Being few in number they had been more easily assimilated into the Spanish population and were generally practising Christians: to expose them to the Moslems of North Africa was a ghastly crime, mitigated only by the inefficiency of the administration to ensure the expulsion of all 500,000 Moriscos; leaving behind perhaps as many as 350,000.

Lerma's retirement did not leave power in the hands of his son for very long, for in 1621 Philip IV became king at the age of sixteen. Cultured, generous and elegant, with a fine taste for the patronage of arts, he was the ablest of Philip II's descendants. Responsive to a strong sense of duty he rarely failed to evince the best intentions in the world; rarely, however, did he succeed in implementing them. His virtues were powerless against his vices. Sensual and self-indulgent to a degree associated more popularly with the Orient than with Europe, his dissipation and debauchery provoked periods of morbid self-condemnation and remorse. He attributed the disasters befalling Spain to the judgement of God upon his sins; 'for no matter how adequate may be the remedies that I adopt, our sins suffice to condemn all our affairs to the most miserable state imaginable'.

Like his father, Philip IV resigned the affairs of state to a favourite, Gaspar de Guzman, count-duke of Olivares; but Olivares, unlike Lerma, was a man of substance and drive. He came from the inner circle of *grandees*, his connections were powerful and he had the energy, the imagination and the perception to become the outstanding statesman of seventeenth-century Spain.

A restless bureaucrat, he was always in a rush about the court, his hat and pockets stuffed with papers, his voice booming down the corridors, his mind as active as his body. His portrait by Velasquez reveals his physical strength, his powerful shoulders, broad bearded chin and fierce black eyes; his contemporaries bore witness to an overbearing manner and violent temper. No man was better equipped to tackle the problems bequeathed by Lerma; no man had so clear a notion of the unity of Spain; no man saw more clearly the map of Europe in relation to the war with the Dutch (see below, pp. 225–6, for his conduct of foreign affairs).

By-passing the cumbersome structure of over-manned and ineffectual councils, Olivares obtained information and executed policy through a series of committees, *juntas*, responsible to him alone. The most important of these initially was the *junta de reformación*, designed to give effect to the opinions of the *arbitristas*. Lerma had to forfeit much of his fortune to purchase an uninterrupted retirement, his son was imprisoned and his unhappy protégé Calderon was executed, but reforming action was not entirely recriminatory and retrospective. Sumptuary laws were designed to put limits to the degree of ostentatious display permitted in public, economies were imposed upon the administration of the court, and taxes were to be reduced. In practice, behind all the excitement engendered by the sense of embarking upon a new venture, nothing much was achieved.

Nor did he succeed in reforming the bureaucracy. The sale of offices, combined with the lack of alternative pursuits in commerce and industry, stimulated in Spain a passion for official employment, with the result that the administration was burdened with incompetent and superfluous officials, Olivares forbade the teaching of Latin in small town grammar schools to reduce the number of qualified applicants; but this was to handle the problem at the wrong end, since by greater economy, by a firm refusal to resort to expedients, the sale of offices could have been checked immediately. However, the renewal of Spain's military commitments in Europe proved so costly that by 1631 a new expedient made office holding even more attractive. In return for *la media anada*, a payment of half the first year's salary, the crown guaranteed to the office holder not only security of tenure but also the right to treat his office as a private possession, to be sold at will or transmitted to heirs. Senior posts alone were excluded from the scheme.

Inefficiency and irresponsibility in the civil service were not peculiar to Spain alone for *la Paulette* in France produced a similar effect, but Olivares faced problems which were more pronounced than those, for example, that confronted Richelieu. The particularism to be found in the outlying provinces of all European countries was encouraged to a fatal degree in Spain by the mountains and plateaux which divided the peninsula so effectively that no one city had good access to the other parts of the kingdom. Furthermore, Spain was in reality a union of separate kingdoms and principalities, Portugal, Aragon, Valencia, Catalonia, Navarre and the Basque, which were virtually independent of each other. In each area the Cortes, the assembly of the Estates, accepted the sovereign of Castile as its own ruler on terms which guaranteed its traditional liberties, or *fueros*. Philip II at his greatest had found it impossible to govern Spain as a unit, and only in Castile had he enjoyed extensive powers of jurisdiction and taxation. In every other kingdom and principality the Cortes stood firmly by its *fueros*, resisting all attempts to impose a more centralised administration. There was much to justify this attitude: centralisation tended to involve subordination as much to Castile as to the king, and the administration of Castile, itself highly centralised, was notorious for its delays and inefficiency. The other kingdoms moreover had never benefited from Castilian enterprises in the New World or the Netherlands, and neither Philip II nor Philip III had visited them with any frequency to hold court and exercise their patronage. In any case there was no wish to become more closely associated with a kingdom burdened beyond belief with overseas commitments and domestic debts.

Olivares recognised the justice of the suspicions and fears
entertained by the other kingdoms, and also the necessity
nonetheless of relieving Castile of some of her burdens. Sensitive
to the grievances of non-Castilians who neither saw the king nor
enjoyed his patronage, he planned the creation of a more
widely-based, Spanish administration to replace the one
dominated by Castile. In return the king would visit the other
kingdoms regularly, listen to their grievances, remedy what he
could and dispense patronage with liberality. As a first step
Olivares proposed a Union of Arms by which each kingdom
would raise its own reserves of troops for service in the defence of
all — 'that when any of the states was at war, the rest should be
obliged to come to its aid and defence.' It was not simply a
military venture but a device to 'familiarise' — using Olivares'
favourite word in this context — the inhabitants of the different
kingdoms with one another and thus to prepare the ground for
closer union in the future.

In 1626 Philip IV appealed in person before the Cortes of
Aragon, Valencia and Catalonia to seek acceptance of the
principle behind the Union of Arms. Aragon rejected outright the
suggestion that she had any duty to aid the king, refused to raise
troops for his European campaigns, but reluctantly consented to
increase her contribution by one million *ducats* the sum to be
spread over ten years. Valencia, after a very spirited resistance,
also agreed to a subsidy, but Catalonia was adamant, insisting
that Philip repaid all the loans made to the crown in the past
before any new supplies were voted. Olivares tactfully withdrew
Philip to Madrid without pressing the point. In 1632 he renewed
his request to Catalonia for aid. Again it was rejected.
Self-regarding and obstinate in all matters, and closer in spirit
and culture to Provence than to Castile, Catalonia was the one
province which Olivares condemned as 'entirely separate from
the monarchy, useless for service and in a state little befitting the
dignity and power of His Majesty.'

When the French invaded Roussillon in 1639,[1] Castilian troops
were welcomed into Catalonia to serve in its defence. As soon as
the French had been driven back, Olivares decided to exploit the
presence of his army to destroy Catalonia's 'provincial pettiness'

[1] See Chapter III, p.203.

In addition to billeting Castilian troops on a population which regarded them as foreign as the French they had beaten, he ordered the raising of Catalan levies, not only to safeguard the frontier, but also to demonstrate his power to compel obedience. The combination of looted billets, forced levies, Castilian interference and a severe drought which threatened to ruin the harvest proved insupportable to the Catalans. In 1640 they revolted. The rebels massacred the Viceroy and other Castilian troops and officials, and declared their state to be an independent republic. Most dangerous of all from Spain's viewpoint, they accepted an offer of support by Richelieu and recognised Louis XIII as Count of Barcelona.

In the same year the Portuguese revolted. Their kingdom had passed to Philip II in 1580 with the strictest provision for the maintenance of its liberties and self-government, but Olivares persistently treated it as an apanage of Castile. Employing Miguel Vasconcellos, himself a Portuguese, to further his plans, he had filled the country with Castilian officials. They sat in the Council of Portugal, inspected the treasury, held Portuguese bishoprics and acquired Portuguese estates. Indignation at the daily violation of their liberties was intensified by anger at Spain's failure to provide an adequate defence for their colonial empire, and the Portuguese looked to their greatest noble, the Duke of Braganza, for a sign. Evading all efforts by Olivares to lure him to Madrid where he might safely be arrested, and undeceived by Olivares's subsequent attempt to win him over by appointing him to command the army in Portugal, Braganza was nevertheless hesitant and shrank from any positive act of rebellion.

In 1636 Olivares ordered the collection of a 5 per cent tax on property, a tax hitherto confined to Castile. This provoked a rebellion, but without Braganza's leadership it was so disorganised as to be easily suppressed. Olivares and Vasconcellos were therefore encouraged to pursue their plans further. In 1640 they proposed to abolish the Portuguese cortes, to enlist the nobles into the Castilian army, and to absorb the kingdom wholly into Castile. So great was the fury that within three hours of the proclamation a revolutionary group had murdered Vasconcellos, seized control of Lisbon and called upon Braganza to become king. In this crisis the decisive figure was Braganza's wife.

She came from one of the proudest families in Spain; her brother
was the Duke of Medina Sidonia and Captain-General of
Andalusia, and her impetuous ambition had long struggled to
overcome the inborn timidity of her husband. The news from
Lisbon gave renewed vigour to her attack, and before the day was
out Braganza had proclaimed himself King John IV of Portugal.
As a further stroke, the Queen persuaded Medina Sidonia to
raise his own standard in Andalusia and to proclaim his
province's independence of Philip IV.

The Years of Rebellion 1641–65

Within six months the work of twenty years was destroyed.
Olivares learned of Medina Sidonia's treason in time to effect his
arrest and to save Andalusia for the crown, but he could make no
headway against the rebels in Catalonia and Portugal. Philip IV,
in a rare moment of inspired leadership, marched out in 1642 to
suppress the Catalans, only to give up when he learned that
French troops had reinforced Barcelona and were advancing into
Aragon. His only solace was to dismiss Olivares, who died insane
with grief at the collapse of his ambitions.

Olivares's ambitions in essence had been those of his great
contemporary Richelieu: why then did he fail so dramatically
where Richelieu succeeded? The difference in character between
the two men was in fact of far less importance than the difference
between their countries. The kingdoms of Spain were not *pays
d'etat*; and the Estates of Languedoc, for all the trouble they caused
Richelieu, were never so independent nor so powerfully united in
the defence of their traditions as the Cortes of Catalonia.
Moreover, the Spanish economy was collapsing and royal
bankruptcy had become commonplace. Whereas Richelieu was
able to send effective aid to the rebels in the peninsula, Olivares
found it impossible to assist the Duc de Rohan's rising in 1629.[2]
Spain, unlike France, could no longer sustain the burden of her
commitments. Above all, she could not afford to be ruled by
Olivares, and it is a point of some significance in her decline that
while inefficient and unimaginative government merely aggravated her weaknesses, an able and energetic one utterly
destroyed her by demanding too much from her depleted
resources.

[2] See Chapter III p.182.

Olivares was succeeded as chief minister by his nephew, Don Luis de Haro. If ability in the seat of government had led Spain into disaster, the appointment of a mediocrity could not reverse the trend, and the government's persistent lack of money compelled it to adopt measures which provoked further outbreaks. In 1646 the French seized the island of Elba, whence they launched attacks on Naples. Arcos, the Viceroy, was ordered to prepare a counter attack, but to finance his expedition he had to impose duties on the sale of fruit, hitherto the one untaxed commodity. Since fruit, however, was all that the poor could afford to eat, rioting immediately broke out in the city.

Masaniello, a young fisherman whose mother had been punished for smuggling corn, put himself at the head of the rioters, retaining their loyalty by acts of violence which daily redoubled their intensity. He led them into Arcos's palace and terrorised the Viceroy into rescinding all taxes imposed since the reign of Charles V. He broke open the prisons, emptied the armouries and attacked the houses of the tax collectors. For ten days the mob was inspired to a frenzy of pillage, arson and murder while its leader, driven insane by the gratification of his lust for power, dressed himself in cloth of gold and executed all whom his demented mind suspected of disloyalty. Suddenly, he too was assassinated, and his funeral provoked scenes of even greater excitement, for it was believed that his severed head miraculously joined itself to his trunk and, thus united, he solemnly blessed the assembled crowd before he was committed to the grave.

Other leaders sprang up, including the Duc de Guise, who claimed the Neapolitan throne, but despite the violence and anarchy which prevailed throughout the winter the rioters never became rebels. Unlike the Catalans and the Portuguese their protest was the protest of poverty. Tradition and centralisation were meaningless concepts to a hungry mob, as the new Spanish commander, Don Juan of Austria[3] was quick to realise. He exploited the differences between the local leaders, and held the nobility firm in their loyalty by threatening to abandon them to the mob. Moreover, French interference was temporarily

---

[3] An illegitimate son of Philip IV who revealed remarkable ability in government and war: see below, p.222. In 1647 he had been appointed captain-general of the fleet.

suspended because of the Fronde. With his limited forces Don Juan skilfully held the ring until the violence of the poorest classes had exhausted itself in its wild career, and then restored Spanish control within the city.

The recovery of Catalonia was not achieved so swiftly. A royal army succeeded in reaching the walls of Barcelona at the end of 1650, and, with naval support from Don Juan, compelled it to surrender after a siege of fifteen months. Its citizens were granted an amnesty by Philip IV, whose chief concern was no longer to enforce the policies of Olivares but to secure the recognition of his authority. Once this was realised by the Catalans the work of recovery was eased, though the French troops, whose presence the Catalans were beginning to find as burdensome as that of the Castilians in 1640, remained in the principality until the Treaty of the Pyrenees (1659).[4]

In order to embarrass the Portuguese in their struggle for independence, Philip IV persuaded the pope to withhold recognition from John IV, secured the exclusion of Portugal from the peace negotiations of 1648, and, in making peace with the Dutch, encouraged them to seize what they could of the Portuguese empire. Less honourably, John's brother, serving with distinction in the Austrian army, was kidnapped and assassinated, and an attempt on John himself was discovered only at the last minute. The Portuguese, however, remained defiant. Indeed, Spain's military strength was so fully extended by the combat with France that the rebels launched an impudent attack into Spain itself, laying siege to Badajoz in 1658. In the following year the Treaty of the Pyrenees deprived them of official support by France, but Charles II of England came to their rescue in 1661 when Catherine of Braganza brought him a dowry of £800,000 along with Bombay and Tangier. By dispensing with imperial outposts they could no longer defend the Portuguese saved their homeland, and the alliance was well purchased. Schomberg, an experienced marshal of France though the son of an Englishwoman, was granted an English peerage, and with French connivance sent to Portugal.

Upon his shoulders rested the kingdom's security, since Don Juan, the ablest Spaniard of his generation, had been transferred

4 See below, p.227.

from his naval command to lead the troops who, after 1659, were no longer needed in Italy and the Netherlands. Don Juan came close to victory in 1663 when Lisbon seemed to be at his mercy, but his men had tasted victory so rarely during the past twenty years that success merely demoralised them. Driven back to the frontier, they were decisively routed by Schomberg at Ameixial. This failure, with the loss of 8,000 men together with the baggage and artillery, led to Don Juan's temporary disgrace, though his successors met with no better fortune. At last Philip IV, in a desperate effort to restore unity to the peninsula before death claimed him, raised every available soldier in his empire and put 23,000 men in the field. At Montesclaros in 1665, in what proved to be the last and the fiercest battle of the war of liberation, Schomberg broke the Spaniards after eight hours of hand to hand fighting. Portugal's independence, though not formally recognised until 1668, was thus assured, and news of the defeat killed Philip IV.

Spain in Europe 1598–1659

Philip II had dominated his age by land and sea; and if modern historians can see the administrative and economic weaknesses behind the facade of power he bequeathed to Philip III, contemporary statesmen did not consider the power of Spain to be illusory. Indeed, by a fortunate turn of events, Spain was able to make peace with France in 1598 and with England in 1604 without loss of face, leaving her free to concentrate upon the Eighty Years War with the Dutch. Accounts of the events of this war, and of their interraction with events in Germany and France can be found in Chapters II, III and V (see pp. 113–44, 154, 197–206, 237–41, 252–8). Two generalisations must be made here.

In the first place the war with the Dutch was the war which Spain most needed to win. It was a war not only with heretics but with rebels: it therefore involved matters of national pride to an acute degree. Moreover it had become an axiom of the government's imperial strategy that unless the Netherlands were recovered, Italy, the Indies and the Iberian peninsula itself would become immediately vulnerable to Spain's enemies.

In the second place the Eighty Years War could not exclude

the rest of Europe. The sea and land routes by which Spain
reinforced her armies in the Netherlands were open to attack at a
number of points and their security often depended upon
temporary agreements. Any shift in the policies of a small city
council or of a major state was alike of tremendous consequences
to the government in Madrid. English neutrality had an
important bearing on communications through the Channel. A
French war with Savoy (see p. 198) virtually resulted in the
closure of a vital section of the 'Spanish Road', and local crises in
Jülich-Cleves, the Palatinate, the Valtelline or Mantua were
transformed into crises of European magnitude because of their
significance for Spain's transcontinental routes. Moreover, the
conflict of two irreconcilable cultures (see p. 115 for an analysis
of this), each representing what the other most hated or feared,
served to polarise the irreconcilable tensions leading to conflict
throughout Europe. Spain and the United Provinces, accordingly, were each looked to, and appealed to for aid, by the enemies of
the other.

In 1609 the Twelve Year Truce was signed, since a form of
military stalemate had been reached and neither side could, for
the time being, sustain a new campaign. The Truce was detested
in Spain, where the persecution of the Moriscos was a direct
consequence of this shattering blow to Spanish pride. Thereafter,
while Philip III's government was restricted in its operations by
a truce which it disliked but could not afford to abandon, his
viceroys and governors and ambassadors throughout Europe did
all they could to strengthen Spains's position against the ending
of the Truce — not least by their actions in the Holy Roman
Empire.

The ambassadors Zuñiga and his successor Oñate were
convinced that the Netherlands could not be held if the emperor's
power was diminished in Germany (see p. 120). Zuñiga,
therefore, helped to mobilise the Catholic League against the
Evangelical Union, which was in alliance with the Dutch, and
Oñate raised the money and troops to help Ferdinand defeat the
Bohemian rebels and their new king, the head of the Evangelical
Union. In addition, Spain's ambassadors in England and France
achieved a diplomatic triumph by securing the benevolent
neutrality of James I and Louis XIII throughout the events of
the Truce. Meanwhile in Flanders, Spinola exploited the crisis

over Jülich-Cleves to take Wesel, which strengthened his hold on the lower Rhineland; and he seized upon the Bohemian war as a unique opportunity to destroy the most dangerous Protestant outpost along the Rhine, the Palatinate. In the same year the Catholic inhabitants of the Valtelline, linking Lombardy and the Tyrol, rebelled against their Swiss overlords, the Protestant Grisons, and the Governor of Milan lost no time in coming to their aid by occupying the pass with his troops.

When the Truce ended in 1621, an event which coincided with the accession of Philip IV and the appointment of Olivares, Spain was in a stronger position in Europe than in 1610, and for the next seven years her power continued to increase. The Palatinate, indeed the Rhineland as a whole, was made safe for Spanish lines of communication to the Netherlands. James I was gulled into neutrality by the prospect of a Spanish match for his son Charles, Breda was seized in 1625 by Spinola and Richelieu failed to recover control of the Valtelline for the Grisons. It was then that Olivares conceived a plan which was not only imaginative but wideranging in its ramifications. Recognising that the Dutch economy depended to a large extent on the trade with the Baltic, he offered the Baltic ports of the Hanseatic League the monopoly of the Spanish trade with Europe provided that they denied the Dutch access to their ports. The Hanseatic towns, however, were afraid of Dutch naval power. Olivares, therefore, proposed in 1626 (see p. 141-2) that while the Catholic league safeguarded the Rhineland from a Danish attack, the emperor's forces, led by Wallenstein, should advance to the Baltic coast, launch a fleet and persuade the Hanseatic towns that they could henceforth count upon Habsburg protection if they turned against the Dutch. It was a brilliantly conceived plan which threatened the economy of the United Provinces at its most vulnerable point. It failed because of the siege of Stralsund and Sweden's intervention in north Germany.

Other setbacks coincided with the collapse of the Baltic plan. In 1627 Spain suspended the payment of interest on her debts; in 1628 Piet Heyn seized the silver fleet in Matanzas Bay; in 1629 Frederick Henry broke through the Spanish defences in Flanders and overran Brabant; in 1629 also, the disputed succession to Mantua and the fortresses of Montferrat and Casale menaced the security of the garrison in Milan, and the Dutch invasion of

Brazil not only compelled Spain to mobilise a trans-Atlantic expedition, which failed, but bred discontent in Portugal (see p. 219).

In the circumstances a peace settlement was the only cure for Spain's ills, but when a chance came during the lull following the death of Gustavus Adolphus in 1632, Olivares refused to consider the idea. He believed, in fact, that Gustavus's death made the continuation of war all the more necessary, on the grounds that Sweden's defeat would result in a revival of Habsburg power and that this in turn would ease the recovery of the United Provinces. The Cardinal-Infante Ferdinand was divested of his clerical robes and sent at the head of an army through the Valtelline. At Nördlingen he met his brother-in-law, the Archduke Ferdinand, and together they crushed the combined forces of the Heilbronn League.

Nördlingen was the last great victory to be won by Spain in Europe. It led directly to a French declaration of war, and in such a war the political stability, the material resources and the firm government of France gave her the advantage. She survived the 'year of Corbie' (1636) when the Habsburg armies made their bid to seize Paris, and thereafter the years of war proved disastrous for Spain. The fall of Breisach in 1638 blocked the overland route to Flanders, the ignominious defeat of the Armada in the Downs in 1639 confirmed Dutch supremacy in the Channel, and the victor of Nördlingen was thus deprived of supplies. With the Catalans and Portuguese in revolt during 1640, and the French armies victorious in north Italy, in Roussillon and at Rocroi in 1643, the collapse of Spain was patent. By making a separate treaty with the Dutch in 1648 she relieved herself of one enemy, but the French too were released from their German commitments by the Peace of Westphalia; and their gains of Pinerolo, Breisach, Philippsburg and the principal fortresses of Alsace and Lorraine, reinforced their stranglehold on Spain's lines of communication.

The Fronde provided an unexpected respite for Spain and an ally in the Prince of Condé, who held his own against Turenne in Flanders, beating him decisively at Valenciennes in 1656. The entry of England into the war, however, signalised by the fall of Jamaica and the Anglo-French victory at Dunkirk, decided the issue. Spain had no option but to accept Mazarin's terms in the

Treaty of the Pyrenees, which was formally drawn up in 1659:

(i) Rousillon and Perpignan; Montmédy in Luxemburg; Artois, and the Netherland towns of Arras, Béthune, Gravelines and Thionville were ceded to France. Dunkirk was given to England.

(ii) All French gains at the Peace of Westphalia were recognised and confirmed by Spain.

(iii) The French withdrew their support from the Catalan and Portuguese rebels.

(iv) The Infanta, Maria Theresa, was married to Louis XIV.

This last clause was to prove the most important in the treaty, since after the reign of Carlos II (1665–1700), it led to the Bourbon succession. Spain might well have been happier if the interval of Carlos's reign could have been foregone.

THE SPANISH SUCCESSION 1665–1714

Carlos II. The Last of the Spanish Habsburgs 1665–1700

Three generations of royal marriages between cousins and nieces[5] produced their dreadful legacy in the pitiful form of Carlos II. Grotesque in appearance, deformed in body and backward in intellect, he seemed barely human: 'He has a ravenous stomach', reported Stanhope, the English ambassador, as though describing some strange Iberian creature, 'and swallows all he eats whole, for his nether jaw stands out so much that his two rows of teeth cannot meet; to compensate which, he has a prodigious wide throat, so that a gizzard or a liver of a hen passes down whole.' The Spaniards, ignorant of genetics, looked upon their divinely appointed leader with dismay and declared him to be in the grip of diabolical spirits, an explanation all the more tragic for being accepted by Carlos himself, so that the anguish of his physical infirmity was increased by nameless fears which denied him sleep unless his confessor and two friars lay in his chamber.

[5] Of 56 of Carlos's maternal ancestors, 48 were ancestors of his father. Carlos's own grandfather was also his mother's; his parents were uncle and niece.

The elaborate administration which had been built around the person of the king collapsed into worthless wreckage since Carlos was unable to play any part in the business of government. Fifteen minutes' work, signing state papers, was reputed to be the most he could do in a day, and the interminable delays for which Spain was already notorious became even more pronounced: 'No head to govern, and every man in office does what he pleases without fear of being called to account' (Stanhope). The blight 'so thick', wrote a Frenchwoman in Madrid, 'that it can be seen, smelt, touched', which settled upon the court and the civil service speeded the progressive deterioration of the economy. The *Mesta*, the *Consulado,* the great Fairs of Castile and all other public and official organs of trade and industry, declined with every decade, and there was little indication that their losses were in any way recouped by gains among private traders and individual farmers. The value of *vellon* continued to fluctuate wildly, with even more disastrous effect after 1680 when the government tried to restore it to its value as in Philip II's day. 'Commerce is in no better state. With the exception of Castilian wool, which foreigners buy, there is no merchandise or manufacture to attract money. The king has no ships now to protect trade and his subjects none to trade with, so that all commerce is done by strangers, and two-thirds of the money from the Indies goes direct abroad, and the other third gradually follows it in payment for goods.'[6]

Material decay found a counterpart in the mood of pessimism which spread throughout Spain, inducing acquiescence and inhibiting self-help. The race which had dominated Europe and opened up a new continent overseas became listless and apathetic, so that the physical degeneration of the royal family merely epitomised the more fundamental deterioration of the national spirit. The single-minded crusading zeal which had once been characteristic of the Spaniard gave way to an exaggerated and dangerous version of the Quietist doctrines of Miguel de Molinos, [7]whose emphasis on the withdrawal of the soul from the world to lose itself in adoration of God was perverted to encourage the utter abandonment of all interest in church and state in favour of the passive, endless waiting for illumination by God.

[6] From *Mémoires de la Cour D'Espagne,* a brilliant and detailed commentary by de Villars the French ambassador.
[7] See Chapter I, p.85.

The political history of Spain after 1665 resolved itself into two successive conflicts, namely to control the king while he lived and to determine the succession before he died. In the first of these Don Juan played a prominent part since his campaigns in Naples, Catalonia and the Netherlands had made his name deservedly popular. He hoped to exploit the marriage of Maria Theresa and Louis XIV to establish closer alliance between their countries, and thus to save Spain from further warfare. Undoubtedly Don Juan was right in his policy and his able qualities clearly marked him out for the direction of affairs. Unfortunately for Spain, both he and his policy were bitterly opposed by Carlos's mother, Mariana of Austria. As an Austrian she wanted to use Spain to protect her own country from Louis XIV: as a mother she was acutely aware of the contrast between the strong soldier and her own feeble infant, and she feared lest Don Juan seize the crown. No doubt Spain would have benefited had he done so, but the principle of legitimacy was not easily set aside. Philip IV, indeed, had wanted to legitimise him, but the jealous Mariana forbade it, and finally he was merely given formal recognition as a royal bastard, an honour denied to the other thirty or so children of Philip's mistresses.

In consequence it was Mariana who secured the direction of affairs on behalf of her son, while Don Juan retired to Aragon. In 1669 he marched on Madrid, and to the delight of the people, cleared the court of the queen's Austrian favourites. More than this, however, he could not do without expelling Mariana herself, and once again he went into retirément. He returned eight years later after Mariana had scandalised the country by taking a lover and making him chief minister. This time Mariana was removed from the court and Don Juan kept control of the king. For two years he enforced his policies against the intrigues of the Austrian faction, and the opposition of the fickle mob which blamed him for Spain's defeats in the war with France (1672–9), undertaken against his advice and one which he was quick to terminate. His triumph was the betrothal of Carlos to Marie Louise, Louis XIV's niece, but his death in 1679 restored Mariana to the court. Although the French princess became queen, her influence with the king was never allowed to challenge that of the queen mother and when she died a second marriage was arranged with the emperor's sister-in-law to confirm the triumph of Mariana and the Austrians. For the luckless king, however, the last years of a miserable existence were made even more intolerable by the presence of a vicious shrew.

The struggle for the control of Carlos II was barely won before it became necessary to determine the succession. Carlos had no children and, whatever the niceties of the genealogical tables, the legality of renunciations and the partition treaties of interested powers[8], the choice before Spain lay between a French and an Austrian prince. Austrian domination at court, which in Vienna was taken to presage the nomination of the Emperor's son, had an unforeseen result: 'The general inclination to the succession', wrote Stanhope, 'is altogether French, their aversion to the Queen having set them against her countrymen.' The lead was taken by Cardinal Portocarrero, who, with powerful support from the grandees, worked actively in alliance with the French ambassador. He played upon Carlos's dislike for his second wife, comparing her unfavourably with the French princess whose short-lived gaiety had charmed the king and whose memory still lived with him. Most astutely, he persuaded Carlos to change his confessor, an Austrian accomplice, for one of the French party. Out of all the intrigue there was one thing the unhappy monarch could apprehend: his empire was threatened with partition, and France alone had the power to guarantee its security. A month before his death in 1700, Carlos made the only significant decision of his life by naming Philip of Anjou as his successor, on condition that he preserved the empire from the indignity of partititon at the hands of Europe.

Spain's survival in the face of continual aggression by France is one of the most startling aspects of the seventeenth century. It was not, however, the result of her own doing for she was saved, in the first place, by her possession of the Spanish Netherlands. In view of the frequency with which these provinces were invaded by the French in the wars of 1667–8, 1672–9, 1684–5 and 1688–97, this may appear to be a paradox; but the advisers of Charles V in the previous century had always stressed the importance of Flanders as 'a citadel of steel, a shield which enabled him to receive the blows of England, France and Germany, far away from the head of the monarchy'. This

[8] See Chapter VII, p.356, for an account of the international negotiations preceding the War of Spanish Succession

appreciation was still valid, and Louis XIV's attacks on the Netherlands not only distracted him from Spain itself but also aroused against him a series of European coalitions. The other powers, but lately combined to destroy Spanish hegemony, found it vital to their interests to prevent the extension of French power in Europe. Spain's late enemies, therefore, rushed unasked to her defence. Secondly, Spain was saved by the chronic illness and infecundity of Carlos II; another paradox, perhaps. If Louis had not been attracted by the lure of the Spanish succession for his sons, Spain would have suffered more severely from his armies. Instead, though many conquests were made, by 1700 France had retained only Franche Comté and a line of garrisons in Flanders. The Partition Treaties, whether with the emperor in 1667 or with William III after the Peace of Ryswick, were in fact a guarantee of Spain's integrity while Carlos II lived.

Philip V and the War of Spanish Succession[9]

On learning that Carlos II had left his empire to a French prince, the Austrians straightway invaded the Spanish possessions in north Italy in the name of the Archduke Charles. Philip V was confident of victory since he could rely upon the support of Louis XIV, but unfortunately it was Louis's rash actions which drove England and Holland, along with most of the German states, into the Austrian camp. When Louis ordered Philip to grant the Asiento[10] to the French Guinea Company; when he expelled the Dutch from their barrier fortresses, in Philip's name but with French troops; when he declared that Philip retained his claims to the throne of France, then the spectre of a universal monarchy, dominating the frontiers of the old world, monopolising the trade of the new, impelled the creation of the Grand Alliance. Guiltless though he was of Louis's blunders, Philip V could not escape their consequences, and his accession was marked by thirteen years of warfare.

The Spaniards welcomed Philip, a cheerful and handsome seventeen-year-old whose determination to fight for his throne

---

[9] See Chapter VII, pp.361–70 for a detailed account of the war.

[10] A valuable concession to foreign merchants, enabling them to supply the Spanish-American empire with Negro slaves

induced a new mood of optimism and awakened a sense of purpose among his subjects. Lethargic though he could be on occasion, and too often inclined to give up in the face of difficulties, he nevertheless provided a remarkable contrast to his predecessors. When the war began in Italy he remarked that Philip II had lost Holland by not leading his armies in person, and added, 'If I lose territories it shall not be for that reason.' During his absence his fifteen-year-old wife, chaperoned and directed by an experienced old Frenchwoman, won the hearts of Madrid by reading out her husband's despatches from the balcony of the palace. Such examples of royal leadership took Castile, at least, by storm; its citizens named Philip *el animoso*, 'the spirited', and fought loyally for him throughout the war.

In any conflict with Spain the English were wedded to the sea-dog tradition of Elizabeth's reign, believing that victory was to be achieved by raids on Cadiz and the West Indies, and by intercepting the treasure fleet. Indeed, Admiral Rooke's expedition of 1702 did this with some success, since he terrorised the citizens of Cadiz for a whole month and seized half the treasure fleet in Vigo Bay. None of this, however, was likely to drive Philip from Madrid and the adoption of a more rational strategy owed much to the skill of Prince George of Hesse-Darmstadt, the Austrian agent in London. He knew Spain well; he had helped to defend her against the French in 1695, and had served as viceroy of Catalonia until the accession of Philip V. His first *coup*, brilliantly devised to suit the Austrian cause, was the completion of the Methuen Treaty in 1703: it secured the use of Lisbon as a military base in the peninsula, it won Portugal from her nominal alliance with France, and it committed the Allies, whose main concern was the defeat of Louis XIV, to an open avowal of the Archduke Charles's claims to Spain. Rooke and Hesse-Darmstadt brought Charles to Lisbon in 1704, along with 10,000 English and Dutch troops. From there they sailed round the peninsula to attempt a landing in Catalonia, where Hesse-Darmstadt had been very popular as viceroy. The expedition failed, however, since the Catalans were not prepared to jeopardise their *fueros* by rebelling against Philip V until they had received some firm guarantee of Allied support. Hesse-

Darmstadt accordingly won a promise from the English government to secure the Catalans 'a confirmation of their rights and liberties from the King of Spain'; and he reappeared in 1705 bringing the Archduke Charles with him. This time the province rose against Philip, and only the citadel of Barcelona made resistance.

In the successful attack on Barcelona, Hesse-Darmstadt lost his life, but his work had ensured that Portugal and Catalonia, the two areas of the peninsula most hostile to Castile, and most easily reinforced by sea, were won for his master. The Allies could thus exploit their mastery of the sea to launch attacks with equal facility from opposite sides of the peninsula. In 1704, before Charles had been transported to Catalonia, an Allied army under Galway had moved eastwards from Lisbon with 20,000 Portuguese in support. French reinforcements led by Berwick,[11] however, blocked its advance, and Philip enjoyed an exhilarating if short-lived invasion of Portuguese territory. Galway returned to the attack in 1705, to be repulsed at Badajoz, but Philip had then to withdraw most of his troops to cross the peninsula in order to face Charles in Catalonia (1706). While his troops were marching across the difficult terrain, the Allies were able to reinforce Charles from the sea, and it was the arrival of the English fleet at a critical moment of the battle for Barcelona which brought about defeat. Since Aragon too had declared for Charles, Philip's only way of escape lay across the Pyrenees. In great humiliation he abandoned his artillery and supply trains, crossed into France and returned to Madrid through Navarre. Galway, however, had realised that Philip's western front had been denuded for the invasion of Catalonia, and his advance was so swift that, within a fortnight of Philip's return to his capital, Galway had seized it, and the king was again a fugitive.

The occupation of Madrid, the culmination of a hundred years of disasters, produced an unlooked-for response among Philip's subjects in Castile and Andalusia. Accustomed as they had become to the ignominious record of defeat, and dulled by a fatalist refusal to believe in the possibility of recovery, they were

[11] An interesting point: Galway was a French Huguenot while Berwick was an Englishman, an illegitimate son of James II.

none the less galvanised into action by the sight of English and Portuguese troops triumphant among their native sierras. At one stroke they discovered alike their self-respect and a talent for guerrilla warfare. Sea power was of no avail to the Allies at this juncture, and Galway's long lines of communication across the Estremadura were harassed and broken. When Berwick's men were reinforced from Navarre, Philip was restored to his capital after an absence of only four months.

In Germany, Flanders and Italy the Allies were victorious: in Spain there was deadlock. The frontier between Castile and Aragon, the historic divide in Spanish history, lay between Philip and Charles, with Aragon, Valencia, Catalonia and the Balearic Islands in Austrian hands. At Almanza in 1707 Philip defeated the Allies but could not consolidate his victory since Louis XIV recalled many of his troops for the defence of France. Charles, on the other hand was freely reinforced from the Austrian bases in Italy, but his incursions into Castile, and even the seige of Madrid in 1710, availed him nothing, since, as Stanhope remarked, 'We are not masters in Castile of more ground than we encamp on'. The deadlock was resolved by events outside Spain. By 1710 Marlborough's successive efforts to invade northern France and to take Paris had failed, and the Allies began to weaken in their resolve. In England the Whig cry of 'No peace without Spain' was repudiated by the Tory majority in the new Parliament; while the sudden death of Charles's brother, the Emperor Joseph, resulted in his own accession to the imperial throne. The spectre of universal monarchy suddenly appeared two-faced; and Philip's timely renunciation of his claim to France induced a general suspicion in Europe of Habsburg rather than of Bourbon pretensions. The Grand Alliance broke up, the Austrians evacuated the peninsula and England defaulted on her guarantees to the Catalans.

By 1714 the final touches had been put to the peace settlement, which affected Spain in the following particulars:

(i) Philip V renounced his claim to the French throne, and was recognised as ruler of Spain and the Spanish-American empire.

(ii) Charles, now Emperor Charles VI, was given the Spanish Netherlands, and the Italian provinces of Milan, Naples and Sardinia.

(iii) Sicily passed to the King of Savoy, who at the same time gained his royal title. (The two islands, Sardinia and Sicily, were subsequently exchanged in 1720.)

(iv) England retained possession of Gibraltar and Minorca, seized in the war; and her South Sea Company was granted the right to sell slaves in the American colonies.

The Aftermath of the War

Spain at last was to be ruled by the man whom Carlos II had chosen. Though the empire had been rudely partitioned, the loss of Flanders and Italy was a source of relief to a government which had found them increasingly impossible to defend; and, if European leadership was denied her, Spain was at least free to enjoy less burdensome privileges, among them the creation of a more efficient administration. The position in 1700 had not been a happy one: 'Extreme confusion reigns in all affairs; it would appear as if the monarchs of Spain had tried by their bad conduct to destroy their realm rather than to preserve it. Thus disorder has grown so much in the last reign that it may be said that there is now in Spain no government at all.' Such was the contemptuous opinion of Louis XIV, a ruler who prided himself on his *métier du roi*, and who had no illusions about the task before his grandson. Accordingly he sent men such as Orry, whose experience of French administration was of great value to a country where there had been no bureaucrat of note since Olivares. Success depended on two factors, the king's control of the peninsula and French control of the king.

The first was assured by Austria's defeat in Spain, since the adherence of Aragon and its attendant provinces to the Archduke Charles was used as an excuse to destroy their *fueros*. The powerfully entrenched liberties of Aragon, which Philip II himself had hesitated to challenge, were abolished outright by Philip V at the head of a victorious army. Catalonia, abandoned by Charles and betrayed by England, held out for thirteen months in a vain endeavour to stave off the final reckoning. Its

new constitution made no mention of its *fueros*, which survived
only in the memory of the people, since no defeat could destroy
the independent spirit of the Catalan race. For the first time in
Spain's history, therefore, the unity of the realm was no longer
personal and dynastic, but constitutional and administrative.
The Cortes became an assembly of representatives from each
province, with no power to defy the crown, and the Council of
Castile was established, as Olivares had once dreamed, as the
controlling body within Spain.

Philip V, for all his good qualities, had not been trained to
direct affairs of state: indeed, his education had encouraged a
quite different quality. 'Younger brother of a violent and
excitable prince', wrote Saint-Simon, 'he was bred up in a
submission that was necessary for the repose of the royal family.'
In Spain he revealed his trait by his emotional dependence upon
masterful women, a dependence so great that whenever he was
separated from his wife he fell into a torpor of inactivity and
indecision. While Marie Louise lived, Philip was dominated by
her, while she in turn was generally open to influence from
France. Galling though it was to Spanish pride, the chief posts
went to Orry and his countrymen, who tightened up the
administration and secured many economies in the treasury.

In 1714, however, Philip married Elizabeth Farnese of Parma.
Reputed to be docile and amenable to French direction, she took
Philip by storm and expelled the French from the court.
Thereafter Spanish policy, temporarily diverted from subservi-
ence to France, was directed once again to the pursuit of power in
Italy, where Elizabeth looked to establish her children's fortunes.
The prospect of peace and retrenchment proferred by the terms
of Utrecht thus soon proved illusory.

── V ──

THE UNITED PROVINCES

THE RISE OF THE DUTCH REPUBLIC

The Eighty Years War and the Truce of 1609

The conflict between Spain and the United Provinces which dominated European affairs in the early seventeenth century (see above p. 113–29) was the second half of the Eighty Years War, the war of independence which the Dutch dated from the execution in 1568 of two famous Netherlanders, Egmont and Hoorn, to the peace settlement at Münster in 1648.

In the beginning all seventeen provinces of the Spanish Netherlands had risen in protest at the destruction of their ancient liberties by Philip II. Essentially a conservative reaction, doomed to failure so long as it sought to restore the customs of a day that could never return, the movement was then revolutionised by the irruption of Calvinism in the northern provinces. The Calvinists were few in number but they seized positions of authority, and, broadly speaking, it was they who ensured by the uncompromising determination of their resolve to fight, that the war was fought to the bitter end. The southern provinces, embarrassed by the religious and political radicalism of the north, eventually compromised with Spain and sank into obscurity. The northern provinces, banded together in the Union of Utrecht, renounced Spain altogether and rose to the rank of a first-class power.

The Union of Utrecht had been forged under the pressure of war. It was not a natural union of provinces based on ethnic or economic foundations, but the fortuitous combination of seven states prepared to accept the leadership of William the Silent and

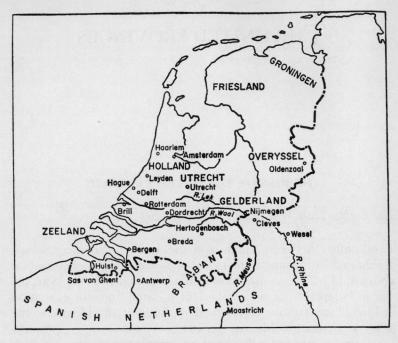

Map 7   The Rise of the Dutch Republic

to subordinate their private interests in the common struggle for
survival against Spain. Individually, the states were very
different in character. Friesland and Groningen were maritime
provinces governed by an assembly of free peasantry; Overijssel
and Gelderland, very similar to their neighbours in Germany,
were continental in outlook, dominated by the nobles and their
semi-feudal followers; Utrecht was formerly a bishopric. Far
different were Holland and Zeeland, where lay the real power
and prosperity of the Dutch Republic. Here the nobility had been
overwhelmed by a wealthy merchant class, and townsmen
outnumbered country-dwellers by two to one. The war with
Spain had stimulated the economy of both these provinces, (see
below, p. 241–8) and in the great towns of Haarlem, Dordrecht,
Delft, Leyden, Rotterdam and Amsterdam, a commercial
oligarchy controlled local government and selected from its own
class the representatives to the Estates of Holland, and to the
States-General of the Union.

Long before the revolt the practice of oligarchy had become almost universal in Holland. In 1445, for example, the charter granted to Delft had allowed the 'wise and rich' citizens to choose forty, 'the wisest and richest, most honourable, notable and peaceful', from whom the duke selected the regents of the town. It was to defend their monopoly of power that the urban patriciate, the regent class, had rebelled against Philip II, and the only change brought about was that, within this closed circle, the sovereign was removed while the urban patriciate consolidated its position.

The burghers were extremely fortunate in this, for rebellion breeds a ferment of ideas, unleashing new social forces, and it is rare that one class, and a small one at that, predominates both before and after a successful revolt. The greatest danger had come from the growth of Calvinism which, organised on democratic lines, won the support of the discontented and unfranchised, who discovered in it a path to salvation and an opportunity for political gain. Though Calvinist regents took the place of Catholics in the towns which fell to Calvinist troops, the new officials came from the same group of families as the old, and their aims were identical: opposed to the intolerance of the ministers, and hostile to the democratic and radical ideas of the Calvinist congregations, they sought to retain the inviolability of their class. By this astute conversion they preserved their monopoly of power.

Calvinism was a vital factor, but not the only one, in the success of the Dutch rebels. At critical moments in the war the natural lines of defence afforded by the waterways of the Rhine delta proved to be essential to Dutch survival, and throughout the period the growing strength of the Dutch economy (see below, p. 241–8) reinforced the war effort. On the other hand it is clear that Philip II of Spain contributed to his own defeat by his involvement in wars with the Turks, the French and the English which, from 1587–8, for example, and again from 1590–2, allowed the Dutch desperately-needed opportunities for recuperation and consolidation.

The role of the House of Orange was also an important factor, and caught the imagination of the people. William the Silent had been the hero of the revolt; Maurice of Nassau, his son, and William Louis, his nephew, added to the family's reputation by the skill which they displayed in the war against Spain. Both Maurice and William Louis planned their manoeuvres with the aid of lead soldiers, trained their men to dig their own positions, and rehearsed them in mock battles during the winter months. In addition to studying Roman methods of warfare, they paid great attention to the inventions of their own day. Maurice, perhaps the first general to use a telescope to study his enemy's position, equipped his cavalry with firearms in place of the lance, introduced the hand grenade, and employed the mathematician Stevin to make surveys for his fortifications. Brilliant in the theory of war, he excelled in action and his routing of the Spaniards at Turnhout (1597) and Nieuport (1600) won him recognition as one of the greatest soldiers of his age.

In order to secure unity of action, William the Silent had been appointed captain-general of the Republic's army, and stadtholder[1] in each of the separate provinces. Maurice succeeded him as captain-general and was elected stadtholder in five of the provinces, while William Louis held the other two. One man largely responsible for this was Jan van Oldenbarneveldt, the Advocate of Holland. Although the regent class regarded with some suspicion the concentration of military power in the hands of one noble family, Oldenbarneveldt persuaded his fellow regents that this was necessary for the conduct of the war. Even more important was his skill in ensuring that the separate provinces of the Union of Utrecht maintained their unity. The federal assembly of the United Provinces, the States-General, was not a sovereign body. The deputies were not free agents but merely the spokesmen of their provinces, and their unanimity was necessary before any action could be authorised. This situation, entailing as it did the constant reference by deputies to their local Estates, could have led to paralysis in the administration; in fact, the tradition of unanimity, observed at all levels of the government, had given rise to another tradition by which the dissentient voices to a majority decision were won over by the chairman of each committee or assembly. Moreover as Holland contributed more than half of the Republic's income, and most of its navy, her

---

[1] Stadtholders had formerly been the representatives of the crown in each province, responsible for defence and good order. After 1579 their office was retained along with its traditional dignity and prestige, but the appointment was controlled by the Estates.

policies were frequently adopted by the other provinces. In these circumstances an able administrator like Oldenbarneveldt, well skilled in manipulating his fellow regents, could, by placing his allies in positions of importance, secure a measure of uniformity in the policy of the Estates of Holland, and subsequently persuade the delegates to the States-General to follow Holland's lead.

By the early years of the seventeenth century a form of military stalemate had emerged. Maurice had won control of all land north of the river line and, by the capture of Breda in 1590, was well placed to invade Brabant and Flanders, but his troops made no headway against the Army of Flanders after the appointment of its new commander, Spinola, in 1603. It was clear, moreover, that the Catholic population of the southern provinces was not prepared to welcome the Dutch Calvinists as liberators. Spinola for his part launched several counter-attacks into Gelderland but achieved no lasting gains. In 1607 the Spanish government defaulted on its debt while the Estates-General calculated that its own debt was mounting by 200,000 florins a month.

A truce had become necessary for both sides. Oldenbarneveldt, despite the reluctance of the military and the opposition of the Calvinists and those merchants lucky enough to be making a profit out of the war, persuaded the States-General to negotiate. The terms secured in the Twelve Years Truce of 1609 demonstrated the weakness of Spain and the wisdom of Oldenbarneveldt's decision. The Spanish government had, for the period of the truce, to treat the United Provinces as an independent state, it was unable to secure guarantees of toleration for the Catholics still living in great number in the northern provinces and it failed to persuade the Dutch to recognise its claim to a commercial monopoly throughout its Far Eastern empire.

The Commercial Foundations of Dutch Power

The commercial supremacy which the Dutch achieved in Europe owed much to the frugality and perseverance of their people, for their country was a small one, with a small population, lacking natural resources.[2] 'Whence do the merchants' profits come

---

[2] The population of the Provinces was about 2,500,000 compared with 4,500,000 in England and 16,500,000 in France.

except from his own diligence and industry?' wrote Calvin, and the habit of thrift, no doubt encouraged by the spread of Calvinism, came naturally to a race which waged a continuous struggle for survival. High tides threatened to breach the dykes and to inundate the polders; storms and pirates took their toll of the herring fleets and merchantmen, and the Spaniards endangered their political liberties for more than eighty years. Nothing came easily for the Dutch; their wealth was achieved by their own labour, by dint of persistent effort and careful husbandry.

The enterprise, inventions and capacity for hard work which characterised the Dutch nation were evident from the earliest days in the way they set about the exploitations of their own land. Between 1590 and 1640 over 200,000 acres were reclaimed from the sea, an operation involving technical ingenuity and vast resources of capital. Having recovered the land they had then to render it fertile, and since it was too precious to lie fallow every third year, as in the rest of Europe, the Dutch invented methods of fertilising the soil and introduced new crops — grasses, turnips, hops and flax — which restored nitrogen to the soil.

A similar combination of thrift, inventiveness and energy was demonstrated by the growth of the fishing industry. From June to December, the Dutch followed the herring shoals along the English coast from Shetland to the Thames Estuary. Recognising that the herring lived near the surface in order to feed upon the plankton, they invented a drift net 107 metres long which they towed at night, when the luminous surface shoals were easily detectable. In addition they designed a new type of boat, the *buizen* or *busses*, which revolutionised the industry. Unlike the open boats they replaced, the *buizen* were decked vessels of up to 100 tonnes carrying coopers and salters, so that the catch could be processed at sea and exported immediately the fleets returned to port. By the time of the Twelve Years Truce, nearly a thousand *buizen* were at work, producing over 300,000 tonnes of salted herrings annually, more than enough to justify the States-General's reference to the North Sea as, 'one of the most important mines of the United Provinces'. It was the experience and the profits derived from the herring fisheries which stimulated the art of shipbuilding and made possible the beginning of the coastal trade.

Unlike the merchants of Flanders and Brabant, however, whose industrial hinterland and long-established fairs allowed them to wait for trade to come to them, those of Holland and Zeeland had to sail out on their own initiative to find cargoes to carry — even those belonging to the enemy — and to undercut their competitors' prices. This they did by underpaying their crews, by borrowing money cheaply on the Antwerp Bourse — later, from the Bank of Amsterdam — and by stringent economy in shipbuilding. Bulk purchases of timber were made; fir was used whenever possible, in place of oak; and the shipyards were equipped with wind-driven sawmills and other labour-saving devices. The Dutch also designed a new type of freight carrier, the *fluyt*, which was virtually a long floating container with enormous holds. Its great length, often six times its beam, created longitudinal stress, but this was compensated for at the expense of the crew's quarters by reducing the superstructure fore and aft. Each *fluyt* was designed for its appropriate trade. Shallow drafts were needed for the silted estuaries of the Baltic, deeper drafts for the Atlantic, and the holds were specially modified for the timber and grain trades.

The energy and courage they displayed in the war with Spain appeared also in their search for markets and commissions; it was the spirit recalled by Joost van den Vondel, the poet of Dutch expansion.

'Wherever profit leads us, to every sea and shore
For love of gain, the wide world's harbours we explore.'

The first area to attract Dutch attention was the Baltic, where the Hanseatic League had forfeited its monopoly of the carrying trade as it lost its cohesion, its members preferring to exploit the short-term advantages of trading independently. The Dutch began in a humble way as contractors for the League and ended by taking over most of the grain trade from Poland, which became the staple of their commerce. In addition they acquired a major share of the valuable exports of the forest regions — amber, furs, wax, potash and the indispensable naval stores of pitch, hemp and timber. As a result the records of the Danish Sound dues, recording the payments made by ships passing in and out of the Baltic, revealed an increase in the annual number of Dutch payments from 1300 in 1500 to 5000 in 1600. Moreover, the average tonnage of each ship had doubled.

From the Baltic the Dutch swept down along the Atlantic coast, and, despite the long years of warfare with Spain, the Atlantic trade never slackened. Spain could not do without grain, fish, metal goods and textiles for herself and her colonies. She also needed timber for her oceanic fleets. There was oak in the interior but it was difficult to transport it to the coast and the expanding iron industry at Vizcaya competed with the shipbuilding yards of Bilbao for what was available. From 1570, therefore, Baltic timber was imported. In return the Iberian merchants needed Dutch vessels to transport Castilian wool and soap to the textile manufacturers of England and Netherlands, salt from Setubal to the Dutch fisheries, and fruits from the Mediterranean, wines from Seville and the Canaries, spices from India and silver from America to the markets of northern Europe. In addition, shortages of raw materials in the Mediterranean, and in particular a dearth of corn after a succession of bad harvests in the 1590s, gave the Dutch a golden opportunity to slip past Gibraltar and tap the rich markets of Barcelona, Marseilles, Naples and Leghorn. Their reputation as enemies of Spain, moreover, helped the Dutch to secure concessions from the Venetians and from the Ottoman Turks.

Trading profits were reinvested in the trading companies, the banks and the schemes for land reclamation rather than in industry, with the result that there was insufficient production at home to supply the export trade. There were, of course, particular cities specialising in industrial manufacture: Rotterdam refined sugar, Amsterdam produced silk, Delft became famous for its pottery, Leyden for woollens, Haarlem for linen, and the Republic generally for its printing, diamond cutting and the making of optical instruments. However, the Dutch differed from other countries since the hinterland of Germany provided what was, in effect, the equivalent of home production, as the English were compelled to recognise in 1668 when they modified their Navigation Acts accordingly.[3] Morever, Dutch wealth depended less on the sale of exports than on the transport of goods between other countries. Provided there was no lack of capital, such trade could continue indefinitely until challenged by another maritime power.

It was an important factor in the commercial success of the

[3] See below, p. 273.

Dutch that the extravagant models of noble households or princely courts, so alien to commercial virtues, were generally held in contempt by the families of the regent class, a point well made by a French observer, Jacques Savery. 'From the moment that a merchant in France has acquired great wealth in trade, his children, far from following him in the profession, on the contrary enter public office ... whereas in Holland the children of merchants ordinarily follow the profession and trade of their fathers. Since money is not withdrawn from trade but continues in it constantly from father to son and from family to family, as a result of the alliances which merchants make with one another, individual Dutch merchants can more easily undertake the Northern and Muscovy trades than individual French merchants can undertake them'.

It was also an advantage that the rise of Dutch commerce coincided with the decline of the south German cities and of the members of the Hanseatic League along the shores of the Baltic and the North Sea (see Chapter 1, p. 16). Above all, the ruin of Antwerp by the Eighty Years War, and in particular by the Dutch blockade of the Scheldt, not only removed a powerful rival but led to the emigration of thousands of skilled artisans, merchants and financiers into Holland. Indeed, half of the original capital of the Bank of Amsterdam was supplied by *emigrés* from the southern provinces.

At Antwerp, in the great days before the revolt, the merchants had inscribed above the entrance to the Bourse the motto *Ad usum mercatorum cuiusque gentis ac linguae*. A similar spirit informed the commerce of the United Provinces. Toleration was offered to men of all creeds and races who came to Holland on business, provided that they practised their religion in private; and Amsterdam, where 5,000 ships, half the entire marine of the United Provinces, found their home berths on the river Amstel, was especially famed for its freedom.

'God, God, the Lord of Amstel cried, hold every conscience free;
And Liberty ride, on Holland's tide, with billowing sails to sea,
And run our Amstel out and in; let freedom gird the bold,
And merchant in his counting house stand elbow deep in gold.'[4]

---

[4] Joost van den Vondel. Cf. the less enthusiastic couplet by Andrew Marvell:
    'Hence Amsterdam, Turk, Christian, Pagan, Jew,
    Staple of sects and mint of schisme grew.'

Toleration, despite occasional outbursts of protest from the strict Calvinist clergy, paid dividends, but it was not only freedom from persecution that the Dutch had to offer. In order to attract a flow of capital into the Republic and to encourage the agents of foreign firms to place their commissions there, the government left the bankers and merchants remarkably free of state control. The economy was sustained by, indeed depended upon, ruthless competition, and there was nowhere else in Europe where the principle of *laissez-faire* was so firmly established. In this commercial society, based on contract, commission and credit, the Bank of Amsterdam held a privileged position. As its deposits were guaranteed by the city council it attracted foreign investment on such a scale that it became the principal money market in Europe, and it served as a clearing house for bills of exchange, a centre of commerical intelligence and a source of cheap credit. Its loans, frequently advanced at less than 5 per cent, enabled the city to bear the heavy taxes imposed upon it by the States-General during the war, and the great trading companies to equip their fleets for operations around the globe.

Free of restriction and provided with a ready fund of capital, the city of Amsterdam was the ideal headquarters for the most recent venture of the Dutch which was the penetration of the Spanish-Portuguese empire. Though vastly less valuable to their economy than the herring fisheries and the Baltic trade, it had nonetheless caught the imagination of individual Dutch merchants, who by 1600 were to be found regularly sailing to the Far East. So great were the difficulties of raising sufficient capital to finance voyages lasting up to three years, and so great the danger of losing it, that Oldenbarneveldt persuaded the free-trading Dutch that the colonial trade was one area in which cut-throat competition and indiscriminate rivalry might be harmful. In 1602 the East India Company was founded with capital of 6.5 million florins.

The directors' aims were commercial rather than colonial, and their agents were ordered 'to keep in view the necessity of peaceful trade throughout Asia from which is derived the smoke in the kitchens here at home'. Nevertheless, like its English counterpart, the company was compelled to defend itself against both European rivals and native rulers; and the ambitions of its more vigorous servants could only be fulfilled by military actions.

One of the greatest of these servants was Jan Pieterszoon Coen who believed that the greatest profits were to be made not by importing silks and spices into Europe but by monopolising the carrying trade of the Indian Ocean and the South China Sea. It was an ambitious undertaking, requiring more ships and bases than the Dutch then possessed, but in pursuit of his vision he expelled the English from Amboyna in 1623, when ten of their number were executed, and set up a base at Jakarta on the north coast of Java. He renamed it Batavia and died in its defence against the Javanese in 1629.

Of his successors, Anthony van Diemen (1636–45) captured Malacca and Formosa and attacked the Portuguese bases in India, but the cost of these operations reduced the Company's dividends by mid-century to a mere ten per cent. It was not until the end of the century (see below, pp. 283–4) that Coen's plans were fulfilled.

Paradoxically, the Dutch were on better commercial terms with their enemy Spain than with England their ally. The

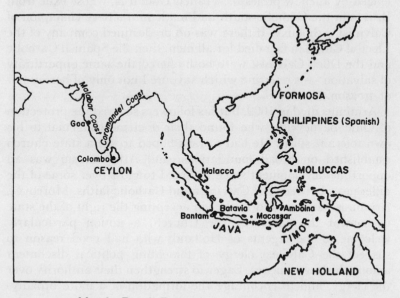

Map 8 Dutch Expansion in the Far East

English of course had Baltic, Levant and East India companies of their own, and complained of their own failure to take advantage of the annual migration of the herring shoals along their coast. In 1607, and again in 1616, James I denied the *buizen* access to his territorial waters, but the Dutch arrested the English ships sent to enforce the order, and continued to fish without interruption.

The Arminian Controversy and the Fall of Oldenbarneveldt

The peace established by the Truce of 1609 was immediately shattered by a theological controversy, the consequences of which were to bring about Oldenbarneveldt's death.

It all began in the university of Leyden where Arminius, a Calvinist theologian of remarkably liberal and humane views, questioned whether a God of love would predestine a man's soul to the horrors of hell. This, he argued, conflicted with the notion of a merciful God and paradoxically made God the author of sin.[5] He was mild, indeed hesitant, in publishing his opinions, and there was no opposition to his appointment to a chair of theology at Leyden in 1602; here, however, he was immediately challenged by a fellow professor, Francis Gomarus, whose exile from Bruges in the Catholic south had made him a fiery champion of Calvinist orthodoxy. If there was no predestined company of the Elect, if Christ in fact died for all men, then the Spanish Catholic and the Duch Calvinist were both offered the same opportunity of salvation — a doctrine which savoured not only of heresy but of treason.

Arminius died in 1609, but his followers secured the protection' of Oldenbarneveldt, who found their doctrine congenial to his own tolerant spirit. He had always hoped to see a state church established on broad foundations, and Arminianism was an opportune development since it served to gloss over some of the differences between the Calvinist and Catholic faiths. Moreover, Arminius had followed Luther in accepting the right of the state to control the affairs of the Church, a notion particularly welcome to the regents of Holland, who had good reason to suspect the Calvinist clergy of fomenting political discontent among the lower classes. Eager to strengthen their authority over the clergy, and to encourage the formation of a more broadly-

5 See Chapter 1, p. 84.

based church, the Estates óf Holland therefore gave approval to a formal declaration of Arminian doctrine, the *Remonstrance,* which had been published in 1610. Every Calvinist congregation became a centre of disaffection, from every pulpit Oldenbarneveldt was denounced, and, oblivious to the fact that the southern provinces had deliberately chosen to remain Catholic rather than ally with the Dutch, a war of liberation was demanded to release them from the yoke of the Spanish Inquisition. The Truce, so beneficial in its effect, was condemned as a compact with the forces of evil, then was extolled as a crusade untimely thwarted in its course by Arminian heretics in the pay of Spain.

It was unfortunate for Oldenbarneveldt that his critics lacked his clear vision of the realities of the situation. He saw that the German Protestant princes were unwilling to champion a Protestant crusade after Henry IV's death in 1610,[6] and insisted on remaining neutral throughout the Jülich-Cleves crisis. When Spinola seized the Rhineland fortress of Wesel, a Protestant stronghold near the Dutch frontier, Oldenbarneveldt allowed Maurice to take possession of other frontier posts in Cleves but not to engage Spinola in person lest the Truce with Spain be broken. His policy, however, only served to confirm the prejudiced views of the Counter-Remonstrants.

As the conflict expanded from the question of Free Will to embrace the issues of war and peace, the quick minds of the Amsterdam merchants awoke to the opportunity for profit which would be afforded by a renewal of hostility with Spain. The burghers of Amsterdam reserved their loyalty to the interests of commerce alone, and, despite their close links with the other regents of Holland, they had opposed the Truce of 1609. The commercial primacy of their city was established by the blockade of Antwerp during the Revolt, and, although the Truce left the Scheldt in Dutch hands, the merchants of Amsterdam were not yet satisfied that their rival was beyond recovery and had sought additional security by continuing the war. Moreover, with appetites enlarged by the success of the East India Company, they dreamed of the still greater profits to be expected from the

---

[6] See Chapter II, pp. 126–8, for an account of the German situation and of the Jülich-Cleves crisis.

creation of a West India Company to promote piracy and trade among the Spanish islands. Oldenbarneveldt had forestalled them by making peace with Spain, and there were many disgruntled burghers who chose to believe that the Advocate did not want to see a rival to the East India Company, with which he was closely connected. As a result, the city of Amsterdam openly came to the support of the Counter-Remonstrants by demanding the dismissal of Oldenbarneveldt and an end to the Truce.

The crisis produced by the Arminian controversy was too good an opportunity for Maurice of Nassau to miss. He had always valued the services of Oldenbarneveldt in the war and had no personal grudge against him but he had not been enthusiastic for the Truce and he was eager to fulfil a lifetime's ambition of leading a victorious army into Flanders and Brabant.

Indifferent to the theological subtleties of Gomarus, disdainful of the profit-hungry merchants of Amsterdam, Maurice realised their value to himself as enemies of the Advocate. To their side he added the weight of his own authority and the support of the petty nobility from the inland provinces who led his army. In all, it was a strange company which banded together in defence of predestination.

Oldenbarneveldt was outnumbered in the States-General by enemies who extolled the House of Orange as the sole guardian of true religion within the provinces. In Holland, however, despite opposition from Amsterdam, he retained his supremacy and at his suggestion the Estates, in 1616, gave authority to individual towns to counter any threat to law and order by raising their own troops. These *Waardgelders* were to swear allegiance to the town which recruited them but it was widely believed that Oldenbarneveldt had ordered them to obey the orders of the Estates, if necessary, against those of the States-General and of Maurice.

Whatever Oldenbarneveldt's private intentions, the levying of the *Waardgelders* was in itself a challenge to Maurice's authority which he could not ignore. In September 1617 he marched through Gelderland and Overijssel, provinces which traditionally were jealous of Holland's predominance in the Union. Each town in turn made open declarations of loyalty to him, and dismissed all regents suspected of Arminianism. In August 1618 his supporters put a resolution before the States-General for the disbanding of local levies, and the regents of Holland who had challenged Maurice's authority were removed from office. Oldenbarneveldt was taken prisoner.

So far the *coup d'état* had been bloodless, and socially it changed nothing. Maurice was not the enemy of the regents as a class: he wanted to make them subservient to his direction, not to destroy their privileged position. Just as Catholics had been replaced by Calvinists during the Revolt, so the supporters of Arminius and Oldenbarneveldt were removed to make way for others more sympathetic to the *Counter-Remonstrance* and to Maurice himself; but new and old were of the same class as before. The high hopes of the Calvinist congregations for innovations in the urban constitutions were disappointed. They were allowed, however, to summon a national synod at Dordrecht in 1618 to draw up a new confession of faith from which all taint of Arminianism was removed, and to secure the dismissal of all Arminian clergy from their livings or university posts.

Oldenbarneveldt was brought to trial and condemned for raising the *Waardgelders* without proper authority. It would no doubt have been dangerous to leave so powerful an opponent alive in prison but it is probable that Maurice desired not his death but his submission. Oldenbarneveldt for his part refused to do anything that might be interpreted as an admission of guilt, and rather than consent to Maurice's triumph he chose death by execution.

Throughout the Truce the Dutch had maintained close contact with the enemies of the Habsburgs throughout Europe, and had entered into agreements with the Elector Palatine and the Evangelical Union and with the Protestant leaders in Bohemia and Austria. In the event, when the crisis broke in the Empire the Dutch were so torn apart by their own internal crisis that they were unable to supply the troops and the diplomatic support on which the Bohemian rebels and the Elector Palatine had implicitly relied (see p. 134). It was indeed ironical that the efforts devoted to the destruction of Oldenbarneveldt, one of the heroes of the war with Spain, should thus have afforded Spain and her allies the opportunity to strengthen their position in the Empire and especially in the Rhineland. In March 1621 the arrival at The Hague of the defeated Elector Palatine and his wife, the Winter Queen of Bohemia, brought home to the Dutch the consequences of the opportunity they had let slip. It also imparted a new degree of fervour to the determination of all the members of the States-General to renew the war under Maurice's leadership when the Truce expired a few months later.

War with Spain 1621-48

Maurice, who had found the years of peace so irksome, was eager to achieve fresh triumphs, planning to overrun the Spanish Netherlands and to restore the Elector Frederick to his Palatinate. It was a personal tragedy for him, and very nearly a national disaster for the Dutch, that his ambitions were rudely checked by Spinola. The Spanish commander had worked fifteen hours a day throughout the Truce to prepare his army for the recovery of the northern provinces, and by his intervention in the German conflict he had gained control of the Rhineland. In 1622 it was he, not Maurice, who seized the initiative by attacking Bergen-op-Zoom, and when the town was finally relieved, renewed his offensive in 1624 by laying siege to the key city of Breda.

Maurice was dying as the siege began, and his immediate concern was to establish the succession of Frederick Henry, his half-brother, to his titles and position in the United Provinces. Unlike Maurice, Frederick Henry had few enemies. After the *coup* of 1619 he had shown sympathy for the defeated party, withdrawing from public life rather than oppose Maurice to whom he was devoted, and his accession was therefore expected to inaugurate a period of greater toleration. Moreover, as the last of William the Silent's sons, he was assured of undivided loyalty from the supporters of his House. His marriage to Amalia von Solms enhanced his popularity, and her buxom charms appeared to even better effect through her position as maid of honour to the most popular refugee in the United Provinces, the Elector Palatine's wife.

Frederick Henry was unable to relieve Breda, which fell to Spinola in June 1625, but he prevented the Spaniards from advancing north and by skilful deployment along the eastern frontier he regained the initiative. Morever, by the end of the year, the Dutch had mobilised a powerful combination to threaten the Habsburg position in Europe. As a result of negotiations at The Hague the Dutch brought England and Denmark in alliance and agreed to furnish 50,000 florins a month to maintain 30,000 infantry and 8,000 calvalry in north Germany. The object of the alliance was to liberate not only the Rhineland but also Bohemia, and to destroy the power of Habsburgs in Europe (see Chapter II, pp. 141–2).

The German campaigns failed to achieve their purpose. The Spanish counter-attack on the other hand, brought Habsburg troops to the shores of the Baltic, and it was only the intervention of Gustavus Adolphus of Sweden (see p. 148) which saved the life-line of the Dutch economy, the trade between Amsterdam and Danzig.

Within the Netherlands, Frederick Henry strengthened and extended his military position. Oldenzaal fell to him in 1626 and by 1629 he had not only recovered Wesel, the Rhineland fortress lost to Spain in 1614 (see p. 127) but had also taken s'Hertogenbosch, one of the most important cities of Brabant.

The inhabitants of the southern provinces were so demoralised by their government's failure to defend them that they considered uniting with the Dutch. Negotiations were in fact begun, only to be cut short by news of the harsh treatment received by the Catholics in Hertogenbosch. A Spanish official in Brussels noted, 'If the Prince of Orange and the rebels were not kept by their fanatical intolerance from granting liberty of worship and from guaranteeing churches and Church property to the priesthood, then a union of the loyal provinces with those of the North could not be prevented.' As in 1576,[7] the hatred between Calvinist and Catholic proved an insurmountable obstacle to the unification of the Netherlands.

It did not, however, prevent the defection of the leading Flemish noble, van der Bergh, when in 1631 he was replaced as commander-in-chief by a Spaniard. In 1632 he joined Frederick Henry in a successful assault upon Maastricht but his appeal to his countrymen to rise in revolt had no effect. The Spanish government in the Netherlands nonetheless recognised the danger and attempted to placate public opinion by summoning the States-General of the southern provinces. Its members, however, demanded that peace negotiations be opened with the Dutch.

Meanwhile, overseas the Dutch had achieved considerable success. In 1621 a group of Amsterdam merchants, many of them

[7] The occasion of the Pacification of Ghent.

emigrés from the south, had established a West India Company which, although it entertained aspirations for the colonisation of north America, was essentially a practical venture to operate in the West Indies. It had won the approval of the States-General because its military enterprises, designed to intercept the flow of bullion from America to Spain, were of strategic value; and the States-General agreed to provide a fleet of twenty warships to protect the company in its operations.

Piet Heyn, one of the most colourful rogues in the Caribbean, brought off a spectular coup in 1624 by seizing Bahia, capital of Brazil. The surprising thing was not the ease of Heyn's victory but the unusual speed with which the Spanish government reacted;[8] within ten months a relief force, 12,000 strong, took the Dutch unawares and compelled them to surrender. The failure of its first great venture almost reduced the company to bankruptcy, but its agents excelled at privateering and so long as there was plunder to be seized the directors were able to pay rich dividends. In 1628, for example, Heyn took captive the entire Spanish silver fleet in Matanzas Bay (Cuba), an occasion which his employers celebrated by declaring a dividend of 50 per cent. The profits derived from this and similar exploits enabled the company to equip an expeditionary force of 8000 men, to be transported across the Atlantic in 65 ships; a military venture far greater than anything ever attempted by the East India Company. Their objective was Recife in Pernambuco,[9] centre of the richest sugar-producing region in America. Recife fell easily, but its capture was of no value without the sugar plantations of the hinterland, and for six years a bitter conflict was waged against the Portuguese settlers who defended their estates with great determination.

The growing cost of the war in Pernambuco which destroyed the profits of the West India Company, and the growing success of Spain's commerce-raiders and privateers based at Dunkirk — which from 1626–34 took 1500 Dutch craft and sank 330 for the loss of only 120 — made the States-General of the United Provinces receptive to the idea, proposed by the States-General of the southern provinces, of a peace settlement. The Spanish

---

[8] Until 1640 in effect, though officially until 1668, Spain administered the Portuguese empire.

[9] At the present time Recife itself is also called Pernambuco.

government too was ready to end the war, but negotiations foundered over the rights of Roman Catholics in the Dutch provinces and a demand by the Dutch that Philip IV assist them in Pernambuco, regardless of the fact that this would have provoked rebellion against him in Portugal.

In the event Olivares abandoned the attempt to secure peace and chose to stake everything on the despatch of yet another army to the Netherlands. The arrival in Brussels of the Cardinal-Infant Ferdinand, fresh from his victory at Nördlingen (see p. 154), caused great alarm in the United Provinces and strengthened the hand of Frederick Henry who had been advocating an alliance with France. There were personal as well as strategic reasons for this since his mother, Louise de Coligny, had brought him up as a Frenchman in all but name, but a Catholic monarchy and a Calvinist republic were strange companions and the Dutch were suspicious of his plan until Ferdinand's arrival in Brussels in 1635.

In the event it was not so much the French alliance which saved the United Provinces as the fact that France, for reasons of her own, declared war on Spain, making it thereafter almost impossible for the Spanish government to preserve its lines of communications. In 1636, moreover, Ferdinand was required to direct his troops, not against the Dutch, but into northern France (see p. 202), and from that moment it seems that the Dutch success was assured.

Frederick Henry established his reputation in Europe, and restored confidence in his leadership at home by the brilliant recovery of Breda in 1636; and, three years later, the Dutch won a momentous victory over the Spanish navy at the Battle of the Downs.

Although Frederick Henry enjoyed, in addition to his other offices, the title of admiral-general, the fleets of Holland and Zeeland were commanded in fact by Maerten Tromp, a man of vast naval experience. In his youth he had twice been captured by pirates and made to serve in their ships, and later he had fought the privateers of Dunkirk for control of the North Sea. He left the sea in 1634, intending to enter the church, but so great was his reputation that the Dutch recalled him to introduce radical reforms in their navy. His efforts were spectacularly rewarded in the autumn of 1639. The fall of Breisach in the previous year had cut the overland route from Milan to Brussels, and the Spaniards, in their desperate need to reinforce their garrisons in the Netherlands with both men and bullion, were compelled to make the attempt by sea. An armada of 75 sail, commanded by Oquenda, left Corunna to sail up the Channel, just as another ill-fated armada had sailed against England in 1588. Tromp had received intelligence of the Spanish plan, but when he encountered the fleet off Beachy Head he had only 13 ships with him. Nevertheless, he attacked with such skill and vigour that Oquenda, for all his numerical superiority, hastily sought the protection of neutral waters by taking shelter in the Downs. For the hard-pressed Charles I of England this was an opportunity not to be wasted: demanding £100,000 from Oquenda as the price of English protection, he sent a squadron to prevent a Dutch invasion of his territorial waters. Tromp patrolled outside the Downs with a fleet that daily increased in size until, after a month of waiting, he decided to ignore English neutrality. Taking advantage of a sea mist on the morning of October 24th, he fell upon the Spanish fleet with such devastating effect that the Dutch broadsides destroyed all but seventeen of the enemy, leaving the English squadron, covered with ignominy, disconsolately protecting the charred remnants of the Spanish navy.

Spain never recovered from the destruction of her naval power in the Downs, and the growing vitality of the French armies in Europe made it impossible for her to redeem her prestige on land. As a result, a strong party began to form among the regents of Holland demanding an end to the war on the grounds that Spain no longer endangered the Republic's security. Indeed, the more far-sighted of them interpreted the French triumph at Rocroi (1643) as proof that their ally had replaced their enemy as the strongest military power in western Europe. Increasingly their suspicions were directed against Frederick Henry, the man who had insisted on the French alliance and who, patently, would derive no benefit from peace with Spain. Once again a conflict broke out between the regents of Holland and the House of Orange.

Frederick Henry had lost a great deal of his early popularity. Military success had induced an autocratic manner, and his temper and tact were the worse for recurrent attacks of gout and jaundice. Moreover, Amalia proved to be a restlessly ambitious woman, constantly urging her husband to strengthen his dynasty by the acquisition of greater authority and of more honourable titles. After his successful invasion of the southern provinces he had secured the consent of the States-General to an Act of Survivance, which declared that his offices were held, not by commission, but by hereditary right. This enabled him to assure the succession of his son to his own pre-eminent position as stadtholder in six of the seven provinces,[10] and as captain-general and admiral-general of the Union's forces. The marriage alliances, too, which he and Amalia arranged for their children were a further indication of their dynastic ambitions. In 1641 William was married to Mary, daughter of Charles I of England, and, a little later, Henrietta Louise to the Elector of Brandenburg.

The regents began to fear for their republican traditions and looked for an early end to the war to restrain the influence and prestige of their leader, who was then in resolute pursuit of the Spaniards. Opposition to his policy came to a head in 1645 when his capture of Hulst and Sas van Gent opened the way to Antwerp. This did not please the Dutch merchants at all, since, if Antwerp fell into their hands they would no longer be justified in blockading the Scheldt: rather than restore the old port and banking centre to its former eminence as a rival to Rotterdam and Amsterdam, they preferred to leave it derelict and abandoned under Spanish control. Worse still, Frederick Henry's dynastic alliances led him to propose Dutch intervention on the side of Charles I in the English Civil War. The regents refused to support his plans and succeeded in carrying the States-General with them. The cost of the war, the dangers of the French alliance, the open ambitions of their prince, the possible recovery of Antwerp and, finally, the proposal to support an Arminian monarch against Puritan rebels, were too great a price to pay for further successes against an enemy which no longer threatened their security.

One thing made possible a settlement with Spain, the death of Frederick Henry in 1647. As Spain was at last convinced that she had no hope of defeating the Dutch, and as her prime concern

---

[10] Friesland was held by a cousin

was to concentrate her forces against the French, she purchased
Dutch neutrality by accepting their demands at Münster (1648):

1 The United Provinces were recognised as independent;
2 The Scheldt remained closed, so that Antwerp remained
   permanently blockaded;
3 Dutch conquests in Flanders and Brabant, including Maastricht and s' Hertogenbosch, were confirmed, without any
   protection for their Roman Catholic populations;
4 Dutch conquests overseas were also confirmed along with
   their rights to trade freely in both the East and West Indies.

It was a triumphant conclusion to the Eighty Years War.

THE UNITED PROVINCES 1648–1714

Culture and Society in the Golden Age

The middle years of the seventeenth century constituted a golden
age for the Dutch. As the tension of the war years was eased by
victory the nation became a self-confident society in which
commercial success induced a mood of mellow affluence.

The freedom allowed to commercial activity brought other
freedoms in its wake. The Dutch presses were prolific; there were
forty in Amsterdam alone in 1664, and their freedom from
government control was a great attraction to writers wishing to
escape the censorship of their native country. Galileo, for
example, could publish his study of mechanics only in Holland,
and frequently the authors themselves followed their manu-
scripts. Descartes moved to Holland to publish his *Discours* and
the *Meditationes*, to be followed later by many fellow countrymen
including the Huguenots and the atheist *philosophe* Bayle. English
victims of the political crises between 1640 and 1690 fled to
Holland to await better times and it was fitting that John Locke
should follow in their tracks to write his *Letter on Toleration* in the
most tolerant society in Europe.

Refugees were welcomed for what they could contribute, but
the Dutch were not dependent on the stimulus of foreign imports,
least of all in the arts and sciences where they produced men of
international repute. The microscope of Leeuwenhoek and the
telescope of Lipperhey led to some of the most important

developments in seventeenth-century science, making possible the accurate calculations of men like Huygens, whose researches in astronomy and the study of light and motion ranked him with Galileo and Isaac Newton.[11] With the practical sense typical of his countrymen Huygens applied his inquiry into the calculus of probabilities to the study of annuities, and Simon Stevin, another great mathematician and the inventor of the decimal system, applied his talents to military engineering and book-keeping, assisting not only in the fortifications of the republic but in reforming the accounting system of the States-General. In the older disciplines of law and philosophy, the Dutch produced two men of outstanding merit; Grotius,[12] whose *De Belli et Pacis* proved to be one of the most influential studies of international law but whose political association with Oldenbarneveldt led to his own exile, and Spinoza, who rivalled the achievements of Descartes, Locke and Leibniz. The Dutch were less fortunate in literature since their authors were tied by their language to a public of less than two millions: whereas Spinoza and Grotius, writing in Latin, won international reputations, only the Dutch themselves could know of Jakob Cats, whose mastery of the language made him one of the most influential figures in Dutch literature until the twentieth centry; of Hooft the lyric poet; of Joost van den Vondel, whose poetry immortalised the daily life of his society and expressed the excitement of a nation conscious of its expansion overseas.

The greatest outburst of creative activity was in the arts and in a manner which accurately reflected the nature of Dutch society.[13] There was little sculpture, save for a few statues of soldiers and sailors, since the Calvinist aversion to graven images had struck root in the national consciousness. It was also a characteristic of the Calvinist to be uneasily self-conscious, even afraid, of the human body with which sculpture is concerned; the more so since sculpture, unlike painting, is pre-eminently an art of the public place. So too is architecture, which gave the Dutch a concrete image of their own ideals. It was essentially domestic.

[11] See Chapter I, p. 55.

[12] See Chapter I, pp. 21–2, 67–70, 78–9 for reference to Grotius and to Spinoza.

[13] The main concern here is to trace the relationship between Dutch art and Dutch society; see Chapter I, pp. 87–112, for a more general survey of European art and architecture.

Innate thrift, Calvinist reticence and the deliberate rejection of monarchy by the Dutch, made it inconceivable for the prosperous merchant to build himself a palace. Even the Mauritshuis at The Hague and the town hall at Amsterdam, where civic pride in any other country might well have found expression in a facade of Baroque magnificence, remained unpretentious but dignified, reflecting the solid, domestic character of the men who commissioned them.

It was above all in painting that the influence of the social environment was most apparent. The revolt had at one stroke removed the Catholic Church and the monarchy, the twin pillars of the artists' world: no longer able to make a living from aristocratic or clerical commissions, the artist had to paint for a very different market. The result, if initially disconcerting, was ultimately liberating, since the market he found was that same vigorous yet frugal, revolutionary yet respectable, middle-class community to which he too belonged. In working for his fellow citizens he was working for himself; he shared their limitations, he reflected their greatness. It was not a patrician aristocracy but an ever-growing body of merchants and farmers who thronged the markets to buy his works on a scale which took the foreigner by surprise: 'We arrived late at Rotterdam,' reported John Evelyn, the English diarist, 'where was their annual mart or fair, so furnished with pictures that I was amazed.'

But it was not a desire to invest mere surplus capital which prompted this unprecedented demand for pictures. It was an heroic age: no people could have been more self-consciously proud than the Dutch in their years of victory, or have taken more delight in their country and in themselves. Before their ardour cooled, before life was reduced once more to terms of profit and loss, they sought the artist to show them themselves, to immortalise the present. The great age of Holland thus found external expression in the great age of Dutch art.

Naturally the Dutch were practical and unsophisticated in their demands: they wanted a picture which would fit conveniently into their rooms; one which could easily be moved from room to room, from house to house, and as easily be sold again. Nor did they want to be perplexed. They wanted pictures which related to their own experience of life, with which they could feel at home, a realist portrayal of familiar scenes, a mirror to life. It was not commercial cynicism which led the Dutch artists to satisfy these demands, since these demands were also their own. Their work displayed a genuine and serene contentment with the ordinary world about them, a world of grey seas and flat fields, of domestic virtues and solid respectability. Never was the sober spectacle of daily life so lovingly portrayed nor such prosaic material illumined by such affection. In one respect only did the nature of the market, and the competition of several thousand painters, influence the work of individuals. Since it was intensely satisfying to the patrons of art to associate one artist with certain constant characteristics in his work, the artist himself, once established as a painter of landscapes or still life, was encouraged to specialise within that genre, to an unprecedented degree.[14]

'The result of these endless pursuits seemed a hitherto unknown revelation of microcosmic life in all its facets.[15] What saved the Dutch from becoming trivial, or stultified by the narrow limits of their specialisation was their intense love for what they painted and their superb gift of observation. The mirror they held up to life was astonishingly accurate, too much so for adherents of the French School whose views eventually triumphed in Holland. Lairesse, in his *Art of Painting*, published in Amsterdam in 1707, wrote scornfully, 'These painters imitate life just as they see it', whereas in his view derived from France, nature should be painted, not as it ordinarily appears, 'but as it ought to be in its greatest perfection'. But the painters of the Golden Age were not so artless as Lairesse implied. No matter how realist his school, the visual impression the artist received of the world he wished to portray could never be wholly comprehensive. He had to select, and by selection he reveals his individual genius.

This is immediately apparent in the work of Frans Hals. Portrait painting was a popular field of specialisation since it was a source of great pride to the middle-class citizen to see himself immortalised on canvas, especially in the company of his fellow citizens. The artist was merely required to make an accurate representation of his patrons, each one paying according to his

---

[14] Of the 3,000 known artists of seventeenth-century Holland, more than 600 are immediately recognisable by their characteristic treatment of a specialised genre.
[15] Professor R. Wittkower, p. 166, of the *New Cambridge Modern History vol. V*—see also, on the same page, a summary list of the varieties of genre painting.

position in the group, so that the occasion might be suitably preserved for posterity. Thus, for the most part, the group portraits are as sober, patient and unspectacular as the men who commissioned them. Yet it was exactly in this prosaic work that Hals, and men like him, discovered opportunities to release the imaginative forces of their genius. Hals's greatest talent was to catch the fleeting expression of his sitters—the artless informality concealing the most skilfully contrived effects; and by his mastery of grouping and movement to give coherence to the crowded scenes of archers and musketeers whose intense pride in their achievements in the war with Spain was celebrated in a succession of convivial portraits. His first great success was such a portrait, *The Officers of the Civic Guard at Haarlem*; in subsequent studies, however, the problem of transforming the solid groups of impassive faces into an exciting, satisfying whole began to tease his imagination so that finally the individual sitters were resolved into an organic unity by the invention of complex patterns of light and shadow. The result did not always please his patrons. Genius is not invariably recognised for what it is, its power to generalise can be disturbing, and the burghers were increasingly perplexed by the image which Hals offered them of themselves. In consequence they turned to other, lesser artists to satisfy their needs and Hals died comparatively poor.

Vermeer's genius, in contrast to Hals's, did not disturb but rather enhanced the expectations of the patron. The prosperous burgher was as eager to purchase paintings of his house, his rooms, his pots, pans and kitchen tables, as he was to secure a portrait of himself. These things were a source of pride, they evinced his attainment of comfortable prosperity, and above all they were an integral part of his life. Dutch standards were domestic; the Dutchman would not have recognised himself in any other setting. So too the miraculous cleanliness and tidiness which pervades these Dutch interiors were not the creation of the artists but accurate reflections of life itself. These houses were furnished as museums, indeed as temples since within these rooms were enshrined both the burgher's treasures and his heart: consequently they were scrubbed and polished to such a degree that no one dared to live in them. 'Even the kitchen was too fine a place for daily use; food was cooked there once a week; on the other days it was heated up in the small oven in the recess behind the kitchen where the family dwelt throughout the winter. When better weather returned, the family went to live outside on the pavement.'[16] In painting interiors such as these Vermeer gave to domesticity a universal significance. Unlike Hals, who appears to be excited by his subject, he seems detached. His paintings are still-lifes with human beings: the cook, caught in the act of pouring milk into a bowl, the lady seated at the virginals, are at one with the objects around them, not in the sense that they are lifeless, but that life itself has been momentarily suspended to permit its meaning to be interpreted with loving precision.

Vermeer developed a technique of floating on the paint so that no trace of brushwork betrays his hand. The surface is translucent, suffused with light, and, indeed, the treatment of light is a common factor in all the genres of Dutch painting. Light radiates from velvet drapes and warm brick, it floods their interiors and permeates their landscapes. No part of Europe, save East Anglia, possesses so much sky as the low-lying Netherlands, and the Dutch were the first to discover the beauty and the variety of its moods. This gave their landscapes a freshness of observation whose power to charm and to astonish is universal. In the canvasses of Albeit Cuyp the mood of perennial high summer, with contented cattle browsing in lush grass, is imparted by a golden glow, an effect he learned from the Frenchman Claude. With Van Goyen the horizon is set low, the river estuaries and mud flats merge in a distant haze, there to blend with the watery skies. More sombre, more consciously dramatic, were the landscapes of Jacob Van Ruisdael: the light gleams across the desolate dunes as the sun breaks fitfully through the cloud; it falls upon a clustered copse, exposing the twisted gnarls, making the shadowy paths mysterious. Ruisdael's love of light and shadow, the poetry he discovered in evening skies, lone trees and castle walls, evoked a romanticism alien to his age and his work was only fully appreciated by later generations.

It is the paradox of genius, and perhaps its explanation, that for all its universality it yet epitomises its own immediate environment. Though the artist never loses his community of interest with his neighbours, he discovers realities of which these neighbours are indistinctly aware. No one was more Dutch than

[16] Dr. D. G. Renier, *The Dutch Nation*, p.99.

Rembrandt; where he excelled was in his power to take everything that was so patently Dutch and to give it universal significance. His first success was a group study in 1632 of the Amsterdam Guild of Surgeons, *The Anatomy Lesson of Dr Tulp*, which was followed by a prosperous decade of fashionable portraiture. Like Hals, however, Rembrandt could not paint to a formula; what had once proved acceptable could not be mechanically repeated since his paintings were stepping stones in his continuous discovery of himself and of mankind. As this developed, the emotions which drove him became increasingly more powerful. In 1642 a company of local defence volunteers in Amsterdam commissioned a group portrait. The result, *The Company of Capt. Frans Banning Cocq*, better known as *The Night Watch*, was a work of tremendous tension and emotion. So overpowering is its effect that its modern custodians at the Ryksmuseum in Amsterdam found it too overwhelming when hanging in a small room and were compelled to set it apart on a separate wall in the largest hall of the gallery. The men who commissioned it were also disturbed since it showed them themselves in a relationship which they could not comprehend.

Commissions were less frequent after this, and until his death in 1669 Rembrandt became more or less dependent on his family. It was during these years, however, that he produced most of the work upon which his subsequent reputation rests, none more famous, and none more illustrative of his genius, than his studies of the life of Christ. In these the figures, the faces and the countryside are those he might have seen from his own doorstep, but their universal significance springs from the insight with which they are interpreted. No less vital a factor in the success of these studies was Rembrandt's integrity, a technical quality, a guarantee of craftsmanship as it were, and a moral sense which repudiated deception of any kind. No one has ever revealed himself with greater candour than did Rembrandt in the series of self-portraits which immortalise the separate moments of his life and which stand for all time among the most brilliant and most sensitive works of autobiography. Few have looked so directly and so honestly upon the figure of Christ. Baroque artists[17] presented a set of idealised concepts which had been adopted

---

[17] See Chapter I, pp. 102–12, on Baroque art.

almost as the official iconography of the Counter-Reformation; Rubens's *Descent from the Cross* in Antwerp Cathedral expresses and enhances the divinity of Christ by the portrayal of His physical perfection. Rembrandt reflects the Calvinist spirit of the northern provinces by insisting upon making his personal comment. For the first time since Giotto the common humanity of Christ and His disciples is emphasised, as for example in the etchings of the Crucifixion where the mood is one of individual human suffering. Sympathetic insight is thus matched with the uncompromising integrity of the Calvinist in a manner which is wholly Dutch.

The Regents and the House of Orange 1648–67

The death of Frederick Henry in 1647 had removed the one man capable of mobilising support for the war in the States-General. The new prince, William II, enjoyed nothing of his father's influence, other than the inheritance to his titles, and the peace party, led by Andreas Bicker, burgomaster of Amsterdam, carried the day.

Once peace had been established at Münster, William had to look to his own position. France was still at war with Spain and he listened eagerly to Mazarin's proposals for an alliance. Moreover, the execution in 1649 of his father-in-law, Charles I, prompted him to consider an attack on the regicide government in England. Bicker, however, countered his aims by calling for a reduction by two-thirds in military expenditure. 'There is no need to have a garrison in every town', wrote one pamphleteer, 'to pay salaries to military governors, colonels and innumerable other officers; it is unnecessary that the military should go about in clothes plastered with gold and silver while the common people have to eat dry bread.'

William retaliated by undertaking a tour of the chief cities of Holland, accompanied by over four hundred troops, in an attempt to intimidate the town councils into withdrawing their support for Bicker's proposals. His action deliberately paralleled that of Maurice in 1618,[18] but history did not repeat itself. The public was weary of war, there were few outside the prince's

[18] See above, p. 250.

entourage who stood to gain by its renewal and the prince's resolve to assist the Arminian Stuarts made him unpopular with the strict Calvinists. William was coldly received: a few of his more outspoken opponents were removed from office as a result of his visitation, but the demands for a reduction in military expenditure were not withdrawn. The tour ended in humiliation at Amsterdam, where Bicker closed the gates and denied William access to the city.

Since the threat of force had failed to have effect, William resorted to active violence by imprisoning at Loevestein six prominent members of the Holland Estates, and by ordering his nephew, the Stadtholder of Friesland, to seize Amsterdam. The attack was bungled, and Bicker seemed ready to conduct a civil war against the prince, but the regents were anxious to negotiate a settlement between them. In 1650 William released his prisoners from Loevestein, Bicker resigned his office in Amsterdam, and the Holland Estates agreed to modify their proposals for reducing the army.

William had won a respite but in November his efforts were dramatically nullified by his sudden death from smallpox. Though his widow was pregnant, there was no immediate heir to take up the Orange cause and the regents celebrated their good fortune by striking a medal inscribed: 'The last hour of the prince is the beginning of freedom.'

Because the Holland regents feared that the States-General might still contain too many adherents of the House of Orange they invited representatives of the Provinces to a Great Assembly in 1651. Their intention was to establish a new constitutional framework to enshrine the principles of republicanism, but they contented themselves finally by condemning William's activities over the past two years. The regents deposed by him were restored to office, and on the advice of a member who said, 'Let us not be so foolish as to hurt ourselves twice on the same stone', the post of captain-general was abolished. Furthermore, since the House of Orange had imposed its leadership by controlling the federal institutions of the Union of Utrecht, the regents affirmed that sovereignty resided with each individual province, and that each province was to be responsible for its own troops.

The principle of states sovereignty was a useful device to forestall any resumption of power by the House of Orange, but the necessity for securing the unanimous assent of seven sovereign states to each decision of the States-General would have led to anarchy had not the regent class of Holland succeeded in imposing their own direction over the republic's affairs; this they did by virtue of the commanding position enjoyed by Holland as the chief contributor to federal funds, and by securing the appointment of their own leader, Jan de Witt, as head of the federal administration.

Jan de Witt was an outstanding example of the best type of regent, devoted to the interests of his country and tireless in its service. His high forehead and long face, its length accentuated by the downward thrust of a powerful nose and chin, made him seem both restless and ascetic in comparison with the cheerfully complacent appearance of his fellow citizens. A man of simple tastes, he sought no private fortune from his public service, and foreigners were astonished to see him walking home through the streets of The Hague accompanied only by a servant carrying state papers in a cloth bag.

A superb civil servant, de Witt was also a skilled politician who directed the republic's affairs from the obscurity of a committee room by means of family connections and personal influence. He belonged by birth to the exclusive oligarchy of the regent class: his grandfather had represented Holland in the States-General; his father had served as pensionary of Dordrecht, and his fame as one of the Loevestein prisoners had eased the son's rise to power. In 1650, at the age of twenty-five, Jan de Witt was appointed pensionary of Dordrecht, and within three years had become grand pensionary of Holland. Subsequently, by his marriage to Wendela Bicker, he became associated with her uncles, Cornelis Bicker and Cornelis de Graeff, both prisoners with his father at Loevestein, who controlled the city council of Amsterdam. Such family ties assured de Witt of supremacy in Holland, but the regents of the other states, jealous of the sovereign powers assured to them by the Great Assembly of 1651, were as suspicious of the leadership of Holland as they had been of the House of Orange. De Witt overcame this by persuading the States-General to delegate much of its work to committees endowed with plenary powers. In these, surrounded only by the seven representatives of the separate provinces, de Witt's personal influence was exerted at its greatest. He overawed his colleagues by his extensive knowledge of the issues which they debated, he flattered their sense of importance in being at the centre of affairs, he exploited by his brilliant chairmanship the ancient tradition of arriving at unanimous conclusions, and, finally, when all else failed, he forced them to recognise that Holland's demands, backed by her financial contribution and her naval power, could not be resisted without dire consequences for the future of the Union as a whole. In the event, the republic, preserving the form of provincial separatism, was run as effectively as a centralised monarchy.

The charges of self-interest levied against the 'Loevestein faction' drew substance from the fact that de Witt tried to fill all positions of importance in the administration with his relatives and friends. This of course was true, but the sincerity of the charges could be discounted since they merely reflected the frustrated ambitions of men who themselves wanted to do the same thing. De Witt, moreover, sought power to benefit the republic as a whole, his policies being given public expression in 1661 by Pieter de la Court in *The True Interest of Holland*. Here, with the title displaying the author's naive belief that what was good for Holland was good for the United Provinces, de la Court provided a sober account of the principles which underlay de Witt's administration.

Hostility to the House of Orange pervaded the book. Its members were accused of gambling with the republic's security in order to further their dynastic ambition, and, heedless of the benefits to be derived from commercial expansion, of seeking to perpetuate their military power by denying the fruits of peace to their subjects. In contrast de la Court claimed that the regents encouraged commercial prosperity to everyone's advantage: 'The inhabitants under this free government hope by lawful means to acquire estates, to sit down peaceably and use their wealth as they please, without dreading that any indigent or wasteful Prince or his courtiers and gentry, who are generally as prodigal, necessitous and covetous as himself, should on any pretence whatsoever seize on the wealth of the subject.'

In the years immediately following de Witt's rise to power there was little to be feared from William's posthumous son, the future William III, but in 1654 the Holland Estates debarred him by an Act of Seclusion from succeeding to his father's appointments. Though de Witt had not prompted the Act, which has been passed more to appease Cromwell than to weaken the Orange family,[19] he issued a *Declaration in justification of the Act of Seclusion*, which rehearsed the main charges of the regents against the House of Orange. To ensure that the point was well taken he also prepared a more pithy version, the *Deduction*, for popular consumption, which reminded its reader: 'And have we not seen with our own eyes that the late deceased captain-general of the States endeavoured to surprise the capital and most powerful city of the land (Amsterdam) with those very arms which the States entrusted to him?'

The decisions of the Great Assembly about the organisation of the army undeniably led to a loss of efficiency, but the regents of Holland pretended that there was no need for concern since the navy was run in the same way, and the strength of Dutch naval power was universally accepted; but since Holland's own fleet, with squadrons from Zeeland and Friesland, was virtually the republic's fleet also, the analogy broke down. In the event, the provinces, even those with the most to fear from land attacks, failed to maintain effective military establishments, with disastrous results in 1672.[20] *The True Interest of Holland* was for once at variance with the policies of the regents, and de Witt, as the one man most able to centralise the administration of the republic, did little to improve the organisation of the army. This, of course, stemmed from his belief that it would never be employed: France and the Rhineland princes were his allies. England was the sole enemy.

The Anglo-Dutch Wars

'There is more to be gotten by us in a time of peace and good trading', wrote de la Court, 'than by war and the ruin of trade'; but though the regents pursued a policy of peace typified by this attitude, de Witt came to power at a time when the Dutch were at war with England. Memories of the Amboyna massacre and of Maerten Tromp's victory in the Downs still rankled in England, conspicuous examples of a long-standing conflict in which the English claimed the sovereignty of the Narrow Seas and the right

[19] See below, p. 272.   [20] See below, p. 276.

to free trade elsewhere, while the Dutch insisted on the doctrine of *mare liberum* in home waters and that of *mare clausum* throughout their commercial empire. It was the Commonwealth's Navigation Act of 1651 which finally brought about the war since it forbade the import of foreign goods unless carried in British ships or in those of the country of origin. This threatened the Dutch carrying trade so effectively that, as an act of defiance, the States-General sent Tromp to enforce Dutch freedom of navigation from Gibraltar to Denmark. When his fleet encountered an English force and refused to salute the flag, the war began.

The advantage lay with England. Between 1648 and 1651 the English had doubled the size of their fleet, whereas the Dutch had reduced theirs after making peace with Spain. Dutch shipping, moreover, had to run the gauntlet of English attacks in the Channel, or seek the stormy routes round Scotland and still risk an encounter in the North Sea. Tromp hoped to keep the sea open for merchantmen by inflicting a series of crippling defeats on the English fleet, but the sea battles, for all their drama, had little effect on the most serious aspect of the war. Whether Tromp won or lost, the lifeblood of the Dutch economy continued to be drained away by the daily loss of merchantmen. England was still primarily an agricultural country and could withstand the temporary dislocation of her foreign trade; not so the Dutch, who had everything to lose from warfare with a rival who could deny them access to the herring shoals and prohibit the passage of their transports through the Channel.

Tromp tried to save the day by a system of convoys, but the intransigent independence and ill-discipline of the civilian captains made convoy duty a nightmare, and a fruitless one since, when Monk or Blake attacked, the merchants scattered in a disastrous attempt to save their own cargoes, and thus delivered themselves into the enemy's hands. At the end of February 1653 Tromp fought a magnificent rearguard action from Portland Bill to Calais Roads in an effort to safeguard a homeward bound convoy of 150 ships, but on the third day his formation was broken and the battle lost. In June he lost again, at the Battle of the Gabbard, when his own naval captains abandoned him, half of them taking refuge in the Texel, the rest in the Maas. Though Monk pressed home his advantage by a blockade of the coast, Tromp ultimately succeeded in reuniting the two halves of his fleet, only to be defeated in August at Ter Heide where he himself was killed.

Such a succession of defeats brought discredit upon the new administration led by de Witt and the government's reputation fell as the price of corn soared on the Amsterdam exchange in 1652 and 1653. The interference with fishing and seaborne trade added to the number of unemployed, and although there were no specific 'Orange' solutions to any of these troubles the Orange party was able to make capital out of them. 'Responsibility for the disasters', de Witt wrote, 'is generally attributed to the bad conduct of affairs by the regents; certain men are fishing in the troubled waters and inspire the commonalty with the idea that an eminent chief is needed to save the country.' The only 'eminent chief' in 1653 was still a baby, but as there was no chance of winning victories de Witt sensibly appealed to Cromwell for peace. Indeed, the threat of an Orange revolt alarmed Cromwell nearly as much as it did the regents since the restoration of the House of Orange would have provided Charles II with an excellent base and willing allies. By harping on this fact de Witt finally secured terms which inflicted little lasting harm on the Dutch. By the Treaty of Westminster they agreed to recognise English sovereignty in the Narrow Seas, to pay for the privilege of fishing in English waters, to make compensation for the massacre at Amboyna and to deny assistance to Charles II.

One further clause, known as the Act of Seclusion, to debar all members of the House of Orange from holding the office of stadtholder or of captain-general, was demanded by Cromwell as a further precaution against an Orange restoration. De Witt convinced him that the clause would never secure the unanimous consent of the States-General, Cromwell agreed to withdraw it from the public treaty provided that de Witt secured its acceptance by the Holland Estates. This was finally done, in a secret session more as a means to end the war and return to trading than as a deliberate attack on the Orange party.

The peace did not last long: as an English hemp merchant remarked to Samuel Pepys, secretary of the Admiralty: 'the trade of the world is too little for us two; therefore one must down'. When the Duke of York, allowing his interests as a director of the Royal Africa Company to prompt his action as Lord High Admiral, sent a naval force to drive the Dutch from Goree, de

Witt swiftly despatched de Ruyter in pursuit. This encounter off
the African coast was the occasion for the renewal of war in 1665.
This time the Dutch were in a better state of preparation. De
Witt and his brother Cornelis had reorganised the Admiralty and
strengthened the navy, and though English public opinion was
jubilant at the news of war, Pepys confided his fears to his diary:
'We all seem to desire it [the war] as thinking ourselves to have
advantages at present over them; for my part I dread it.' In fact
the war began well for England. The Bishop of Münster invaded
Overijssel as Charles II's ally, and at Lowestoft in June 1665, the
Dutch commander Opdam, having held the weather-gauge for
two days to no advantage, lost it on the third, together with the
battle, his flagship and his life. The survivors were rallied by
Cornelis Tromp, who fought a skilful rearguard action to bring
sixty sail back to the Texel. Despite his youth, the government
rewarded him with the command of the fleet, but at this moment
de Ruyter returned from his successful mission to Goree and
superseded him. This caused much bitterness and resentment
though the two served together well enough in the famous
Four-Day Battle of June 1664.

By 1667 the Dutch were confident of victory but de Witt
desired to end the war quickly to restore the flow of peace-time
trade into Dutch harbours as well as to leave his country free to
face up to the implications of the French invasion of the Spanish
Netherlands (see p. 274). To achieve this he planned with de
Ruyter one of the most daring and effective naval *coups* of
European history. Since the English fleet was laid up at
Chatham, because Charles II had no money to put it to sea, de
Ruyter sailed up the Thames and the Medway to the dockyards,
where he held his position for two days and nights, destroying
much of the fleet and making off with its latest acquisition, the
Royal Charles. The humiliating effect of the raid on a public
demoralised by the great plague and the fire, and on a government already bankrupt, was wholly devastating. 'Thus in all
things,' wrote Pepys, 'in wisdom, courage, force, knowledge of
our own streams, and success, the Dutch have the best of us and
do end the war with victory on their side.' In the Treaty of Breda,
1667, de Witt wisely refrained from provoking the English by
imposing further humiliations, especially since he had an eye to
an alliance with them against Louis XIV. He accepted the right

of the English to a salute in the Channel; but in the important matter of the Navigation Act he won a vital modification by the recognition of Germany and the Spanish Netherlands as a sort of Dutch hinterland for the purpose of importing goods from there into England in Dutch ships.

The Triple Alliance and the French Invasion, 1667–72

De Witt's achievement in bringing the second Anglo-Dutch war to a successful conclusion in 1667 had been only one of his many services in the conduct of the Republic's foreign policies. The imperialist ambitions of Charles X of Sweden[22] had been as dangerous to the Dutch as the commercial rivalry of the English, since they threatened the Dutch monopoly of Baltic trade, the mainstay of the economy. On Charles X's invasion of Poland in 1655 de Witt remained unmoved by the fate of inland cities such as Cracow and Warsaw, but when Swedish troops laid siege to Danzig, a city significantly referred to by the Dutch as their 'breadbasket', he promptly despatched a squadron to its aid. His action served its purpose, though a more serious situation developed in 1659 when Charles inflicted a crippling defeat on the Danes and compelled them to deny passage through the Sound to ships of any country hostile to Sweden. When warfare broke out again between Charles and Denmark in 1660 de Witt sent a fleet to the Sound to enforce the Peace of Roeskilde, interpreted in a manner favourable to the Dutch, and was given diplomatic support by both England and France. In the final settlement, the Peace of Oliva, de Witt ensured that the Dutch were confirmed in their freedom of access to the Baltic.

In order to discourage Portuguese attacks on the West India Company in South America,[23] de Witt ordered a blockade of the Portuguese coast in 1657, but as nothing could save the Dutch in Brazil from ultimate ruin, he wisely came to terms in 1661. Though the treaty put a formal end to the company's activity in South America, it none the less made provision for Dutch merchants to trade freely in Portuguese territories, an agreement which in the long run was more profitable to the Dutch.

---

[22] See Chapter VIII, pp. 390–92, for an account of Charles X's Baltic campaigns.
[23] See above, p. 255, for a description of the West India Company's activities in South America.

Above all de Witt could rely on the friendship of Louis XIV, whose ambassador, d'Estrades, had orders to support the administration of the regents against the intrigues of the Orange party. Nevertheless, Louis's friendship could be embarrassing when it involved de Witt in his ambitions to seize possession of the Spanish Netherlands. *Gallicus amicus sed non vicinus* was no doubt a sound maxim for de Witt to adopt, but there was little he could do to apply it.

In the event he accepted an English proposal that Spain should be urged to agree to some of Louis' demands and thus to restore peace. With great reluctance he also accepted a further, and secret, proposal that if Louis should then be tempted to increase his demands, England and the United Provinces would stand together to oppose him. This agreement, later endorsed by Sweden, became known as the Triple Alliance (1668), and as Louis, for reasons of his own (see p. 337–8) made peace a few months later, it appeared to have achieved its intention.

De Witt had not sought to deny Louis XIV's claims upon the Spanish Netherlands, but only to moderate the extent of his demands. Nor was he prepared to abandon the French alliance for an English one: as he informed the English ambassador, 'the States-General would think it like to prove too sudden a change of all their interests, and that which would absolutely break them off from so constant a friend as France, to rely wholly upon so new and uncertain a friend as England had proved'.

De Witt was not alone in suspecting Charles II's intentions: Pomponne, Louis's foreign secretary, also had his doubts. 'I shall not say what intentions motivated England on this occasion, nor whether, at the time when she appeared to enter more deeply into the sentiments of the States-General and to second more sincerely their ardour for the Triple Alliance, she had in mind vengeance upon them or upon France.' There is no doubt that Charles II was seeking not only to placate his Parliament and perhaps to compel Louis to buy him out of the Triple Alliance, but also to embroil de Witt with Louis to the advantage of Charles's relatives, the House of Orange. It is significant that the secret clauses of the Alliance were discovered by French agents not at The Hague but in London, and it was this revelation which ruined Franco-Dutch relations. De Witt, in apologising to d'Estrades for his part in signing the Triple Alliance, had explained that his hand had been forced and that there was nothing in the treaty to give offence to Louis. His assurances were accepted until Louis discovered the full story, when, to Charles II's delight, the United Provinces, and de Witt in particular, became the principal object of Louis's hatred and indignation.

In these circumstances the celebrations marking the Peace of Aix-la-Chapelle rang hollow in de Witt's ears. His government commissioned a medal, 'After having made the laws secure, reformed religion, reconciled kings, maintained the freedom of the seas and established peace in Europe, the Council of the Netherlands has caused this medal to be struck.' It read ominously like an epitaph. From this moment, in fact, de Witt was engulfed by forces over which he had no control. He was reappointed as grand pensionary at twice his former salary but the bases of his power were weakening. Even in Amsterdam he could no longer secure the election of a friend as pensionary of the city since there were many there who opposed de Witt's attempt to preserve good terms with France. They feared that France might one day occupy Antwerp and restore it to its former power, and they were angered by the French tariffs of 1667 (see p. 321).

As de Witt became more isolated, popular support for the young Prince William was becoming more apparent, and de Witt's device of treating the boy as a 'child of state', in order to supervise his education, had only served to emphasise his special position. Though the Estates of Holland secured the acceptance of the other provinces to a Plan of Harmony to prevent a captain-general from holding administrative office, it was clear that agreements of this sort would have no effect if 'the public found it necessary to demand the strong government of a prince of Orange. The time was not long coming: in 1672 the French invaded the United Provinces.

Louis's act of vengeance for the secret clauses of the Triple Alliance had been well prepared. De Witt could not prevent the governments of England and Sweden selling out to France, and it was too late to organise an effective defence force after the years of provincial indifference and separatist control.

In a lightning attack, made easier by the abnormally low level of the Rhine, the French advanced to Utrecht and the Dutch could gain a respite only by flooding large areas south of the

Zuider Zee.

In the crisis all eyes turned to the young William III. In July the Estates of Holland appointed him Stadtholder, as did those of Zeeland, and within days the Estates-General conferred upon him the titles of Captain-General and Admiral-General. De Witt resigned his office in August, and it was while he was visiting his brother Cornelis, who had been arrested, that both men were seized by the Civic Guard of The Hague and torn to pieces in the street.

William III and Louis XIV

The shock of de Witt's murder steadied the Dutch. Nerved by the crisis and invigorated by the leadership of William III they rose to resist the French, whose army was held in check only by a few square miles of water. Luck favoured them with a mild winter, but it was their own determination in the spring which led them to recover Naarden and to strike at the long lines of communication which supplied the invading army. Spain and the Empire, moreover, declared themselves their allies, Cologne was invaded by both Imperialist and Dutch forces, and, in the Grand Alliance of The Hague, William revealed his diplomatic skill as the architect of the first great European coalition against Louis XIV. As far as the war on land was concerned the Dutch were safe.

At sea the Dutch faced the English in their third encounter of the century. Charles II had returned to the haven of French subsidies in 1670, and from that moment the English had revived their traditional disputes with the Dutch. In March 1672 they attacked a convoy homeward bound from Smyrna: in June they joined the French in an attack upon the Dutch coast. Though both these ventures failed, the Dutch were none the less in great danger and William III's first act was to effect a reconciliation between Cornelis Tromp and de Ruyter, the one a zealous Orangist, the other a friend of de Witt, in order to restore unity to the fleet. In the event the two rivals combined to defeat the English in a series of naval battles in 1673. Accordingly, since Charles II was bankrupt and the English Parliament was alarmed by the consequences of his alliance with Catholic France, the Dutch secured peace in 1674, when the Treaty of

Westminster virtually renewed the clauses decided at Breda in 1667.

William's resolution in prosecuting the war both with England and with France had not been anticipated by Charles II — nor for that matter by de Witt. Both had expected that William, in return for the triumph of the House of Orange, would make concessions to the House of Stuart. William, however, revealed a deep sense of patriotism. With Charles II he was content simply to force his withdrawal from the war: with Louis XIV he sought his defeat. This in the course of time became the overriding purpose of his life. Nature had equipped William for single-mindedness, compensating for the deformed back and for the body wracked by asthma, with an indomitable spirit which made him independent of the affection and support of others. Trained by the circumstances of his childhood to practise unnatural restraint, he remained ascetic and aloof, and in his unimaginative mind the simple concept of defeating Louis XIV became the all-consuming passion of his lifetime.

William's triumph at home, though accompanied by wide-spread rioting against the regents, did not result in victory for the lower classes who had traditionally identified their cause with that of the House of Orange. The Estates of Holland, 'so that the citizenry should not take it upon itself to restore order', invited William to 'change the laws', a request that he temporarily accept exceptional powers to alter the composition of the town councils of the state. Of about 400 hereditary councillors 160 were replaced. Many of the new appointments were regents who had been dismissed or excluded by de Witt, and many more were de Witt's own supporters who had hastened to acclaim William, believing that only the prince could save the regents from the lower classes, and all of them from the French. The traditional antagonism of the regents and the House of Orange was resolved in a new synthesis in which both sides at last recognised a cardinal principle of their conflict that whoever won or lost, no third party was to benefit.

William in fact acted as de Witt had done. Using his powers of patronage to fill key positions in the government, he built up a powerful following in Holland, and, in the States-General. Where de Witt had exploited Holland's overwhelming wealth, William exploited the jealousy aroused by this wealth among the other provinces. When the French began to withdraw from Utrecht, Gelderland and Overijssel, the two maritime provinces, Holland and Zeeland, attempted to secure their readmission to the Union as subordinate members only. William's intervention not only forestalled their design but, in return for his support, he demanded the right to appoint the new regents in the liberated provinces. Unlike de Witt, William could always fall back on force, though, as his father had experienced, it was a double-edged weapon and he avoided its use. Far more radical, however, as a move to end for ever the internal conflicts of the republic, was his attempt in 1675 to secure recognition of his house as the ruling family of the Netherlands. It came about when the Estates of Gelderland offered him the title of duke: this created a paradox in that William as the commissioned servant of the United Provinces was to become hereditary sovereign of one of them. The solution which William desired was for all the others to follow suit; accordingly he sounded the opinion of the provinces as to whether or not he should accept Gelderland's offer. Zeeland opposed the move but the crucial decision lay with Holland. The nobility cast their vote in the Estates in favour, together with Dordrecht and four other towns; Rotterdam, however, and three other towns gave only reluctant approval, and the remaining eight were either opposed or observed a studied neutrality. William accepted the mixed verdict as a defeat. It was clear that the Dutch, while accepting him as stadtholder of the separate provinces and as captain-general of them all, would never receive him as their monarch.

The limitations of William's position were revealed most clearly in 1678. Once the French had ceased to menace Dutch territory, and the burden of the war had passed to the republic's allies, the regents decided to make peace in order to restore the full flow of trade through their ports. William opposed the suspension of warfare, inspired as much by his consuming determination to defeat Louis XIV as by fears that his authority might subsequently be reduced. He failed to halt the negotiations, however, and not even a last-minute attack on Mons when the French were off their guard believing the war to be over, stopped the Peace of Nijmegen, which represented a victory for the very regents whom he had confirmed in office after the 'change of the laws'.

In 1684 William suffered a further setback when the city of Amsterdam threatened to withhold supplies when William proposed an alliance with Spain against France. In the following year, however, the Revocation of the Edict of Nantes provoked hostility to Louis XIV and an increasing number of the regents began to accept the fact that William's belligerent attitude towards France was justified. Anthony Heinsius, a former opponent of William, became a convert to this view when he was sent on a mission to Versailles in 1683. There he was struck by the arrogance of Louis's ambitions and from that moment became one of William's most fervent supporters, and in 1689 was appointed grand pensionary.

The closer understanding which was emerging between the prince and the regents made possible William's invasion of England in 1688. His wife, James II's elder daughter, was heir-apparent to the throne, and her staunch protestantism had already encouraged many an Englishman to suggest her immediate accession backed by William's army. Though the acquisition of England as a second base from which to prosecute his crusade against Louis XIV was an attraction of prime importance, William made no move until he had received firm assurances of English support. That the Catholic policies of James II were unpopular was obvious to everyone; that the people would rise against them was uncertain, and, unlike the ill-fated Monmouth, who had landed in 1685 to be welcomed only by peasants, William was not to be lured into action by vague promises. In June 1688 he received as specific a guarantee of support as any invader could require, signed by seven of the most influential politicians in the land: 'If the circumstances stand so with your Highness that you believe you can get here time enough, in a condition to give assistance this year sufficient for a relief under the circumstances which have been represented, we, who subscribe this, will not fail to attend your Highness upon your landing.'

William began immediately to raise German troops for the invasion force, and, when their presence in Holland could no longer be concealed, took the Estates into his confidence. The *réunions* of Louis XIV and his revocation of the Edict of Nantes gave point to William's argument that France was daily becoming more dangerous, and though the States-General feared for the future if William were to rule in London it ultimately agreed to take into public service the troops which William had privately raised. The last restraint was the fear that once William was at sea the French might invade, and this was removed in September 1688 when Louis attacked the Palatinate[24]. Straightway an unwieldy fleet of 200 transports, protected by 49 warships, exposed itself to the hazards of the Channel. Vulnerable though it was, it was swept on its way by a 'Protestant' wind, a steady north-easterly which penned the English navy in the Thames while sweeping the Dutch triumphantly round to Torbay. William was joined there by all who had invited him, the royal army deserted piecemeal as he advanced upon it, James II fled to France, and on 25 December William entered London without having fired a shot.

The Revolution Settlement which followed, vital though it was to the English, was only one side of the bargain so far as William was concerned. He had not risked everything in a dangerous venture merely to bring constitutional monarchy to England, and though the English protested at what they termed 'Dutch William's War', they were compelled to fight alongside the Dutch in the War of the League of Augsburg. The Dutch for their part shared William's hostility to Louis and supported him loyally but, wiser than him in this respect, they were prepared to settle for a secure frontier instead of outright victory. The quest for a barrier against French expansion was to dominate their foreign policy for nearly a generation, and the Peace of Ryswick (1697) took them one step towards its attainment by granting them the right to post garrisons in the Spanish Netherlands, at Ypres, Namur and Menin.

William's death in 1702 led to rioting in the United Provinces and another shift in the struggle between the House of Orange and the regent class. On this occasion popular opinion opposed the election of new stadtholders to succeed William and the republican character of Dutch politics was re-affirmed. This, however, did not affect the States-General's foreign policy since the newly-appointed regents unhesitatingly endorsed William's foreign policy, knowing that their republic was as vulnerable as ever to French invasion.

[24] See Chapter VII, pp. 350–55, for an account of this, and of the war of the League of Augsburg which followed.

For this reason Anthony Heinsius, who as Grand Pensionary had worked in the closest co-operation with William since 1689, survived his death and remained the indispensable officer of the republic, responsible for prosecuting the war with France. His excellent personal relations with the other leading regents and with Marlborough ensured close co-operation between England and Holland in the early years of the war. There were tensions. The field-deputies who directed the troops of the United Provinces were alarmed at Marlborough's proposals to leave the Netherlands for the Danube valley, thus leaving the republic dangerously exposed to the threat of invasion. More serious was the fact that, as in the War of the League of Augsburg, the Dutch were restricted to military operations on land, leaving England increasingly to dominate the war at sea. Naval supremacy, as both countries knew well, led to commercial supremacy, and the Dutch had further reason for complaint in the Methuen Trade Treaty of 1703 which gave them no advantages at all.

As allies of the English the Dutch began to lose not only the primacy in overseas trade which they had preserved through three wars with England, but also, since they ceased to be masters of their own destiny, their status of a first-class power. Even over the vital question of the barrier they were shamelessly betrayed. With the occupation of the Spanish Netherlands, for which the Dutch had contributed half the cost and half the troops, they insisted on the right to garrison the principal towns at the expense of the local population. The emperor, who expected to acquire the Spanish Netherlands after the war, refused to approve the plan, but the English, for fear lest the Dutch make a separate peace with Louis XIV, guaranteed, in the Barrier Treaty of 1709, Dutch possession of eighteen towns and also a share in Spanish-American trade. Thereafter, a General Election in England resulted in a new government which, far from trying to keep the Dutch in the war, was itself resolved to back out at almost any price.

Heinsius should have made his own peace with the French, but he adhered loyally to the Allies' policy of 'No peace without Spain', even when it was no longer viable. In addition, he failed to understand the significance of the Tory victory in 1710 and continued to correspond with the Whig leaders as though they were still in power, instead of facing impeachment as in fact they were. His gaffe gave the Tories an excuse to betray the pledges of 1709, and it was ironical that a peace conference from which the Dutch were virtually excluded should have been held at Utrecht. The paltry concession of seven barrier fortresses was a public demonstration that France, Great Britain and Austria no longer considered the Dutch Republic as an equal.

The Economic Position of the Dutch in 1714

Political decline was not immediately marked by economic stagnation or decay. The great artery of European trade, from the Baltic by way of the North Sea to the Iberian coast, was still dominated by the Dutch. The English had not only expanded the average annual number of ships passing through the Sound from 592 in the period 1681–90 to 791 in the 1720s, but also increased the tonnage of each ship, but far more dangerous than English competition had been the Swedish attempt to create a *dominium maris balticae*. After 1707 the Dutch showed remarkable resilience in recovering their position there. The annual average number of ships passing the Sound fell from 1902 in the 1680s to 1612 in the 1720s but this still left the Republic in a commanding position. In any case, so great had been the extent of Dutch commerce at its height, amounting to a practical monopoly of European trade, that it could not be overthrown in a generation. What was perhaps significant for the future was that although the Dutch retained a higher level of prosperity than their rivals, they had ceased to outstrip them, their rate of expansion had fallen and the English in particular were beginning to catch them up. It was not until the middle of the eighteenth century, and perhaps later still, that the economic decline of the Dutch became evident.

Overseas, the West India Company had failed, but a new company, founded in 1674, began to profit from the slave trade between West Africa and America. The East India Company continued to flourish. The value of its sales in Europe continued to increase throughout the seventeenth century and did not reach a peak until after 1720. While other nations found that trade with the east merely drained them of their precious metals, the Dutch had overcome this by monopolising the entire carrying trade between Ceylon, 'the cinammon garden,' Malabar, the centre of a flourishing cloth industry, and the spice islands of the

Moluccas. This, however, necessitated not only the driving out of European interlopers but also the defeat of the Indonesian princes who themselves engaged in competition with the Dutch or gave succour to their rivals. The Company's rules forbidding territorial expansion had been well observed: Batavia on the island of Java was the only settlement of any size, and this was merely a small enclave wedged between the kingdom of Mataram and the sultanate of Bantam. Elsewhere, apart from Ternate, which was governed through puppet rulers, the Company owned nothing more than trading stations. In 1666, however, Jan Maetsuycker, the governor in Bantam, decided that the Dutch would never monopolise the spice trade of the Moluccas unless they occupied Macassar in Celebes, since its ruler not only patronised Portuguese and English interlopers but encouraged his own people, a race of bold seafarers, to attack Dutch shipping.

Cornelis Speelman, who led the successful attack on Macassar in 1669, subsequently became governor in Bantam and extended Dutch conquests throughout Indonesia. Under the Bantam Treaty of 1684 the Dutch gained full control of the pepper trade and all other foreigners were expelled. The unification of Indonesia under Dutch rule had thus been forwarded, and a commercial system founded from Japan and Formosa to India and Persia. So valuable did this inter-Asiatic trade prove to be that the profits from it exceeded those derived from the cultivation and export of spices to Europe, and made it possible for the Company to accumulate in Bantam a reserve fund of over twenty million gilders.

Within the Dutch Republic itself the pattern of the economy was changing, and it was perhaps natural for contemporaries to interpret the symptoms of change as indications of economic decline. They pointed to the stagnation of the textile industry in Holland, to the increasing number of the poor, to the falling off in trade as witnessed by the fall of customs receipts, and to the collapse of shipbuilding, so marked that in 1727 the city of Amsterdam had to send to England for shipwrights.

The energy, frugality and sheer inventiveness which had characterised the earlier years of the century were now lacking. Indeed as early as 1688 the English consul in Amsterdam had noted of the regent clan that, 'the older, severe and frugal way of living is now almost quite out of date'. Yet a shift in emphasis did not necessarily connote decline. The wealthier families, less interested than in the past in trade and manufacture turned their attention to land and foreign investment. The Dutch became a race of commission agents, and the Bank of Amsterdam retained its primacy in Europe, supported by the private fortunes of its stockholders and growing rich on the interest of the enormous loans which helped to finance the wars against Louis XIV. Whatever disasters the eighteenth century was to hold for the Dutch, the bases of their economy were still sound in 1714.

VI

LOUIS XIV: A STUDY IN ABSOLUTISM

LOUIS XIV AND THE STATE

Louis XIV: his métier du roi

Her territories compactly joined, her land fertile and her population[1] the largest of any European state, France was held back from pre-eminence in Europe only by the recurrent civil war and rebellion that had plagued her since 1559. Bodin[2] in 1577 had been the first to comprehend the need for an absolute monarch to save France from disorder, and since his time the French had learned from experience to discredit all theories of a monarchy tempered by constitutional checks and balances. The tempering had too often been at the hands of overmighty subjects.

The English in 1660, the French in 1651, alike had welcomed the return of their kings to their capitals; but whereas the English retained with undiminished powers the Parliament that had defeated Charles I, the French, condemning the bitter feuds that had jeopardised the prosperity, the security and the prestige of their country, entirely repudiated the action of the Frondeurs. This popular instinct towards absolutism found formal utterance in the writings of the clergy, notably in those of Bossuet whose *Politics based on the very words of Holy Scripture* repeated the political maxims of the day and reinforced them with the sanction of biblical authority: the king was God's *vive image* upon earth, his authority was absolute and he answered for his actions to God alone. The lawyers too acclaimed the power bestowed upon kings by invoking the precepts of Roman law most apposite to their

[1] About 18,000,000 in 1660
[2] *Six Livres de la République.*

brief, and all alike owed much to Hobbes's brilliant anatomy of Leviathan,[3] despite his disreputable status as an atheist and an Englishman.

Ready as they were to accept the theory of absolutism, the French only awaited a monarch capable of practising it. Henry IV, of course, had been an ideal hero king, but the royal authority which he had done so much to restore had since been exercised by cardinals. 'Ci-gît l'Éminence deuxième', wrote a wit in eager anticipation of Mazarin's death, 'Dieu nous garde de la troisième.' Louis XIV delighted his subjects by taking the wit at his word. When, after Mazarin's death, the Archbishop of Paris and the principal secretaries asked the king to whom they should report for instructions, they received the terse reply, 'A moi'. In two words Louis determined the destiny of France for the next sixty years.

'It was the moment for which I had waited', wrote Louis in the *Mémoires* he compiled for his son's instruction, 'and which I had dreaded', he had the honesty to add, yet he was not wholly lacking in experience. Mazarin had been an accomplished tutor and the Fronde a valuable if painful lesson in practical politics.

Moreover, he was well equipped by nature for the role of king. John Evelyn, the English diarist who witnessed his return to Paris after the Fronde, described him as 'a young Apollo...a prince of a grave yet sweet countenance'. He was well built, toughened by long hours of hunting, with a dignified bearing and a keen eye which commanded respect. Though he lacked a sense of humour he could yet be lively and charming; and if he took himself too seriously, if he positively savoured the formality of court etiquette, this was no disadvantage in a king who was resolved to show himself to his subjects as no ordinary mortal but as God's *vive image* upon earth.

When Mazarin died Louis made his dramatic *début:* 'I resolved never to appoint a first minister nor to leave to another the function of royalty while reserving to myself the mere title.' For Louis, monarchy was a specialist occupation; he liked to term it his *métier du roi*, and he took it as seriously as any other man might undertake his own profession. His ideas were already fully worked out. Each country, he believed had its own 'true maxims'

[3] Translated into French in 1649. See Chapter I, p.18, for a more detailed analysis of seventeenth-century political theory.

of state, rooted in the natural order whose author was God. Good statesmanship consisted in identifying and applying these maxims and it was only kings with absolute authority who could do this consistently. Absolutism, however, was not to be confused with despotism. Louis was essentially conservative in his view of the orders of society and of the laws necessary for the protection of religion, property and the state: he had no desire to alter the former nor to dispense with the latter — his treatment of Fouquet proving to be a rare example of royal interference with the due process of law. Conventional in his attitudes, imbued with a live sense of tradition — especially so far as his dynasty was concerned — his object overall was to increase the grandeur of his kingdom and of his royal house. He was exceptionally strongminded, and his ministers whom he respected for their ability had in turn to respect both his grasp of affairs and his industry and energy.

Once Louis had assumed the responsibility of governing France he allowed nothing to interfere with his task. He did not abandon his mistresses, but the amusements, balls and hunting trips which had occupied his youth became the strictly regulated relaxations of a busy man with a crowded time-table. Bishop Burnet, an English visitor to Paris in 1667, commented, with an implied reproof of his own sovereign Charles II, that he was 'diligent in his own councils and regular in the dispatch of his affairs'.

The *métier du roi* required regular attendance at the numerous councils by which France was governed. The *conseil d'état*, later known at Versailles as the *conseil d'en haut*, met for long sessions on three days a week to determine policy on all the major issues of the day: the *conseil des finances* met weekly, and the *conseil des dépeches*, supervising the law courts and the working of the administration, met two or three times a month. These, and many other councils, Louis attended in fulfilment of his belief that 'the right of deliberation and resolution belongs to the head alone, and all the functions of the other members consist in executing the orders given to them'. In a typical day, described by his minister Colbert, he was in council from 10 a.m. until 1.30 p.m.; after lunch he attended another council, devoted two hours to improving his Latin in order to read Papal documents unaided, and was in council again until 10 in the evening. None of this was for Louis the mechanical performance of a tedious duty, for he not only attended but possessed a rare faculty for active listening. The ministers whom he inherited from Mazarin were among the most talented administrators of the century, with a genius for planning and innovation. In their specialist fields Louis could not rival them, but as chairman of their discussions he revealed his own genius for committee work and an ability to take an overall view.

No one attended the councils by right of birth or office. Membership was determined by the king alone, according to the problem in hand. The great nobles and the great churchmen who had hitherto played a decisive part in the government of France were replaced by men of the *noblesse de la robe*, Michel Le Tellier, Jean-Baptiste Colbert and Hugues de Lionne, who had been trained by Mazarin in the discipline of royal service. Sons frequently succeeded fathers in the great affairs of state but on merit not of right. The *Maison du Roi* and the *Marine*, for example, were controlled in turn by Colbert and his son Seignelay, to be succeeded by two generations of the Ponchartrain family: Colbert's brother, Colbert de Croissy, was later to superintend foreign affairs, in which post he was followed by his son, Colbert de Torcy. The secretaryship of war was held by three generations of the same family; Michel Le Tellier, his son Louvois and his grandson Barbézieux. Family rivalry and dependence upon the king were all to Louis's advantage, but he himself had the common sense to choose men who were not merely sycophants or squabbling rivals. Once his authority was recognised, his servants were allowed great responsibility since he valued their talents and gave them full play.

Nicolas Fouquet alone among those who had served Mazarin failed to appreciate Louis's intention. He had acquired great wealth and power from his position as *Surintendant des Finances* and had hoped to succeed to Mazarin's place, but thwarted in his ambition by Louis's resolve to be his own first minister, Fouquet brought about his own downfall by a series of foolish mistakes. It was tactless to make advances to La Vallière, the current royal mistress, and to display his wealth in prodigious *fêtes* when royal revenues were pledged in advance. It was dangerous to give prominence to his motto, *Quo non ascendam,* and to fortify his home at Belle Isle. His behaviour smacked of the irresponsible and over-mighty subjects who had dominated Louis's childhood, and the king decided upon his downfall. The assiduous Colbert, eager for the reversion of Fouquet's office, supplied evidence of his malversation of royal funds, and a royal court condemned him to exile. At this point Louis intervened to increase the penalty to one of life imprisonment at Pinerolo. Fouquet's punishment served as a useful warning to his colleagues from which they did not fail to profit. When Colbert secured an appointment for his son Seignelay, he passed on the lesson which he had made his own: 'Never as long as you live send out anything in the king's name without his express approval'.

Versailles: Symbol of Absolutism

Louis XIII had built a small château at Versailles to save himself the fatigue of returning to Paris after a long hunting trip in the Forest of Marly. It was a simple building, a rectangular block, framed to the right and left by two wings, which Louis XIV often visited in his youth, and for which he had much affection. In 1661 he began to enlarge the gardens without altering the main building, but in 1668 he determined upon a more radical transformation: the original château was to be preserved, but around it he ordered the construction of a new palace, large enough to serve as a permanent home for the royal family. By 1682, though building continued for the rest of his reign, he had moved into residence. From that date until the Revolution, Versailles replaced Paris as the seat of government.

Louis's decision sprang from many sources. He shared his father's love of walking and hunting, but the spaciousness of Versailles satisfied more than his physical needs. The splendour of monarchy, as Louis believed in it, had not been reflected in the unhappy events of his youth. His coronation at Reims (1654), conducted in haste as a manœuvre to outwit the Frondeurs, had been an undignified ceremony from which most of those who traditionally attended upon the king, including the Archbishop of Reims himself, had been absent. The Fronde, moreover, left him with a permanent distaste for the narrow streets of Paris with their frequently erected barricades, and for the noisy mob who had once swarmed through his palace. To compensate for these indignities he sought a more splendid and more spacious environment for his court. The abode of *le roi soleil* was not to be stumbled upon around a street corner; and in revenge upon his unruly capital he removed himself from its midst. Personal gratification, however, was not the only consideration in Louis's mind. As France became the most important power in Europe he wished to epitomise her greatness, which was his own, by creating a more magnificent stage for his actions. He had already been offered a model in Fouquet's superb chateau at Vaux-le-Vicomte, built by Le Vau, with Le Brun to direct the internal *décor* and Le Nôtre to lay out the gardens. Here for the glorification of Fouquet, the most famous poets, musicians and dramatists — La Fontaine, Lully, Molière — presented their work and enjoyed his patronage. With Fouquet's disgrace all these were immediately taken into royal service, and the reign-long task of constructing the great palace at Versailles was begun.

The men who built Versailles had an excellent understanding of Louis's purpose. It was not only the Roman Church that had discovered the power of art to impress and overwhelm:[4] the Baroque style had been applied to domestic architecture, grouping façades and wings, arcades, terraces and pavilions in a manner calculated to awaken in the observer a sense of movement and of grandeur. Le Vau, the first of Louis's architects, lengthened the wings of the original château to create an impressive *cour d'honneur* awaiting the visitor from Paris; while on the garden side he built a new central block which, with its two wings, presented a massive façade. To heighten the effect he broke the façade at its centre, recessing the upper storeys to leave the ground floor covered by a marble terrace, decorated with a fountain. He was succeeded, however, by Hardouin-Mansart, who represented a different tradition to the Italian style of Le Vau, opposing the Baroque with a more severely classical style. This classical tradition accorded admirably with the requirements of order, discipline and harmony which characterised the ideal of Louis's absolutism. By removing Le Vau's central recess, Mansart imposed a uniform façade on the garden side, and strengthened its horizontal line by adding two further wings, slightly recessed, which brought its overall length to 550 metres. The elevation remained the same but the whole effect was transformed: the sense of movement was destroyed and in its

4 See Chapter I, p.88.

place was created a mood of restrained magnificence, majesty and order.

Le Brun superintended the decoration within the palace. His taste was similar to Le Vau's, and the Ambassador's staircase, no longer extant, was a masterpiece of baroque illusion, intended to astound the foreign dignitaries who called upon Louis. Around it was placed a balustrade, between the pillars of which was painted a throng of courtiers who seemed to press forward to watch the stately processions as they ascended. Later, however, Le Brun bowed to Mansart's influence and the famous *Galerie des Glaces* was designed in a more restrained fashion, following the classical traditions which Louis found more apposite to his austere sense of majesty. The gardens were laid out by Le Nôtre in a similar style. The rough terrain where sandy scrub and marshland competed for precedence was reduced to order by thousands of workmen who levelled the earth and laid pipes to supply the 1,400 fountains with water from the Seine, since there were no springs in the area. From the palace there stretched countless *parterres* of flowers, vast sheets of water, and an apparently endless succession of stately avenues. Here, where man had wrought his will upon nature, was reflected the well-ordered society of which Louis was the centre.

It mattered little that several thousand workmen died from fever and pneumonia in the work of constructing the palace and its gardens; that ten thousand courtiers and servants crowded upon each other in perennial confusion and dirt; that the great corridors resembled frozen alleyways in winter, and that the chimneys smoked because their height had been reduced to preserve the dignity of the façade. It mattered little, since the prime purpose had been so notably achieved: Versailles epitomised the grandeur of Louis XIV.

If Versailles had been designed and constructed to enhance Louis's glory, life within its walls was directed towards the same end, and the complexity and rigidity of court etiquette became the marvel of Europe. To some extent this resulted from Louis's own humourless personality; taking himself so seriously, he saw nothing strange in the highly organised society that revolved, like the planets, in stately progression around its sun. He acted his part so convincingly that it is doubtful if he ever conceived of it as a part at all. Even his moments of relaxation were conducted with ceremony and dignity: he played billiards, as one lady remarked, with the air of being master of the world. The laws of etiquette and precedence, however, had also a political value, since they demonstrated the inferior rank of all who attended upon the king. The most minute distinctions between the greatest of his courtiers, and indeed among his own family, were reflected in the degree of familiarity permitted to them. The seriousness of Louis's purpose is made clear from a revealing passage in his *Mémoires:* 'About this time I learned that my brother was thinking of asking that his wife might be allowed to sit in the Queen's presence on a seat with a back to it. My friendly feelings towards him made me unwilling to refuse him anything; but seeing of what great moment this matter was, I let him know forthwith, with all possible gentleness, that I could not possibly give him satisfaction;...that I did not feel able to grant this which would seem to be an approach to my own elevation.'

The king's day began with the *petit lever* to which over a hundred people were admitted in six successive parties, each one a shade less select than the one before. Those of the highest rank were permitted to see the king leave his bed; the least favoured had to be content with observing the final stages of his dressing. At Mass, it was said, the king worshipped God while the court worshipped the king; dinner, *au grand couvert,* was eaten by the royal family alone, in the presence of the hushed congregation of the court; and at the *petit coucher* the favoured few, who had watched the king rise, attended him to his bed. 'Given an almanac', wrote the Duc de Saint-Simon, 'and a watch, one could always tell what the king would be doing.' This constant parade before the court demanded from Louis as much care as attendance at his councils, and never did he neglect either. Seven days before his death, the old and broken king yet managed to dine *au grand couvert,* even though he could barely sip a little liquid, to demonstrate that the life of the court still revolved around him alone.

Versailles made the great noble families more dependent than ever upon the king. The standards of conspicuous expenditure expected of them rose as the general economic depression after 1680 reduced the income from their lands, and it was necessary for them to approach the king for favours — positions of profit, commissions for their sons, gifts of land, loans. In order to secure these, however, it was necessary for the nobles to live at court. 'C'est un homme que je ne vois jamais,' was Louis's coldest rejection of a suitor for preferment, and the exorbitant expense of court life ensured that once a noble had secured charity from the king he was as quickly reduced to petitioning for more.

Trapped within the confines of the palace, the nobles who had ridden roughshod over the crown in the past were transformed into servile courtiers, submitting eagerly to the laws of precedence for fear of seeing someone of inferior status gain closer access to the king than themselves. To be at Versailles was in itself a privilege, to attend the more intimate ceremonies of the king's life was a peerless distinction, and the offer of holding the royal candle at the *petit coucher* reduced Saint-Simon, for one, to mute ecstasy. Petitioning for favours to stave off bankruptcy, jostling for precedence to assuage their dignity, their lives an artificially gay succession of balls, hunts, gaming and gossip, the nobility was tamed more effectively by the etiquette of Versailles than by the harsh edicts of Richelieu. To quit the court of Louis XIII had been an act of defiance: to be sent from Versailles was a shameful disgrace. 'Loin de vous, Sire', breathed a fervent noble released from exile, 'on n'est pas seulement malheureux, on est ridicule.'

Unhappily for the future, the life of those at court became divorced from that of the people who worked their estates: France ceased to exist beyond the borders of Le Nôtre's gardens, and the dusty miles between Versailles and Paris seemed to grow longer with every year.

Yet another vital function of Versailles was to attract the services of poets, artists and musicians to enhance Louis's fame. Louis's offer was an attractive one of generous pensions, a permanent audience of the most distinguished kind, and a magnificent *milieu* from which their fame might radiate throughout the civilised world. Louis himself was no connoisseur. He had no interest in promoting the nascent talents of young men, but exploited for political ends the genius of men who had already made their name. Molière, Bossuet, La Fontaine, Le Brun, Lully, Le Vau and Le Nôtre were established before 1661 and the only great name to appear as a result of Louis's patronage was, perhaps, Racine.

Adherence to the classical tradition was demanded not only of the architects of Versailles but of the poets and dramatists. Nicolas Boileau's *Art Poétique* was acclaimed a masterpiece of literary criticism because it urged the literary world to take its subjects from classical mythology and history, and insisted, for example, that in the drama the Aristotelian unities of time, place and action be preserved.

Molière alone was allowed to analyse and expose the foibles of his own society without censure, since his wit and perception appealed to the king: he took care, none the less, not to direct his comic genius at the institution of monarchy. Fenélon and La Bruyère, whose works revealed criticism of Louis's government, and Descartes and Bayle, who were suspected of atheism, did not receive bounty from the king. Patronage proved to be a more effective weapon than censorship; and the foundation of the *Académies* was undertaken to ensure a better control over their members. The *Académie de Peinture et de Sculpture,* for example, met monthly to discuss a work of art; from its discussions the members formulated rules to be observed so that a common spirit informed their work. As the *Académies* met under Le Brun's direction, Louis was assured that novelty, or any other trend unsuitable to an absolute regime, would be immediately suppressed, and he succeeded in his purpose. The fine arts supported and gave lustre to his political supremacy. No other court in Europe could display the talents of so many gifted men, and primacy in the arts, once the proud boast of Italy, was won for France. While other states combined to attack the armies of France, they competed with each other in adopting French fashions and in imitating the achievements of the civilisation created at Versailles.

Royal Control in the Provinces

The work of Henry IV and Richelieu had done much to extend the authority of the king throughout France, but administrative uniformity had yet to be achieved. Although the *pays d'élections* had been reduced to obedience and conformity, the *pays d'état,* which had been heartened by Richelieu's failure to defeat Languedoc, and by the temporary collapse of the central government during the Fronde, still retained particular liberties which made nonsense of Louis's concept of *l'état, c'est moi.* It would be misleading to compare the Estates of Languedoc, for example, with the Cortes of Catalonia or with the East Prussian Diet: self-regarding as they were, they did not claim a nationality separate from the rest of the kingdom nor did they repudiate the king's action in foreign affairs. Their loyalty to Louis XIV was not in question, nor did they deny his right to financial assistance. Their concern was simply to safeguard their local jurisdiction, and their pockets, from interference by the central government, and when they voted their annual *don gratuit* to the king, they jealously preserved its original meaning.

The task of bringing the *pays d'état* into line with the rest of France was entrusted to Colbert, and his treatment of Languedoc in particular will serve as an illustration of his actions in general. Sessions of the Languedoc Estates were effectively controlled by securing the election of the Archbishop of Toulouse as President. As an eminent local dignitary there could be little objection to him by the members: as one of Colbert's clientele, however, seeking to further his career by service to the central government, he was able to exercise great influence over their actions. Speakers favourable to the crown were given the floor, their opponents were cut short by operation of the closure, and the agenda was carefully supervised. Some members responded to bribery, prompting Colbert to remark that 'perhaps ten or fifteen thousand *livres* distributed in this way might have a good effect on all other matters that might arise in the future': others were reduced to silence by the presence of Colbert's agents who, with great ostentation, made notes of their speeches. The recalcitrant few, who determined to contest this manipulation of their debates, suffered from interference in their private lives, their friends and relatives found it difficult to secure the reversion of vacant offices, and, in the last resort, their arrest was ordered by *lettre du cachet* which removed them from the public eye without the compensation of a public trial.

As a result by 1665 Languedoc was voting its *don gratuit* on the advice of royal intendants, and, as the king's hold tightened on the province, it became unnecessary to employ these methods further. Colbert had originally proposed to abolish the Estates outright: in the long run, however, he found them invaluable as a means of enforcing royal policy under the guise of local consent. The device was scarcely a state secret. In 1671 Madame de

Sévigné attended the session of the Brittany Estates and reported that these would be short. 'They have only to ask what the king requires; no one will say a word, and so it will be done.' The Estates on this occasion voted 2,500,000 *livres*, of which the king remitted 300,000 'wishing to repay them for the good grace with which they obeyed him by this result of his liberality'. For the rest, 'an infinity of presents, some pensions, some repairs of roads and bridges, everlasting hospitality and gaming, eternal balls, three comedies a week; in all a magnificent show'.

The account of the session of 1671 did not mean that what was voted was administered without difficulty. The period 1675–6 was one of serious unrest and revolt throughout the province, to the extent that 10,000 troops had to be sent in to restore order. Within all the provinces, moreover, there existed groups and individuals whose privileges, derived from custom or authorised by charter, might check the smooth running of the king's writ. The authority of provincial governors had already been drastically curtailed; Louis reduced it further by limiting their term of office to three years, thereby ensuring that the real direction of provincial affairs was assumed by intendants operating on a permanent commission from the *conseil d'état*. Nonetheless, the personal position enjoyed by the governor, his family's standing in the province and above all his powers of patronage ensured that he could never be reduced to a cipher.

The position of the *parlements*, too, was altered. After the collapse of the Fronde had dealt a death blow to their pretensions they were subsequently supervised by the *conseil des dépêches*. Cases in which the crown had a particular interest were removed from their jurisdiction, and judgements adverse to royal policy were swiftly revoked by edict.[5] 'It is no use writing about speeches made in the *Parlement*', wrote Colbert to his intendant at Grenoble, 'As you know, the noises made by *parlements* are no longer in season.' Yet again it was one thing for open opposition to cease: it was quite another to outwit the talents of legal experts engaged in circumventing royal decrees. Petty obstruction lacked glamour but it was effective, and if the government could no longer be defied, its orders could very easily be evaded.

There remained the municipal corporations, invested with considerable autonomy by their charters of incorporation, but

[5] See, for example, the case of the Widow Falempin of Amiens, below, p. 319.

whose affairs were notoriously mismanaged by the small group of families which controlled each town. Incompetence and dishonesty in the administration of civic funds gave the crown an unimpeachable excuse for intervention — as at Saint-Quentin where the citizens had been hoodwinked into paying for the maintenance of walls which had never been constructed. In 1683 Colbert ordered each corporation to submit an annual report of its finances to his intendants, who were then charged with the significant duty of liquidating their debts. Finally, in 1692, when effective control had been firmly established by the intendants, the farce of election was abolished and civic offices were sold for life as profitable sinecures.

In one respect, therefore, it seems that the traditional system of government was thus preserved in appearance only. Governors, mayors, members of the Estates and of the *parlements* maintained the ceremonial trappings of their office and enjoyed their accustomed perquisites: the right to govern was transferred to men wholly dependent upon the king. The duties of the intendants were exhaustive, and some idea of their extent can be gathered from the *Mémoires* of Nicolas Foucault, who served successively in Montauban, Pau and Poitiers. He was variously employed in supervising the sessions of the Estates and the *parlements;* in police work, censorship and in scrutinising the activities of tax-collectors and municipal officers; in surveying roads and rivers; in superintending conscription, vagrancy, tobacco farms and industry, and in reporting to the central government on every matter under the sun, from the behaviour of Huguenots to the state of the harvest. Professionally competent and always accountable to the *conseil d'état*, the intendant served as the principal agent of Louis's absolutism.

On the other hand, at all the lower levels of the administration Louis's absolutism was compromised by the very servants he was compelled to employ. The intendants, of course, were endowed with unprecedented powers of direction and coercion but the *généralités* they controlled were often the size of a province. Of necessity they had to work through the *officiers* who constituted the civil service of the day, and without whose co-operation as a class nothing could be done. To the intendants, schooled by Colbert to serve the state with professional skill and utter loyalty, the body of *officiers* represented an incubus. It was not that the *officiers* were necessarily inefficient or fraudulent but that their interests were their own rather than the king's. Having purchased their posts for profit, they were entrenched in positions of authority from which they were virtually irremovable. They could rarely be called to account and they reflected the narrow outlook of their neighbourhood. Wise enough not to challenge the government by open opposition, they relied instead on their capacity for private or passive resistance. They exercised an informal surveillance over royal edicts, quietly ignoring those which threatened their position or offended the traditions of their locality. Months might pass before the intendant had noted and reported their offence; still more before the council's indignation was brought home to them. The *officier* merely shrugged his shoulders. The edict had never arrived, it had been lost, it had been misunderstood, it would be enforced tomorrow, and the intendant remained uncomfortably aware that the matter would again be ignored on his departure.

The stranglehold which the *officiers* exercised over the administration seriously affected the commercial and religious policies of the crown, but it is best revealed by Colbert's failure to secure a more systematised legal system. The seigneural and church courts touched upon the daily life of the subject far more than the royal courts, and these could not be abolished without serious opposition from the nobles and clergy. Colbert did not attempt to do so, especially as the crown had evolved a procedure for evoking from their jurisdiction any case in which it was interested. His concern was to remedy the confusion in the royal courts themselves. There existed, for example, two distinct areas of law, the *droit coutumier* based upon custom and precedent, and the *droit écrit* derived from Roman law, and court procedure varied from one place to another. To create a standardised code, a *droit français,* applicable to the whole kingdom and uniformly enforced in every court of justice, was a prospect to delight the tidy minds of Colbert and his uncle Pussort. As the law itself presented so great a tangle, their first step was to establish methods of procedure, which they did in 1667 and 1669 respectively when they issued the *ordonnance civile* and the *ordonnance criminelle.* The codes which followed were concerned with the laws themselves. The *Code Savory* (1673), named after the merchant who inspired it, established uniform trading and commercial practices; the *ordonnance de la marine* (1680) related to maritime cases; the *Code Noir* (1685) regulated the government of the colonies.

The total effect was to demonstrate Colbert's skill as a legislator; but whatever virtues the codes and ordonnances possessed they lacked enforcement. The magistrates, possessing to the full the deep-rooted conservatism inherent in all legal bodies, and resenting the necessity of adopting new procedure, opposed them from the first. Moreover, they had paid a high price for their positions and they knew only the traditional methods of recouping themselves. No matter what the royal councils decreed, their edicts were ignored. Passive resistance triumphed, and Pussort reluctantly admitted failure; 'France', he wrote, 'has the honour of having the most wonderful and the wisest ordinances to be found in Europe, but she has also the reputation of enforcing them more inefficiently than in any other state.'

There was only one remedy, to abolish the sale of offices and to create an entirely new bureaucracy subservient to royal direction, but this was impracticable. Though Louis XIV had never forgiven the *officiers* for their part in the Fronde and despised their *bourgeois* origins, he nevertheless had a sound respect for their strength. Moreover, to the Treasury the sale of offices was an indispensable source of revenue. 'One of the most wonderful privileges of the kings of France', wrote Desmarets, himself an *officier*, 'is that when the king creates an office, God, at that very instant, creates a fool to buy it.' It was true that the demand never slackened, but the purchasers were not fools. From the *premier president* of a *parlement* to the village bailiff and clerk, the *officiers* formed a privileged estate, and not only every middle-class family but many a noble family centred its hopes on acquiring office. It was a profitable investment since it often purchased exemption from taxation and provided a means to secure valuable fees and other perquisites. 'When a villager has learned three words of Latin', ran one report, 'he at once stops paying the *taille*; he becomes a procurator, a syndic or a sergeant and proceeds to ruin his neighbours.' Not only wealth but honour awaited the successful *officier* and the highest positions carried with them noble status, the *noblesse de la robe*. The president of a *parlement* was received in his province with honour accorded to princes; while he lived the greatest persons gave him precedence; when he died all the church bells were rung.

So attractive was the sale of offices to the purchasers and to the Treasury, so powerful were the *officiers* themselves, that the government was unable to reform the system. The king, against whom all open resistance had ceased, and whose authority was recognised by every institution which had formerly claimed some degree of autonomy, was thus exposed to the silent opposition of the men who administered the laws in his name. The existence of the *officier* class thus explains the paradox that the most absolute ruler of the seventeenth century was so frequently disobeyed.

One class which out of despair still frequently erupted from disobedience into revolt was the peasantry, the overtaxed, under-privileged section of the community. Many differences of degree existed among them. A million or so still endured the shackles of serfdom in the eastern provinces; a million, perhaps, owned their own land; several million were landless labourers; but about half the peasants, were *métayers*, paying as much as half their produce in rent to their lords. Collectively, however, the peasantry bore the brunt of the *taille* and the *gabelle*, sustained the church by tithes, and the nobility by seigneurial dues. Many of these dues had become nominal, but the lord could still compel his peasants to grind their corn in his mill, to bake their dough in his oven, and to crush their wine in his presses, for all of which he exacted payment. The *métayers*, in addition, paid him a tax whenever their lease was transferred by inheritance or by sale.

Worst of all was the effect of the high level of taxation, which led to many popular revolts in the first two decades of the reign. In 1662, for example, the Boulonnais rose — in vain, and hundreds were sent to the galleys : in Bordeaux in 1675 order was restored by quartering eighteen regiments among the disaffected families. By the middle years of the reign revolts were less frequent, although the despair remained, since the government had succeeded in collecting enough taxes to maintain a vast army which in turn was capable of enforcing, when necessary, the collection of more taxes.

To add to the general misery a succession of bad harvests across the entire country during the Fronde, in 1661–2 and again in 1693–4 led to starvation, sickness and death on such a scale that the population did not return to its levels of 1648 until after

1720. Moreover, in one area after another subsistence crises became more common as local harvests failed with greater frequency in the last decades of the century.

As for the nobility, it is important to avoid generalised statements. Although most nobles shared the common characteristics of landowning, of social privileges and of exemption from taxes, all enjoyed different standards of living and different degrees of social and political importance. There were the princes of the blood and the great aristocratic families whose names were an essential part of the fabric of French history; these had the *entrée* to Versailles with all the advantages and disadvantages which this involved (see above, p. 292). There was the *noblesse de la robe* where wealth and importance were derived from government service. Finally, the majority, the *nobles de province* who suffered as the reign went on from the agricultural depression which set in after 1680 and from the growing poverty of their peasants. The government made things worse. Land held by tenants was subject to taxation and Colbert refused to exempt it if a noble recovered direct possession in order to work it himself. Moreover a noble employing more than four ploughs for his personal use became liable to taxation.

Under the rules of *dérogeance* a noble lost his status and exemptions if he engaged in a 'demeaning' occupation. There were therefore few opportunities for the nobles in commerce and industry, there were not enough wealthy benefices in the church to satisfy all who sought them, and the army offered a career only to those who attained to the high professional standards demanded by Le Tellier and Louvois (see Chapter VII, pp. 331–2). Even for those prepared to swallow their pride by marrying the daughter of a successful businessman the opportunities for such a *mésalliance* were all too limited. The number of impoverished nobles increased throughout the reign, and at the very lowest of the class the *hobereau*, the petty noble, became an object of scorn. 'Useless to his country, his wife and himself', wrote La Bruyère, 'often without a roof, clothing or any merit at all, the provincial noble tells himself ten times a day that at any rate he is a gentleman.'

As a class, the nobility was no longer the dangerous force it had been in the past, partly of course because Louis XIV, while insisting upon the most severe penalties for any act of rebellion, was careful to guarantee the nobles their special privileges, their freedom from taxation and their privileged status in French society.

To the envious princes of Europe, Louis XIV appeared as the very epitome of absolutism. Absolutism, however, in seventeenth-century France must not be equated with totalitarianism in the present age, since its practice was limited and restrained by several factors.[6] Absolute control of the state is only possible in an egalitarian society, in which each member is equally exposed to the power of the government: French society resembled a privileged hierarchy, and, arbitrary though the *ancien régime* might be, it retained countless bulwarks against encroachment by the king. The individual was powerless before the majesty of the throne, but the class to which he belonged was hedged about and protected by time-honoured privileges which prevented radical changes in the distribution of wealth, power or social esteem. Uniformity could only be attained through social revolution, and it is significant that it was the Revolution of 1789 which gave birth to the truly absolute powers of a Napoleon.

CHURCH AND STATE

The Gallican Clergy

To all appearances Louis XIV had the French Church well under control. As a result of the Concordat of Bologna (1516) he controlled the appointment to all abbeys, priories and bishoprics in France; and as most of the candidates for higher office were of noble birth, with little prospect of success in any other career, they made it their business to be as accommodating as possible to the king. Opposition, even on theological grounds, was a luxury they could not afford and many remained securely ignorant of theology. The Catholic revival in France[7] owed little to the leadership of such men who sought benefices by the same means as their elder brothers sought pensions and places at Versailles. Their sisters, too, joined in the struggle for preferment; and

[6] See Chapter I, pp. 18–26 for a general study of this phenomenon.
[7] See Chapter I, pp. 82–3.

Angélique Arnauld, appointed at the age of eleven as Abbess of the convent at Port-Royal, proved a disconcerting exception to the general rule by allowing herself to be converted by a visiting preacher when she was nineteen.

In such circumstances it was not difficult for Colbert and Le Tellier, acting on the king's behalf, to build up a loyal clientele among the clergy. Colbert's brother, the Archbishop of Rouen, and Le Tellier's son, the Archbishop of Reims, could of course be relied upon implicitly, as could the de Carbon brothers, who held the archbishoprics of Toulouse[8] and Sens. There were many others, and in Harlay, appointed to Paris in 1671, they found their exemplar. Sufficiently scholarly to win attention, astute enough not to take his studies too seriously, he served Louis XIV with constant devotion and unflagging self-interest; his influence was equalled only by the royal confessor, de la Chaise, his sole colleague in the *conseil de conscience* which advised the king on Church affairs. Against their policies it was always dangerous, and generally useless, to protest, and the Church became very much a mere department of state.

There was, however, another side to the coin; one which explains why, if the clergy were so amenable to discipline, the king and his ministers were perennially concerned to ensure their co-operation: indeed, the Assembly of the Clergy was the only representative body in France to be consulted with serious intent by Louis XIV. He knew that though his clergy were anxious to gratify his wishes, they were also determined to maintain what they termed their 'Gallican liberties'. Gallicanism, in essence, repudiated the authority of the pope over the Catholic Church in France. The orthodox prelate might have hesitated to put it so bluntly; but the laymen of the *parlement,* jealous of all ecclesiastical jurisdiction, whether papal or episcopal, had sharply defined the limits of the pope's authority in France. They denied him any temporal jurisdiction, his bulls were valid only after approval by the king and his *parlements,* and his decisions in spiritual matters were capable of amendment by the councils of the Church. The Sorbonne, however, where most of the bishops read their theology, disliked this attempt by the lawyers to subject the clergy unconditionally to the crown. Accepting the general principles of

---

[8] The Archbishop who performed valuable service as President of the Languedoc Estates: see above, p. 295.

Gallicanism, it interpreted them rather as a safeguard of a bishop's autonomy within his diocese, an attitude as dangerous to king as to pope. The result was that in conflict with the pope, Louis had no more devoted allies than his own clergy: it was less certain whether they would support him as readily if he invoked papal assistance to discipline one of their number.

The *cause célèbre* of Gallicanism in Louis's reign arose from the conflict between Louis and two of his bishops. Throughout most of France Louis enjoyed the right of *régale*, which allowed him to appropriate the revenues of a vacant bishopric and to make appointments within the diocese. The mounting cost of the Dutch War (1672–9) prompted Colbert to advise the king to assert his lucrative prerogative in the twenty-nine dioceses hitherto exempt. The extension of the *régale* went unopposed by all but two of the bishops, Caulet of Pamiers and Pavillon of Alet, who challenged the legality of Louis's actions. Unfortunately for themselves, they antagonised the rest of the clergy by appealing directly to Pope Innocent XI to champion their cause.[9] Pavillon died in 1673, his successor accepting the *régale,* but Caulet remained recalcitrant. He was dispossessed of his see, but the canons of Pamiers refused to elect a new bishop and the Archbishop of Toulouse ordered their prosecution. Innocent XI then intervened to condemn the extension of the *régale* and to threaten de Carbon with excommunication if Caulet were not reinstated.

To repel the attack from Rome, Louis summoned an extraordinary Assembly of the Clergy in 1681. Behind the scenes Colbert and Le Tellier mobilised their adherents, and Harlay led them into action in the Assembly. In pleading the cause of Gallicanism Louis's anxiety was not that the clergy might refuse to follow him against the authority of the pope, but that they might outstrip him and precipitate a schism: he welcomed the moderate views of Bossuet, Bishop of Meaux, who, in asserting the liberties of the French Church, nevertheless reminded the Assembly of its duty to preserve unity with Rome. In 1682, the Assembly drew up Four Articles, which gave force and clarity to opinion which had hitherto been loosely, even carelessly, defined. Their effect was to

[9] It is some indication of the confused politics of the French Church that it was only a few years previously that Caulet and Pavillon had joined with other bishops in support of Jansenism (see below, p. 311), claiming the protection of the Gallican liberties against the pope.

reduce the pope's authority in France to nought, and to deny his infallibility in matters of faith[10]. Trenchant though the Articles were, they raised no novel issue to complicate the *régale* crisis still further, but gave Louis the means he sought to force the pope's hand. An edict of March 1682 ordered the Articles to be registered in the *parlements*, and demanded subscription to them from all candidates for degrees in theology. Innocent was not to be intimidated. As bishoprics fell vacant he refused bulls of institution to any cleric who had taken part in the Assembly: Louis would nominate none who had not.

The deadlock was prolonged until Innocent's death in 1689, by which time thirty-five dioceses were without bishops. Only mutual compromise could avert schism, yet both sides were reluctant to make concessions. Important though France might be to the Catholic Church, the publication of the Assembly's Articles was a grave affront to the papacy. Orthodox though Louis was at heart, he was obstinately resolved to secure the extension of the *régale*. Tension was eased at last only by a change of circumstances. A new pope, Innocent XII, was less bitterly involved than his predecessors; Louis had good reason to desire Italian neutrality in his war against the League of Augsburg (1688–97); moreover, the unwelcome views of a section of the clergy on an entirely different issue[11] offended equally both king and pope, and these could only be suppressed by effective co-operation between Rome and Versailles. Louis revoked his edict enforcing the Four Articles, and the clergy apologised to the pope, but in terms, however, which did not explicitly renounce their opinion, and in a manner so unpublicised that few outside their number were aware of it. The *parlements*, in fact, never withdrew their registration of the Articles: nor for that matter did Innocent XII give more than tacit consent to Louis's extension of the *régale*. Through the mists of compromise and secrecy which finally shrouded the issue it is at least clear that the cause of Gallicanism had suffered a set-back. Louis himself was unperturbed. He had merely used Gallicanism as a means to compel the withdrawal of papal support for Caulet, who had died in the meantime without securing a retraction of the *régale*.

Neither Gallican nor Ultramontane, neither schismatic nor

[10] The Assembly, influenced by Bossuet, had actually avoided the word infallibility, stating that the pope's judgements were not *irreformable*.
[11] The Jansenists. See below, pp. 310–12.

subservient to Rome, Louis's interest in the Church, as in all other matters, was political, his policy opportunist. Whereas in 1682 he denied the validity of papal authority, by 1693 he was preparing to invoke that same authority to discipline a section of his own clergy. The religious history of his reign reflected the view of an absolute monarch from whose ways none might dissent, and who practised the maxim enunciated by Bossuet, *un roi, une loi, une foi.*

The Huguenots

Since the Grace of Alais had destroyed their military powers,[12] the Huguenots had maintained an exemplary record of loyalty and obedience. No longer did they cherish political ambitions: the nobles and *officiers,* whose grandparents had fought against the Catholic League, renounced their faith to seek preferment at court or in the royal administration; of their more resolute brethren, 1,500,000 at the most, many resorted to industry or commerce in which their abilities won at least the respect of those who hated their religious convictions. Louis XIV had nothing to fear, and much to gain, from their presence in the kingdom. Their freedom from persecution was a factor of great importance in winning the alliance of Protestant states against the intolerant Habsburgs, and their contribution to the economic strength of France was out of all proportion to their numbers. Nevertheless their very existence became an outrage to the government. The French clergy appealed to their unshakeably orthodox monarch against 'this wretched liberty of conscience which destroys the liberty of the true children of God'; and Louis was reminded that the Edict of Nantes[13] had been wrung from the crown at a moment when Henry IV had had no other means of silencing Huguenot opposition than by concession. What had once been granted out of weakness could, logically, be reversed from strength. Louis's concept of the state allowed no room for dissent, and the Huguenots, as a separate community within his body politic, were a blatant example of irreconcilable nonconformity.

If Louis's *Mémoires* can be trusted, he was not at first in favour

[12] 1629. See Chapter III, pp. 182–3.
[13] 1598. See Chapter III, p. 166.

of revoking the Edict of Nantes outright: 'I thought that the best way to reduce the Huguenots of my kingdom was to avoid using any new severity against them, and to maintain all the concessions which they had obtained from my predecessors, but to give them nothing more and to limit the execution even of these within the narrowest bounds that justice and decency would admit.' The Assembly of the Clergy was eager to assist Louis's definition of these 'narrowest bounds', and set up a commission to investigate the administration of the edict, construing its terms as literally as possible. So stringent were its recommendations that Colbert was forced to protest at the damage to the economy which might result from Huguenot emigration, and Louis's diplomats advised him of the concern displayed by his Protestant allies. For the moment Louis agreed to restrain the ardour of his clergy, but the respite lasted only a decade.

Nor was it without incident. Irritating restrictions were imposed by overscrupulous interpretation of the edict and a number of Protestant churches were closed. Moreover, as the morale of the Huguenots began to weaken, many of their leaders, Turenne for one, and large numbers of their pastors abjured their faith. So marked was this development that Conversion Bureaus — *Caisses des Conversions* — were established to encourage further conversions by the offer of payment.

As a result the number of Huguenots fell to about 500,000 by the time that the end of the Dutch War (1679) made it easier to ignore opinion abroad. Louvois, moreover, anxious to preserve his importance in Louis's eyes, applied himself to urging the king to adopt more positive measures.

His action was well timed. Embarrassed by his public controversy with the Pope over the *régale*, Louis was eager to demonstrate his orthodoxy by persecuting Huguenots. Moreover, he had abandoned his vivacious mistresses for the sedate companionship of Madame de Maintenon, whom he subsequently married after the queen's death. Her personal devoutness made itself felt in the improved morals of the court, and both she and de la Chaise urged Louis to atone for the sins of his lusty youth by eliminating heresy within France. 'The king is beginning to think seriously of his salvation,' she wrote. 'If God preserves his life there will soon be only one religion in this kingdom.'

After 1680 a series of edicts attacked the Huguenots at every point. Churches built since 1598 were demolished on the grounds that the Edict of Nantes protected only those churches in existence at the date of its issue; the professions were formally closed to all save Catholics; Huguenot academies were closed, and children aged seven were taken from their parents to make a 'free choice' between the two faiths. In areas where the Huguenots were most numerous, in Alsace, Picardy, the Midi and the provinces along the west coast, many of them had purchased office and were thus able to protect local congregations from the full force of the edicts. Against the *dragonnades*, however, they were powerless. The billeting of troops had been used in the past to punish the inhabitants of a region for non-payment of taxes. In 1681 Louvois ordered Marillac, the intendant of Poitou, to adopt the same device in order to 'force the Huguenots into conversion'. By looting their billets, by brutal and bestial conduct, the troops terrorised their hosts into renouncing their faith. Whole villages were 'converted' overnight, but such was the influence of the *officiers*, even of Huguenot *officiers*, who by the recent edicts should not have held office at all, that when those of Poitou protested Louis made a public show of disapproval by reprimanding Marillac and by ordering the *dragonnades* to cease. Louvois, however, understood the true wishes of his master and extended his activities. Both Louis and the court privately applauded what Madame de Sévigné described as 'the astounding success of the magistrats and provincial governors, aided by a few dragoons'.

Thirty thousand conversions were reported from Poitou alone, and Louis claimed that the Edict of Nantes was no longer relevant, 'as the best and largest part of our subjects of the so-called reformed religion have embraced the Catholic faith'. In 1685 the edict was revoked. Henceforth, Huguenot services were forbidden, all children were to be baptised by a priest, and, though the pastors were exiled, laymen who tried to emigrate were to be executed or sent to the galleys. To enforce the decrees the troops were again employed, and Louvois officially approved their excesses, 'since these people are distinguished by their refusal to submit to the king's decrees, you need not observe in their case the restraints which have been prescribed to you, nor can you make too severe and burdensome the quartering of the

5. *The Karlskirche, Vienna*

6b The Church of the Sorbonne, Paris

6a The Church of Les Invalides, Paris

7a. *The Orléans Wing, Blois*

7b. *The Louvre, East Front, Paris*

8. *Versailles: the Garden Front*

troops upon them'.

At least 200,000 Huguenots risked their lives to flee abroad. Sixty thousand came to England, and the remainder found refuge in Switzerland, Denmark, Brandenburg and the United Provinces.

The consequences of their arrival cannot be exaggerated in so far as their presence nourished hostility to France. The city of Amsterdam put aside its disputes with William of Orange and supported the formation of the League of Augsburg, the elector of Brandenburg abandoned the subsidies of France for those of the emperor and the English, on the brink of removing a Catholic ruler, were encouraged in their horror of Catholicism. The economic consequences were equally serious. The Revocation is no longer held to be the major cause of French industrial decline in the later years of Louis's reign but its effects were nonetheless harmful. Most of the *emigrés* were merchants or craftsmen, since the less wealthy had not the means to escape. France could ill afford this exodus of talent: her ironworks, paper-mills, tanneries and textile centres were grievously affected, and Nîmes, Lyon and Reims lost more than half their number of skilled workers. A new impetus was given to the industries of France's rivals by the influx of *emigrés* who established, for example, the manufacture of glass at Copenhagen, of lace at Nottingham, and of silk in London, Amsterdam and Geneva.

'The Revocation, without the least pretext of necessity, depopulated a quarter of the kingdom, ruined its commerce and weakened it in all parts. It authorised tortures in which thousands of both sexes died, split families in twain, drove manufacturers abroad, profited the foreigner at the expense of France and filled the country with the perjury and sacrilege of those who sacrificed their conscience to their prosperity and quiet.' Saint-Simon, of course, exaggerated and, furthermore, he wrote in secret. In public the revocation was acclaimed. 'The greatest and most wonderful thing that has ever been imagined or achieved', wrote Madame de Sévigné, and the official view was given utterance by Bossuet: 'Proclaim this miracle of our times. Send up to heaven our praises and say to this new Constantine, this new Theodosius, this new Charlemagne, it is the worthy achievement of your reign. By you heresy no longer exists.'

In fact heresy stubbornly persisted: the majority of the Huguenots took refuge in passive resistance, sometimes protected in Huguenot areas by the *officiers* of their own faith, and by 1698 Louis had been persuaded to oppose the excesses of the more violent intendants. The forced conversions and the passive resistance of those who could find no refuge in flight, did nothing to improve the condition of the French Church, but this was beside the point. The king's absolutism had been expressed in a satisfyingly dramatic manner, and uniformity, no matter how superficial, had been achieved.

Catholic Nonconformists

During Louis XIV's minority a small but extremely devout section of the French clergy had begun to identify itself with the teaching of Cornelius Jansen, a theologian of Louvain in the Netherlands. Jansen had revived the perennial questions of Free Will, Justification by Faith and the nature of Divine Grace:[14] he taught that man was saved only through the love of God which created faith, that this love was awakened by an act of conversion and that conversion came about solely by the operation of God's irresistible Grace. A convinced Catholic, who owed his inspiration to the writings of St Augustine, he not only opposed the Jesuits who emphasised the value of man's own efforts towards attaining salvation, but his doctrine smacked of predestination. His followers were attracted mainly by the emphasis he placed upon the sense of personal conversion, resulting in a life of personal devotion and piety: without it, he claimed, morality became little more than the performance of prescribed duties.

Jansen died in 1638 but his close friend, the Abbé de St Cyran, introduced his ideas into France; and before his death in 1643 he had found two loyal adherents in Angélique Arnauld, the Abbess of Port-Royal, and her brother Antoine, a doctor of the Sorbonne. In their hands Jansenism developed as a spiritual movement with a strong bias against the Jesuits, whom they accused of encouraging too worldly an attitude to religion. The Jesuits retaliated by charging them with heresy and enlisting the support of the government. Largely due to Mazarin's intervention, five

---

[14] See Chapter I, page 83, for a more detailed examination both of his doctrine and of his followers

propositions extracted from Jansen's writings were condemned by Pope Innocent X in 1653, and, three years later, Antoine Arnauld was censured by the Sorbonne and deprived of his doctorate. More dangerous than the hostility of the Jesuits was Louis XIV's own disapproval of the movement. He was not a theologian but he made up in prejudice what he lacked in understanding. The Jansenists offended him beyond measure, since, as Racine put it, 'they had dealings with many people in disgrace at court, who came to them to seek spiritual consolation and sometimes even to adopt a life of penitence'. Many of these people were former Frondeurs, among them Madame de Longueville, who had discovered at Port-Royal an austerity and a discipline which provided a welcome change from their previous life. This, though bad, was not all. By embracing a particular mode of life and by defending doctrines which the orthodox Catholic found suspect, the Jansenists stood accused of nonconformity, the very sin which Louis XIV most abominated.

The first attack, in 1661, was directed against the community at Port-Royal, where the nuns were required to sign a Formulary condemning the five propositions attributed to Jansen by the bull of 1653. Mère Angélique died just before the crisis broke, but despite her loss the nuns refused to submit to Louis's orders, and were consequently removed from Paris to confinement in the convent of Port-Royal des Champs. When the Formulary was presented to the clergy, however, Louis found it less easy to discipline his opponents. Four bishops, among them Pavillon and Caulet, declared that though the pope's condemnation of the propositions had to be accepted, his ruling that these propositions represented Jansen's teaching was only a matter of fact, and therefore open to question. It was an ingenious distinction, made in the first place by Blaise Pascal, whose *Lettres Provinciales* had made him the most effective propagandist of Jansenism. Moreover, the bishops were on good ground in denying the pope's authority to intervene in this matter, since they could invoke in their defence the liberties of the Gallican Church. Nineteen other bishops supported their stand, and so loth was Louis to provoke a crisis in the Assembly of the Clergy that he handed the affair over to his diplomats. Lionne, in particular, was expert at reconciling diverse views,[15] and he finally secured a settlement, the *paix de*

[15] See Chapter VII, p. 334.

l' église (1668) which allowed the clergy to preserve a 'reverent silence' as to whether or not the condemned doctrines were in fact those of Jansen. Louis was beaten for the time being: the Formulary was withdrawn and the nuns at Port-Royal des Champs were permitted to live there freely, preserving their doctrines and even teaching them in the convent school.

For some time an uneasy truce prevailed, but the action of Caulet and Pavillon in defying the king a second time, over the *régale*, revived Louis's indignation against the Jansenists in general who, while the *paix de l'église* was prolonged, were able to grow in strength. One of their books, Quesnal's *Réflexions Morales sur le Nouveau Testament* enjoyed remarkable success and was even approved for use in his diocese by Noailles, the influential Bishop of Châlons, who later succeeded Harlay as Archbishop of Paris. Louis could wait no longer, and, despite the thorny problem of Gallicanism, he resorted to Rome for assistance. Clement XI was as eager as Louis to suppress the Jansenists and the bull *Vineam Domini* (1705), worded with meticulous care to avoid affronting the Assembly of the Clergy, forbade any further recourse to 'reverent silence'. Port-Royal des Champs was closed and, by a petty act of vengeance which revealed the personal spite behind Louis's policy, the graves of former members were desecrated. Quesnal's book, however, had not been specifically condemned by Clement's bull, and Noailles's approval of it required an effective answer. Louis appealed to Clement yet again, and in 1713 he was rewarded with the bull *Unigenitus,* which handsomely condemned no less than 101 of Quesnal's moral reflections.

Unigenitus gave rise to such confused debate within the Assembly that, among its opponents it became impossible to distinguish Gallican from Jansenist. At first Louis tried to appease them by modifying its terms; but Clement refused to countenance any further interference with the pope's power to condemn heresy, and Noailles preferred to defy the king than to endure the humiliation of retracting his approval of Quesnal. When all else had failed, Louis used force, and the bull was accepted only after its opponents had been exiled to their dioceses. This resort to personal intimidation, in the last months of Louis's life, destroyed the working alliance he had always sought to maintain with his clergy; yet, paradoxically, it identified church and state more closely than ever since Louis had thus made himself the sole arbiter in a theological dispute. The king's will was expressed not only in law but in dogma: his absolutism extended beyond the realm of politics into the recesses of the individual conscience.[16]

THE SOURCES OF FRENCH PROSPERITY AND POWER

Colbert and Royal Solvency

Jean-Baptiste Colbert was perhaps the most talented, certainly the most ubiquitous, of Louis XIV's ministers. He had served a long apprenticeship, first under Le Tellier, then as Mazarin's principal agent, until finally, after Fouquet's disgrace, he became Louis's chief adviser and servant in domestic affairs. Finance, industry and trade were his greatest interests, but he also proved invaluable in matters relating to the navy, the administration of justice, the control of the clergy, the dispensation of patronage and the creation of a centralised administration. To most people he seemed a colourless man, meticulous and coldly ruthless, but without the pompous idiosyncrasies of Sully or the dominating personality of Richelieu. In fact his life was filled with the endless satisfaction of directing the affairs of state from the privacy of his office. A true bureaucrat, he had a genius for planning and organisation; he loved the collation of reports, the preparation of agenda, and the compilation of instructions. He was, in short, the best type of *officier*.

The fiscal system was as bad as it had always been.[17] The privileges of the nobility, the clergy and the *officiers* prevented the Treasury from taxing the wealthier sections of the community, an anomaly constantly indicated by Colbert's intendants: 'Less than half the land in the kingdom is liable to the *taille*: the nobles who own the greater part of it pay nothing; the citizens of several towns who own land in the surrounding countryside are exempt by privilege, office or favour; only the miserable peasant has to pay.' The taxes, moreover, were levied at different rates in different parts of the country. If the incidence of taxation was unfair, its collection was inefficient and unreliable. In the villages

[16] For yet another incident revealing Louis's obsessive hatred of religious nonconformity, see the account of Madame Guyon and the Quietists in Chapter I, p.86
[17] See Chapter III, p. 173, on Sully.

it was necessary to conscript one of the peasants as tax-collector, and if he failed to secure the full amount from his neighbours, by means of methods which could in any case only imperil his future social life, he himself was mulcted of the deficit and imprisoned. Higher up the scale, the *officiers* through whose hands the taxes then passed made a fortune by falsifying their accounts. Colbert estimated that of the 85,000,000 *livres* collected in 1661, more than 53,000,000 *livres* were lost to the crown before the remainder finally reached the Treasury.

The fundamental faults of the system could not be remedied. In an age when the civil service lacked a tradition of honesty and efficiency, and when the government possessed no effective means of speedy communication and law enforcement, Colbert's imaginative concept of a uniform fiscal system was incapable of execution. Although the *pays d'état* had been compelled to accept royal direction in matters of taxation there was a limit to the amount which could be demanded — witness the Brittany revolt of 1675 (see above, page 296) — and Louis XIV was too concerned with foreign affairs to allow his minister to initiate radical changes which might result in revolution. Colbert himself recognised this, though he never abandoned his efforts to achieve some measure of reform. Each tax in turn was scrutinised in the hope that its incidence might be extended or its collection improved. Some provinces, for example, paid the *taille personelle*, a kind of poll tax based on estimates of personal income, while others paid the *taille réelle*, a property tax which spared the landless labourer but in general imposed heavier burdens upon the taxpayer. Colbert attempted to make the latter universal, though first of all it was necessary to undertake an effective land survey. This he did in the *généralité* of Montauban and the increased yield from taxation was immediately apparent; unfortunately it was also clear that the organisation of a land census on a national scale was beyond the resources of Colbert's staff. It was not simply a matter of handling and interpreting the statistics: the application of mathematical techniques and principles to the science of administration, termed political arithmetic, provided no formula to account for the passive resistance to be expected from the threatened provinces.

Colbert recognised the poverty of the peasantry and made every effort to reduce the *taille*. In its place he set out to tap the pockets of the wealthier members of society by increasing the indirect taxes from which there was less exemption. By 1683 indirect taxes produced half of the government's revenue, although there was little that was uniform about them. Even the *gabelle*, the compulsory purchase of salt from the government's licensed retailers, lacked the degree of uniformity essential for exploitation and development on a national basis. Some indication of its efficacy was afforded by the universal hatred it aroused, especially as the retailers frequently augmented their profits by wholesale adulterations: the Bordeaux peasants who rebelled in 1674 echoed the plea of thousands when they shouted, *'Vive le roi, sans gabelle.'* Unfortunately for Colbert, its incidence varied from thirty-five to forty-eight *livres* on each hundred pounds of salt between the Somme and the Loire, the region of the *grande gabelle*, and from six to thirty in the southern provinces.

What could not be reformed had nevertheless to be made to work. Colbert hit out at peculation by using the *chambre de justice* appointed to condemn Fouquet to investigate the activities of his subordinates. The shock administered by Fouquet's disgrace, and the obvious determination of the king to reinforce Colbert's efforts, proved remarkably salutary. By 1669 over 100,000,000 *livres* had been recouped by the Treasury from the pockets of its agents. At the same time, Colbert reduced payments on the *rentes*, which he abhorred as a parasitic growth on the Treasury since they consumed money that was needed for the king's government. In December, 1664, Madame de Sévigné recorded a rumour in Paris that 'the *rentes* were to be paid off at a rate which would send them all to the workhouse'. Her report was exaggerated, but Colbert's action was none the less severe. Some of the *rentes* were paid off at their value in 1639, others were repudiated altogether, and the interest on the remainder was revised. In all, this represented a virtual repudiation of the debt by about 60 per cent. From Colbert's point of view it was a satisfactory achievement, but the blow given to public credit was to have harmful effects later.[18]

Colbert, like Sully, compelled the tax farmers to accept rates more favourable to the Treasury, and he scrutinised patents of exemption with the result that in Provence alone he claimed to have discovered more than a thousand *faux nobles*. His inten-

18 See below, p. 321.

dants, the only men he could trust, were ordered to supervise the *officiers* engaged in tax collection, and an improved system of accounts was introduced in order to make peculation more difficult. Within the Treasury he kept a *registre de fonds* and a *registre de dépenses* to record the anticipated revenues and expenses of his department, while the actual payments and receipts were recorded in a daily balance sheet, the *journal*. From this he compiled an annual *état au vrai*, of which a simplified summary, the *abrégé des finances*, was presented to the king. By this means the collectors and other agents of the Treasury discovered that Colbert had established a clear idea of the sums to be expected from them. Consequently, their falsified reports had to be hastily amended to the Treasury's advantage. The system was not foolproof: Le Pelletier reported several discrepancies when he succeeded Colbert, but for this Colbert's idealism was to blame. Denied the chance to establish good order throughout the kingdom, it was some small consolation to make his books reflect an ideal statement of his intentions.[19] His achievement was none the less remarkable. Taxation in 1683, the year in which he died, produced 116,000,000 *livres* as compared with the 85,000,000 *livres* of 1661; but the significant figure which revealed the value of his work was the reduction of the amount lost in collection from 53,000,000 *livres* to 23,000,000.

The government's debts in 1660 exceeded 700,000,000 *livres*, without taking into account the capital value of royal offices, calculated by Colbert to be worth 420,000,000 livres. Within ten years Colbert had more or less balanced his books and it was only the outbreak of the Dutch War, prompted in part by his own tariffs, which compelled him to accumulate new debts of about 230,000,000 *livres* by 1683. (See R. Briggs, *Early Modern France*, Appendix, Graph 6.) It was nonetheless a tremendous achievement and the reputed glory of Louis XIV's reign, the expenditure on Versailles and warfare, was thus made possible by the indefatigable efforts of an honest minister who increased the net value of a corrupt and out-dated fiscal system from 22,000,000 *livres* a year to 93,000,000.

The nature of Colbert's genius when untrammelled by vested interests is best revealed by his management of crown lands, a

[19] Cf. the comment of E. Lavisse, *Histoire de France*, 'Il y a l'abîme entre ce qu'il a voulu et ce qu'il a fait', a verdict which applies to so much of Colbert's work.

sphere in which he was entirely free to apply the principles of good order that delighted his imagination. First he prepared a survey of all lands, waters and forests belonging to the king, scrutinising all charters of alienation to ensure that nothing had been forfeited during periods of anarchy in the past. Then he examined the activities of his staff and prepared a comprehensive code of instructions for the better management of the royal estates. During his term of office, the value of the forests alone increased from 168,000 *livres* a year to over 1,000,000; while the other crown lands produced 5,500,000 *livres* in place of the 800,000 recorded for 1661. It is a sad comment on the *ancien régime* that no proportionate increase in revenue could be achieved in the national system of taxation.

Colbert and National Prosperity

Colbert's comprehensive programme for the expansion of industry and trade had been formulated during his long period of service under Mazarin. As early as 1653 he prepared a statement of policy which embraced every section of the economy, and, though Mazarin had ignored it, it was to be the basis of Colbert's work after 1661: 'We must re-establish or create all industries, even luxury industries; a system of protection must be developed by means of a customs tariff; trade and traders must be reorganised into gilds; financial hindrances which burden the people must be lightened; transport of commodities by land and sea must be restored; colonies must be developed and commercially bound to France; all barriers between France and India must be broken down; the navy must be strengthened to afford protection to merchant ships.'

The plan was not designed to benefit Louis XIV's subjects so much as Louis himself, since any increase in national wealth was to result in an equivalent increase in taxation. Colbert realised the intimate connection between economic and military powers and attempted to construct an economic system geared to the needs of warfare; 'the commercial companies,' he wrote, 'are the armies of the king, and his industries act as his reserves'.[20]

For a country which maintained such vast armies and paid such generous subsidies to its allies, it was natural to identify

[20] See Chapter I, pp. 26–9, for a general discussion of mercantilism.

national wealth with the possession of gold: gold, moreover, was considered to be a limited commodity, and the value of trade was accordingly assessed by Colbert by its success or failure to bring bullion into France. Trade itself, he believed to be as limited as gold, and he accepted as a basic fact that 20,000 ships were all that was required for the commerce of his age. 'The Dutch have of this total 15,000 to 16,000, and the French 500 or 600 at the most.' Whether or not his figures were correct the moral was obvious; and if it was easy for historians of a free-trade era to condemn the economic theory informing Colbert's work, it is less so now in an age pre-occupied with the need to avert an adverse balance of payments.

The first task was to stimulate productivity, but curiously enough Colbert paid little attention to the essential problem of food production.

He believed that agricultural production was essentially static, in contrast to the manufacturing industries which, if handled correctly, could attain to unlimited heights of prosperity: it was these which he described as 'the fertile sources of a kingdom's prosperity'. In the event, therefore, little was done for French agriculture, and the peasant was left to fight his own struggle for existence unaided.

To revive old industries and to introduce new ones Colbert recruited skilled craftsmen from all over Europe: tapestry-makers, dyers and paper-makers from the Netherlands; silk-workers, glassblowers, embroiderers and lace-makers from Italy; leather-workers and hatters from Spain; engineers, mining experts, engravers, ironfounders and naval constructors from England, Germany and Scandinavia. To train Frenchmen in the best techniques, Colbert envisaged a national system of technical education, but his ambitions once again outran the facilities at his disposal. Nevertheless, teams of craftsmen were despatched to demonstrate their methods in the provinces, the *Académie des Sciences* was mobilised to study techniques of production, and the *Journal des Savants* gave publicity to its findings. The experts were also employed to make detailed recommendations which Colbert embodied in a series of edicts of an exceptionally high standard. The object of his legislation was best expressed in the preamble to an edict affecting most of the textile workers, and dealing with the length, width and quality of cloths, serges and other stuffs of linen and wool: 'to render uniform all those products of the same type, name and quality, in whatever place they may be made, both to increase their sale inside and outside our kingdom, and to prevent the public from being cheated'.

A staff of inspectors was appointed to administer the edicts, penalties were laid down for all irregularities in production, and the gild system was revived, by making membership compulsory (1673), in order to establish a more effective control over the artisans themselves. As was only to be expected, Colbert's regulations were disliked by those who had become accustomed to their own traditional methods of work, and even more by the *officiers* who resented this detailed interference in their local industries. Their resistance frequently jeopardised the system, and the case of the Widow Falempin was by no means untypical. Obstinately refusing to conform to the standards required by Colbert, she was punished by the inspectors, but successfully appealed to the *parlement* of Amiens to rescind the penalties. Colbert immediately drafted a new edict to reverse the verdict, and emphasised the moral that 'if such frequent contraventions as those of the Widow Falempin, and such enterprise as her appeal to the *parlement*, were not severely repressed, the *échevins*[21] of Amiens would lose prestige, the regulations would be violated with impunity, and industry and trade would be ruined'. Colbert's words revealed perhaps a trace of hysteria, but the magistrates frequently refused to impose the penalties demanded by the industrial edicts, and it was impossible for him to interfere in each case. Moreover, there were many thousands of workers who supplemented their living from the fields by part-time spinning or weaving[22]. Scattered across the countryside, and working in their own homes, they evaded the supervision of the gilds and could ignore Colbert's edicts with impunity.

Despite Colbert's difficulties, French industry was revitalised, and the production of textiles, his favourite concern, was greatly improved. France began to produce lace of a quality which sold abroad. The Gobelins factory in Paris, one of Colbert's *manufactures royales* established to introduce new industries, became a showpiece for visitors, and its tapestries, along with those of Beauvais and Chaillot, were eagerly purchased outside France.

[21] Inspectors
[22] In Picardy 19,000 or more worked at home, against the 6,000 officially registered in the town gilds.

At Arras the production of heavily embroidered fine cloths was established with the help of government subsidies, while in Languedoc half a million skilled workers were similarly employed in the neighbourhood of Carcassonne.

If industry as a whole were to expand, the transport of heavy goods had to be radically improved. Colbert, as *Grand Voyer*, reorganised the departments of state responsible for roads and bridges, provided a national freight service, and encouraged the widespread use of stone setts to make the *pavés du roi*. Once again he was confronted with the opposition of local authorities; indeed, there were many landowners with a vested interest in bad roads since they were lawfully entitled to all spilt merchandise. Coach travel between Paris and Orleans, a distance of 120 kilometres, took two days, and eight more were needed to continue the journey to Lyon: heavy transport made slower progress. Colbert therefore turned to transport by water. Great stretches of the Seine, the Loire and the Rhône were opened to navigation, and the most spectacular of his ventures was the construction of the Languedoc Canal. The engineering genius of Riquet, and later of Vauban, was employed in damming an entire valley to create a reservoir supplying water at the summit, and in constructing a hundred locks and three great aqueducts. The two ends were linked by blasting a tunnel of 180 metres, the first time that gunpowder was used for this purpose. With a depth of 1.8 metres and 9.7 metres wide, the canal was able to carry barges of 200 tonnes from the Mediterranean to the Atlantic, a feat of civil engineering which far surpassed any other since the time of the Roman Empire.

An even greater handicap to internal trade than the state of the roads was the exorbitant number of tolls and taxes levied on goods in transit across France. The *péages*, payments to local corporations or landowners, had outlived their original purpose since the collectors were no longer required to maintain roads and bridges in their area; but like so many other features of the *ancien régime* they had become the perquisite of a privileged class, and Colbert was powerless to reform them. The *traites* were government taxes, and though Colbert was free to establish a more rational system of collection, they were too lucrative to be abolished. Colbert divided France into three free-trade areas, the central provinces, the outlying provinces which ringed them, and the newly acquired towns of Alsace. By this means internal trade was encouraged, but it was still possible for the *traites* to be levied more than once in a single journey, thus making the whole transaction unprofitable.

The tariffs on goods passing in and out of France were another matter, since Colbert intended to use these to protect French industry. To begin with, the import of raw materials was encouraged by reducing the tariff, while goods manufactured abroad were heavily taxed, but a new tariff code in 1667 carried his plan a stage further. All imports of Venetian lace and glass were forbidden, and the tariffs on imported textiles were doubled; fine cloths, for example, were taxed at 80 instead of 40 *livres*, and worsted stockings at 8 instead of 3 *livres*. In this way Colbert intended not to raise revenue but to discourage foreign competition: above all, he hoped to strike a blow at the Dutch by limiting their exports into France. This, of course, was an important factor in the war which broke out between the two countries in 1672. Unfortunately for Colbert, the cost of the war, prolonged by the spirited defiance of the Dutch, made his tariff policy impracticable. The state needed money urgently, and tariffs had to be exploited as a source of revenue rather than as a means to benefit French industry and trade.

Another of Colbert's plans to stimulate production was by seeking control of markets overseas, a difficult task since English and Dutch companies were already established in this field. Colbert nevertheless believed that the formation of properly controlled companies might yet establish France as *l'arbitre du commerce* . The plan was well conceived but the companies were handicapped from the start. The middle classes could not be persuaded to invest in them. Traditionally, they preferred to employ their capital in buying offices in the administration, and Colbert's drastic revision of the *rentes* discouraged investment in government funds. The Treasury could only afford to make initial grants to the companies, and then only during the rare periods of peace. The activities of French merchants aroused the hostility of the English and Dutch governments, and commercial rivalry was an important factor contributing to the wars of 1688–97 and of 1701–14. The recurrence of warfare was the final blow, since a government preoccupied with defending its frontiers would afford time only for the most cursory attention to the well-being of its trading companies. Indeed, its sole action was to apply Colbert's regulations after his death in a rigid, mechanical way that inhibited commercial activity, whereas the companies directed by private merchants in England and Holland continued to expand their operations.

In short, none of Colbert's companies achieved anything more than partial success, and after his death in 1683 they collapsed. The Senegal Company challenged the Dutch in West Africa to good effect, but to undercut its rivals it had to forgo its own profits, and thus failed to attract the investment needed for consolidating its position. In the Baltic the French maintained so favourable a balance of trade, selling wines, textiles and West Indian sugar for naval stores, that the English and Dutch governments made it a specific feature of their policy during the war of 1688–97 to drive French shipping from northern waters. The Levant Company had a longer life: based on Marseilles it was better placed for trade with the Middle East than its rivals in London and Amsterdam, but Colbert disliked its operations since the import of silk, leather, rice and cotton had to be paid for in gold. Repeatedly he urged the Marseilles merchants to sell the fine cloths of Carcassonne, deliberately designed for export, but no amount of regulation could create any enthusiasm for them in the markets of the Levant. The most immediately successful of Colbert's projects was the West Indies Company. By its efforts the production of sugar in the islands was increased from an annual total of 5,500,000 kilograms in 1674 to 8,150,000 kilograms in 1682, and twenty-nine refineries were established in France to process the entire crop. Tobacco, too, did well, until the Dutch War when the tobacco monopoly was farmed out to speculators. But while Colbert surpassed himself in recruiting Dutch experts to create his refineries, he failed to attract settlers to run the plantations. Indeed the men he most needed, men of independence and resourcefulness, were discouraged by his paternalist regulations and chose to live instead in the backwoods of the St Lawrence or join La Salle in opening up the Mississippi delta.

The internal peace and security afforded by Louis XIV's reign no doubt accounted in part for the expansion of trade and industry between 1660 and 1685, but it was also a period of general economic depression throughout Europe and, in a contracting market, the merchants of Holland and England were well placed to preserve their virtual monopoly of European trade. Colbert, moreover, had to combat the privileged nature of French society, the power of the *officiers* to resist his orders, and the persecution of the Huguenots which deprived France of thousands of skilled workers — faults for which he was not responsible, and which he was powerless to amend. Nonetheless the degree of regulation was excessive, the tariff of 1667 contributed to the very war which destroyed the peace-time economy upon which depended the success of his policies, and his inability to provide more than 2,000,000 livres from the government funds from 1661–72 left all his companies and industrial projects hopelessly underinvested.

THE PRICE OF WARFARE: FRANCE 1683–1715

In the glorious aftermath of the victories of Condé and Turenne, Louis XIV conceived of Versailles as a seat of government worthy of his majesty and might, but it was the sad irony of his reign that the palace was completed only to receive the news of Blenheim, Oudenarde and Ramillies.[23] Indeed, the growing failure of French troops to hold their own against the combined forces of a hostile Europe was reflected in the malaise which afflicted the court after 1690. The younger nobles deserted Versailles for the livelier atmosphere of their hotels and *salons* in Paris, and the ceremonial constructed around the sun king began to lose its meaning as his mortality became all too evident. 'The years pass one after the other,' wrote Louis to his grandson Philip in Spain; 'time slips by without our being aware of it; we grow old like ordinary men, and we shall finish like them.' The dauphin died in 1711, to be followed within a year by his elder son, his daughter-in-law and his grandson. Saddened by their loss, the king lived on in lonely isolation.

If Louis himself had died in 1688, at the age of 50, he might have left an unblemished reputation for majesty, power, efficiency and success. Moreover, because of his own active contribution to affairs of state he would have deserved the credit for managing the brilliant team of servants bequeathed him by Mazarin. It was

23 See Chapter VII, pp. 366–8.

his tragedy to outlive them by a generation. Lionne died in 1671, Colbert in 1683, Le Tellier in 1685, and their talented sons, Seignelay and Louvois, in 1690 and 1691. There were still some men of ability, notably Colbert de Torcy, but the golden age was over. The practice of minutely regulating the affairs of France to benefit both king and country was succeeded by the mere habit of regulation for its own sake. The informing genius which had breathed vigour into the agencies of government was lost, and the administration congealed. So great a burden had been imposed on the Treasury by the relatively short campaign against the Dutch (1672–3), that even Colbert had been forced to run into debt. His successors, none of whom had that minister's ability and were faced with a period of almost continuous warfare, were therefore doomed to failure. The increasing cost of financing Louis's campaigns, combined with the greater laxity of the tax collectors led to a desperate situation. Expenditure rose from 130,000,000 *livres*, in 1689 to 211,000,000 in 1698, 264,000,000 in 1711 and 213,000,000 in 1714 (see *MCMH* Vol VI page 299 and Briggs, *op.cit.*, Appendix). Most of this went on the war and in financing the debts incurred by expenditure on warfare.

Taxes were increased, but they fell upon an ever-shrinking section of the community, on those who were too impoverished to purchase exemption, and so imminent was the danger of bankruptcy that a more effective system of taxation was attempted. During the war of 1688–97, the government introduced the *capitation*, under which the population was graded into twenty-two classes, the first to pay 2,000 *livres* a year, the lowest one *livre*. The provinces of Alsace, Franche Comté and Flanders immediately purchased their exemption, as did the clergy, and the rest of French society rushed in to be downgraded on the scale. The tax produced 22,000,000 *livres* in its first years, but it became so riddled with exemption that in 1710 it was supplemented by the *dixième,* a tax claiming one tenth of all incomes. Powerless to enforce it uniformly, the Treasury discovered that most of the revenue it produced was immediately offset by decreasing returns from the other taxes still in existence.

The government resorted to an endless variety of expedients. Leases were limited to a period of nine years so that the Treasury might secure frequent fees from their renewal; coffee, tea and chocolate joined the ever-increasing list of state monopolies;

forced loans were imposed on municipal corporations, natural-
ised aliens, the newly ennobled, and the remaining Huguenots
whose wealth secured them unofficial toleration. The government sold even its personal credit: the contracts for the tax farms
of 1693 were revoked after they had been purchased, and sold a
second time at a profit of 10,000,000 *livres*, while bills on the
Caisse des Emprunts were so dishonoured that they fell to 30 per
cent of their nominal value. More general and more injurious in
their effect, were the nine adjustments made between 1689 and
1709 in the relative values of bullion and currency, and the issue
of paper money (1702), which within three years had become so
inflated that royal edicts were powerless to compel its acceptance.

Worst of all was the excessive sale of offices: 'The powers of
protecting innocence,' wrote La Bruyère, 'of punishing crime and
of providing justice for everyone were sold to the last penny, as
though the administration were a business firm.' When legiti-
mate posts had been duplicated beyond all measure—at Besançon, for example, a new chamber had to be added to the *Parlement*
to accommodate the new *officiers*—the government resorted to the
creation of ludicrous ones. Controllers of *perruques* were appointed
in 1706. More fantastic still was the sale of offices to supervise the
registration of baptisms: in 1691 Guardians of Registers were
appointed; in 1697 their work was duplicated by Controllers of
the Registers, in 1706 by Controllers of Extracts from the
Registers, in 1709 by Bailiffs of the Registers. Baptism became an
expensive affair when each of these *officiers* demanded his fee. The
device, moreover, recoiled upon the Treasury. Between 1690 and
1715 it raised over 900,000,000 *livres* by selling offices, but each
new *officier* was not only exempt from taxes but had to be paid a
salary. Whereas 23,000,000 *livres* were spent in salaries in 1683,
the cost in 1699 was 47,000,000—and in 1715, 84,000,000.

As a result the government's indebtedness became more acute.
Excluding the capital value of its own offices, the debt exceeded
400,000,000 *livres* in 1688, 1,200,000,000 in 1708 and
2,000,000,000 in 1715. (See Briggs, *op.cit.*, Appendix). With the
ending of the war the whole financial machinery of the government was in such confusion that recovery had not been achieved
by the time of the Revolution in 1789.

It was the fundamental weakness of the *ancien régime* that it
failed to tap the real sources of wealth within the country, and the

true condition in France should not be judged by the plight of the Treasury. Nevertheless, the withering influence of the government's unimaginative policies brought about a serious economic decline. The trading companies collapsed because the government was too preoccupied with warfare to direct them efficiently; the revocation of the Edict of Nantes deprived industry of many of its skilled workers; and heavy taxation, along with the uncertainty of money values and fluctuation of wheat prices, led to a fall in consumption and productivity. The gilds resorted to restrictive practices and the masters exploited the powers conferred on them by Colbert, not to improve the quality of their work but to discipline and to underpay their journeymen and apprentices. Strikes broke out frequently, and it was not only the Huguenots who sought refuge abroad: 4,500 Catholic weavers suffered so severely from the depressed condition of their industry in Normandy that they emigrated to England. The government's attempt at remedial action made matters worse, since it resulted in a spate of new edicts which merely parodied those prepared by Colbert. In trade and industry alike the hope for the future lay solely with a few merchants and manufacturers whose personal initiative and enterprise overcame the stultifying effect of the government's policies. Indeed, by the end of the reign, this unlooked-for development was beginning to take effect. In the *chambre de commerce* the need for a change in policy was indicated by one of its members: 'Colbert's companies', he said, 'served their purpose forty years ago; but now we need more freedom from control.' Hence, in 1715, the system of protective tariffs was modified in order to secure reciprocal trade agreements with neighbouring countries. In the hands of private individuals the outlook for the French economy was not without hope.

But the major blows to the French economy in this period were delivered neither by war taxation nor by administrative interference but by the weather. The great agricultural crises of 1693 and 1708 led to famine and threw the economy into confusion, as did the appalling winter of 1708–9 which froze the rivers and paralysed commerce. It is remarkable that rebellion was only sporadic; but spirits had been cowed by the intimidating power of the army and the distress in most quarters was so great that what little energies remained were devoted to survival. The most serious disturbance was the revolt of the *Camisards*[24] among the hills and forests of the Cevennes. Here, a peasant population which had jealously preserved its attachment to the Huguenot faith, was driven to revolt by persecution and by lack of food. In 1702 a Catholic official was murdered, and the act became a signal for a general rising. The *Camisards* knew their countryside well, and, at a time when Louis XIV was at war with the rest of Europe, they maintained an open struggle against the royal troops for four years.

In 1707 Vauban's *Projet d'une dîme royale* expressed a loyal soldier's concern at the poverty which assailed him as he journeyed throughout France. 'I have come to the clear conclusion', he wrote, 'that one-tenth of the people is reduced to beggary and does as a matter of fact live by begging; of the nine-tenths remaining, five cannot give alms to the first tenth because they are very little better off; of the other four-tenths, three are in far from comfortable circumstances.' Once convinced of his case, Vauban laid siege to the Treasury as he had once laid siege to Maastricht, and the solution he sought was as methodically organised as the saps and trenches of his campaigning days. The king, he claimed, owed equal protection to all his subjects and therefore the privileges granted to any single class could only harm the whole state. Accordingly, he proposed the *dîme royale,* a tax of 5 per cent on the yearly produce of all land, and a graduated tax on all incomes derived from other sources. The book was circulated privately among his friends in the government; but its analysis was too penetrating, its proposals too well informed, for the comfort of the king, and it was condemned by royal edict.

Louis XIV could silence criticism: he could not alleviate the distress caused by his policies. In his earlier days he had written for the Dauphin's instruction: 'In working for the state, the monarch is working for himself; the good of the one is the glory of the other; when the former is happy, noble and powerful, he who has brought this about is glorious'. France, during the war of Spanish Succession, was neither happy, noble nor powerful: by his own criterion, Louis XIV stood indicted.

[24] So called because they concealed themselves on raiding parties by wearing nightshirts over their clothes.

VII

WESTERN EUROPE
1660–1714

THE ASCENDANCY OF FRANCE 1660–85

Louis XIV

The initiative in Europe had passed to France: the Dutch, powerful as they were, looked anxiously for other states with whom they might combine to provide an effective balance to French influence, but Spain was a spent force, Austria dared not relax her concentration over the Hungarian plain, Sweden was preoccupied with her struggle for Baltic supremacy, and England, after the triumphs of Cromwell, returned to her subordinate role. France, on the other hand, had seen her power confirmed by the Treaties of Westphalia and the Pyrenees, and in Louis XIV she had a king who delighted in the conduct of war. His ministers cast wide their net of diplomacy to entangle every other state in his plans, his armies marched with confidence against all comers, and for nearly thirty years his ambitions determined the course of events in Europe.

Historians have not agreed in their identification of the motives behind Louis' foreign policy, especially as the period of his reign covered over half a century. It has often been suggested that whereas Henry IV and Richelieu had worked to strengthen their frontiers and to weaken their enemies, Louis was concerned to satisfy a desire for fame and empire, to be the heir of Charlemagne and yet greater. Mazarin had failed to secure his election to the imperial throne in 1656 but Louis never abandoned his dream, always referring to his candidature in his frequent negotiations with the German Electors. 'The German Emperors', he wrote scornfully, 'are neither the heirs of the Romans, nor the successors of Charlemagne'. He alone was

destined for that honour; Versailles, not Vienna, was to house the
temporal overlord of Europe. It was a sad blow when Leopold
lived out the century and thus forestalled the possibility of a
Bourbon triumph in the Electoral College.

Mazarin had bequeathed him yet another imperial vision, that
of the Spanish empire, since Maria Theresa's renunciation of her
claim had been invalidated by Spain's failure to pay her dowry.[1]
In 1661, indeed, his hopes seemed about to be realised. On 1
November Philip IV's sole surviving son died; on the same day
Maria Theresa gave birth to the Dauphin. For five days the heir
apparent to the Spanish throne was, in Louis's eyes, his own son,
until on 6 November the Spanish court celebrated the birth of the
future Carlos II. Nevertheless, the child's sickly nature gave rise
to Louis's hope that soon the Bourbons would succeed to the
Spanish empire. He lived in this hope for forty years.

On the other hand Louis was as preoccupied as any of his
predecessors with the security of his frontiers. The attempt to
tidy them up, by further acquisitions, especially in the north-east
and east, in short to make France more secure, was an important
feature of his policy throughout his reign. Unlike Henry IV and
Richelieu he was more strongly placed to get his own way.
Moreover, though Louis was undoubtedly an aggressive
monarch it is true that the conventions of the century required
that kings achieve military success, and the point was made
clearly by Louis himself in 1688 when he wrote, 'to extend one's
territory is the pleasantest and the most worthy occupation of a
king.'

Le Tellier, Louvois and Colbert: the Army and Navy

Louis XIV's pursuit of glory depended upon the fact that his
army increased in size more rapidly than that of any other state:
72,000 men were under arms in 1660; 120,000 in 1672; 300,000 or
more during the critical years of the War of Spanish Succession.
Recruitment on so vast a scale created unprecedented problems
not only of finance and of leadership in the field but especially of
administration. It was not enough to exploit every device known
to the Treasury until the state fell into bankruptcy, nor to enjoy
the services of such brilliant commanders as Condé, Turenne and

[1] See Chapter III, p. 206.

Luxembourg: if the army were not to collapse under the weight of its own numbers an administrative revolution at the war office was necessary. This was achieved by Michel le Tellier and his son, the Marquis de Louvois, who between them controlled the army from 1643 to 1691.

Le Tellier protested to Mazarin in 1643, 'The army has become a republic with as many cantons or provinces as there are lieutenant-generals.' The Fronde made matters worse, since commanding officers disposed of their troops as they saw fit, changing sides and making treaties without reference to any authority but their own. Such a condition of anarchy derived in part from the arrogance of the French nobility before it had been tamed by Louis XIV, but its basic cause was the system of recruitment. Companies and regiments were raised by noble contractors, who then bargained with the king to determine their conditions of service, with the result that the men of these regiments owed a greater loyalty to the employers who protected their interests than to the king who had played no part in their recruitment. It was necessary therefore to destroy the independence of the contractor by reducing his status to that of a regimental officer subject to the authority of general officers and the commander-in-chief; but this could not be done overnight since it was only by the existing system of contracts that the army could maintain its numbers. The day of feudal levies was long past, and its revival in 1674 at a critical stage of the Dutch war produced so motley a force of ill-equipped and untrained men that Turenne disbanded them at once; nor was conscription a satisfactory alternative since, on the rare occasions when it was adopted, the men deserted in their thousands. Le Tellier and Louvois achieved no radical reform, but by piecemeal modification and improvement, by more stringently worded contracts, and in Louvois's case by means of a formidable, overbearing personality, they extended royal control throughout the army as relentlessly as Colbert had done throughout France. As a measure of their success, 72 of the 78 infantry regiments in existence at Louvois's death, were no longer known by their colonel's name but bore permanent titles as regular units of the royal army.

A serious fault was the dishonesty of commanders who falsified their muster rolls. Having contracted to raise a company of 60 men at a rate of 75 *livres* a month, they would often recruit less than thirty: if the company were to be inspected the remainder, popularly known as *passe-volants*, were enlisted from the streets and taverns for a day's pay. To remedy this, Le Tellier appointed *intendants de l'armée*, inferior in rank only to the commander in chief whose task was not merely to check the muster rolls but also to examine the standard of training in every company and regiment. Men like Martinet, who became a household word for his stringent application of military regulations and whose name significantly was given to the twelve-thonged whip used for military punishment, did much to raise standards of discipline and training throughout the army, and by exposing the *passe-volant*, hastened his departure.

Two further weaknesses of the system were that the man who contracted to raise a body of troops inevitably commanded them, and that commissions were bought and sold like offices in the civil administration. Wealth alone was thus the prerequisite of command. Le Tellier and Louvois therefore limited where possible the advantages of wealth by keeping down the cost of purchasing commands, an infantry regiment in 1689 could be bought for 22,500 *livres*, a company for 12,000, but for a fashionable company of Guards it was still possible to pay as much as 80,000. Of greater service to the poor but talented officer was the new system of promotion, designed by Louvois to allow men to rise to the specially created rank of brigadier-general without first having purchased a colonelcy. A much more positive solution, however, was to accept that wealth was an indispensable factor but to ensure that the serving officer possessed other attributes as well.

Nine colleges were established by Louvois along the northeastern frontier, each with roughly 500 cadets, whose professional training in the colleges was supplemented every summer by practical experience in the field. Existing officers were subjected to promotion examinations and to constant supervision, and Louvois's persistence in setting the highest standards began to produce results since none was spared his displeasure. His treatment of one offender who preferred Versailles to the camp was gleefully recorded by Madame de Sévigné for the entertainment of her daughter:

'M. de Louvois spoke very haughtily to M. de Nogaret the other day.

"Sir, your company is in very poor shape."

"Sir," said he, "I did not know it was."

"You should know," said M. de Louvois. "Have you had a look at it?"

"No," said M. de Nogaret.

"You should have done."

"I will issue some orders about it."

"They should have been given already. You must make up your mind, Sir, whether to declare yourself a courtier or do your duty as an officer."'

Despite the innate conservatism of many officers, Le Tellier and Louvois successfully overcame their resistance to new weapons. The typical company of 1660 comprised two rows of musketeers, whose match-fired *mousquets* were so cumbersome that an additional row of pikemen had to be provided to protect them during the processes of reloading. By 1679 the *fusil* with its flintlock action had replaced the *mousquet*, the plug bayonet the pike. The transformation was completed in 1688 by the introduction of the ring bayonet, which made it possible for the same infantryman both to fire and to thrust, and also brought about a consequent revolution in tactics in that the infantry were no longer compelled to seek the shelter of a square but could form line to repel a cavalry attack. The *carabine rayée*, a rifle, was another innovation which Louvois adopted, when he formed a company of carbineers in 1680 to give protection to the cavalry. So successful did the weapon prove that within ten years he had created no less than 107 companies of carbineers. In other fields the work of specialisation and improvement was continued: grenadiers, bombardiers and sappers made their appearance in the army; schools of artillery were established; the commissariat was no longer left to private enterprise but directed by the government, and the value of Louvois's supply dumps was dramatically demonstrated in 1674.[2]

The total effect of the inspired efforts and the painstaking administration of both Le Tellier and Louvois was to create the first modern standing army. None the less, by modern standards it was still incredibly haphazard: not all the troops wore uniform,

2 See below, p. 344.

most of them were still sent home for the winter, and little was done to provide medical care or accommodation. Nor, for all its improved efficiency, could the army escape the horde of camp followers which still clung to its heels. The seventeenth-century army, 'had not yet lost all resemblance to a confused tribal migration'.[3]

In 1665, Colbert was appointed to control the *conseil de la marine* where he fought a single-handed struggle to expand the French navy. Louis XIV frankly disliked the sea, and his prosaic imagination could not encompass the benefits to be derived from sea power. Moreover, there was little to show for the efforts of Richelieu a generation before; few of his ships had survived, and their crews had dispersed to the merchant navy or to the fleets of England and Holland.

Colbert attacked the problem with characteristic vigour. Brest, a village of fifty inhabitants, was transformed by 1680 into one of the greatest dockyards of France with a population of 6,000. Rochefort was the next to be developed, then Toulon, and finally Dunkirk. A vast programme of shipbuilding was undertaken and nearly 300 vessels were constructed ranging from the 40 great ships of the line, with armaments of between 60 and 120 guns, to the humble but still effective Mediterranean galley. The greatest problem was recruitment. Each galley needed at least 250 men, and it was customary to use slaves, criminals, and, eventually, Huguenots to man the oars: but these men were not satisfactory material for the Atlantic fleet. In 1673, therefore, Colbert instituted the *inscription maritime*, a roster of all sailors in French ports who were required to serve with the fleet for a period of six months, and to stand by on half pay for another six months. At the end of the year they were released to seek more congenial employment in the fishing and trading fleets for two years. It was in fact a highly selective press gang with many defects and with many loopholes for evasion, but it certainly produced more men of a suitable nature for the fleet. As for officers, Colbert faced the same problems as did Pepys in England; unfortunately he administered too many other departments to emulate the patience and single-mindedness of his rival. Many naval captains used their ships for private trade, and there was bitter rivalry between those trained at sea and the so-called land admirals

[3] G.N. Clark, *The Seventeenth Century*, p.III.

whose appointment resulted from royal favour or was purchased outright. In order to enforce naval regulations Colbert appointed intendants to serve with the fleet, although they were not permitted to interfere with the handling of the ships.

Though Louis XIV remained indifferent to the navy, and though its strategic importance to France was bound to be secondary to that of the army, Colbert's achievement was none the less remarkable. Within less than 20 years, handicapped though he was by lack of money and by many more onerous tasks in the government, he created a navy which succeeded in holding its own against the English and Dutch until its disastrous defeat at Cap La Hogue in 1692[4].

Much of Louis' success in the early years of his reign was due to the skill of Hugues de Lionne. International relations were no longer left to dignitaries of church and state, embarked on special embassies for particular occasions. Since the sixteenth century, when the Italians had demonstrated the value of a regular and organised corps of diplomats, diplomacy had become a specialised profession: in Lionne it found one of its most brilliant practitioners. He had acquired from the part he had played in the complex negotiations preceding the treaties of Westphalia and the Pyrenees an unrivalled knowledge of European politics, and his personal experience was daily reinforced by the systematic reports he demanded from his agents in every capital city. These agents were trained not only to observe but to advise their hosts, and to impress upon them the value of a French alliance by means of the generous subsidies they had to offer. Moreover, as representatives of Louis XIV they were to reflect his majesty throughout Europe, and insults, real or imagined, to his honour were not to go unchallenged. When, in 1661, Lionne learned that the Spanish ambassador in London had insisted on taking precedence over the French ambassador, despite the recent defeat of Spain by France, he advised his agent how best to retaliate. Consequently, when Charles II next rode in state, a running fight broke out between the servants of the rival embassies as they jostled their carriages to secure the place of honour. Not content with this, Lionne demanded from Philip IV an apology for the presumption of his representatives, a special audience being convened in the Louvre to witness Spain's

[4] See Chapter VII, p. 352.

submission.

Apparently trivial, this kind of incident served a useful purpose in augmenting Louis's prestige, and assured his agents of deferences throughout Europe. Such matters, however, were merely tactical exercises: Lionne was also a strategist on the grand scale, skilled in the art of gaining allies and in isolating an enemy.

The War of Devolution 1667–8

The 'year of Corbie[5] (1636) had demonstrated the weakness of France's frontier to the north-east, for which the only remedy was to occupy the Low Countries: as Mazarin had said, 'they would provide an impregnable rampart for Paris which would then become the real heart of France'. It was here that Louis tried to strengthen his frontier by pressing his wife's claim to the Spanish Netherlands. His case was ingenious if illogical, taking advantage as it did of the local laws of inheritance peculiar to the Netherlands. In Brabant, for example, all property devolved upon daughters by a first marriage in preference to sons of a second. When Philip IV died in 1665 Louis XIV claimed that his own wife, Maria Theresa, should succeed in place of Carlos II, her younger stepbrother, in all provinces which observed this custom of devolution. At one stroke he thus demanded possession of Brabant, Antwerp, Limburg, Malines, Upper Gelderland, Namur, Cambrai and those parts of Hainault and Artois still unoccupied by France. In Luxemburg, local custom was not so amenable for it allowed sons to inherit two shares of the property to the daughter's one. In this case Maria Theresa with one stepbrother and one sister, was only entitled to a quarter of the duchy. In Franche Comté, where equal division was made among all the children, she claimed a third.

Naturally enough, the Spaniards resisted Louis's argument that what applied to property within the provinces applied equally to the sovereignty of the provinces themselves, and Philip IV declared in his will that the Spanish Netherlands were an integral and indivisible part of Spain. He also insisted that his daughter had no claim upon any part of his estate. Louis immediately published a statement of his wife's claims and announced his determination to enforce them. As a pretext for

[5] See Chapter III, p. 202.

aggression the devolution claim served its purpose, but it could scarcely be taken seriously in itself, and the lengthy justifications and refutations which streamed from the pens of French and Spanish lawyers were vain manœuvres in a battle of books. Louis had stronger weapons in readiness.

While Le Tellier and Louvois had built up the striking force of the French army, Lionne had achieved a diplomatic triumph by isolating its intended victim. Sweden, Denmark and Brandenburg assured him of their neutrality in the event of war between France and Spain, and Portugal was assisted in her struggle for independence with an annual subsidy of 2,000,000 *livres*. The emperor, of course, as Spain's natural ally, could not be won over, especially as his victory over the Turks in 1664 had freed his hands to some extent on the Danube[6]. To prevent his intervention in the Netherlands, therefore, Lionne approached the League of the Rhine Princes, but the League, a pliant tool of French diplomacy in the days of Mazarin, was on the point of breaking up. Moreover, its members were at that time more sympathetic to Leopold I after his repulse of the Turkish invasion than to Louis XIV, whose troops had occupied Lorraine in 1662.[7] Their fears, however, were ultimately allayed by lavish subsidies, and though the League itself made no official alliance, Lionne secured separate, if expensive, agreements with its individual members.

Lionne had anticipated no difficulty in winning Dutch support against Spain, but on this occasion the Dutch were alarmed by Louis's plan to advance his frontier to the Scheldt. While agreeing that France should strengthen her northern frontier by the seizure of some Spanish towns, the Dutch wanted to leave the intervening territory as a buffer state between themselves and the French. Their leader, de Witt, was handicapped in his negotiations by the outbreak of the Anglo-Dutch War in 1665, but, since both combatants were allies of France, the war also raised a problem for Lionne. He solved it by sending troops against England's ally, the Bishop of Münster, a move which assisted the Dutch without alienating Charles II, whose need for French

---

[6] See Chapter IX, p. 422.

[7] Louis had purchased the succession to Lorraine from its ruler, Charles IV, in order to secure easier access to the Alsatian towns acquired in 1648. When Charles showed signs of going back on his word, French troops immediately occupied the duchy.

subsidies made him receptive to Lionne's secret assurances of friendship.

As a result of Lionne's efforts not a single European state was prepared to go to the aid of Spain when, on May 20th, 1667, Turenne marched north from Amiens with 35,000 men. Against a commander of such experience, the most talented French soldier of the seventeenth century, the Spaniards had little hope of success. Possessed of great patience and tenacity, Turenne's particular skill lay in the deployment of troops against forces which outnumbered his own, but in 1667, however, these talents were scarcely to be required since the Spanish governor in Brussels had but few men to put in the field. By the end of June Turenne had seized a dozen towns, while Lille, the most important city in Flanders, fell to Vauban after the first great siege of his career.

The swift advance of the French took Europe by surprise, and evoked an unexpected response from the emperor. Alarmed by the French successes against Spain and by the threat of further Ottoman attacks against his own territories, Leopold was moved by a yet deeper concern for the continuance of his dynasty. The sick condition of Carlos II in Spain, and the advice of his own doctors that the Empress was unlikely to bear him heirs, caused him to believe that the Habsburg family was doomed. In order to gain time, he offered to divide the Spanish empire with Louis on the death of Carlos, giving France Luxemburg or Franche Comté, Naples, Sicily, Navarre and the Philippines. In return, Louis was to content himself for the moment with the towns he had already siezed, or with Frenche Comté. Leopold believed he was acting in the best interests of his family, but he was also conscious of betraying his cousin of Spain, and he insisted that the treaty, ratified by Louis in January 1668, should be kept secret in the safe-keeping of the Duke of Tuscany. Ironically, he was to marry a second wife in 1678 who produced two sons, while Carlos survived in Spain until 1701.

At this moment of apparent triumph Louis was suddenly disconcerted to learn of the defection of England and the United Provinces: Charles II and de Witt, having made peace at Breda (1667), had joined with Sweden in January, 1668, to form a Triple Alliance.[8] De Witt was anxious to check Louis' progress

[8] See Chapter V, p. 274.

without breaking the French alliance, but some of his colleagues, notably the regents of Amsterdam, were becoming hostile to France on commercial grounds (see pp. 275–6). The public clauses, therefore, urged Spain to concede the towns taken by France in 1667, but the secret ones pledged the allies to oppose Louis if he advanced further north. Louis's anger was intense, but the alliance of the three maritime powers at a time when Colbert had not yet fulfilled his plans to revive the French navy, made him circumspect in action. Diverting his attack from the Netherlands, he launched his next campaign in February against Franche Comté. This time it was Condé's turn to demonstrate the speed and efficiency of the French army. Turenne's closest rival, he waged war more passionately and had earned a reputation for impetuosity and courage. Under his spirited leadership, an army of 15,000 overran Franche Comté within three weeks and occupied Besançon, the capital.

This lightning campaign destroyed the remnant of Lionne's system of alliances and when Spain made peace with Portugal and when the German princes threatened to join the Triple Alliance, Louis at once decided to end the war. Reassured by the terms of his secret agreement with the emperor, he saw no need to antagonise European opinion by demanding territory which he expected to acquire by peaceful means in the near future. His terms, therefore, appeared to be disarmingly magnanimous. By the Treaty of Aix-la-Chapelle, May 1668, he evacuated Lorraine, restored Franche Comté to Spain, having first dismantled its fortresses, and retained only the towns seized by his troops in the Netherlands.[9] Their possession in no way strengthened his northern frontier since they lay too far inside the border, but as forward positions, threatening Ghent and Brussels, they might prove valuable in the event of further conflict.

It can be argued that Louis had made a serious error of judgement. The alliance between England and the United Provinces was insecure and the German princes had as yet shown little interest in the defence of the Spanish Netherlands. It might, therefore, have been possible for Louis to fight on to secure substantially better gains and a more defensible frontier when there was little to stop him. By deferring the issue to the future he made his task the more difficult to achieve.

[9] Bergues, Furnes. Armentiéres, Oudenarde, Courtrai, Douai, Tournai, Ath, Charleroi and Lille.

The Dutch War and the Grand Alliance of The Hague 1672–9

Louis regarded the formation of the Triple Alliance as an act of presumption and betrayal. His anger was especially directed against the Dutch since he had believed de Witt to be a reliable ally, a view he never held of Charles II, and in his mortification he vowed to teach the Dutch a lesson. Though such a step ran counter to the policies of Henry IV, Richelieu and Mazarin, who had always looked for support from the other enemies of the Habsburgs, Louis was able to find many reasons to justify his personal vendetta against de Witt. The campaigns of 1667–8 had demonstrated that Spain was no longer to be reckoned a major power and it seemed to Louis that Dutch opposition to his wholesale occupation of the Spanish Netherlands was likely to be more of a stumbling block than the resistance of Spanish troops in the field. Indeed the Republic's action in striking a medal depicting Joshua holding the sun in the heavens was a clear indication that it was congratulating itself upon restraining the action of *le roi soleil*. In this respect Louis's decision to attack the United Provinces was a logical development of the devolution policy.

In many ways Louis had never been able to consider the Dutch suitable allies of so eminent a sovereign as himself. Their Calvinism outraged his Catholic orthodoxy, their republicanism was an unpardonable affront to his concept of monarchy. There were other matters, too, which had rankled for some time, on which Colbert was well equipped to brief his master. Dutch ships controlled the carrying trade in the Baltic, the Atlantic and the Levant which Colbert sought to win for his own trading companies, and he denounced the evils of the Dutch monopoly which he desired so fervently for France. 'As we have crushed Spain on land, so we must crush Holland at sea. The Dutch have no right to usurp all commerce...knowing very well that so long as they are the masters of trade, their naval forces will continue to grow and to render them so powerful that they will be able to assume the role of arbiters of peace and war in Europe and to set limits to the king's plans.' Commercial warfare had in fact preceded military conflict by a decade or more. In 1664 and, more dramatically, in 1667, Colbert had altered tariffs in order to drive Dutch competitors from French ports. Refined sugar, a major

French import, was virtually excluded if carried in Dutch ships, lace was taxed at 60 *livres* instead of 25, and fine cloths paid 80 instead of 40. In such a conflict the Dutch were the losers since it was difficult to discriminate effectively against the few French ships which entered Dutch ports. None the less, retaliation had to be made and new tariffs were promulgated in 1670 and 1671. Finally in 1672 when war seemed imminent in any case, the Dutch banned all French imports from their territories for a whole year.

In order to isolate the Dutch, the alliances of 1667 had to be refashioned by Lionne, a task made the more difficult by the swift successes of the French army which had to some extent alarmed Louis's neighbours. Indeed, the Archbishop-Elector of Mainz was proposing an alliance of German states to resist French aggression, and his arguments were strengthened in 1671 when Charles of Lorraine was once again expelled from his duchy. Lionne counter-attacked by exploiting the habitual lack of common purpose among the German princes. With great skill he caused them to suspect each other's good faith, revived their latent distrust of the emperor's ambitions, reassured them individually that France intended them no harm, and when the moment was ripe clinched the agreement with a generous subsidy. Münster, England's ally in the Anglo-Dutch war (1665–7), was delighted to secure a more powerful ally against her traditional enemy: Brandenburg was won by the promise of assistance against the Dutch in Cleves and the Swedes in Pomerania: Bavaria was flattered by the Dauphin's marriage to the Elector's daughter: Hanover, the Palatinate and Cologne were bought outright. Since Cologne also controlled the bishopric of Liège, which ran like a wedge through the Spanish Netherlands from France to the Rhineland, Lionne had thus opened up for Louis a safe route through the Rhineland to the United Provinces. Moreover, his allies afforded some protection to the eastern frontier of France in the event of imperial intervention in support of the Dutch. Leopold, in any case, was afraid that French agents in Germany were planning to form a league against him, which in addition to his perennial fear of an Ottoman attack, made him agree by the Treaty of Vienna (1671) to remain neutral.

At the same time it was vital to destroy the Triple Alliance of

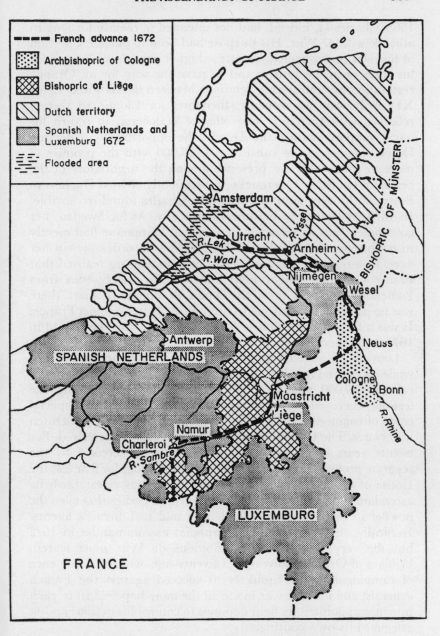

Map 9 Warfare in the Netherlands, 1672–3

1668. Charles II, indeed, had not intended to remain for long in alliance with de Witt. His purpose had been to placate a section of his own parliament, to secure a higher price from France for his services in the future, and to pave the way for an Orange restoration by embittering relations between de Witt and Louis XIV.[10] It was not difficult, therefore, for 'Lionne to restore relations with England. The offer of Walcheren in return for naval support against the Dutch, the opportunity to destroy Dutch commerce, the subsidy of £166,000 with the promise of more to come, and the presence among the negotiators of the beautiful Louise de Querouelle, subsequently created Duchess of Portsmouth, were temptations which Charles found irresistible. In 1670, at Dover, he became Louis's ally. As for Sweden, her government was so seriously in debt that Pomponne had merely to double the Dutch offer of 200,000 *livres* in order to win her over. As a result of this the Elector of Brandenburg realised that France could no longer help him to clear the Swedes from Pomerania, and sold out to the Dutch. Brandenburg apart, there was no power left in Europe to support the Dutch against France. It was a fitting conclusion to Lionne's career, since he retired in 1671 to be succeeded by Pomponne.

Louvois, as meticulous and as skilful as Lionne, had meanwhile been making his preparations for war. In addition to raising 120,000 men, he established supply bases along the frontier, surveyed the route through Liège, and trained a special corps of engineers in the use of pontoons for crossing the Dutch waterways. The Dutch, in contrast, were wholly unprepared. For twenty years control of the army had been exercised by the separate provincial administrations of the Union, for fear lest the House of Orange secure control of it and thus re-establish its ascendancy. So incompetent were these local bodies that even the powder in their magazines had been sold to Louvois's agents. Ironically, there was no one to appoint as commander in 1672 but the very prince whose ambitions de Witt most feared. William of Orange, however, at twenty-one, with no experience of campaigning, was unlikely to succeed against the French generals; and his task was made all the more hopeless since each province appointed its field deputies to control his actions and to safeguard its own contingents.

[10] See Chapter V, pp.274–6.

In April 1672 Louis joined Turenne at Charleroi, one of the forward bases acquired in 1668, and the army of 60,000 advanced through Liège. The Dutch, foreseeing this obvious move, had strengthened the fortifications of Maastricht, which lay along the frontier. Contemptuously by-passing the city Turenne joined forces with 30,000 men under Condé and marched swiftly down the Rhineland brushing aside the Elector of Brandenburg's troops in Cleves as he did so.[11] When William moved his men into trenches behind the Yssel, at the point where it flowed into the Rhine from the north, Turenne smartly turned his flank. Since prolonged drought had reduced the water level of the Rhine, the French army crossed on pontoons to the south bank, marched past William, now impotent on the further bank, and recrossed the river below him at Arnheim. The Dutch were therefore cut off from their base, and William retreated rapidly to Utrecht.

Condé, with his flair for the penetrating thrust, urged Turenne to race for Amsterdam, ignoring the other towns as Turenne himself had ignored Maastricht; but the plan was too daring for Louis and Louvois, who attended the army, and they overruled it. Louis, moreover, enjoyed receiving the surrender of each town in turn, and it was the long succession of these petty triumphs which lost him the opportunity to win the war. On 18 June the dykes were breached, leaving Holland and Zeeland in temporary security behind the water line.

In the crisis de Witt was compelled to resign — and was later lynched in the street. The young William of Orange was appointed to command the Union's forces and the States-General offered to purchase peace by ceding the land south of the Maas. It was an opportunity which Louis failed to exploit. Either on his own account or advised by Louvois, who had a vested interest in maintaining his usefulness to the king by prolonging the war, he rejected the offer. Instead he demanded not only the surrender of large tracts of Dutch territory and an indemnity, but also full liberty of worship for Roman Catholics in the United Provinces. The Dutch had no option but to fight on.

The French settled down to await the coming of winter when the flooded polders would become a frozen pathway to Amsterdam, but the weather proved unexpectedly mild and the enemy

[11] After this the Elector temporarily became Louis's ally by the Treaty of Vossem.

unexpectedly active. By 1673, Leopold found it impossible to stay neutral any longer, and his general, Montecucculi, fought his way across Cologne to join forces with William in the capture of Bonn. This unexpected move threatened the French lines of communication: the main body of the French army was withdrawn from the Dutch provinces, Turenne marching eastwards to protect Munster, while Vauban retired southwards to capture Maastricht in order to give the French more effective control of the line of the Meuse. From there they repulsed an audacious thrust by William at Charleroi.

The character of the war had altered radically. Holland and Zeeland were fighting back vigorously in company with the Imperialists, and it was the turn of the French to be concerned with the lines of communication and defence. In 1674 William and Leopold were joined in the Grand Alliance of the Hague by Carlos II, Charles of Lorraine, and the rulers of Mainz, Trier, Brandenburg and the Palatinate. France was threatened from every quarter. Meanwhile England, defeated at sea, made peace with the republic at Westminster (1674)[12] and for the next six years Charles II was to be preoccupied with the domestic consequences of the Treaty of Dover and the Popish Plot.

The French army was at last put to the test and its conduct in 1674 justified the great efforts of Louvois to make it the finest in Europe. Condé fought a successful defensive action to contain William in the Netherlands, while Vauban and Louis occupied Franche Comté with a speed that rivalled the lightning campaign of 1668; but it was Turenne who outshone the others by his famous defence of Alsace and Lorraine against Montecucculi. Throughout the summer months he held his own against superior numbers and devastated the Palatinate in order to deny the enemy the opportunity of revictualling in the Rhineland. He then feigned retreat to lure them further into Alsace. Here, in November, just as Montecucculi was about to withdraw his troops for the winter, he equipped his own from the supply dumps prepared by Louvois and launched a new offensive. A forced march of seventeen days brought him to Turckheim, south of Strassburg, where he took the enemy by surprise and drove them across the Rhine. The advantage thus gained was maintained for the next six months until Turenne's death in battle (July 1675) temporarily demoralised his army . His pupil, Créqui, had not yet acquired the patience of his master, and an impetuous attack resulted in his own capture. At this crisis, Condé was transferred from the Netherlands to hold the Rhine leaving Luxembourg to defend the northern frontier against William. Towards the end of the year, however, Condé was forced by ill health to resign his command, and Louis lost his second great general. The security of France after 1675 was to depend upon the abilities of Vauban and Luxembourg, and of a chastened Créqui, who was ransomed from the emperor.

Sweden, meanwhile, had met with disaster. La Gardie, the Chancellor, had never anticipated that France might call upon him for assistance; his intention had been to do nothing more strenuous than to receive the liberal subsidies of Pomponne, but the change of circumstances by 1675 compelled him to relieve the pressure on his ally by intervening in north Germany. The Swedish army, however, was defeated at Fehrbellin by the forces of the Elector of Brandenburg, which then overran Pomerania, while Denmark invaded the mainland provinces of Scania and Bleking.[13]

Throughout 1676 and 1677 the overall situation became one of stalemate. The armies of the Alliance of the Hague could not penetrate the French lines of defence; the French were unable to launch a major offensive. Louis led a sudden attack into the Spanish Netherlands in 1677, seizing Cambrai and other frontier towns, including Valenciennes which was taken by Vauban after an assault in daylight, thereby confounding the pundits who were horrified by such a venture; but there was no breakthrough to the Dutch frontier. Both sides had become mesmerised by the conduct of sieges; outright victory was clearly denied to either side, and negotiations were begun for a peace treaty. In Holland the fanatic determination of William to fight until Louis had been destroyed was overruled by a powerful group of merchants. These men were entirely unconcerned about the fate of Spanish Franche Comté, imperial Alsace or Swedish Pomerania; their one desire, now that their country's safety was assured, was to return to the conditions of peacetime commerce. So precipitate, in fact, were their efforts to end the war that their allies were denied the opportunity of exploiting their own bargaining positions. Wil-

13 See p. 394.

liam indeed tried to undermine their negotiations with Louis by making a sudden attack on Mons in 1678, but the French refused to be drawn. At Nijmegen the terms were finally settled, and by 1679 western Europe was again at peace.

The settlement was a comprehensive one since nearly every state in western Europe has been involved in the war.

(i) The French restored Maastricht, their sole conquest in the Dutch provinces, and reduced the exhorbitant tariffs imposed before the war in an effort to damage Dutch commerce.

(ii) The French returned their forward bases in the Spanish Netherlands, gained in 1668, in exchange for a strip of territory 160 kilometres long, running from Dunkirk to the Meuse, which afforded a more effective means of strengthening their northern frontier.

(iii) Louis, abandoning his belief in the immediate death of Carlos II, retained Franche Comté, and provided Carlos with a French wife, the Princess Marie-Louise.

(iv) Charles of Lorraine refused to accept any of Louis's terms, with the result that France retained possession of his duchy.

(v) The Emperor, owing to the haste with which his allies made peace, had no option but to agree to Louis's retention of the principal Alsatian towns along with Freiburg, but recovered Philippsburg for the Empire.

(vi) Brandenburg and Denmark, though they were not a party to the Treaty of Nijmegen, were subsequently compelled by Louis, who threatened their Rhineland territories, to restore to Sweden the lands they had occupied since 1675.[14]

In their justifiable enthusiasm for the peace settlement, the French forgetting the anxieties they had undergone, and ignoring the massive debt which burdened the Treasury, hailed their king as 'Louis le Grand'. The Dutch had yet to restore their scarred towns and flooded fields; Spain had again revealed the feebleness of her resistance; the German princes had gained nothing, and were anxious only to restore the flow of French subsidies into their depleted treasuries. Frederick William of Brandenburg

[14] See Chapter X, p. 395.

voiced the general sentiment: 'In the present state of affairs, so far as human prudence can judge, it seems that no prince will henceforth find security and advantage except in the friendship and alliance of the king of France.'

Nevertheless, the Dutch had not been defeated. The motives which had driven Louis to declare war had eluded achievement, and in William of Orange the French had made an implacable enemy. Moreover, the Alliance of The Hague was an ominous indication that Europe had learned the need to unite against French aggression.

The Corrosive Peace 1679–85

In the years following the Dutch War the influence of Louvois on French policy seemed especially evident. It was partly that the autocratic manner in which Louis conducted his government encouraged perhaps the advocate of firm, clear-cut aggressive policies, discouraging the advocate of mediation and compromise. Equally, Louvois may well have suggested the very things which Louis most wanted to hear. Either way it was unfortunate for France since the government was less careful to cultivate European opinion by propaganda and diplomacy. Instead it purchased support, contemptuously, with bribes or compelled acquiescence by the threat of force. As a result, while almost all the decisions of the next decade could each be justified in terms of national security, their cumulative effect on European opinion was to convey an impression of rampant aggression.

Louis's next venture was directed primarily against the German princes. Since 1648 the French had acquired piecemeal many towns and provinces along their frontiers, and Louis was concerned to integrate them more closely with France by eliminating the enclaves of other powers which separated them from each other or from the main body of the kingdom. In addition, he wished to extend his influence within the Holy Roman Empire in preparation for the day of Leopold's death: Louis renewed his treaties with the Electors of Brandenburg and Bavaria and hoped, by securing control of the Rhineland, to be able to coerce the Elector Palatine and the Archbishop-Electors of Cologne, Mainz and Trier. To achieve his purposes, Louis exploited the military unreadiness of his neighbours to blackmail them into conceding what he required. The years of peace were to be made as profitable to France as those of war. It was scarcely a wise policy to antagonise the former members of the Grand Alliance of The Hague, and Pomponne was dismissed for saying so, but with Louvois abetting him, Louis had become over-confident. In Colbert de Croissy they found a new foreign secretary who could offer them the means to achieve their ends, and they were eager to make a start.

Croissy, brother of the great Colbert, had formerly served as intendant in Alsace, and the experience he had gained there in unravelling the complex network of rival jurisdictions, which were a legacy of the Peace of Westphalia, prompted him to develop his *réunion* policy. In the first place he sought to clarify the status of towns ceded to France in the past, and thus to ensure that within their boundaries the absolute sovereignty of Louis XIV was universally recognised. In Alsace, for example, the towns acquired in 1648 had retained their immediacy to the Holy Roman Empire, a term which had been invented in order to reconcile the emperor to their loss. Croissy proposed to break this tenuous link, and to enforce the recognition of Louis's *supremum dominium*. This was reasonable enough, but his second step was to examine the archives of all the towns ceded to France along with their dependencies, another ill-defined term employed by the peacemakers of Westphalia, to ascertain what these dependencies were in order to appropriate them. By this means he hoped to extend the boundaries of each of these recently acquired towns and provinces until they formed a coherent frontier, embracing all positions of strategic importance.

The *réunion* policy, in short, was nothing less than a calculated gamble that the German princes would sooner accept the loss of some territory than risk another war with France. In 1680 Louis appointed *chambres des réunions* at Besançon, Breisach and Tournai with jurisdiction over Franche Comté, Alsace and Flanders respectively, and a fourth chamber at Metz to investigate the duchies of Bar and Lorraine and the bishoprics of Metz, Toul and Verdun. Their decisions were swiftly made, and as swiftly enforced by the French army, so that by 1681 the frontier from Dunkirk to Grenoble had been strengthened by the systematic annexation of towns and villages which were deemed by Louis to have become dependent upon France. Since it controlled a Rhine crossing of great importance, the most valuable single acquisition was the free city of Strassburg, which had previously been in the anomalous position of owing a degree of loyalty to both Louis and the emperor. In addition, the French seized Casale, the capital of Montferrat, though this was less of a *réunion* than an act of outright confiscation.[15]

Europe was outraged, but none of Louis's neighbours dared to challenge the legality of his action by resorting to war. The German princes had no option but to submit; Sweden was unable to defend her Rhineland base of Zweibrücken, and Spain was powerless to recover Casale. It was not until French troops marched into Luxemburg to enforce their claims there (1682) that the victims of the *réunions* made some show of protest. Led by William of Orange, Louis's most resolute enemy in Europe, many of the lesser German princes, particularly those of Franconia and the Rhineland, met at Laxenburg to seek an alliance with Sweden, Spain and Austria, in an effort to halt the course of French expansion. Louis deemed it wise to withdraw for the moment, announcing that a new Turkish threat to Austria made it necessary for Europe to remain at peace, an ironical term to describe the condition of Europe after 1679. Louis indeed offered to assist at the siege of Vienna,[16] but the emperor refused his aid since its acceptance would have implied his own tacit consent to the *réunions*. As soon as Vienna had been saved, but before Leopold was free to intervene in western Europe, Louis renewed his assault on Luxemburg (1684). Spain, unable to countenance this final blow to her dignity, attempted armed resistance, but without the support of allies her efforts were ineffective. The Laxenburg powers had evolved no plan of military action: William's plan to support Spain was over-ruled by the States-General: Leopold could do nothing. Thus, after the French had taken Luxemburg, bombarded Genoa and invaded Catalonia, the Spaniards had no option but to make peace in 1685. By the Truce of Regensburg (Ratisbon), they recognised for a term of twenty years all Louis's acquisitions since 1679.

'After 1672', wrote Leibniz in his effort to stir up German feeling against Louis XIV, 'the French decided that the king no

---

[15] See Chapter II, p. 144, for an account of Montferrat's value to France in controlling Spanish troop movements in north Italy.
[16] See Chapter IX, p. 431.

longer needed to justify his enterprises to the world.' The immediate fruits of Louis's aggressive policy gave him a position of unrivalled power in western Europe: their long-term effect in provoking the opposition of all his neighbours was to prove less advantageous.

THE EUROPEAN COALITIONS AGAINST FRANCE 1685-1714

The War of the League of Augsburg 1688-97

The ruthless exploitation of his military power since 1679 had left Louis XIV without the support of allies. Worse still, his victims were becoming accustomed to combining against him, and the habit of regular opposition to French expansion was producing a new sense of solidarity in western Europe. Louis remained insensitive to it. To celebrate his triumphs he commissioned a monument which inconsiderately displayed the rulers of Sweden and Brandenburg as his chained vassals; and the revocation of the Edict of Nantes despatched a thousand fervent embassies throughout the Protestant states to confirm the growing legend of an arbitrary and irresponsible monarch. In 1686 the princes of Franconia and the Rhineland entered into a defensive league at Augsburg; within two years they had been joined by Brandenburg, Bavaria, Saxony, Spain, Sweden, Savoy, the United Provinces and the emperor. That such a coalition, on the scale of the Grand Alliance of The Hague (1674), could be formed in peace-time was a significant indication that Louis's disregard for European opinion had been carried too far, and that the initiative in Europe was slowly passing to his enemies. Moreover, the emperor was at last becoming free of the Ottoman threat to his territories which had paralysed his previous attempts to limit the expansion of France. In 1687 the Turks were defeated at Mohács,[17] Transylvania and Hungary were cleared, and by 1688 Belgrade was once again in European hands, for the first time since 1521.

When Louis tried to extend still further his control of the Rhineland, a European war became inevitable. In 1685, on the death of the childless Elector Palatine, William of Neuburg

[17] See Chapter IX,p. 435.

claimed the succession. As a member of the League of Augsburg, and as father-in-law to both Carlos II and the emperor, he was in Louis's eyes an undesirable neighbour, so the French put forward a claim on behalf of the former Elector's sister who had married Louis's brother. While the dispute was being referred to the Diet, there fell vacant another Rhineland throne, the archbishopric of Cologne, which, like the Palatinate, possessed not only a position of great strategic value but also a vote in the Electoral College. Louis resolved to secure this too by proposing the Bishop of Strassburg, Cardinal Fürstenberg, in whom he had implicit confidence. Unfortunately, the Bavarian Electors had long been accustomed to look upon Cologne as a family possession, to be used as a lucrative refuge for younger sons: a Bavarian candidate was therefore put forward, but since he was a minor and had not yet been admitted to holy orders, the pope was required to adjudicate in the matter. Louis considered that he had shown uncommon restraint in accepting a resort to arbitration in two cases which so closely touched his interests: he was, therefore, all the more indignant when both the Diet and the pope decided against him, and straightway reverted to those stronger measures which had so often stood him in good stead. In 1688 he installed Fürstenberg by force in Cologne, and invaded the Palatinate.

No diplomatic preparation, no husbanding of allies, preceded this stroke, save for a published *Mémoire des raisons qui ont obligé le roi à reprendre des armes,* a piece of empty rhetoric to lay the blame at Leopold's door. Louis, in fact, intended nothing more than a simple coup such as he had recently become accustomed to, and did not believe that his action would result in a general conflict; but Europe sprang to arms with surprising speed. Leopold planned a march on the Upper Rhine, while Saxony and Brandenburg advanced upon its lower reaches, and the defensive League of Augsburg was transformed into an offensive coalition at Vienna. The invasion of the Palatinate, moreover, by diverting Louis's troops from the Dutch frontier, enabled William to sail for England;[18] before the year was out, James II was an exile at Versailles. As soon as Louis realised that he was committed to a war in which all his frontiers were threatened with invasion he abandoned his forward position in the Palatinate, ordering its devastation in order to deny its use as an enemy base. The work

18 See Chapter V, p. 280.

was done with systematic brutality. Turenne in 1674 had been content to destroy the crops but Louis destroyed the cities too. Heidelberg, Mannheim and Speyer were sacked and their fortifications razed; several thousands died at the hands of the troops and from starvation, and many more fled to recount their pitiful tale among the member countries of the Vienna alliance. Louis had thus succeeded, where every emperor had failed, in creating a unanimous body of German opinion hostile to France.

At sea the French immediately seized the initiative. It was indeed remarkable that their navy should be prepared to challenge the acknowledged naval might of England and the United Provinces, and it was due to the devoted efforts of Colbert, before his death in 1683, that they were able to do so.[19] De Tourville landed James II in Ireland with a small force to lead the Irish rebellion against William, but a repulse at Bantry Bay compelled him to abandon his plan to establish control of the Irish Sea. In consequence, the English transports conveyed William's army safely to Ireland, there to inflict a crushing defeat on James at the Battle of the Boyne in 1690. On the very day of William's triumph, however, de Tourville scattered both the English and the Dutch fleets off Beachy Head, one of the gravest disasters in British naval history. For two years he retained mastery of the Channel until defeated by the English admiral, Russell, at Cap La Hogue. The loss of fifteen ships of the line so weakened the French that subsequent operations in the Atlantic were left to the privateers, like Jean Bart, who raided allied merchantmen from the fortified harbours of Dunkirk, St Malo and Dieppe. So successful were their attacks that the French government leased them naval vessels and stores on easy terms; thus equipped, squadrons of privateers ranged the Atlantic from the North Sea to West Africa. England, Holland and Spain were peculiarly vulnerable to this kind of attack, and their losses were heavy. In 1693 over a hundred merchantmen of the Smyrna convoy were captured off Lagos, and in 1697 an audacious raid as far afield as the Caribbean led to the capture of Cartagena, the entrepôt of Spanish-American trade.

On land the French remained secure behind frontiers which had been strengthened, not only by the *réunions*, but also by the hand of Vauban. In the south they invaded Catalonia, and would

have taken Barcelona but for Russell's timely relief of the city by
sea. In 1697, however, de Tourville escaped from an allied
blockade of Toulon to assist a second, and successful, campaign
against Barcelona. French troops also crossed the Alps and
defeated Victor Amadeus of Savoy at Stafforda in 1690. The
Savoyards then rallied under Prince Eugène and invaded
Dauphiné. Eugène had spent his youth in France, but when
Louis XIV who wanted to make a churchman of him refused to
give him a military command, Eugène took service with the
emperor and soon demonstrated his talents as a soldier. So
invaluable were his services that Leopold recalled him in 1692 to
drive off a Turkish counter-attack in the Danube; deprived of his
leadership the Savoyards collapsed, being defeated at Marsiglia
in 1693 by Catinat, who held the Alpine passes with ease for the
rest of the war. In the Rhineland, though the French lost Mainz
and Bonn, the allies were unable to force their way into Alsace
and Lorraine. The three great natural barriers of the Pyrenees,
the Alps and the Rhine had proved insurmountable.

It was in the Netherlands that the allies launched their main
attack, but the campaign was predestined to a form of stalemate

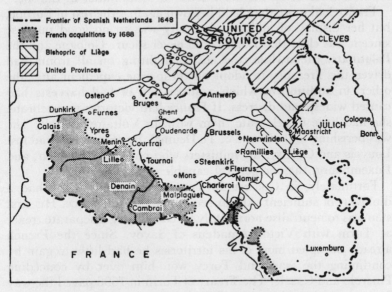

Map 10 Warfare in the Spanish Netherlands, 1688–1714

since both sides held firm lines of defence, the allies the rivers and waterways, the French the fortresses of Vauban. The armies became accustomed to a sluggish crawl from one siege to another, although Luxembourg showed himself a lively successor to his tutor, Condé. At Fleurus in 1690 he defeated the Dutch, preventing them from joining with the Brandenburg army in Cleves, and held the ring while Vauban reduced the fortifications of both Mons in 1691 and Namur in 1692. In this latter year William launched a surprise attack on the French at Steenkirk, but his plans were badly made, and the French, leaving their quarters *en déshabille,* routed him; this victory was celebrated at Versailles by the ladies who adopted a new hairstyle, dishevelled *à la Steenkirk.* Luxembourg triumphed again in 1693 at Neerwinden where he took 15,000 prisoners and sent so many standards in triumph to Paris that he was named *le tapissier de Notre-Dame.* William had realised already that the allies could not attain their aims and that peace talks would have to begin; but he caused something of a sensation by recovering Namur in 1695. It was rare indeed for a fortress defended by Vauban to fall, and its capture provided some solace for the man who was fast earning a reputation for being the most defeated commander in Europe.

France had more than held her own against the rest of Europe, but her display of military virtuosity was to no good purpose since it was clear that Louis could never secure Cologne and the Palatinate. Meanwhile, the cost of fighting on all fronts had driven the Treasury to adopt one desperate expedient after the other, in addition to which a succession of bad harvests had caused widespread distress. If France had victories to celebrate, she had little to celebrate them with: in Voltaire's words, 'she was perishing to the sound of Te Deums'. By 1696 Louis had lost Louvois and Croissy, the ministers who had urged the war, and Luxembourg, the one general capable of winning it.

Fortunately, in Colbert de Torcy, Croissy's son, he had a diplomat of sufficient skill to see how to secure peace. His first step was to neutralise north Italy by concluding a separate treaty at Turin with Victor Amadeus of Savoy. Since the French already occupied most of his territories he had little to gain by continuing the war, and Torcy won him over by conceding Pinerolo and Casale. The Treaty of Turin in 1696 paved the way for a general settlement. William was aware of opposition in

England to the 'King's War', as it was termed; and both he and Leopold were as anxious as Louis to end the conflict when they learned that the death of Carlos II, so frequently anticipated, was at last imminent. The problem of determining his heir made it imperative to end the deadlock in Europe. The terms of the Peace of Ryswick in 1697 did not altogether reflect the true course of events of the war:

(i) William of Neuburg secured the Palatinate.

(ii) Prince Clement of Bavaria became Archbishop Elector of Cologne.

(iii) Louis recognised the accession of William as King of England, and promised to withdraw his support of James II.

(iv) Lorraine, after more than thirty years of French occupation, was restored to the grandson of Charles IV.

(v) Luxemburg, Charleroi, Mons, Courtrai and Barcelona were restored to Spain.

(vi) Territories gained by the *réunions* were restored to their original rulers, with the exception of Strassburg and the towns of Lower Alsace.

(vii) In addition, by a private treaty, Spain allowed the Dutch to garrison a series of frontier towns, including Ypres, Menin, Courtrai and Luxemburg, to act as a barrier against future French aggression.

Louis thus renounced all the acquisitions, save Alsace, which he had made since 1679, and also gave up Lorraine and Pinerolo whose occupation had been of longer standing. His most difficult obligation was to recognise his most persistent enemy as king of England, since this involved the repudiation not only of his ally James II but also of his whole concept of monarchy and divine right. Nevertheless, the burden of waging a prolonged war was proving too great for France to bear, and Louis was prepared to accept the losses of 1697 in order to realise his dream of peaceably acquiring the Spanish Empire, which, at long last, seemed to be within his grasp.

The Problem of the Spanish Succession 1697–1702

Louis, for once, had learned something from his mistakes. The arbitrament of war had proved to be too uncertain a means of securing his aims, both against the Dutch and in the Rhineland, and its brief moments of glory were overshadowed by its excessive cost. Moreover, the emperor's reconquest of Hungary, confirmed by the Treaty of Karlowitz in 1699, and William's accession to the throne of England, made it all the more dificult for France to ride roughshod over Europe. If Louis were to secure the Spanish Succession then it could only be by negotiation and diplomacy.

It was clear that the Dauphin had a good claim to the Spanish throne since his grandfather and his father had married the elder daughters of Philip III and Philip IV, but the prospect of one prince inheriting both Spain and France was one which appalled not only the rest of Europe but the Spaniards themselves. Louis wisely instructed his ambassador in Madrid that the Dauphin would renounce his claim in favour of his younger son, the Duke of Anjou, 'in order to remove all grounds for fearing that Spain and France might ever be united'. Leopold, too, could urge a strong claim on behalf of his family: both he and his father had married the younger daughters of the Spanish kings who, unlike their elder sisters, had never made public renunciation of their rights of inheritance. The strongest candidate was therefore Joseph Ferdinand of Bavaria, Leopold's grandson by his marriage to Carlos's sister, but Leopold in fact reserved his affection and ambition for Joseph and Charles, the sons of a later marriage to Eleanor of Neuburg. It was Joseph who was to inherit the Austrian empire, and for him Leopold sought the Spanish empire too. Once again this caused the prospect of a union of thrones. Though Leopold was less eager than Louis to conciliate opinion on this, ultimately he agreed to the candidature of Joseph's younger brother, the Archduke Charles.

It was not merely a question of avoiding a union of thrones. The future king of Spain would also rule the Netherlands and control the commerce of the Spanish empire: in both matters the English and Dutch were vitally concerned. Having fought to repel Louis from the Netherlands they had no desire to see his grandson acquire them by inheritance, and they believed that

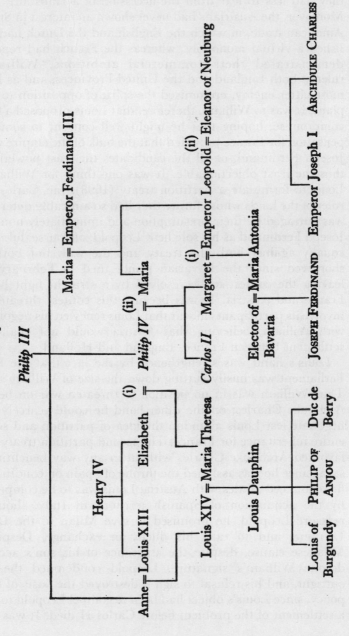

Genealogical Tree showing the Descent of the Three Chief Claimants (shown in capitals) to the Spanish Throne.

they had less to fear from the accession of a Habsburg prince. Moreover, the Austrians had never shown an interest in Spanish-American trade, in which the English and the Dutch had established a virtual monopoly, whereas the French had repeatedly demonstrated their commercial ambitions. William, as ruler of both England and the United Provinces, and as Louis's most bitter enemy, epitomised the spirit of opposition to Louis' plans. It was to William, therefore, that Louis proposed a form of compromise, hoping that he might well consent to some compensation for France provided that the bulk of the empire went to Joseph Ferdinand, of all the candidates the least powerful and thus the least objectionable. It was one thing for William and Louis to formulate a partition treaty (1698), but Carlos II, as ruler of the lands whose future they had so amicably determined, was outraged by their presumption and immediately nominated Joseph Ferdinand as his sole heir. Leopold, of course, fulminated equally against both the treaty and the will, but both were shortlived since the Bavarian prince died in February 1699, leaving the contest to be resolved by a straight fight between France and Austria. It was because this contest threatened to involve its participants in war that Louis renewed his negotiations with William, believing that Austria would not challenge a settlement between France, England and Holland.

Louis's hand was strengthened by the fact that the English Parliament was busily cutting down the size of William's army. Thus William was in no position to threaten war on behalf of Archduke Charles; on the other hand he could scarcely fail to negotiate lest Louis abandon the idea of partition and seek the entire inheritance for France. The second partition treaty in fact favoured Archduke Charles without in any way benefiting Austria, since he was assigned the throne of Spain on condition that he renounced all ties with Austria; Louis was to be compensated by the acquisition of Spanish territory in Italy, though, to reassure Leopold, he promised to give Milan to the Duke of Lorraine, and to take his duchy in exchange. Despite the Milanese clause, despite the assurance of his son's accession, despite William's signature, Leopold condemned the treaty outright, and his refusal to sign it destroyed the basis of Louis's policy, since Louis's object had been to compel Leopold to accept a settlement of the problem before Carlos II died. It was Carlos himself who finally exposed the unreality of the negotiations. In a last spirited effort to preserve the unity of his empire he drafted a new will in October 1700 naming Philip of Anjou as his heir, on condition that he renounced his claim to the French throne. While his choice of the French prince owed much to the influence of Harcourt, Louis's ambassador in Madrid, it was also a recognition of the fact that only a prince supported by the might of France could hope to preserve the Spanish empire from partition.

One month later Carlos died, leaving Louis with the choice of rejecting the will or of repudiating the partition treaty. The Dauphin, Torcy, Ponchartrain and the Duc de Beauvilliers were summoned to a historic meeting in Madame de Maintenon's rooms. Beauvilliers urged Louis to stand by the treaty: it was guaranteed by the governments of both England and the United Provinces, and it assured to France the permanent acquisition of Lorraine, Naples, Sicily and the Tuscan ports. The will was defended by Torcy and Ponchartrain, for if Philip refused his inheritance the Spaniards would offer the empire to Archduke Charles; it was unlikely in such an event that William would be willing to join France in a war to enforce the treaty; moreover, though Philip's accession offered France no territorial gains, there were many commercial and strategic advantages to be derived from it. In short, since Leopold would certainly contest both the will and the treaty, Louis should fight for the greater gains offered by the will. To this argument both the Dauphin and Madame de Maintenon assented, and Louis informed the Spanish ambassador that he might acknowledge Philip as his new king. The decision was undoubtedly correct, since the treaty had already been rendered worthless by Leopold's refusal to sign it.

William expressed his anger in a letter to Heinsius, the Grand Pensionary of Holland: 'I never relied much on engagements with France but I must confess I did not think they would on this occasion have broken in the face of the whole world a solemn treaty before it was well accomplished;' but he was also compelled to admit 'I am troubled to find that nearly everybody prefers the will to the treaty.' His Parliament was indeed already pursuing the impeachment of those who had negotiated the partition treaty, and though Leopold had launched a campaign in north Italy on behalf of Charles, the neutrality of both

England and the United Provinces seemed assured. There were only two things to guard against, as Louis was warned by his ambassador in London: 'Your Majesty cannot take too great pains to exhort the Spaniards not to make any changes in their commercial relations with England and Holland, nor to behave too circumspectly with regard to the security of the Low Countries.'

At this crisis of his reign, when the prize he had sought for forty years was in his hands, Louis seems to have lost his sureness of touch. Historians have found it difficult to understand how Louis, after demonstrating such sound judgement in the late 1690s could suddenly make a series of blunders. Yet, whether through loss of nerve, overweening pride or simple lack of perception, this is what happened, with the result that he brought about the very coalition of enemies which formerly he had striven to avoid.

In February 1701 he reaffirmed Philip's rights of inheritance as third in line to the French throne, an unnecessary act which foolishly drew attention to the close links binding the French and Spanish crowns. In the same month he sent French troops into the Spanish Netherlands in order to seize the barrier fortresses held there by the Dutch. Since the States-General had not yet recognised Philip as King of Spain there was some justification for Louis's action, but the cavalier use of French troops in a matter relating to Spanish territory provoked a universal suspicion that Louis, not Philip, was to be the arbiter of Spain's fortunes. In August he secured from Philip the right for French companies to trade in the Spanish colonial empire. If this was intended to coerce the English then Louis had badly miscalculated: from this moment William was assured of support from the powerful merchant houses of London and Amsterdam. When news came that Eugène had driven the French and Spanish troops from Lombardy, the English and Dutch governments were emboldened to ally with Leopold in the second Grand Alliance of The Hague (September, 1701).

The allies agreed that none of them should make a separate peace with Louis; the French and Spanish thrones were to be kept separate; French trade in the Spanish empire was to be forbidden; Leopold was to acquire Italy and the Netherlands; the English and Dutch were to seize what territory they could in the

West Indies and America. Significantly, no mention was made of Spain herself, though Leopold's determination to place his son in Madrid was understood if not acknowledged. The maritime powers in fact were concerned to fight only for commercial advantage, leaving Leopold to pursue his dynastic ambitions as best he could. With the allies so divided in their aims, Louis might still have won the neutrality of England and the United Provinces by repudiating his actions of the past months. Instead, on the death of James II he recognised James's son as James III of England. No doubt he was concerned to safeguard James's position as much at Versailles as in London, since an unrecognised pretender had few claims to precedence in the rigid hierarchy of court life. Moreover, William was dying and the possibility of a Stuart restoration could not at least be ignored. Yet in England, Louis's action was regarded as a flagrant violation of the Treaty of Ryswick, and for Englishmen the War of Spanish Succession became a war to protect the Protestant succession at home. William, in his last months, recaptured the wholehearted support of his subjects for the first time since his arrival among them in 1688, and his death in March 1702 did nothing to prevent a declaration of war on France.

The War of the Spanish Succession 1702–14

In 1702 France possessed none of the advantages she had enjoyed at the outset of her previous wars. Of her allies, Portugal and Savoy were on the brink of defecting to the Grand Alliance, and Philip V ruled a kingdom which had proved so incompetent in defending its territories that it was more of an incubus than an ally. Louis's sole diplomatic triumph was an alliance with Maximilian of Bavaria and his brother the Archbishop of Cologne, whose appointment Louis had contested in 1688: in return for their support, Maximilian was to receive the Spanish Netherlands of which he had been governor since 1695. As a result, Louis secured a useful foothold across the Rhine, and the compact *bloc* of Spain, France and Bavaria gave him the advantage of interior lines of communication. In every other respect, naval, military and financial, France was inferior to the combined strength of the Grand Alliance. Against her were ranged the maritime powers of England and the United Provinces; the

Elector of Brandenburg, who hoped to secure the title of king in
Prussia by loyal service to the emperor; Leopold himself, his
Danubian provinces secured from Turkish attack; the Elector of
Hanover, an experienced imperial general whom the English had
named heir presumptive to Queen Anne; the king of Denmark;
and almost all the minor German princes. In all, the Grand
Alliance could muster more than 200,000 men, several thousand
more than the French, while in Marlborough and Eugène it
possessed two generals who were to prove their outstanding
brilliance. Marlborough too was an astute diplomat who well
understood the petty jealousies which continually threatened to
disrupt the Grand Alliance, and whose winter visits to the allied
capitals did as much to hold the allies together as his summer
campaigns against the French. At sea the fleets of England and
Holland were supreme, and the wealth they derived from
commerce ensured the financial stability of the alliance. France,
in contrast, was virtually bankrupt.

Despite their advantages, the allies achieved little success in
1702, and it was the French who seized the initiative in the
Netherlands. Advancing through Liège and Cleves, their plan of
campaign so closely resembled that of 1672 that the Dutch were
thrown into a panic, until Marlborough adroitly halted the
invading force by a swift attack on its lines of communication in
Liège. His action revealed his revolt from the static pattern of
limited marches and perpetual sieges which Vauban had imposed upon his age. He sought to meet the enemy in the open, to
ignore the scattered garrisons beleaguered within their own
earthworks, and to deliver a series of penetrating thrusts into the
heart of France. His very training of the infantry indicated the
adventurous role he had evolved for them. Equipped with the
new flintlock and the ring bayonet, they were no longer condemned to huddle in defensive postures, repriming their clumsy
matchlocks while the pikemen protected them from marauding
horse, but were trained to advance in the open as aggressively as
the cavalry. As soon as it was clear that the French invasion of
the Netherlands had failed, and their army was withdrawing in
confusion, Marlborough planned to exploit his advantage by
invading France up the Moselle valley: unfortunately the Dutch
field-deputies who accompanied him were slow to abandon their
traditional outlook on war and could only think in terms of

defence. The opportunity to catch the French at a disadvantage was thus forgone, and it was many years before the allies were again in so favourable a position for striking at Paris.

Elsewhere in 1702 the French held their own. In Italy, where fighting had begun in the previous year, Eugène captured Marshal Villeroi, whose failure to halt the Imperial advance caused the French to celebrate his loss as a victory, but he was unable to drive Vendôme from the Alpine passes of Piedmont. The support of Bavaria made it easy for Louis to repel attacks in the Rhineland, and the only dramatic gain for the allies was the destruction of a Spanish fleet in Vigo Bay.[20]

Secure in their control of the Atlantic, the English were badly in need of a naval base in the Mediterranean, and planned to seize Toulon. The French were already weakened in that area by the revolt of the Camisards,[21] and when Victor Amadeus had been persuaded to join the Grand Alliance in 1703 and to allow the Imperialists to march through Savoy, the project seemed feasible. In the event Leopold was too suspicious of Victor Amadeus's ambitions in north Italy to co-operate satisfactorily with him, and an Anglo-Dutch fleet bombarded Toulon to no effect. Of greater importance was the Methuen Treaty with Portugal in the same year, by which the harbour at Lisbon was opened to the allies. In return, England and the United Provinces undertook not only to expel Philip from Spain and to install Archduke Charles in his place, but also to pay and equip half the Portuguese army. The English and Dutch were therefore pledged to assist Charles in Spain, a point which had been avoided during the formation of the Grand Alliance, but England at least had no immediate cause for worry since the military treaty was followed by a commercial one, granting her valuable concessions in the export of wool to Portugal. The Dutch on the other hand gained nothing: moreover, they had further cause to be restive since, by agreeing to England's policy of prohibiting all trade with France, they were causing themselves a great deal of hardship. England, it seemed to them, was becoming far more dangerous as their ally than as their enemy. Not surprisingly their field deputies forestalled Marlborough's plan to seize Ostend: caring nothing for its strategic value, they knew only too well that with such a base in his hands Marlborough would equip

20 See Chapter IV, p. 232.   21 See Chapter VI, p. 327.

his army direct from England instead of via the Dutch ports. In any case, the field deputies still distrusted Marlborough's plans of invading France, although one of them made an astonishingly handsome confession of his own faults in the campaign of 1702: its success was, 'solely due to this incomparable chief, since I confess that serving as second in command I opposed all his opinions and proposals'. His colleagues remained obdurate, and throughout 1703 Marlborough's only conquests were Bonn and Spanish Gelderland.

If anything the advantage in 1703 lay with France. Not only did the allies fail to cross her frontiers but she herself launched a new offensive in Germany, using Bavaria as a base from which to advance down the Danube. Eugène was held in north Italy; Hungary rose in revolt; Regensburg fell to Villars and the Elector of Bavaria, and the way was open to Vienna. The Elector, however, was more interested in the future of Milan, and wasted five months in an unsuccessful attempt to secure control of the Tyrolean passes. Villars, denied the opportunity of acting independently of his wayward ally, could only await his pleasure, occupying himself meanwhile in keeping the Imperialists at bay and in the taking of Augsburg. When, in September, the Elector returned, Villars urged upon him that there was yet time to take Vienna. The Elector demurred, and a violent quarrel between the two commanders led to Villars's recall in disgrace. In this manner France lost not only one of her best generals, but also her best opportunity of ending the war.

During the winter Eugène was recalled to Vienna where he turned the general panic to good account by making himself president of the council of war. He was desperately short of men with which to face both the Hungarians and the French in the campaigns of 1704, and appealed to his allies for aid. Though it was no new thing for the Imperialists to operate several hundred miles from their base, the English and Dutch governments had no experience at all of campaigning in central Europe, and the prospect appalled them. Nevertheless, to his great credit, Heinsius, Grand Pensionary of Holland, comprehended the danger of the situation and persuaded a reluctant States-General to allow Marlborough to leave the Netherlands in a bold but dangerous venture to save Vienna. How he was to do this no one knew: Marsin, Villars's successor, had already joined forces with the

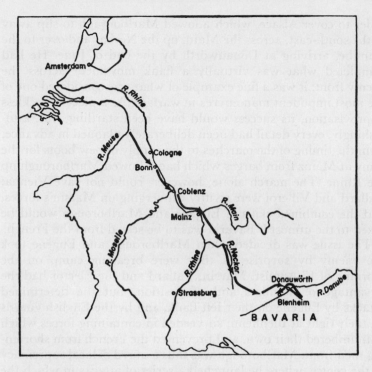

Map 11   Marlborough's Danube Campaign, 1704

Bavarians, and while Tallard protected his lines of communication across the Rhine, Villeroi stood guard against Marlborough in the Netherlands.

In the event Marlborough deceived both friend and foe by one of the most brilliantly planned marches in history. Leaving Jülich in May 1704, he advanced up river along the west bank of the Rhine, and tricked Villeroi into anticipating an attack from Coblenz up the Moselle valley. Villeroi in consequence was mystified on learning that Marlborough, far from leaving the Rhine at Coblenz, had merely crossed over to the farther bank, there to continue his march up river. Suspecting a ruse, Villeroi dared not abandon his position in the Moselle, and Marlborough made his way safely to Mainz. His appearance there brought Tallard back from Bavaria to the French side of the Rhine in order to cover Alsace, which allowed Marlborough to slip away to the south-east, across the Main, up the Neckar and over to the Danube, arriving at Donauwörth by the end of June. He had completed what was virtually a flank movement across the enemy front; it was a fine example of what was considered one of the most impudent manœuvres in warfare. As a piece of reckless improvisation, its success would have been startling, but, astonishingly, every detail had been deliberately planned in advance, from the timing of the marches to the supply of new boots for the army at Mainz from barges which had followed Marlborough up the Rhine. The march alone, however, could not save Vienna: Tallard and Villeroi were swiftly converging on Marsin's forces, and the combined skills of Eugène and Marlborough would be taxed to the utmost if Bavaria was to be seized from the French.

The issue was decided when Marlborough and Eugène took the enemy by surprise as they were breaking camp on the morning of 17 August. Marsin, Tallard and the Elector had the advantage of numbers and of position, but the determined attacks by Eugène on their left flank, and by the English guards on their right at Blenheim, succeeded in containing forces which outnumbered their own, and prevented the French from shortening their front. Marlborough was thus assured of local supremacy in the centre, where he launched a series of attacks in which the infantry, true to his training, ran into battle behind the cavalry to take advantage of the breaches made in the enemy line. Marsin and the Bavarians were driven off into the hills, and Tallard was taken prisoner in Blenheim. As a result of this, the most crucial engagement of the war, Vienna was saved, Bavaria occupied and the legend of French invincibility destroyed. Elsewhere the allies were only moderately successful in 1704: Rooke beat the French fleet off Malaga, and captured Gibraltar and Minorca, but the attempt to land Archduke Charles in Catalonia was repulsed.[22]

In 1705 a second attempt was made to establish Charles in Catalonia, but its success was overshadowed by Marlborough's failure to invade France in that year. France appeared to be secure behind her frontiers, and the allies were faced with the prospect of a long conflict against the loyal population of Castile. Moreover, the Emperor Leopold had died and his successor Joseph showed more interest in his Danubian territories than in

22 See Chapter IV, p. 232.

his brother's ambitions in Spain. Marlborough sensed a weakening of purpose within the Grand Alliance and resolved in 1706 to restore its morale by a second great victory. Louis too wanted a victory to strengthen his hand before negotiating for peace, and sent Villeroi to meet Marlborough with the troops of the *Maison du Roi*, the cream of the French army. The armies met at Ramillies. A vigorous attack on Villeroi's left wing succeeded in drawing his reserves from the centre, at which Marlborough withdrew half his attacking force behind the cover of a ridge of high land and sent it, without Villeroi's knowledge, to strengthen his other wing, an example not only of tactical skill but also of perfect timing and control. The allied left, thus reinforced, outflanked the French and drove them from the field. The towns of the Spanish Netherlands, in revulsion against the warfare which ravaged their territories, declared for Archduke Charles, and the allies gained immediate control of Brussels, Antwerp, Ghent and Bruges. Meanwhile, the year of victory was crowned by Eugène's swift campaign in north Italy. Although the emperor refused to withdraw troops from Hungary, Marlborough persuaded the German princes to send contingents to Eugène's support, and his victory at Turin not only saved Savoy from occupation by the French, but ensured allied control of the Alpine passes.

Blenheim, Ramillies and Turin loosened the French hold in Germany, the Netherlands and north Italy: it was less easy to penetrate the frontiers of France herself. After a year of fruitless campaigning (1707), Marlborough defeated the French again, at Oudenarde in 1708, but his subsequent capture of Lille, the first French city to fall to the allies, was achieved only at a cost in casualties five times greater than those at Oudenarde. Louis judged the moment ripe to appeal for peace. He had every reason to believe that France could no longer sustain the burden of war, and he tried desperately to conciliate the allies: England was to have Newfoundland and his guarantee of the Protestant Succession; the Dutch were to acquire a formidable range of barrier fortresses in the Netherlands; the emperor was to have Strassburg; Charles was to inherit Spain and Philip would be denied French support. The allies, however, replied by raising their terms too high. They had suffered too much from Louis's aggression in the past to believe in his good intentions in 1709 and interpreted his offer as a diplomatic trick to split the Grand Alliance[23]. Marlborough too led the allies to believe that in one more campaign they would enter Paris in triumph. Consequently they demanded of Louis that he join them in expelling Philip from Spain, a demand which he rejected with dignity, 'While I have to make war,' he said, 'I prefer to fight my enemies than my grandson.'

To his own people Louis made a spirited appeal against the conduct of the allies: 'Though I love my people as much as I love my own children; though I share in all the evils which the war has brought upon my faithful subjects; though I have shown how sincerely I desire to give them the blessings of peace; I am persuaded that they themselves would refuse the terms which are offered, as contrary to justice and dishonourable to the French name.' Short of repudiating Louis altogether, the French had no alternative but to stand by him in the defence of their country; and in the event their resistance was to bear fruit. Marlborough, in pursuit of his promised victory, invaded France in 1709, to be met at Malplaquet by Villars with an army mainly composed of recruits. Although the French were driven from the field, the allied losses exceeded those of the French, who, moreover, retired in sufficiently good order to re-group between Marlborough and Paris. Meanwhile, in Spain, Philip's army had defeated the allies at Almanza in 1707. The allies, though they did not yet fully realise it, had shot their bolt. The English Tories, who shared none of the Whig determination to establish a weak naval power like Austria in control of Spanish commerce, repudiated the cry of, 'No peace without Spain,' and came to power in the general election of 1710. Their hostility to Charles's candidature was reinforced in 1711 by the death from smallpox of the Emperor Joseph and the accession of Charles to the Austrian and imperial thrones. There was no good reason to prolong the war in order to secure for him a third crown, especially as Philip had made himself master of all but Barcelona. Marlborough was recalled and disgraced: Ormonde, his successor, was ordered by an infamous memorandum to co-operate as much with the French as with Eugène, who was thus exposed to defeat at Denain in 1712.

[23] See Chapter V, p.282 for the crisis which resulted in Anglo-Dutch relations.

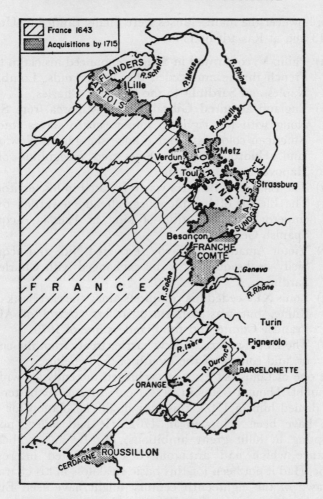

Map 12 French Territorial Expansion, 1643–1715

From 1710 the movement of diplomats took precedence over the march of armies; and the allies, encouraged by England's example, betrayed each other's interests in order to secure their own. Their confusion of purpose resulted in a series of treaties, negotiated at different places, at different times and between different parties, and not infrequently between the allies themselves; however the main clauses were finally ratified at Utrecht in 1713 and at Rastadt in 1714.

(i) Philip V, confirmed in Spain, renounced his claim to the French throne and ceded the Netherlands, Lombardy, Naples and Sardinia to the Emperor Charles.

(ii) England acquired Gibraltar and Minorca from Spain, along with the right to import negro slaves into the American colonies; from France she gained Newfoundland, Hudson Bay, St Kitts and recognition of the Hanoverian Succession.

(iii) The Elector of Bavaria was reinstated in his territories.

(iv) The Elector of Brandenburg, already rewarded by the emperor with the title of king in Prussia, acquired Spanish Gelderland.

(v) Victor Amadeus of Savoy recovered Nice and acquired Sicily—subsequently to be exchanged with Charles for Sardinia.

(vi) Louis XIV ceded his conquests along the east bank of the Rhine, but was confirmed in his control of Alsace, Franche Comté and the Flanders line of 1679.

(vii) The Dutch secured a new barrier treaty from the emperor, and control of the mouth of the Scheldt.

Not one of Louis XIV's wars achieved the ends for which it was fought. Though Louis in 1714 secured terms far better than those denied him in 1709, this was small consolation for what might have been achieved in 1702. He had failed, not by attempting to fulfil great ambitions, but by an overbearing arrogance which had antagonised every vested interest in Europe. Had it not been for this basic weakness in his character, the dawn of the eighteenth century might have seen Europe under the domination of a Bourbon dynasty, secure in both France and Spain.

VIII

SWEDEN AND THE STRUGGLE FOR SUPREMACY IN THE BALTIC
1600–1700

THE RISE OF SWEDEN

Gustavus Adolphus 1610–32

The inhabitants of north-eastern Sweden, led by Gustavus Vasa, had rebelled against Danish rule in 1523 and the fact that both countries subsequently adopted Lutheranism had in no way diminished their hostility. By the end of the century the Danes had in Christian IV (1588–1648) a vigorous and intelligent king who was determined to recover the ground lost by his predecessors. Sweden was ill equipped to resist. The southern provinces of Blekinge, Scania and Halland remained under Danish occupation and her one Atlantic port, Älvsborg (Gothenburg) was easily blockaded and almost impossible to defend. Denmark, moreover, by her possession of the islands of Bornholm, Gotland and Osel was able to dominate the Baltic from Copenhagen to the Gulf of Riga.

In order to strengthen their position in the Baltic Gustavus Vasa and his sons, Eric XIV and John III, had established bases along the coasts of Finland and Estonia, but this had served only to bring them into conflict with Russia. To complicate matters further, John III had married a Polish princess and his son Sigismund, brought up by her as a Roman Catholic and elected king of Poland in 1587, was therefore unacceptable to the Lutheran Swedes when he succeeded John in 1592. After six years of dispute and unrest, he was deposed in favour of his uncle Charles in 1598. Sigismund, no less vigorous than Christian IV of Denmark, was equally as determined to recover the throne, and Sweden accordingly was threatened on all sides by dangerous enemies.

Even more dangerous to Sweden were the symptoms of internal dissension. The nobles considered themselves the natural leaders of Sweden; they had been affronted by Gustavus Vasa's assumption of royalty in 1523, and their jealousy had not been allayed by his gifts of Church land. They argued that the monarchy should be elective, and the subsequent depositions of Gustavus's eldest son Eric XIV, and of Sigismund I, the one for being insane, the other for being a Catholic, gave practical force to their theory. They objected in particular to their exclusion from the council (the *riksrad*) and to the novel practice of the Vasa kings in summoning representatives of the Estates (the *riksdag*) to approve matters which, in the nobles' opinion, were beyond their competence. As disaffection grew, many of the nobles returned to their Danish allegiance, others chose to follow Sigismund, while the remainder determined to withhold allegiance from Charles IX's son when he should succeed his father, unless he agreed to guarantee them a monopoly of power both in making policy and in administering it.

When Charles died in 1611 the nobles found his successor unexpectedly conciliatory. Though Gustavus Adolphus was not a man to be readily intimidated he recognised that Sweden was too small a country to withstand the secession from public service of so important a section of the community. In order to bring the nobles back into responsible political activity, therefore, he disarmed them by wholly conceding to the demands presented by their leader Axel Oxenstierna. The working out of his promises, enshrined in the charter of 1612, was to transform the government of Sweden over the next twenty years.

The successful implementation of the Charter depended upon the close co-operation which developed between Gustavus and Oxenstierna. In the latter were personified the best qualities of public service, and he proved to be an admirable foil to the volatile king, being practical, cautious, diplomatic and a gifted bureaucrat: when Gustavus complained, 'If we were all as cold as you we should freeze', he retorted, 'If we were all as hot as your majesty we should burn'. Gustavus was indeed a fiery monarch, and it was his personality as much as his concessions which transformed a jealous nobility into a body of loyal officials. A big, clumsy man with tawny beard and hair, *il re d'oro* to the Italian mercenaries, immensely strong, with the fierce temper, the easy manners and the blunt directness of an infantry officer, he inspired others with his boundless self-confidence: 'He thinks the ship cannot sink that carries him,' wrote the English ambassador. But self-confidence and a manly gait were not all. His father had prepared him well for the task of kingship, training him in military skills, making him fluent in five languages and able to understand four more, and instilling in him a respect for the institution of monarchy as intense as his devotion to the Lutheran Church. In addition to his education, Gustavus possessed natural powers of leadership which made him a national figure, able to win the nobles back into public life without forfeiting the affection of the other estates. The nobles followed him despite themselves because, like Henry IV of France, he commanded both loyalty and affection.

Important changes, nonetheless, were made as a result of the Charter, and the first affected the composition of the *riksrad*. The low-born secretaries and the bailiffs who ran the royal estates in the provinces, were replaced by members of the nobility with authority to review royal policy. In the initial stages this was not of any great significance since meetings were infrequent and few attended: Gustavus, moreover, was so personally acceptable that the suspicions of the leading nobles were soon swept away. Before long, in place of scrutinising royal policy they had begun to identify with it and in 1625 the *riksrad* under Oxenstierna's chairmanship became a Regency council, the government of Sweden to all intents and purposes while Gustavus fought abroad.

In their criticism of the *riksrad* in 1612 the nobles had complained not only about their exclusion from it but equally about its inefficiency. The Vasa kings with their handful of secretaries and bailiffs had failed to cope with the growing complexity of government work. Primitive and peripatetic, the system depended upon the king's capacity to be his own chief bureaucrat when what was needed was an expanded civil service, operating permanently in Stockholm. As a consequence of the charter, therefore, members of the noble families were recruited to staff a number of new departments of state. The development was piecemeal, the differentiation of function determined by a series of experiments. The Judicature Ordinance of 1614 created the Supreme Court under its High Steward, the Exchequer

Ordinance of 1618 regularised the work of the Treasury, and in 1635 the experience of the past two decades was given expression in the Form of Government. This established the main structures of an administration organised into five colleges (departments), under the admiral, the treasurer, the high steward, the marshal and the chancellor. The nomenclature was that of medieval government, and so were the sources of revenue, since the administration was maintained by the produce of crown lands assigned to the separate colleges; but because of the co-operation between king and nobles the system worked admirably, with-standing the burdens of perpetual warfare, of assimilating con-quered territories and of governing in the absence of a king whose reign was spent with the army.

Co-ordinating and directing everything was the chancellor, Oxenstierna, and since two of the other four senior offices were held by his relatives he was able to supervise the entire adminis-tration to good effect. The Chancery, in addition to serving as the principal channel of communication between the king and his civil service, handled matters of foreign policy, religion and local government. The reform of local government was in fact one of the most crucial achievements of the reign, and the administra-tion of the royal bailiffs was superseded in 1624 by the creation of twenty-three districts whose governors enjoyed power not unlike those of the intendants of France.

Among the other reforms of the reign the position of the *riksdag* was regularised. In 1617 its composition was confirmed, with its four estates — the nobility, the clergy, the townsmen and the free peasantry — and in 1632 its consent was declared necessary for changes in taxation. The nobles, however, remained suspicious of its rôle lest a future king use it to by-pass their control of the *riksrad*, and although the *riksdag's* legislation was declared valid it was denied the power to initiate legislation on its own account.

The extent of the reforms achieved by Gustavus and Oxen-stierna should not be exaggerated. Inefficiency was not always eliminated, it was many years before the shortage of trained administrators had been overcome and the lines of demarcation were never as clear in practice as the Form of Government suggested. The main achievement was to recruit the nobles into government service, cementing the new alliance between them and their king, and to create an administrative system capable of governing not only Sweden but also an empire which, under Gustavus' direction, expanded along the shores of the Baltic into the heart of Germany.

Indeed, perhaps the most important consequence of the Charter of 1612 was that it left Gustavus free to deal with his enemies abroad. Chief among these was Christian of Denmark whose forces had taken Älvsborg and were poised to strike at the heart of the kingdom. Christian, however, was unaware of the true weakness of the Swedish army, and lacked the funds to finance a new campaign: in addition, his troops around Älvsborg had been disconcerted by the bitter resistance maintained by the local peasantry. The conquest of Sweden, though conceivably within his grasp, appeared to involve a prolonged war of attrition, too expensive to sustain, and he settled instead for the retention of Älvsborg. By the Treaty of Knäred (1613) Älvsborg was assigned to Denmark until it could be redeemed for 1,000,000 *riksdaler*, a price well beyond the Swedish king's resources. This saved the day for Sweden. The Danes' success, moreover, brought the Dutch upon the scene, (see p. 243) anxious to re-establish Sweden as a counterweight to Danish power in the Baltic, and it was with the help of Dutch loans that Älvsborg was redeemed in 1619.

Meanwhile on the eastern frontier the Russians had become involved in a civil war which afforded Swedish troops the opportunity to seize the important city of Novgorod. When a new tsar, Michael Romanoff, had defeated his rivals he secured peace with Gustavus by offering generous terms at Stolbova in 1617. Sweden evacuated Novgorod but was left in possession of Ingria, Karelia, Ingermannland — the bridge between Finland and Estonia — and the isle of Kexholm (see map 14). This deprived Russia of her access to the Baltic and made Sweden controller of her Baltic trade.

As for Poland, a series of short-term truces were agreed upon until Gustavus, attracted by the valuable customs duties to be collected at the mouths of the Polish rivers, invaded Livonia in 1621 and laid siege to Riga. Standing at the mouth of the Dvina and controlling one-third of Poland's exports, Riga was one of the great cities of the Baltic: it was also a great fortress, and it was the measure of Gustavus' success that within ten years he had brought his kingdom so successfully from the brink of defeat that

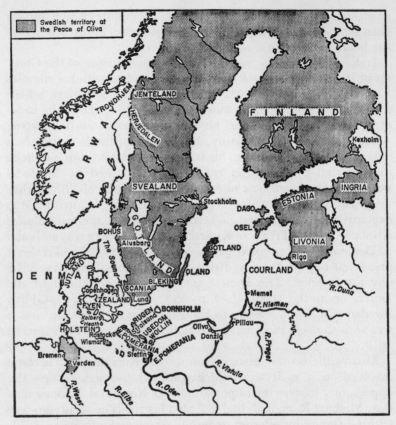

Map 13   The Swedish Empire in the Baltic, 1610–60

he could now achieve so great a prize. The conquest of Livonia afforded Gustavus a golden opportunity to reward noble families with new estates — and unruly peasants were transported to work them. By 1650, in fact, the Swedish nobility controlled nearly half of the province and government offices were reserved for Swedes or Swedish-speaking Livonians.

From 1626 to 1629 Gustavus challenged Sigismund for control of Polish Prussia, a coastal region between the mouths of the Niemen and the Vistula, whose ports provided an average income of over 600,000 *riksdalers* in customs duties. Sigismund, having other enemies to contend with in the Turks and the Russians (see p. 424), was unable to contain the Swedish advance, and was fortunate that Gustavus allowed his own attention to be distracted by events in north Germany. Wallenstein's growing power and his assumption of the title 'Admiral of the Baltic' compelled Gustavus to send aid to Stralsund in 1628 (see p. 143).

Wallenstein's military ambitions were the more ominous since the Habsburg emperor who employed him was both a champion of the Counter-Reformation and an ally of Poland. His victories in north Germany had been exploited to enforce an Edict of Restitution: it was not too fanciful to suppose that further victories in the Baltic might presage a restoration of the Catholic Vasas to the Swedish throne. 'All the wars which are going on in Europe,' wrote Gustavus, 'are linked together and are directed to one end' — the triumph of the Habsburgs and the defeat of Protestantism. So great was the emergency that he even invited Christian of Denmark, one of his bitterest enemies, to make common cause with him to save Stralsund. 'I now see with little difficulty that the projects of the House of Habsburg are directed against the Baltic; and that by a mixture of force and favour the United Provinces, my own power and finally yours are to be driven from it.'

Many years later when it would have been only too easy to disassociate himself from it all Oxenstierna endorsed Gustavus' action. 'It is certain that had his late Majesty not betaken himself to Germany with his army, the emperor would today have a fleet upon these seas. And if the emperor had once got hold of Stralsund, the whole coast would have fallen to him, and here in Sweden we should never have enjoyed a minute's security.' This was not however his judgement in 1629 when he argued that Gustavus should concentrate all his efforts to secure the defeat of Poland and strongly opposed his decision to free himself for Germany by seeking a truce with Sigismund.

It was not in any case a propitious moment for negotiation since Sigismund, reinforced by Wallenstein, had just defeated Gustavus at Stuhm, but the Polish Diet, unlike its ruler, wanted peace and the representatives of France and the United Provinces worked hard on Sweden's behalf. France was eager to enlist Gustavus' help against the Habsburgs without delay, and

the Dutch were desperately anxious to put an end to the war
which for three years had more than halved the profits of their
staple trade with the Polish Prussian ports. The outcome was the
Six Year Truce of Altmark, and Sweden, for the period of the
truce was to occupy Livonia and enjoy the revenues of the
Prussian ports. Within months Gustavus had landed in Pomerania to intervene with dramatic effect in the events of the Thirty
Years War. (For an account of Gustavus' campaigns, see pp.
148–52).

Historians are agreed that the French subsidies, offered in the
Treaty of Barwalde (1631) were an inducement but not the main
reason for the invasion of Germany: for the rest there is general
disagreement about Gustavus' underlying purposes. Some maintain that he was a military adventurer, fighting for the sake of
fighting and ready to chase the horizon on any pretext whatsoever: others interpret his actions more sympathetically and identify
his inner preoccupation with the idea of a just war: others, again,
stress the defensive strategy behind the relief of Stralsund.
Nonetheless, when Gustavus told the *riksrad* that he proposed to
occupy Pomerania, 'to guarantee Sweden's position for a few
years to come', he had more than defence in mind. Pomerania
was not only, after Livonia and Polish Prussia, the next target to
offer itself as he conducted his successful campaign along the
Baltic littoral, but also a base from which he could threaten both
Denmark and Poland. At the same time Gustavus believed his
own propaganda, which cast him in the role of Protestant
Champion against the fell hand of the Habsburgs, so that for him
the cause of Sweden and that of the Reformation were insepar-
able. His purposes were summarised, therefore, in two key
words: *assecuratio,* the need for a secure base in northern Germany, and *satisfactio,* the indemnity he required from the north
German Protestants to recompense him for saving them from the
Edict of Restitution and the Counter-Reformation.

No matter how precisely Gustavus defined his terms they were
in the event capable of infinite expansion.

'If we should conquer,' he said in council, 'it will be in our
power to do as we please.' If, as is possible, his words were
deliberately vague in order to evade precise definition of his
ambitions, it is none the less true that once launched upon his
campaigns these ambitions fed upon success. The victory at

Breitenfeld and the triumphal progress through the Rhineland enlarged his appetite. The saviour of north Germany required payment. It was no longer Pomerania alone but Magdeburg too. Moreover, as the Rhineland cities fell to his onset, south Germany beckoned alluringly.

By 1632 Gustavus had no doubts about his mission to dominate Germany. Continued success brought out in him the autocratic streak and the arrogant conceit of the presumptive world conqueror. Justly perhaps, he scorned the military ability of the Lutheran princes, and compelled their assent to treaties of contingent federation, a form of subsidiary alliance which gave him full control of their armies. If any protested the right, as an ally, to be consulted, he was brusquely informed that his lands were already at Sweden's mercy by right of conquest. It required a special mission by Oxenstierna to smooth the ruffled vanities of his sovereign's allies; but there was more at stake than vanity. The treaties of contingent federation could too easily become stepping stones to a political federation with Sweden, a *corpus bellicum et politicum* which Gustavus actually proposed when encamped at Frankfurt.

If Gustavus' aims have perplexed posterity, his genius for military affairs astounded his contemporaries. A great admirer of Maurice of Nassau (see p. 240) he learned from him to adopt new tactics and to develop new weapons: indeed, where Maurice had armed his cavalry with pistols in order to fire into the enemy and wheel away to reload, Gustavus trained his to charge with the sabre after discharging their firearms. His greatest achievement was to revive the role of the infantry who had become accustomed to scrumming together in massive formations, whether in defence or attack.

Gustavus regrouped them in smaller units and thus enabled them to change front and to move their ground with speed and efficiency, as was well demonstrated at Breitenfeld when the Saxon army fled exposing the Swedish flank. Since the smaller units were more exposed he provided groups of cavalry to defend them, and equipped them with light artillery. His famous 'leathern gun', a three-pounder with a very thin bronze barrel, bound with rope and mastic enclosed in a sheath of hard leather, was developed by him before 1627, though its successor in 1629, an all metal four-pounder, proved rather more effective. The value of these guns was that they were easily portable and, relatively speaking, quick-firing. Three men were enough to transport and to operate one in the battlefield, and it was the possession of forty-two of these at Breitenfeld, against Tilly's ponderous twenty-four pounders, which helped to give the Swedes their victory.

Regulations introduced in 1620 improved the recruitment and payment of conscripts. These were assigned to designated royal estates from which were derived the rents which paid their wages and where they could be billeted when not on active service. Swedish troops, however, although they provided a useful stiffening among the ranks of Gustavus' army, comprised barely one-fifth of his strength at Breitenfeld and the proportion diminished as the range of his operations extended. Indeed, contrary to the legend, embroidered by later ages, of blonde Nordic giants fighting with matchless valour for their king and their faith against the mean spirited mercenaries of north Germany, the Swedish army was almost as polyglot as its rivals. What distinguished it was the regularity with which it was paid, the vital factor which made recruitment easy and reconciled troops to the harsh discipline and training upon which the success of Gustavus' tactics depended.

The cost of maintaining a standing army of ever-increasing size imposed heavy burdens of taxation upon a relatively impoverished kingdom. Stockholm, the capital, was an established commercial centre and Älvsborg thrived by reason of its position west of the Sound — supplying timber and hemps to the Dutch dockyards without payment of dues to Denmark — but the other cities lagged behind them in wealth. The government therefore encouraged foreign merchants and craftsmen to settle in Sweden, and Alvsborg in particular became virtually a Dutch colony.

Among the immigrants one of the most enterprising was Louis de Geer who, in co-operation with the Swedish government, virtually created an armaments industry and played a major rôle in the exploitation of the country's mineral resources. In the Stora Kopperberg at Falun, Sweden enjoyed possession of the largest deposit of copper in Europe, at a time when copper was in great demand for the manufacture of coinage and artillery. In 1619 Gustavus Adolphus set up a company to exploit the mine so that, with the aid of Dutch capital and Dutch engineers, 3,000

tons of copper were produced annually until the ores were
exhausted by the middle of the century. From this production the
Swedish government initially enjoyed over 300,000 *riksdalers* in
annual royalties. Iron too was mined, again with Dutch aid, and
production was raised from 5,000 tons in 1620 to 20,000 by
1630.

Sweden nonetheless could not afford to finance her army
overseas from her own wealth and resources. It had taken more
than six years of heavy taxation, and a Dutch loan, to raise
1,000,000 *riksdalers* to redeem Alvsborg: one regiment of foot cost
approximately 1,000,000 *riksdalers* a year. In 1626 moreover, the
copper market collapsed for a period of years when the first
imports of Japanese copper arrived in Amsterdam and the
Spanish government abandoned its copper currency and returned to silver.

By 1629, of course, Sweden had secured the right to collect the
customs duties of the Polish Prussian ports, worth up to 600,000
riksdalers a year. In the same year the Swedish navy raised a
further 584,000 *riksdalers* by levying tolls on all ships entering the
Baltic ports under its control. On top of this Gustavus derived
considerable help from his allies. The French promised 400,000
riksdalers a year by the Treaty of Barwälde and the Russian
government, Sweden's ally against Poland since the Treaty of
Stolbova, sold grain at a subsidised price to Gustavus' agents
who in 1630 made a clear profit on the Amsterdam market of
400,000 *riksdalers*.

Despite these additional and valuable sources of revenue
Gustavus found it impossibe to undertake the invasion of Germany without making further demands upon his subjects at
home. In addition to meeting the normal expenses of government
the Swedes raised over 2,300,000 *riksdalers* in 1630 to send to
Germany. It was an intolerable burden and one which could not
be sustained, even though the nobility voluntarily agreed to make
its own contribution. In 1631, however, Gustavus was master of
Germany, and as a result of the forced contributions levied by the
army the additional taxes demanded at home fell to 1,147,278 in
1631, to 476,439 in 1632 and to 128,577 in 1633. From 1631 in
fact it had become the unchallengeable assumption of Swedish
foreign policy that warfare was required to pay for itself.

The Regency and Reign of Queen Christina 1632 – 54

Although it was well known that Gustavus always fought along-side his men in battle and thus incurred the risks which beset the humblest soldier, Sweden was utterly unprepared for his death in 1632 and the succession of his young daughter Christina. His chancellor, Oxenstierna, was in the Rhineland when the news broke and moved swiftly to Dresden in order to keep a watchful eye on John George of Saxony. From there, too, he arranged matters in Sweden where the *riksdag*, summoned at his orders to receive the news of Gustavus' death, entrusted the conduct of the regency to the *riksrad*. This in effect gave Oxenstierna all the power he needed. Not only was he an able and loyal public servant, but in addition his leadership was acknowledged by the other noble families. Moreover, he held the most important office in the administration while two of the other four great offices were held by a brother and a cousin.

The situation in Germany was less easy to control. Saxony was a reluctant ally, as were the other German Protestants, and Richelieu was eager to mobilise the anti-Habsburg states of the Empire under the leadership of France. In the event the forma-tion of the Heilbronn League (see p. 152), despite the unwel-come intrusion of the French in its councils, served Sweden's purpose well enough in the aftermath of Lützen.

After Nördlingen, however, (see p. 154) Oxenstierna was in serious difficulties. When the Swedish army mutinied for lack of pay he was more or less made prisoner by the garrison in Magdeburg: the German princes began to make their peace with the emperor; France offered assistance in the Treaty of Com-piègne but only on condition that Sweden renounce her claims in the Rhineland; Denmark threatened war, and the Truce of Altmark with Poland was about to expire. Of all these problems the most crucial was the need to avert a renewal of war with Poland, but the *riksrad*, in Oxenstierna's absence, completely bungled its own negotiations with the Poles by making public its minimum terms before the settlement had been concluded. In the event the truce was renewed at Stuhmsdorf and Sweden re-mained in occupation of Livonia, but the Prussian ports and their valuable revenues reverted to Poland.

Against the odds Baner, the Swedish commander-in-chief,

held together the remnants of the Swedish army so that Oxenstierna could return to Stockholm to reassert his authority and to
prevent the Queen Mother marrying Christina to a Danish
prince. Denmark was indeed the enemy Oxenstierna most feared
after Poland. Germany was of less importance provided that
Gustavus' conquest of Pomerania be preserved and to this end he
abandoned Sweden's pretensions in the Rhineland in order to
secure the French subsidies which Baner desperately needed
(Treaty of Hamburg 1638). Baner tried to exploit his improved
position for his own advantage rather than his country's (see p.
556), but when his successor Torstensson had re-established
Swedish authority in north Germany at the second battle of
Breitenfeld (1642), Oxenstierna decided that the time was propitious to deal with Denmark.

'We find' he wrote, 'that Denmark is not less hostile to us than
Austria, and a more dangerous enemy because she is nearer to
us'. Christian IV's diplomacy moreover had been devoted since
1635 to weakening Sweden's position, so that Oxenstierna was
justified in his complaint that Christian 'had repeatedly tucked
us under the chin to see if our teeth were still firm in our heads.'
The latest dispute arose over the Sound dues. Sweden's exemption from these was not in question but Denmark refused to
exempt ships plying from Baltic ports under Swedish occupation
and no longer countenanced the deception by which many Dutch
ships sailed under a Swedish flag.

Late in the autumn of 1643 Oxenstierna ordered Torstensson
to abandon a campaign in Silesia and take Denmark by surprise.
By January Torstensson was master of the Danish mainland,
waiting impatiently for the Little and Great Belts to freeze to
allow his troops access across the ice to Copenhagen. Louis de
Geer, the Dutch entrepreneur with a fortune invested in Swedish
metallurgical industries, had commissioned a private fleet in the
United Provinces which gave Sweden temporary command of the
Sound and made easy the capture of Gotland and Osel, two
islands belonging to Denmark which commanded shipping lanes
in the eastern Baltic. Meanwhile Horn attacked the Danes in
Scania, one of the provinces of Danish-occupied Sweden, in the
hope of reaching the coast and of launching an invasion across
the Sound.

In the event, the Little Belt failed to freeze and Horn was

delayed by unexpected resistance at Malmo. Torstensson was therefore trapped in the Jutland peninsula and, if Gallas, who had had the wit to chase after him, had also had the sense to keep sober, the emperor might well have recovered his influence in northern Germany. Torstensson left Wrangel to hold the mainland and with almost contemptuous ease gave Gallas the slip at Kiel. When Gallas turned to follow he defeated him. Denmark was therefore still in danger from Swedish armies in Jutland and Skåne, but Christian saved the day at sea. He drove off de Geer's fleet in May, and for several weeks engaged the Swedish navy in a running battle among the Danish islands. The battle reached its climax on 1 July off Kolberg Heath, between Kiel Fjord and the island of Fehmarn, when Christian was victorious. The survivors however joined with other Swedish ships to seize the island of Bornholm, and a form of stalemate ensued in which Sweden could not overrun Copenhagen but the Danes had little hope of counter-attacking successfully.

Into this mood of hesitancy intruded the personality of Christina, perceptive, imperious and uncompromisingly determined to end the war, not merely with Denmark but with all Sweden's enemies. She was convinced that war served no other purpose than to justify Oxenstierna in excluding her from the direction of a purely masculine occupation. In September 1644 she came formally of age on her eighteenth birthday; and with the termination of the regency came an end to the war. In one respect, however, her strictures on the futility of the war were unfair since the campaign against Denmark resulted in important gains for Sweden in the Treaty of Bromsebro, 1645:

(i) Denmark ceded the provinces of Jemteland and Herjedalen along the frontier between Norway and Sweden;

(ii) Denmark ceded the islands of Gotland and Osel, both of strategic value in the Baltic;

(iii) Denmark agreed that not only Sweden but all the ports throughout her empire should be exempted from the payment of the Sound dues. In pledge of this Sweden was to occupy the province of Halland on her south-western coast for a period of thirty years.

In the event, the acquisitions made at Bromsebro proved to be of much greater value to Sweden than those gained four years

later at Westphalia. Despite the successful campaigns led by
Torstensson against the emperor after 1645 (see p. 156),
Sweden gained less in 1648 than Gustavus II Adolphus had held
at the end of 1631. Denied an electoral title or any voice in the
Imperial Diet, she was bought off with a payment of 5,000,000
riksdalers and confirmed in her possession of Western Pomerania,
of Stettin, Stralsund and Wismar, and of the offshore islands of
Rügen, Usedom and Wollin. In addition, the secularised bishoprics of Bremen and Verden gave her control of the river mouths of
the Weser and the Elbe.

The ending of the war went almost unnoticed in Sweden where
the country was swiftly moving to the brink of civil war, as a
result of the wholesale alienation of crown land which had taken
place since 1632. The departments of the administration depended on the produce of the royal estates assigned to them, but
as rents in kind were sometimes difficult to convert into negoti-
able currency—salted hides and bales of corn were scarcely
liquid assets—Oxenstierna had decided to alter the fiscal system.
He began by giving land outright in lieu of payment for good
service in the army or in the administration, or by selling it to
raise immediate capital. His next step was to recoup the administration by providing it with a more efficient source of revenue
from indirect taxation and he hoped that the development of the
towns and the expansion of Sweden's Baltic trade would provide
alternative sources of wealth for the government to tap.

Unhappily for Sweden, Oxenstierna lost control of his colleagues in the *riksrad*, who became so excited by the opportunity
afforded them by the disposal of royal estates that they ignored
the second, essential part of his plan. From 1632, without
Gustavus's physical presence to overawe and to inspire them, the
nobles forgot their recent conversion to the ideal of public
services, and, brushing aside the protestations of Oxenstierna,
began to plunder Sweden with the irresponsible selfishness of
triumphant mercenaries. Two-thirds of the Crown's territorial
revenues had vanished by 1654. Twenty-two of the most influential families obtained lands worth one-fifth of the ordinary
revenue of the state, their lesser colleagues gaining less in
proportion to their status. With land they also sought honours
and titles, the number being more than doubled during the
Regency: where three men had held the title of count, twenty

were to glory in the honour, and the barons increased from seven
to thirty-four.

The consequences for the peasantry, a vigorous and self-reliant
estate, were serious. Those living on crown lands, who had
enjoyed a position of virtual independence under an absentee and
generally tolerant landlord, were subjected to the mercy of a
profit-minded noble in their midst, anxious to exploit his investment. Worse still, and much more frequent, was the sale not of
land but of the tax revenues from the freeholding peasantry, since
the nobles who thus collected these taxes for themselves fell very
easily into the habit of treating these freeholders as though they
were their tenants. The threat of degradation to the status of
servile labourers, made all the worse by the seigneurial habits
acquired by the nobles from their experience of serfdom while on
service in Germany, brought the peasantry very close to rebellion.

At the same time, the administration began to founder without
its accustomed revenues: offices in the civil service went unpaid,
and the army had to plunder to survive. When the *riksrad* at last
took up Oxenstierna's proposals for indirect taxation it could not
introduce these without the *riksdag's* consent, and on this issue
the peasantry, the clergy and the townsmen were united in
opposition: 'When the nobility have all the peasants subject to
themselves,' declared Archbishop Lenoeus 'then the Estate of
Peasants will no longer have a voice at the diet, and when the
Estate of Peasants goes under, Burghers and Clergy may easily
go under too.' The *riksdag* demanded *reduktion*, the restoration of
all crown lands, and when the *riksrad* refused to surrender its
gains, the *riksdag* refused to pass the indirect taxes.

In this impasse the decision lay with Christina, a woman of
such intrepid self-assurance that it was unlikely that she could
stay out of any controversy for long. In many ways she resembled
her father; physically tough, capable of great endurance, trained
to diplomacy and the command of foreign languages, she was as
autocratic and self-willed. Her ebullient mind extended beyond
the confines of statecraft and war: these alone bored her, and she
looked for companionship to men of letters and philosophy—she
patronised both Grotius and Descartes—delighting in the excitement of intellectual debate. Unlike Gustavus, Christina had no
concept of duty: if ruling Sweden should prove tedious then with

wilful disregard of the consequences she was ready to give it up: if ruling Sweden meant that she would have to provide an heir, she was too imperious to submit to the servitude of marriage and chose rather to abdicate. In her place she resolved to be succeeded by her cousin Charles, who had commanded the Swedish army at the end of the German war.

Her first move was to secure the assent of the *riksrad* to the nomination of Charles as heir to the throne. It was a difficult task since the nobles could see no reason why this was necessary: moreover they intended, when the day came, to impose stringent conditions before allowing Charles to become king. To achieve her purposes, therefore, Christina decided to champion the *riksdag's* demand for *reduktion*. It was a cynical manoeuvre. Of all the lands alienated by the crown more than half had been lost since Christina herself came of age in 1644, and she had shown herself as indifferent as any self-seeking noble to the needs of the peasantry. In 1650, however, she discovered in the threat of peasant revolt a weapon with which to coerce the *riksrad*.

In that year the failure of the harvest, the worst of the century, brought peasant discontent to a head. The *riksdag* met for the unprecedented period of four months in one year, and the speeches of the lower estates, in conjunction with the demonstrations of hungry villagers, caused consternation among the nobles. Oxenstierna confessed that he was afraid to visit his country house, and another noble drew an unhappy parallel with events elsewhere: 'They all want to do as they have been doing in England, and make us all as like as pig's trotters.' The more the nobles panicked, the more they played into Christina's hands. Cynical though she was of the *riksdag's* demands, she incited it to attack the nobility and pretended to embrace the cause of *reduktion*. At this the nobles had no option but to capitulate: Christina, in return for withdrawing her support from the campaign for *reduktion*, won acceptance of Charles as Hereditary Prince.

Christina's remaining years as queen were spent in filling in the details of her abdication. She was determined to live as lavishly in retirement as she had done on the throne, and, by one of the ironies of her reign, compelled the *riksrad* to recover certain crown lands in order to assure her of a fixed income. Occupied also in preparing for her spiritual comfort, she entertained in secret a succession of priests through whom she was received into the Roman Church. In May 1654 she abandoned her throne.

Christina's romantic vision of herself as an exiled queen holding. literary court in Rome before the astonished eyes of Europe was not fulfilled. After the initial shock people found her merely absurd. Her punishment was to live to an old age, ignored by her former subjects and bored by her friends.

Charles X 1654 – 60

Christina's abdication solved none of Sweden's problems except that it left the throne vacant for a successor with a more profound sense of public duty. If Charles X had little experience of anything but the military life, which he passionately enjoyed, he had nonetheless observed the difficulties facing Christina's government and had declared in advance his opinion that crown lands would have to be recovered. Herman Fleming, the treasurer, agreed with him. The administration was bankrupt, unable to pay its servants, provision the navy or supply hay for the royal horses.

Fleming and Charles X overrode the opposition of the *riksrad* — which had, after all, accepted Charles as Christina's successor only to avoid *reduktion* — by appealing to the *riksdag*. For a moment there was a serious risk of rebellion until Charles agreed to a compromise. Royal estates deemed to be 'indispensable' for the administration of the court, the armed forces and the mining industry, were restored to the crown along with one quarter of all other crown land. This represented the recovery of roughly 3,000 farms and homesteads although it took Fleming several years to implement the agreement. In return, the nobles were guaranteed permanent possession of the other crown lands they had acquired.

One important reason for insisting upon a compromise was that Charles X was about to declare war on Poland. As commander-in-chief in the last months of the German war he felt he had been cheated of victories by the settlements made in Westphalia: now, aged 32, he could still hope to rival the achievements of Gustavus Adolphus. There were also more fundamental issues at stake. Having acquired an empire Sweden lacked the resources necessary for its defence. Since the government could not afford to maintain its garrisons in idleness, the only alternative to disbanding them was to send them to wage war abroad where they could keep themselves alive by plunder. 'Other nations make war because they are rich,' said one Swede sadly, 'Sweden because it is poor'.

Warfare could prove profitable in one other respect. For the first time, perhaps, in the century economic considerations ranked as important in the councils of Sweden as motives of security, the defence of Protestantism, military strategy or national ambition. Oxenstierna set up in 1651 the *Kommerscollegium* to encourage the growth of Swedish shipping and hoped ultimately to solve the government's financial problems by providing it with a rich and permanent flow of revenues from customs dues and shipping tolls. To this end the government would have to establish control of every major port and estuary in the Baltic and, finally, to wrest control of the Sound from Denmark.

In the meantime the government faced a more immediate problem in Poland. Sigismund's son, John Casimir, had reasserted his father's claim to the Swedish throne, while the Swedish government coveted the revenues of the Prussian ports which it had briefly enjoyed during the Truce of Altmark (1629–35). John Casimir moreover was challenged by rebellious subjects and his country had been invaded by separate forces of Magyars, Cossacks and Russians. Although it seemed to be an opportune moment for Sweden to settle old scores with Poland, Charles X was more concerned with the success of the advancing Russian army. Ever since the treaty of Stolbova (1617), when Sweden had acquired Russia's foothold on the Baltic coast, the two countries had remained on surprisingly friendly terms because of their common hostility to Poland. When, however, the Russians threatened to break through to the Polish Prussian coastline Charles X feared they might well attack the Swedish bases in Livonia and Estonia and re-establish themselves as a force in the Baltic. As a result he offered to assist John Casimir against his enemies in return for possession of the Prussian ports, and only when this offer was rejected did he prepare to invade on his own account.

The invasion of 1655 was both swift and successful. The Polish army could not withstand simultaneous attack from four quarters, and there were many disaffected nobles, Sobieski among them, who welcomed Charles's approach and recognised him as king. Within a few weeks Charles entered both Warsaw and Cracow, the joint capital cities, and John Casimir fled into exile. A tentative move by the Elector of Brandenburg to sneak advantage from the Swedish invasion by gaining full independence for his duchy of Prussia, a Polish fief, (see p. 400) was firmly checked by Charles at Königsberg in January 1656 where the Elector was compelled to recognise Charles as his overlord, to supply him with troops and to pledge him half the revenues of his duchy.

By this time, however, Charles X, although he had had precise reasons for invading Poland, showed that he had very little idea how to attain them in the long run. Moreover his troops by their depredations, and even more by their deliberate desecration of Catholic churches, had roused the peasantry to revolt. For reasons which are not at all clear, Charles plunged blindly into the interior, reaching Lwow, in February 1656, while behind his back John Casimir returned to Warsaw and the Russians invaded the Baltic Provinces.

With 800 kilometres between himself and his base in Pomerania, Charles demonstrated his brilliance as a soldier by bringing his troops back safely to the coast. Unhappily he then wasted his advantage by laying siege to Danzig, a move which immediately antagonised the Dutch government, ever dependent upon free trade with the city, and brought it to the aid of the Russians and the Poles. It was in these difficult circumstances for Charles that Frederick William demanded and secured full sovereignty in Prussia as the price of his continued support.

Frederick II of Denmark, meanwhile, decided that Charles' predicament afforded Denmark an opportunity to recover the losses of 1645. Whatever its dangers Frederick's declaration of war in June 1657 at least gave Charles an excuse to abandon a position which was rapidly becoming untenable, and to demonstrate again his excellence in attack. Within eight weeks he brought his army by forced marches across Pomerania to the shore of the Little Belt, separating the Danish mainland from the island of Fyen. But unless he could win control of the sea the point of his swift campaign would be lost, and a Swedish fleet which ventured into the Little Belt in September was driven back by the Danes. Charles's subsequent conquest of Jutland won him no advantage: as a show of force it made no impression upon Frederick who knew he was perfectly secure in Copenhagen, and who drew confidence from the news of Casimir's restoration in Poland and of Brandenburg's desertion of Sweden.

Poised on the brink of the sea yet impotent to cross it, Charles became daily more exasperated until at last a desperate opportunity offered itself. In January 1658 the waters of the Little Belt froze and the Swedish army marched across to Fyen, losing two squadrons of horse and the royal carriages through the ice. More dangerous than the crossing was the situation it created, for Charles had merely isolated himself in Fyen instead of in Jutland and once the ice melted there would be no escape. But the cold held, and intensified until the Great Belt too was frozen. For seven days, in a thrilling race against the thaw, Charles with 5,000 men and his artillery, leaped from one island to the next until he arrived on Zealand with Copenhagen at last at his mercy. Frederick, betrayed by the elements, could only surrender.

The Treaty of Roskilde, concluded in February 1658, was the most important in Swedish history since it established the boundaries of modern Sweden. Whatever Charles's faults of judgement the result of his military escapades was to expel the Danes once and for all from Swedish mainland. Halland, pledged to Sweden for twenty years in 1645, was ceded in perpetuity along with the coastal provinces of Scania, Bleking and Bohus. In addition the Danes surrendered Trondhjem in Norway and the island of Bornholm.

By losing Scania the Danes lost control of the Sound, which could thus be closed only by the two countries acting in co-operation. Charles X immediately demanded that it be closed to Dutch armaments, in revenge for Dutch intervention at Danzig, but Frederick refused to commit himself. He was playing for time in which to find allies, and he wasted no opportunity to inform the Dutch of his efforts to preserve their access to the Baltic. Charles X was not given to patient negotiation. The difficulties and delays prompted him to teach the Danes a sharp lesson, and no doubt he considered the advantages of deposing Frederick in order to take for himself the triple crown of

Scandinavia. Moreover, the reversion to peace merely revived his original problem of what to do with the army. He could not afford to maintain it in idleness; he dared not dismiss it. Within five months of the Treaty of Roskilde he had invaded Zealand.

This time the Danes in Copenhagen resisted him so strongly that instead of the swift success upon which he had reckoned he was forced to undertake a siege which promised to be both long and bloody. Simultaneously the inhabitants of Trondhjem and Bornholm rebelled against their change of ruler. Most serious of all was the sudden blockade of the Sound by the navies of France, England and the United Provinces, acting in rare concert. Their trade with the Baltic was too lucrative to depend upon the whim of a Swedish king, and indifferent though they were to his quarrel with Denmark they could not permit him to control both banks of the Sound. Charles was thus unable to defeat Denmark, but neither could he be defeated. The impasse was only resolved by his death from camp fever in 1660.

In the Treaty of Copenhagen Charles' successors restored Bornholm and Trondhjem to the Danes and abandoned the attempt to close the Sound to other states: in every other respect the Treaty of Roskilde was confirmed. At the same time, in the Peace of Oliva, John Casimir renounced his claim to Sweden and the Elector of Brandenburg won general recognition of his sovereignty in Polish Prussia. Finally, by the Treaty of Kardis (1661), the Russians formally confirmed Sweden's possession of the Baltic provinces. For the first time in the seventeenth century the Baltic was at peace.

The Regency and Reign of Charles XI 1660–97

The death of Charles X, though it gave Sweden a respite from war, resulted in other ills so serious that the fruits of peace could not be enjoyed. Since Charles XI was a minor the *riksrad* seized power in his name and dismissed from office such men as Herman Fleming who had begun to implement the *reduktion* of crown lands. In their place were appointed Gustave Bonde as treasurer and Magnus de la Gardie as chancellor. De la Gardie was both rich and handsome, a glittering figure at court and a great patron of the arts. Unhappily for Sweden he had little understanding of government finance although he was able at first to rely on Gustav Bonde to husband the slender resources of the state. The Polish war had left a debt of 10 million *riksdalers* and Bonde succeeded in paying off most of this before his death in 1667, but thereafter the worst excesses of Christina's reign were repeated. Not only were new loans contracted without the means to redeem them, but the sale of crown lands was resumed at a prodigal rate.

De la Gardie successfully negotiated the treaties of Copenhagen, Oliva and Kardis (see p. 392) but the situation abroad was dangerous; indeed the problems of Gustavus Adolphus in establishing the Swedish empire in the Baltic were as nothing to those facing his successors who sought to preserve it. The separate provinces were bound together by no emotional or racial ties, and as an empire were strategically indefensible. Scattered around the Baltic shores, they were open to attack from all quarters, nor was it possible to penetrate into the interior in search of natural boundaries; there were none to be found east of the Urals or north of the Alps. Instead, they perpetually excited the hostility and greed of the inland powers. To this problem there seemed to be no simple, satisfactory solution. Gustavus Adolphus and Charles X had reacted to the situation, 'by pre-emptive strikes, anxious aggressions, swift exploitation of opportunities which might well prove transient, in the hope thereby of buttressing their defences or deepening the protective zones which surrounded them'. (M. Roberts, *The Swedish Imperial Experience*).

At first sight De la Gardie's foreign policy was in essence cautious and pacific, but the bankruptcy of his government compelled him to run down the garrisons overseas and seek out foreign allies prepared to offer Sweden protection and subsidies. In the event the search for subsidies took precedence over other considerations. 'Let us act like merchants', said one of his colleagues, 'so as to get money enough and do naught else for it than to sit still'. After a brief association with the Dutch in the Triple Alliance of 1668 (see p. 274), the Swedes sold out to France for an annual subsidy of 400,000 *livres*. When Louis XIV invaded the United Provinces in 1672 la Gardie deceived himself that Sweden would have nothing more onerous to do than to close the Sound to Dutch shipping, a task made even more easy by the fact that Denmark too was in the French camp. Unfortu-

nately, when the Dutch found an ally in the Elector of Brandenburg (1674), a Swedish army had to be sent to Pomerania in
order to neutralise the Elector's forces in north Germany. La
Gardie had no intention of provoking a fight with Brandenburg—his sole concern being to satisfy Louis XIV that his
subsidies were being put to good use—but so badly were his men
supplied that within a few weeks they were compelled to cross the
border into Brandenburg in search of food. There they were
defeated at Fehrbellin in February 1675.

The battle itself was little more than a minor engagement, but
so consistently had Sweden triumphed in the past that the news
of her defeat by a north German princeling had important
repercussions. The immediate result was to advertise her impotence before all her enemies, who were quick to take advantage of
it. The Elector's troops overran Pomerania, the Bishop of
Münster occupied Bremen and Verden, and Christian V of
Denmark set about the recovery of the provinces lost in 1660.
The Danish fleet reinforced by the Dutch, captured Gotland and
won command of the Sound, and an invading army swarmed
across Scania, to the great delight of the peasants who ransacked
the houses of the nobility and hailed the Danes as liberators.

The crisis served one good purpose in that it galvanised
Charles XI into action. So backward and shy had he been as a
boy that many had believed him illiterate, and it had been an
easy matter for la Gardie to win complete ascendancy over him.
Even when Charles came of age in 1672 he passively accepted his
uncle's leadership, until he discovered in 1674 that his army, the
one thing to interest him, had virtually ceased to exist. This
prompted him to demand, and to secure, the *reduktion* of several
hundred homesteads whose income had traditionally maintained the army. When, in the succeeding year, he saw his empire
on the brink of dissolution, he abandoned la Gardie altogether
and put himself at the head of his people. It was almost too late.
With 15,000 men he fought a harsh campaign against the Danes
in Scania, a campaign made all the more bitter by the peasantry
who formed guerilla bands to harass the royal army.

After many difficulties and without proper equipment and
supplies for his troops, Charles won a major victory at Lund in
the late autumn of 1676, which led in the following year to the
withdrawal of the Danes from Scania but had no effect on the

guerilla bands who remained active until the end of the war. The Danes moreover retained their supremacy at sea and even the miniature navy of Brandenburg successfully blockaded Stettin and Stralsund.

By 1678 the mainland had been secured, but it seemed that the north German territories were lost for ever. Ironically, however, what had been lost on account of the French alliance was recovered immediately by the same means. Louis XIV could not afford to earn a reputation for deserting allies; consequently, when a peace settlement was being negotiated at Nijmegen, he made separate treaties with Denmark at Fontainebleau, and with Brandenburg at Saint-Germain, compelling them to evacuate their troops from Wismar, Holstein-Gottorp and Pomerania. It was in its way a gesture typical of Louis's arrogance since Charles was not consulted by the French, and so angry were both he and Christian that they salved their pride by embodying the terms of Fontainebleau in a special treaty between themselves.

The war had a profound effect on the domestic history of Sweden. Charles XI knew only too well whom to blame for the crisis which had endangered his kingdom. Alongside him in the desperate campaign to save Scania from the Danes were men like John Gyllenstierna who planned with him not only the means of effecting a recovery when the war was over but also the retribution to be demanded from those responsible for beginning it. As early as 1675 Charles appointed a commission of enquiry into the conduct of the regency, but in 1680, at the insistence of the *riksdag*, he replaced it with two separate commissions, one to investigate the 118 families which had been involved in de la Gardie's administration and to punish them for the consequences of their misrule, the other to recover all crown lands alienated since 1638.

The *riksdag's* support was important to the success of the commissions, and in this respect the critical factor was the action of the lesser nobility who sided with the clergy, the townsmen and the free peasantry. Angry at the incompetence which the magnates had demonstrated and jealous of the wealth they had amassed, they were also aware that a bankrupt government could not afford to pay the salaries upon which many of their class depended. Even the magnates themselves, conscious of their isolation, acquiesced in the demands of the other Estates, hoping that the political storm might blow itself out in due course. In this they were to be mistaken. In 1682 the *riksdag* endowed the commissioners with even greater powers to ensure the success of their work. By the end of the reign one commission had collected four million *riksdalers* in fines, while the other had recovered more than 80 per cent of all land alienated by the crown, assuring it for the future of an additional annual revenue of over two million *riksdalers*.

This development was accompanied by constitutional changes of fundamental importance. The *riksdag,* believing that the king was indeed the only true guardian of its interests, was determined to remove the last vestiges of noble oligarchy by creating a royal absolutism. As early as 1680 it declared the king's authority over all the institutions of government, saving that he must govern 'according to the law'. Subsequently, by a series of decisions of the *riksdags* which met over the next decade or so, the king was authorised to levy extraordinary taxes at will on all classes including the nobility, to determine the membership and the duties of the *riksrad,* and to make laws and regulations without consulting the Estates. The climax to all this was the Declaration of Sovereignty of 1693 which declared Charles to be an 'absolute-sovereign king'. The words of the declaration of 1680 that the king must govern according to the law were redrafted to read 'according to his pleasure and as a Christian King'. No longer tied by temporal laws, the king of Sweden was responsible to God alone.

In the years following the war, and assisted by the plans discussed with Gyllenstierna before his death in 1680, Charles reformed and expanded his civil service. A table of ranks was published to make it clear that positions in civil and military life depended upon merit rather than birth, and with the income provided by the *reduktion* commission the government was able to pay good salaries to recruit good candidates. As the new class of officers, coming in the main from the lesser nobility, grew wealthy in Charles' service they began to purchase the lands of the dispossessed magnates — though some of these, bowing to the inevitable, came back into royal service to rebuild their fortunes.

The collegiate system remained as before, but the nature of local government was developed to a degree of excellence unparallelled in Europe. The smallest unit, the *socken*, was made up of a small group of peasant farmers under their headman, who joined with the pastor and the elected magistrates to assess each taxpayer's contribution. The system demanded a peasantry wealthy enough to sustain the burden of taxation, in which Sweden was fortunate, but even more striking was its fairness and efficiency, demonstrated by the general readiness of the peasantry to pay their due amount. Above the *socken* came the district of one thousand hearths with its staff of magistrates and permanent officials: seven or eight districts comprised the province whose affairs were directed by a governor and four other officers: their work in turn was integrated with the five colleges of the central administration. The result was a highly organised system, methodical and meticulous and particularly successful in the assessment and collection of taxes. Even during the disastrous years which followed Charles XI's death, when Sweden was burdened with the continuous and extensive campaigns of his successor, this local administration, based on honesty, justice and efficiency never collapsed.

One of the most important tasks of the government in the post-war period was to integrate the Danish speaking inhabitants of Scania and the other mainland provinces, acquired in 1659, more closely with the rest of the kingdom. Little attempt had been made before the war to change the language, laws and customs of these provinces but the vigour with which they had welcomed back the Danes in 1675 prompted the government to take steps to prevent this happening again. It introduced garrisons, linked by an effective road system, and Swedish colonists along with the Swedish legal systems, the Swedish church and the Swedish language. By the end of the reign the process of cultural colonisation was virtually complete.

As the government's revenues began to exceed its expenditure Charles XI could afford to establish permanent garrisons, employing about 25,000 troops in all, throughout his overseas possessions. In addition, by introducing a territorial system — the *indelningsverk* — Charles could maintain an army of 38,000 at home by assigning its units to specific estates recovered by the crown. Officers and men lived in the same district and the men, when not engaged in training exercises, could help the farmers produce the crops on which their livelihood depended. The officers were regularly seconded to gain experience in the Dutch and French armies. A similar territorial system maintained 11,000 men for the Swedish navy, re-equipped with 34 ships of the line and 11 frigates, and whose officers trained in the Dutch and English navies. In addition Charles moved the naval head-quarters from Stockholm. The city was too far to the north — its waters remained frozen one month longer than those of Copenhagen, allowing the Danes too great an advantage. Even when the ice had melted, the islands and reefs off the harbour could, when the wind was unfavourable, compel the fleet to take two months to take to the sea. Karlskrona on the coast of Blekinge was vastly better situated for naval warfare in the Baltic.

Abroad Charles XI was both cautious and pacific. The international situation in which Gustavus Adolphus had been able to exploit the weakness of Poland, the turmoil within Russia and the defeat of Denmark at the hands of the emperor had been profoundly altered. The Baltic Provinces, for example, which constituted the very bastion of Sweden's power in the Baltic had become increasingly vulnerable to the growing power of Russia; and the Danes had demonstrated only too clearly their ability to threaten Swedish territory. Moreover, the readiness of the Dutch to support Sweden against Denmark could no longer be relied upon as a matter of course, nor were the major powers interested any longer in cultivating allies capable of thwarting Austria and Spain. In a world dominated by the rivalry of France, Austria and the Maritime Powers of England and the United Provinces it was wise for Sweden to avoid becoming involved.

For this reason Gyllenstierna had urged Charles as a matter of urgency to come to terms with Denmark. In the Treaty of Land, 1679, Charles was betrothed to Christian V's sister, and it was agreed that neither side would make alliances without consulting the other. This new and uncertain amity did not last long. Denmark could not feel secure until she had possession of Holstein-Gottorp; Sweden dared not relinquish her interest in that quarter. In 1682 Christian allied with France, without Charles' agreement, and occupied the duchy; Charles in return secured the restoration of its duke, his cousin, through the good offices of England and the United Provinces in the Treaty of Altona, 1689.

One problem, the full significance of which did not become clear in Charles XI's reign, arose from the operation of the *reduktion* commissioners in the Baltic Provinces. The Swedish colonial landowners in possession of crown lands were expropriated as in the mainland provinces, but the native nobility of Livonia protested strongly that it too should have to give up the lands it had acquired. Moreover, the commissioners in their enthusiasm claimed the repossession of lands which had been alienated long before the 1630s. The Estates, summoned to Riga in 1681, refused to give way to the royal commissioners and *reduktion* had subsequently to be carried out by force. The bitter resentment experienced by the Livonian nobility found a voice in John Patkul who led a deputation to Stockholm in 1692. Unhappily he was ill suited to so delicate a mission. Violent and intemperate, his outspoken words only angered Charles XI who ordered his arrest. Later, after his escape into exile, he was condemned for treason.

Livonia nonetheless remained quiet if resentful, and Denmark, though hostile, was effectively restrained by the maritime powers of England and the United Provinces. The Swedish empire, for all the strategic weakness of its position, extended so vulnerably along the Baltic littoral, was nonetheless more powerful and more capable of defending itself than at any time in the seventeenth century.

THE GREAT ELECTOR OF BRANDENBURG

Brandenburg to 1660

Sweden's defeat by Brandenburg at Fehrbellin took Europe by surprise and marked the emergence of the Elector Frederick William as a major figure in Baltic politics. Thirty-five years earlier, at the time of his accession in 1640, the position had been very different. One of the largest principalities in Germany, Brandenburg had no assets: it was cut off from the sea, its towns had ceased to be centres of trade, it lacked natural resources, and because of its poor soil it was known as the sandbox of the Holy Roman Empire.

The depopulation of the countryside and the impoverishment of the towns, evident before 1618, were accelerated by the Thirty Years War, especially as Brandenburg was in the unhappy position of a buffer state between Sweden and Austria. Her ruler, however as one of the seven imperial electors, had an important title, and as a Hohenzollern he was the heir to many carefully planned marriage alliances which had extended his territories. The duchy of Cleves, with the counties of Mark and Ravensberg, had been salvaged in 1614 from the Jülich—Cleves crisis (see p. 127); the duchy of East Prussia had been acquired in 1618 as a Polish fief; in 1637 the last duke of Pomerania had bequeathed his duchy to the Hohenzollerns. These separate duchies were each of strategic and political importance, which, in the circumstances, was their chief disadvantage since this made them highly desirable to other powers. Cleves had close links with the United Provinces, and in 1640 was actually under Dutch occupation in order to protect it from Spain: Prussia was coveted by Poland, with whose king the Prussian nobility had more in common than with the Elector of Brandenburg: Pomerania with its valuable ports on the Baltic was under Swedish occupation.

Scattered though his territories were across Europe, and sharing no common institutions, bound together by no ties and virtually controlled by the armies of other powers, the new Elector was none the less inspired by a vision of a Hohenzollern state which should be both independent and united. His character was well suited to his self-appointed task. Like his father, George William, he was a tall big man, but it was only the son whose spirit could match the frame: where his father had been hesitant, timid and unimaginative, Frederick William was a man of enterprise with a talent for bold decision. Determined, opportunist and resourceful, he was able to interpret the run of events more skilfully than his father had done and, if rewarded on occasion with some remarkably good fortune, had the wit to recognise it when it came his way.

Although his father had allied himself with the emperor after the Peace of Prague (1635), Frederick William spent his youth in the courts and camps of Austria's enemies. At the age of ten he was presented to Gustavus Adolphus on his landing in Pomerania, he accompanied Frederick Henry of Orange at the siege of Breda, and so marked did his hostility to Austria become that his

father summoned him home in 1638. Two years later he was free
to pursue his own policy. The Peace of Prague and the Austrian
alliance were, in his opinion, of no value. They guaranteed no
conquests since George William had made none, and imposed
upon his people the burden of maintaining troops to serve an
emperor who was unable to protect them from Sweden. With
hindsight this view may well seem selfevident: in 1640 it was not
so, and by abandoning the emperor to make his own arrangements with Sweden Frederick William undertook a dangerous
course of action which the other German princes were reluctant
to follow.

In the Diet, moreover, the new elector demonstrated his
independence in debate, spoke openly against the Peace of
Prague and refused to accept the emperor's ruling that the
individual princes should not be separately represented in the
peace negotiations which began in Westphalia. Here he was
fortunate since the Dutch and the French were willing to support
his presence, if only to embarrass the emperor, and Frederick
William paid them careful attention. He married a princess of the
House of Orange and attracted Mazarin's friendly interest as the
one German state worth backing against Austria.

Despite the relative weakness of his position and the need to
solicit help from the major powers Frederick William nonetheless
refused to give way over Sweden's demand for Pomerania, and
demonstrated his ability to play a weak hand consummately well.
In the event he offered to partition Pomerania with Sweden,
accepting the eastern section despite its lack of useful harbours in
return for compensation elsewhere. Mazarin concluded that it
was valuable to restrain the emperor in the future by making
Brandenburg as strong as possible, and in the event, Frederick
William was given territory much greater in extent than that
surrendered to Sweden, and of greater strategic importance for
the future, because it established a series of links in a chain
binding the Rhineland duchies to Brandenburg.

  (i) The emperor confirmed the Treaty of Xanten (1614),
      which had assigned Cleves, Mark and Ravensberg to the
      Hohenzollern claimant;
  (ii) Ravensberg was strengthened by the acquisition of its
      neighbour, the secularised bishopric of Minden;

(iii) The Elector also acquired the secularised bishoprics of Cammin and Halberstadt on Brandenburg's frontier, together with the reversion of the secularised archbishopric of Magdeburg after the death of its existing ruler. This prince did not die until 1680, but as early as 1650 Frederick William ensured that an electoral garrison was posted there;

(iv) Sweden took possession of Western Pomerania, with Stettin and the mouth of the Oder, but the eastern half of the duchy, barren of ports, was restored to the Elector.

Once the war was over the elector turned his mind to something more ambitious than survival. His object was to strengthen his authority within each of his scattered territories and to bring these territories together in an administrative union, making them as he put it *membra unius capitis*.

The most powerful opponents of his policy were the *junkers* of Brandenburg. Unlike the landed nobility of western Europe, receivers of rents and feudal dues, the *junkers* were large-scale entrepreneurs who ran their estates with serf labour and made their profit from the sale of corn and beer. They dominated the economy, the administration and the politics of Brandenburg — and paid no taxes. Local clergy were under their thumb, local government was staffed and directed by local assemblies (*regierung*) which they managed and their voice in the Diet was vastly more powerful than that of the townsmen. The Diet moreover not only controlled the granting of taxes but also their assessment and collection. The *junkers'* political creed was quite simple. They disliked warfare which interfered with their trade and brought foreign troops to ravage their fields, they preferred to dominate the elector than be dominated by him and they had no interest whatsoever in his other territories.

This was made clear in 1650 when, in order to raise troops to settle a frontier dispute with Sweden in Pomerania the elector appealed to the Diet of Brandenburg for money and was refused point blank. The elector returned to the attack; as he later put it for his son's instruction, 'a ruler is treated with no consideration if he does not have troops and means of his own', and in 1652 he was determined to have both. Accordingly, he summoned a full session of the Diet. This in itself was an innovation since representative committees usually met on behalf of the Estates, but the surprise of the members at being summoned was nothing to their indignant alarm on learning the Elector's proposals. Instead of the excise on beer and the customary contributions levied separately on the towns and countryside, he demanded a general excise on the Dutch model, a series of indirect taxes on such goods as beer, wine, salt and cattle which all his subjects were to pay. Moreover it was quite clear that the excise if granted would make him virtually independent of the Diet in the future.

In the angry debate which followed, the *junkers* counter-attacked with every possible grievance they could bring against the elector. Finally they came to terms with him in the Recess of 1653, which concluded the Diet.

(i)   The serfs were to be abandoned more completely than ever before into the hands of the *junkers;*

(ii) The practice of the elector, a tolerant Calvinist, of employing Catholics in his service was to stop;

(iii) All treaties contracted by the elector were to be ratified by the Diet;

(iv) The excise was not to be adopted;

(v) A sum of 500,000 *thalers*, to be collected over a period of six years, was granted to the elector.

The Recess appeared to be a victory for the *junkers* who wanted absolute control over their serfs, who hated Catholicism, who distrusted their ruler's diplomacy, and who refused to pay taxes. Their one concession cost them nothing, the burden of the contribution falling upon the towns since they themselves were exempt. But Frederick William as the greatest landowner in Brandenburg, shared the prejudices and emotions of his class so far as the serfs were concerned. The other concessions mattered very little when set against the award of enough money to raise 1800 troops. It was only a small beginning, but if his vision of a Hohenzollern state was to be given reality he could not manage without it.

The invasion of Poland by Sweden, Russians and Cossacks (see pp. 389–90) almost destroyed his plans. By the treaty of Konigsberg (1656) he surrendered to Charles X not only half the revenue of his East Prussian ports but also the use of his hard-won troops. Worst of all he had to recognise Charles' title to Poland and do homage to him for his fief of East Prussia, an act for which he might forfeit it for ever should John Casimir return victorious. In the event Frederick William proved to be both fortunate and resourceful. When Charles X ran into difficulties the elector demanded full independence in East Prussia in return for his aid. Later still, when Charles abandoned Poland to invade Denmark, Frederick William survived unscathed because John Casimir, with Cossack and Russian armies plundering his kingdom, could not afford to refuse the elector's offer of assistance. In return, by the treaty of Wehlau, he confirmed Frederick William's sovereignty in East Prussia.

The Creation of the Hohenzollern State 1660 – 1700

After the general peace of Oliva in 1660 Frederick William retained as many as 12,000 troops in service despite the heavy expense they incurred. He had of course the revenue from his own estates in Brandenburg. Over the past decade he had succeeded in freeing them of interference from the local assemblies (*regierung*) so that he was better able to develop them to good advantage. Over the next twenty years he managed to centralise their administration under a central Chamber which provided him eventually with nearly 40 per cent of his income.

Since this was insufficient to maintain the army the elector employed the army itself to collect the balance. There was no pretence of winning popular support. The Diet complained repeatedly, but ineffectually, of the army's fiscal activities and it failed to prevent the elector replacing in some areas the traditional contribution by the excise. The towns were fatally handicapped by social divisions. Many burghers resented the close oligarchy of the older families, and advocated the excise in order to win the elector's favour in their local conflict. Others preferred the excise since it was at least paid by everyone whereas the older families had in the past exempted themselves from payment of the contribution. For these reasons several towns voluntarily submitted to the excise in 1667; in 1682 it was imposed on the remainder.

The Diet lost the power not only to vote taxes but also to

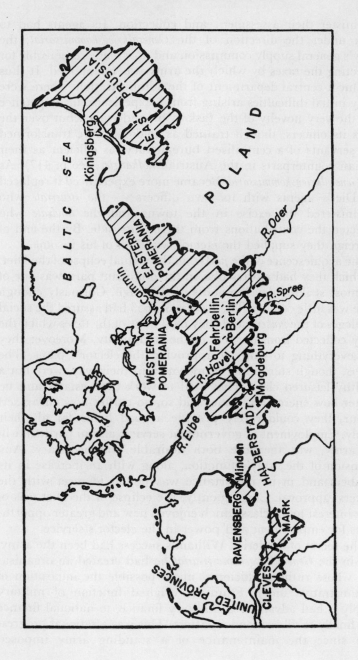

Map 14 The Territories of Brandenburg, 1660

administer their assessment and collection. Its agents had to work under the direction of the *Generalkriegskommissariat*, the army's general supply commission and now made responsible for collecting the taxes by which the army was maintained. It thus became a central department of the administration. There were many initial difficulties arising from inexperience, incompetence and the very novelty of the task to be undertaken but over the years its officers, though trained as soldiers, were transformed into servants of a centralised bureaucracy, as efficient as their civilian counterparts in the Austrian *hofkanzlei* (see p. 417). As the *Generalkriegskommissariat* became more experienced it replaced the Diet's agents with its own officers — the *steuerrate* who administered the excise in the towns and the *landrate* who collected the contributions from the countryside. By the end of the reign they supplied the elector with half of his income.

The acquiescence of the *junkers* in the virtual eclipse of the Diet, in which they had always played the dominant part, was one of the most striking developments of the reign. Curiously enough there was little conflict. The Recess of 1653 had assured the social privileges of the *junkers,* and they paid none of the taxes which the army collected from the rest of the community. Moreover they had everything to gain by approving the elector's plans. The *junkers,* though substantial landowners in their way, were not a wealthy leisured class. They had to work their estates and no matter how energetically they did so, no matter how cheap serf labour, they could rarely provide a good living for all their family. Employment in government service, and in particular in the army, was therefore both desirable and necessary. Any extension of the army's function, along with an increase in its numbers and in its importance was bound to meet with the junkers' approval. Consequently, the eclipse of the Diet was of little interest to the class which enjoyed new and greater opportunities for employment and power in the elector's service.

The secret of Frederick William's success had been the army, and in the *Generalkriegskommissariat* he had created an organisation whose ruthless efficiency made possible the imposition of administrative unity. From its original function of military supply it had advanced to military finance, to national finance and finally to all economic matters. This was a rational progression since the maintenance of a standing army imposed tremendous strains upon the state's resources: by 1688 a population of 1,000,000 supported a standing army of 30,000, in contrast to France at that date where 18,000,000 maintained no more than 300,000.

About one-tenth of the cost was met by foreign subsidies, four-tenths from the elector's domains and half from taxation — which could not be increased without greater natural prosperity. As a result the *Generalkriegskommissariat* was assigned the task of supplementing with state aid the scanty resources of private initiative.

The elector's propagandists did their utmost to blacken the picture of Brandenburg's plight in 1640 in order to enhance the achievements of his reign, but there was little need for exaggeration. The economy which had been gravely weakened by the decline of the Hanseatic League and the by-passing of transcontinental trade routes, was well-nigh destroyed by the perpetual passage of armies during the course of the Thirty Years War. The process of recovery was both slow and spasmodic.

A Dutch merchant, Raule, whose audacity and enterprise were such that it became necessary for him to leave the United Provinces, found a welcome at the Elector's court, and became Director-General of the navy in 1672. Four years later, appointed to direct the electoral Board of Trade and Admiralty, he sent out privateers to win silver from the Spanish treasure fleets, and in 1682 he established the Brandenburg African Trading Company. It was a waste of time. The Dutch discouraged competition, and Brandenburg was scarcely in a position to offer any. Though his commercial ventures failed, Raule did equip a fleet of Ruritanian proportions, boasting a frigate and two small craft at Königsberg, and a North Sea squadron of seven other vessels at Emden.

Much effort was made to improve communications, the most striking work being the construction of a canal from the Oder to the Elbe, via the river Spree and Berlin, designed to divert Silesian traffic away from the Swedish commissioners in Stettin. In addition to improving communications, Frederick William did much to encourage immigration. Settlers not only brought new skills and industries to a population which had been traditionally agricultural, they also bred more consumers to stimulate industry and more taxpayers to support the army. The *Generalkriegskommissariat*, therefore, helped immigrants to set up companies to manufacture textiles, glassware, iron, copper and brass. The Dutch were especially welcome since their skill in land reclamation was invaluable in transforming the sandy wastes and marshy swamps of Brandenburg into fertile farmland, and the elector offered them leases free of rent for ten years. He was quick to respond to the revocation of the Edict of Nantes, moved as much by anger as a fellow Calvinist as by national self interest. The Edict of Potsdam offered the Huguenots 'a free and safe refuge in all our lands and possession', and 20,000 found a home in Brandenburg. Though they did much to establish horticulture around Berlin, it was in the manufacture of textiles that they made their greatest contribution. The elector's army was soon equipped with uniforms of their making, and was swollen by the addition of five infantry regiments of French refugees.

In pursuit of his goal of a unified Hohenzollern state, the Elector had to extend his administration to his other territories, but the Rhineland duchies were in no mood to welcome interference from Berlin. Their towns were wealthy, and in the Estates the burghers joined with the nobles to oppose the Elector's plans. In two sessions of particular importance, in 1649 and 1653, they won substantial concessions, among them the right to meet on their own initiative, to negotiate independently with foreign powers, and to prevent the appointment of any official not locally born: in addition, the Elector could not raise taxes nor introduce his troops into the duchies without their consent. All these liberties were violated during the Swedish war of 1655–60, when, in spite of the threat of a general rising, over a million *thalers* were collected by the army. In 1660 the Elector challenged the opposition to show its hand by sending an ultimatum: unless their liberties were curtailed he would march upon the duchies. The fact that after the Peace of Oliva the Dutch were on good terms with Frederick William meant that the towns could not rely upon them for assistance as in the past; there were also many nobles who were eager to follow the example of the *junkers* by selling out to the Elector in return for privileges and employment.

The result was a compromise. By the Recesses of 1660 and 1661 the Estates gave up their right to negotiate with foreign powers, to exclude electoral troops and to appoint and dismiss all officials. In return they retained their right to assemble at will and to vote their own taxes. Although on occasions the army

subsequently collected forced taxes, the process of integrating the
Rhineland duchies with Brandenburg went no further, and they
remained an exception to the general pattern of Hohenzollern
despotism.

At first sight the problem of Prussia seemed greater than that
of Cleves. The administration was headed by four locally
appointed *oberrathe*, whose collective powers were those of a
viceroy, save that they answered to no king. Frederick William
found their arrogance intolerable: 'These Prussians make the
inhabitants of Cleves seem like little saints.' The Prussians had
only to look across into Poland to see the type of anarchy which
most appealed to them. Consequently they would rather have
been integrated with Warsaw than with Berlin, and when
Frederick William removed all hope of this by winning Prussia's
independence in 1660 he was faced with revolt. The city of
Königsberg, a great Baltic city which aspired to the freedom
enjoyed by its great rival, Danzig, challenged the legality of the
treaty of Wehlau, and its spokesman, Hieronymus Roth, urged
John Casimir to recover his rights in East Prussia. Frederick
William, faced with the loss of the sovereignty he had so recently
acquired, sent troops to Pillau where they disembarked and
marched on Königsberg in 1612. Roth was arrested and in a
Recess of the Diet in 1663 Frederick William's sovereignty was
reaffirmed. The Diet even voted a tax but it retained controls
over its administration, refused to allow further taxes without
consent and required the elector to recall them at least every
three years.

The compromise between independence and integration did
not last long. A powerful group of nobles was soon deep in
conspiracy, and when Kalckstein, its leader, suspected that the
elector was informed of the plot he simply crossed the frontier
into Poland in 1669. Such immunity, creating a dangerous
precedent for other traitors, could not be tolerated. Kalckstein
was kidnapped by the elector's Resident in Warsaw and smug-
gled across the frontier to Königsberg. There, after torture, he
was executed in 1672. Two years later, when Königsberg refused
to allow the elector's troops to collect taxes, the citizens found
themselves the unwilling hosts of the army, which remained
billeted upon them until the taxes had been fully paid. Strong
measures won the day. After 1674 there was no further conspira-

cy, the administration was geared to that of Brandenburg, and the independent power of the *oberrathe* was destroyed: 'They are councillors and servants who derive their power only from their lord', wrote Frederick William, 'without his will and approval they have no power to do or decide anything in his affairs, except in conformity with their instructions and commission. It belongs to His Electoral Serenity to make the decisions which he thinks best and most useful.'

Of all the diverse and scattered elements of his inheritance the elector could scarcely make one nation. His achievement was to make one state, and though it was two hundred years before Berlin became the capital of a territorially united Hohenzollern empire, by 1688 it had been established as the administrative centre of the elector's territories, directing and controlling all the important features of their political life.

In his foreign policy after 1660 Frederick William was unable to achieve triumphs to be compared with those of his earlier years. At first he seemed content to avoid dangerous commitments and to join his fellow German princes in accepting French subsidies. When war broke out between France and the United Provinces in 1672, however, he intervened on the Dutch side, partly because of his close relations with them in the past, partly in return for subsidies and also because it placed him conveniently in opposition to Sweden which had joined France. The encounter at Fehrbellin in 1675 was more of a skirmish than a battle, but it did wonders for the Great Elector's reputation. His army overran Pomerania and Stettin, the Baltic port he had long coveted, fell to him in 1677, but the conquest was shortlived. Louis XIV in 1679, when the peace settlement was made (see p. 395), was too powerful, and Cleves too vulnerable to his power, for the Elector to withstand him. The territories were restored to Sweden. Thereafter Frederick William returned to the receipt of French subsidies, foreign subsidies being an important element in his annual revenue, and played an unheroic part during the *réunion* crises. In 1688, however, the year of his death, he was stung into action by the French invasion of the Palatinate, offered his alliance to the emperor, and sent aid to William of Orange on his voyage to England.

It was left to his son Frederick to join in the War of the League of Augsburg, and in return for his offer of 8,000 troops in the War of Spanish Succession the emperor gave him a subsidy of 100,000 *thalers* and permission to call himself 'King in Prussia'. In 1640 the Prussians had been the most recalcitrant of Frederick William's subjects, and Prussia itself a fief of the Polish crown: in 1700, tamed and transformed, it was deliberately chosen to give its name to the Hohenzollern monarchy since, lying beyond the frontiers of the Holy Roman Empire, it symbolised the emergence of a new and independent power in Europe.

IX

THE CREATION OF THE DANUBIAN MONARCHY

AUSTRIA, POLAND AND THE TURKS

Austria and Western Europe

In the eyes of western Europe the decline of the Austrian Habsburgs in the seventeenth century seemed to be as obvious a fact as the decline of their cousins in Spain. The Peace of Westphalia appeared to have exposed their position in Germany as nothing more than the nominal leadership of the loosest and most impotent federation in Europe. Their position in Germany, however, was not the result of the Thirty Years War, since the Holy Roman Empire was not and had never been in the least like a nation state. Ferdinand I's acceptance of the Augsburg principle of *cujus regio, ejus religio*[1] was proof that real power had passed to the princes long ago.

What gave the Thirty Years War its special importance in this respect was that from 1619 to 1629 Ferdinand II had successfully overcome the limitations which had crippled his predecessors. His imperial projects, like the creation of a military force independent of the German princes, the conquest of north Germany, and the restoration of secularised lands to the Catholic Church, were destroyed, not by the German princes who proved utterly unable to make their protests effective, but by the intervention of France and Sweden. Consequently, though the Peace of Westphalia recognised that the revolutionary plans of Ferdinand II had failed, the authority of Ferdinand III and Leopold was neither more nor less effective than that of Matthias, Rudolf and Ferdinand I. Moreover, if the ambitions of the emperors were buried in 1648, so were the attempts of many protestant princes to transform the empire into an aristocratic

[1] See Chapter II, p. 122.

412

republic in which the emperor's role would have been nominal, a view which had gained much publicity in 1640 through the writings of Martin Chemnitz [Hippolithus] who claimed that sovereignty was an attribute of the princes and not of the emperor.

Of far greater importance than the effect of the Thirty Years War was the fact that other developments were taking place which made it all the more unlikely that any future emperor might imitate the action of Ferdinand II. Not only were the princes following the pattern of the age in claiming to be the independent and absolute sovereign of their territories; some of them were becoming too great to be confined within the archaic structure of the empire. Since his accession in 1640, Frederick William of Brandenburg had begun the long process of integration which was to transform his territories, scattered between Poland and the Rhineland, into a powerful kingdom of two million subjects.[2] Equally significant was the growth of Saxony, Bavaria and Hanover, each with a population of 1,500,000, whose dynastic ties with Poland, France and Great Britain respectively were to encourage them to act outside the framework of the empire. The lesser princes followed suit by forming regional groups, such as the League of the Rhine Princes, which treated independently with foreign powers.

As the German states looked beyond Germany to satisfy their ambitions, and as Sweden and France intruded their own disruptive influence by controlling Pomerania and Alsace, the empire lost cohesion. The Diet continued to deliberate imperial affairs, and in 1663 it was even transformed from an occasional assembly of no fixed abode into a permanent one meeting at Regensburg, but its discussions were rendered pointless by the envoys who wrangled interminably over precedence and who, if an occasion for decision should arise, merely referred the issue back to their princes: 'Those who are unacquainted with the proceedings of this assembly would wonder that, where so many ministers are met and maintained at so great a charge by their masters, so little business is done, and the little that is so slowly...'[3] Moreover, the traditional concept of the Holy Roman

[2] See Chapter VIII, pp. 399–411.
[3] The Letterbook of Sir George Etherege, quoted in *New Cambridge Modern History*, vol. v, p.447

Empire as a metaphysical ideal to which the institutions of Germany ought to approximate, a model as it were for their behaviour, was being overthrown by the new philosophy of the scientific revolution,[4] which denied the independent existence of all metaphysical ideals. The empire, far from being an idea in the mind of God, was reduced to the level of a mere contractual association, with the obvious implication that what could be once made could later be broken.

The power of Austria to influence the destinies of Germany had not, however, been diminished. The peace of Westphalia (see pages 157–60) had left the Austrian Habsburgs more surely based than ever in their hereditary territories on the Danube and in Bohemia, and from time to time they were able to intervene in German, and indeed in western European affairs with commanding force. Contemporaries did not always believe this to be possible, and misinterpreted the rise of France to imply the decline of Austria. This was in part because Leopold, in the early years of his reign, seemed to be powerless in 1667 to prevent the invasion of the Netherlands, and his subsequent attempt to buy off Louis with the promise of partitioning the Spanish empire was interpreted as a confession of weakness.[5] It was true that he sent Montecuculi to invade Cologne in 1673 and thus gave dramatic and invaluable aid to the Dutch at a critical moment in their history, but this was an unexpected occasion. In general, he seemed to play the part of a reluctant enemy, submitting even to the *réunions* rather than openly challenge Louis for the mastery of Europe.

After 1697, however, Leopold confounded the prophets of Austria's doom by showing unwonted determination in urging the succession of his sons to the Spanish empire. Not only was Austria the first power to declare war on the Bourbons, not only were her armies more continuously engaged against the French than those of any other member of the Grand Alliance, but she gained possession, if not of the Spanish empire, at least of the Netherlands, of Lombardy and of Naples and Sicily. In addition, if Leopold no longer had authority to order the armies of the German princes, as the most important leader of the Germans

[4] See Chapter I, page 59.
[5] See Chapter VII, p. 337.

Map 15   Austrian-Habsburg Territories in 1630

against French aggression, his influence within the empire was increased immeasurably.

This dramatic reversal of Austria's role in the west was not fortuitous. Leopold in fact had achieved so little in reviving Imperial power in Germany and in halting the advance of Louis XIV because he had deliberately chosen to fulfil his great ambitions in the east. It was a wise choice: the defeat of the Ottoman Turks[6] was an event of the utmost importance to Austria, compared with which the loss of imperial sovereignty in Alsace and the indignities suffered at the hands of Louis XIV were of little consequence. The recovery of Hungary and the creation of the Danubian monarchy, by which the peoples of the upper Danube valley were restored to the community of Europe, was not only of considerable value to Austria, enabling her to play a much more commanding role in western Europe after 1697, but ranks as one of the greatest events in the history of Europe in the seventeenth century.

[6] This is described below pp. 426–38.

The Austrian Empire

The Austrian Habsburgs ruled over a fragmented empire, the chance result of two centuries of marriage contracts; its separate territories, stretching from the Alpine valleys to the middle reaches of the Danube, were dissimilar in race, language, religion and custom. Austria alone comprised the two separate duchies of Upper and Lower Austria, each with its own Estates and traditions, and each with Protestant minorities entrenched amid the Catholic population: the only common factors they shared with each other, and with the duchies of Carinthia, Carniola, Styria and the Tyrol, were the German language and a habit of regarding Vienna as the capital city of the Habsburg family. Utterly different in every way were the kingdoms of Hungary and Bohemia which had been more recently acquired, and in which the practice of elective monarchy made uncertain the continuous succession of Habsburg rulers.

It was clear that the Habsburgs could not achieve pre-eminence in Europe until they had consolidated their diverse possessions into an effective administrative unit. The first step was taken when the practice of allocating these possessions among the younger members of the family was checked by Matthias; the next occurred in 1665 when the Tyrol escheated to Leopold I who thus became the first Habsburg ruler to exercise personal control over the entire Austrian empire. It was Matthias who began to extend his authority in Upper and Lower Austria by undermining the traditional privileges of the Estates, and by attacking the Lutheran communities whose nonconformity had political as well as religious implications. The young Archduke Ferdinand was meanwhile performing a similar task so effectively in Styria that he was selected by Matthias to succeed him in 1619. It was Ferdinand's great achievement to weld the non-Germanic kingdom of Bohemia to the bureaucratic system directed from Vienna.[7]

This system was never so efficient as that of France, for example, since Louis XIV could raise taxes at will whereas the emperors could only augment an inadequate income by bargaining with the separate Estates. The idea of a States-General for the Danubian territories as a whole had been proposed, but the

[7] See Chapter II, p. 137.

Habsburgs decided that such an assembly would only aggravate the problem of disunity by revealing the fundamental differences between the representatives. Nevertheless, without a central legislature to override the authority of the local Estates the task of centralisation was made all the more difficult for the civil servants who had, by 1600, created the nucleus of an imperial administration. With a privy council (*Geheime Konferenz*), a war council (*Hofkriegsrath*), an imperial treasury (*Hofkammer*), and a chancellery (*Hofkanzlei*), the division of powers seemed to be well organised, but in practice the separate departments were not equally effective. The *Geheime Konferenz* was an advisory rather than an executive body. The *Hofkriegsrath* had no control over the recruitment of troops within the Habsburg empire, and could only suggest quotas which the local authorities might or might not fulfil. The *Hofkammer* controlled only mineral rights and indirect taxes; the assessment and collection of direct taxes was jealously preserved by the Estates. In the long run the importance of the departments was determined less by the tasks assigned them than by the character of the men who staffed them, and it was the administrative genius of the 'cameralists', as they were called, which transformed the *Hofkanzlei* from a legal and judicial body into the most active force in the creation of the Danubian monarchy, and ultimately its administrative centre.

The work of the cameralists was impeded by the local nobility who had little comprehension of the arguments of chancellery officials, and who stubbornly defended the validity of their franchises, immunities and traditions. Such opposition to bureaucratic centralisation was common to the rest of Europe, but in the Danubian territories it was all the stronger since the entire character of local government was coloured by the existence of serfdom. This was no antique survival from past centuries but an economic necessity for landlords who sought to exploit their demesne lands in an age of rising prices.[8] The relation of landlords to serf was reflected in local law and local institutions, and made it impossible for any but landlords to control local government. All the cameralists could do was to reinforce the landlords' authority by applying the principles of Roman law, which made a harsher distinction between bond and free than did customary law, and to expect in return a greater degree of

8 See Chapter I, p. 5.

co-operation. It was, in short, an extremely cautious policy whereby local institutions were not destroyed but fitted into the loose framework of the centralised administration; and had it not been for special, extraordinary circumstances the work of one century would scarcely have been completed in three.

The Bohemian revolt, so dangerous in its initial stages, was ultimately to prove beneficial to the Habsburg monarchy. In the years before 1618 the *Hofkanzlei* had made little headway in its efforts to establish a centralised regime: indeed, the Letter of Majesty in 1609[9] had given formal protection to the disruptive forces of nationalism, separatism and heresy. Attempts were made by Lobkowitz, the most able of the cameralists, to whittle away the terms of the Letter but he could do nothing radical until the election of Ferdinand II as Matthias's successor in 1617. It was then that he secured the appointment of two fanatical Catholics, Martinitz and Slavata, to lead the council of regency in Bohemia. The consequences of his action were greater than he had intended. The immediate effect was to provoke rebellion, during which the Estates of Lower Austria were also emboldened to make their own demands for toleration and autonomy; but because the rebels failed and because the rebellion was engulfed in the larger issues of the Thirty Years War, Ferdinand II was free to impose his own terms upon Bohemia. Returning to Prague at the head of a triumphant army there was no need to placate nor to win the support of any section of the community. He ruined the gentry by confiscating their lands, the townsmen by deliberate inflation, and the Protestants by proscription. Advised by Lobkowitz he then created a new class of Roman Catholic and mostly German landlords, who depended upon him utterly for protection in their new titles and estates, and who ruled as his agents in occupied territory.

By 1627 it was safe to summon the Estates in order to give the appearance of popular consent to a new constitution which destroyed the traditional liberties of the Bohemians. The monarchy was declared to be hereditary in the house of Habsburg; Austrian legal customs and administrative practices were to be adopted throughout the kingdom; the Bohemian chancellor was to accompany the king at all times. In short, the government of Bohemia was to be determined henceforth in Vienna. It re-

[9] See Chapter II, p. 129.

mained for Ferdinand II's successors to achieve a similar result in Hungary.

The Ottoman Turks

Hungary presented a challenge which the cameralists of the *Hofkanzlei* were not equipped to meet: it was not that the privileges of the Magyar nobility were protected by the Golden Bull,[10] a document so far reaching in its concessions that it made the Letter of Majesty seem innocuous by comparison, but that most of Hungary was occupied by the Ottoman Turks.

Since their conquest of the former Byzantine empire, straddling the Balkans and Asia Minor, the Ottoman Turks had expanded not only into Egypt and Persia, but also further into Europe. Until 1521 they had been held back at the line of the Danube and the Save, but in that year they had seized Belgrade, standing at the junction of the two rivers, and burst northwards into the Hungarian plain. From that moment the fortunes of the Habsburgs became indissolubly bound with those of the Turks, as became evident in 1526 when the Turks routed the Hungarians at Mohacs and killed their king. His widow, a Habsburg princess having no children of her own, secured the election of her brother Ferdinand to the thrones of Hungary and Bohemia. Important as this was to be for the future the immediate course of events made Ferdinand's election seem pointless since the Turks then overran the whole of Hungary and, in 1529, besieged Vienna.

Fortunately for Europe the siege was abandoned after twenty-eight days, and though other attacks were launched on later occasions the walls of Vienna proved to be the high water mark of Turkish expansion into Europe. Ottoman lines of communication were too dangerously extended to permit of a long campaign in Austria, and the largest section of the army, the Spahis,[11] insisted on being free to return home at the onset of winter. Moreover, the Turks had to undertake a long series of campaigns against the Persians which prevented them making anything more than sporadic attacks up the Danube. In the event, as was

10 See below, p. 429.

11 The *Spahis*, a feudal levy of cavalry, numbered about 130,000 though not all would serve at the same time: the regular standing force of highly trained infantry, the *Janissaries*, was only 12,000.

recognised in the Treaty of Sitva-Torok (1606), the line of effective Turkish occupation lay midway between Buda and Vienna, which left to the Habsburgs a strip of Hungary varying in depth from forty to eighty miles, constituting barely a quarter of the kingdom, for which they paid tribute to the sultan.

Occupation by the Turks was not so intolerable for the Balkan peoples as western observers believed. The Turks had inherited the culture of the Seljuks, of the Arabs and of Islam; moreover, both as neighbours, and later as conquerors, of the Byzantine empire, they had learned much from Hellenistic civilisation. The capture of Constantinople, therefore, 'was not a victory of barbarism but rather of another and not undistinguished civilisation. The four slender minarets that the Turks added to the Church of Santa Ṣophia may be, for the Christian, a desecration. They are not a defacement.'[12] Though the Turks were capable of occasional acts of great cruelty, and though they conscripted a fifth of the young men every five years for the army, their rule had its compensations. The records of registers and travellers alike testify to the steady increase in wealth and population, for the people could live in peace, their frontiers protected by the Ottoman army. Things were not so satisfactory in Hungary where frontier warfare continued for nearly two centuries, but the estimated decimation of the population[13] was caused more by a combination of plague, emigration and starvation resulting from the inadequate cultivation of poor soil, than by Turkish brutality. Many Hungarians were Protestants and thus enjoyed a great measure of toleration, no matter how capriciously withdrawn on occasion, than they could expect to receive from the Habsburgs, their self-appointed liberators. Above all, since the seigneurial jurisdiction of the Magyar nobility was replaced by that of Ottoman fief-holders who demanded taxes but not forced labour, the peasantry had no cause to envy the serfs of central Europe.

The Turks were nomadic warriors and the basic character of their empire remained that of an army on the march, so that whenever their advance had reached its limits they lost their vigour. The periods of consolidation and settlement which have marked the history of other empires were denied to the Turks.

---

[12] 'Europe and the Turks: the Civilisation of the Ottoman Empire.' Bernard Lewis, *History Today*, October 1953.

[13] See *New Cambridge Modern History*, vol. v,p.479.

They occupied vast tracts of territory but never settled in them. They exploited but never assimilated their subject races, and none save the conscripted Janissaries could identify themselves with their conquerors as men in the Roman empire had proudly done by winning Roman citizenship. The military nature of the empire left all powers in the hands of the sultan. If he were gifted the empire prospered, if he were insane or feckless there was no other authority to direct events and the empire fell into decay. Apart from Murad IV (1623–40) the only ruler of the century to reveal any ability, the sultans exchanged their imperial responsibilities for the intrigues of the harem, or gave way to a life of debauchery so excessive as frequently to induce insanity. The effect upon the empire was disastrous: the efforts of the wives to secure the succession for their own favourite son caused faction in the army, the fief-holders grew independent, the Janissaries relaxed their rigorous standards of discipline, and the frontiers began to contract. Shah Abbas the Great of Persia drove the Turks from Azerbaijan, Georgia and Kurdistan, the Poles recovered Moldavia, and in Transylvania, among the Carpathian mountains of eastern Hungary, George Rackoczi set up an independent Magyar kingdom.

The accession of Murad IV in 1623 restored the efficiency of the empire since he proved to be a successful soldier; so successful that it was fortunate for Europe that he chose to fight against Persia instead of intervening in the Thirty Years War. Shah Abbas was a powerful opponent but Murad triumphed in 1638 when, after the fall of Baghdad, the Peace of Sehab re-established Ottoman rule in Mesopotamia. The moral effect of military success was startling. The army abandoned its political intrigues to become once again the well-drilled agent of the sultan's conquests, and the feudatories returned to their obedience. Though his successors were inept, Murad's death in 1640 did not lead to disaster since an astute Albanian, Mahomet Köprülü, came to power in the next reign as Grand Vizier. Köprülü, recognised that only by constant warfare could the disintegration of the empire be averted, and he was fortunate enough to win the ear of the sultan's mother. Knowing that her son, Mahomet IV, was incapable of anything but hunting and debauchery, she drew up a contract with Köprülü which virtually gave him absolute authority within the empire provided that he maintained efficient government and waged war effectively. Köprülü did both. Credited with ordering the execution of 60,000 dishonest tax-collectors, officers and soldiers, he was obeyed as no grand vizier had ever been before, while the armies renewed their conflict with Europe. They seized Tenedos and Lemnos from the Venetians in 1657 and then, having driven the Rackoczi family from Transylvania, began a long campaign to subdue the local nobility who still clung to their independence.

Köprülü died in 1661, to be followed by his son Ahmed, the finest Ottoman soldier of the century. By 1663 Ahmed had defeated the Transylvanian nobles and sent 80,000 Christians into slavery; he then advanced on Austria. The great fortress of Neuhaussel, the proud creation of Ferdinand I to guard the Waag valley north of the Danube, fell in November, 1663, but its spirited resistance and Montecucculi's brilliant rearguard action ensured that the main Turk attack was delayed until the following year. Nevertheless, many detachments broke through to the north to raid Moravia and Silesia. Immediately the Ottoman Turks ceased to be the private problem of the Habsburgs: Pope Alexander VII called for a Holy League and a cosmopolitan force assembled for the defence of Austria. As a result of experience gained in the Thirty Years War Europe at last was no longer inferior to the Turks in cannon and cavalry, and in 1664, at St Gotthard in the Raab valley, the Turks were defeated on European soil for the first time.

The Habsburgs derived little positive benefit from their victory. Their allies withdrew as soon as it was clear that Europe was no longer in danger, and Montecucculi advised Leopold that there were not enough men to make possible the recovery of Hungary. Moreover, since Louis XIV was preparing to enforce his devolution claims upon the Spanish Netherlands, Leopold decided to purchase a respite in the Danube. By the Treaty of Vasvár (1664) Ahmed Köprülü agreed to a twenty-year truce.

Poland

Poland in the seventeenth century was the sick man of Europe. Its territories, sprawling across the continent from Silesia to Kiev, from the Baltic to the Balkans, were coveted by aggressive and expansionist neighbours against whom Poland was singularly

Map 16 Poland and her Neighbours

ill equipped to defend them.

Since the fifteenth century when the Ottoman Turks had captured her ports on the Black Sea, and thus disrupted the overland trade routes to the Baltic which had invigorated the commercial life of the inland cities, Poland had become a kingdom dominated by the nobles. They alone had wealth, exporting grain, flax and timber from their estates by shipping them down the Vistula; they alone had political power, electing their sovereign and imposing upon him whatever conditions they wished. The *pacta conventa*, a formal statement of the concessions he was willing to make, was signed by the elected candidate before his coronation, and the nobles held him to his promises by threat of rebellion. Unlike the rulers of other states, the kings of Poland were unable to influence their assemblies to make laws of benefit to the crown since the dissentient voice of one representative alone was enough to prevent the passing of any measure. No matter how successfully the kings played off one group against another or employed the arts of intimidation, flattery and bribery, there always remained the obstinate opponent whose resistance could not be overcome by the votes of the majority.

Occasionally a king was elected whose vigour and military skill, if they did nothing to strengthen the monarchy, at least helped to stave off the endless succession of invaders. Such a man was Sigismund III (1587–1631). His greatest victories were against the Turks, who had won control of Moldavia by 1618 and who then seized Chotin on the Dniester. From there they threatened to overrun Podolia, the narrow corridor between the Dniester and the Bug along which Poles and Turks had fought for more than a century. Inspired by Sigismund's leadership, the Poles made such valiant resistance that they recovered Chotin in 1621 and secured the restoration of Christian rulers to Moldavia, so that the principality might lie as a buffer state between themselves and the Turks. Against his other enemies Sigismund was less successful. He failed to defend Kiev against the Russians and could do nothing to prevent the triumphal progress of Gustavus Adolphus through Livonia and Courland.[14] Fortunately for Poland, Gustavus was so eager to intervene in north Germany that he allowed his French allies to negotiate the Truce of Altmark (1629), by which he withdrew his troops in return for control of the Baltic ports.

Sigismund's elder son, Ladislau IV (1631–48), was elected to succeed him, and so effectively did he wage war against the Russians that his army entered Moscow in 1634. There he compelled the tsar to renounce his claim to White Russia and Little Russia, to the areas surrounding Smolensk and Kiev respectively, which the Poles had seized from Russia in the Middle Ages.

The achievements of Sigismund and Ladislau were all the more striking when set against the disasters of John Casimir's reign (1648–68). John Casimir was Ladislau's brother, and so little expectation had he of ascending the throne that he had entered the church as a Jesuit priest. In the year of his election he was awaiting appointment to an altogether different seat in the College of Cardinals. He was not the man to deal with the Cossack revolt which broke out within a few months of his

[14] See Chapter VIII pp. 375–6.

accession.

The Cossacks of the Dnieper were Russian in race, language and religion, though they enjoyed their position as nominal vassals of Poland since it left them free to practise piracy on the lower reaches of the Dnieper and brigandage along its banks. Fierce and warlike, they might have served Poland well, especially against the Turks, if the Poles had not regarded them with suspicion, disliking both their independent behaviour and their loyalty to the Russian Orthodox Church. Attempts were made during Ladislau's reign to convert them to Roman Catholicism, and intendants had been appointed to strengthen royal authority in their territory. By 1648 the Cossacks were near breaking point. Finally, when their leader, Bogdan Chmel'nyckyj, left home to protest to John Casimir against the tyranny of the intendants, one of these raped his wife and killed his son, and thus provoked the most serious rebellion of the century in Poland. Foreign invasion was dangerous enough but civil war was far more so since the Polish nobles, who rarely lacked courage in facing an invader, behaved then at their most factious for fear of strengthening the crown. Even when the Cossacks seized Lwow with ease, they made no move to support John Casimir, who was compelled to appeal to Vienna, pleading his cause as a Catholic crusader against heretics of the Orthodox Church. With Austrian aid he defeated Bogdan Chmel'nyckyj's army in 1651, but, in their desperate stand along the Dneiper, the Cossacks too could call upon allies, the Russians, who were eager to avenge their defeat of 1634. The Russians had soon occupied all Polish territory east of the Dneiper, and in 1656 they overran Little Russia, seized Lwow and advanced as far as the middle reaches of the Vistula. In that same year Rackoczi, the Calvinist ruler of Transylvania, crossed the Carpathian mountains to invade Poland from the south, while Charles X of Sweden[15] attacked from the north, captured Cracow and Warsaw and compelled John Casimir to fly into Silesia.

It was only the fact that Poland's invaders were so bitterly opposed to each other which saved her from immediate partition. In the event the consequences were severe though not disastrous. Sweden gained nothing since the Dutch intervened to save Danzig and a Danish invasion of his homeland caused Charles to

[15] See Chapter VIII for this and subsequent references to Sweden and Brandenburg.

withdraw in haste from Poland; the Turks under Mahomet Köprülü chose this very moment to drive Rackoczi from Transylvania; the Great Elector of Brandenburg exploited the crisis to win full independence of Poland for his fief of East Prussia; Russia, after a further decade of warfare, was confirmed in possession of Kiev and Smolensk with their surrounding territory by the Treaty of Andrussovo (1667).

No sooner had the Russians been bought off than Poland was again torn by civil war, as a result of Louis XIV's ambitions to win the kingdom as a permanent ally against the Habsburgs. John Casimir, who had married a French princess, and who sought to retire to the calmer life of a rich benefice in France, undertook to secure the election of the great Condé's son as his successor. To strengthen his hand he appointed Jan Sobieski, who too had married a French wife and who supported Louis's ambitions, as commander-in-chief of the army. Sobieski had previously betrayed John Casimir to Charles X during the Swedish invasion, but French influence had subsequently effected a reconciliation between them. This support was well worth having: not only could he supply the entire army from his own estates, but, by pledging these, he could if necessary raise sufficient money to pay the troops himself. His appointment provoked the opponents of the French party into civil war, and when in 1668 John Casimir gave up the struggle by abdicating, the crisis was resolved by the election of Michael Wisnowiecki. A native Pole, Wisnowiecki had the advantage of being tied to no party, but he was wholly lacking in ability and leadership, qualities which were sorely needed four years later when the Turks again invaded Poland.

Since the defeat at St Gotthard had halted his plans of conquest on the Danube, Ahmed Köprülü knew only too well that his retention of office depended upon the achievement of military success elsewhere. For some years he fought in Crete to expel the Venetian garrisons, but he looked for some more dramatic occasion to silence his detractors. This presented itself in 1671 when the Cossacks west of the Dnieper, who were still under Polish control, again rebelled and appealed to the Turks for assistance. Ahmed championed no cause but his own in this tangled conflict along the Dnieper, and he exploited the crisis brilliantly. Within a few months (1672) he had taken Lwow and

Kamenets Podolskiy, overrun Podolia and laid claim to the Ukraine. Michael Wisnowiecki, himself incompetent and unable to discover ability in others, ceded all these conquests without dispute, and by his supine acquiescence in defeat stung a large section of the nobles into doing what they might well have done before. Under the leadership of Jan Sobieski, whose factious refusal of support had been partly responsible for the recent humiliations, they raised 40,000 men and in 1673 routed the Turks at Chotin. Michael Wisnowiecki died on the eve of this great victory and so great was the enthusiasm for Sobieski that he was elected king. Thereafter he harried the Turks between the Dniester and the Bug until much of Podolia had been cleared, drove them from Lwow, and, finally, in the Treaty of Zurawno (1676) forced them to cede all their conquests save Kamenets Podolskiy, the capital of Podolia, and its surrounding districts.

The campaigns of 1673–6 brought about a great change in Sobieski. The factious noble, the tool of French diplomacy, became obsessed with a desire to crusade against the Turks. Louis XIV, who had welcomed his election as a triumph for France and who had offered to secure the recovery of East Prussia from Brandenburg if Sobieski would assist the Magyar rebels in Hungary,[16] stood condemned in Sobieski's eyes as the unofficial ally of the sultan, and it was to Leopold I that he offered his alliance. His determination to drive the Turks out of Poland was clearly of political value, since it enhanced his prestige and assured him of the support of the nobles; but when he dreamed of something greater than the recovery of Kamenets Podolskiy, greater even than the reconquest of Moldavia and the Black Sea ports, he subordinated the true interests of Poland to the achievement of his private ideals. Sobieski, of all Poland's kings, might have exploited his military skill and prestige to strengthen his country's defences and to improve its administration: he might have recognised that Poland, threatened as she was on all sides by powerful and aggressive neighbours, was in no condition to undertake a crusade. To all this he remained blind. His determination grew, 'to give the barbarian conquest for conquest, to pursue him from victory to victory over the very frontiers that belched him forth upon Europe, in a word, not to conquer and curb the monster, but to hurl him back into the

16 See below, p. 430.

deserts, to exterminate him, to raise upon his ruins the empire of
Byzantium; this alone is noble, chivalrous and wise.' Noble and
chivalrous, in terms of the medieval world which Poland still
inhabited, but in terms of seventeenth-century politics it was
scarcely wise.

LEOPOLD I AND THE RECONQUEST OF HUNGARY

Habsburg Hungary

On the death of his elder brother in 1654, the future Leopold I
was hastily snatched away from his theological studies in Spain
in order to prepare himself for the task of succeeding his father.
Three years later Ferdinand III died and Leopold, at the age of
sixteen, became head of the Austrian empire. Intellectually he
was well equipped and he had a clear sense of vocation and his
duties. He admired and envied the style of monarchy established
by Louis XIV, and he likewise announced his intention of being
his own first minister, but he lacked both Louis's commanding
appearance and his ability to command. The lolling jaw which
disfigured the Habsburgs merely gave physical emphasis to
Leopold's characteristic irresolution, for while he enjoyed the
task of administration, the burden of decision was too great for
him. For such a ruler, faced with so many dangers from both east
and west, this was a serious failing, scarcely remedied by implicit
reliance upon divine intervention: 'If I were permitted to say so',
wrote the Papal nuncio, 'I would personally wish that the
emperor's trust in God were a bit less, so that he might deal with
somewhat more foresight with those dangers which threaten, and
when he has decided, act.' None the less, unfitted though he
seemed to be, it was left to this self-conscious prince, who longed
for glory but distrusted his ability to attain it, to determine the
relationship of Hungary to the growing unity of the other
Habsburg possessions.

Habsburg Hungary was little more than a frontier province
where the Habsburgs fought a double battle against Turkish
aggression and domestic disaffection. A few German officials held
posts in Pressburg, the capital, but the country was in reality

controlled by the Magyar nobles whose privileges had been preserved intact since their donation in the Golden Bull of 1222. Irresponsible and ungovernable, they paid no taxes and claimed the *jus resistandi* or right of insurrection. As a result of a great missionary campaign undertaken by Cardinal Pázmány early in the century most of the landlords were Catholics, but total conversion had been denied because of the assistance given to the Protestants by the Calvinist rulers of Transylvania. Moreover, so suspicious were the Hungarians of all things Austrian that it was almost a point of honour for many of them to be heretics. The Protestants tended to fear the Ottoman pashas in Buda less than the Catholic emperors in Vienna, but Ahmed Köprülü gave them a rude shock when he sold 80,000 Christians into slavery after his conquest of Transylvania (1663). This act assured Leopold of unanimous support from the Hungarians at the battle of St Gotthard, but the ensuing Truce of Vasvar merely increased his problems. Excited by the prospect of a campaign to release the rest of Hungary from Turkish control, the Magyars felt betrayed: on the grounds that Leopold had not first consulted the Hungarian Diet, they denounced the Truce which they interpreted as a device to win for Leopold twenty years of peace in which to do to Hungary what his grandfather had achieved in Bohemia. The construction of a new fortress at Leopoldstadt, which was allowed for by the Turks in the treaty, was seen not as a bastion against the enemy but as a citadel from which to subdue the local champions of Hungarian independence.

In 1666, when one of the leading nobles married into another prominent Magyar family, the celebrations were organised on so lavish a scale that the nobility attended in great numbers. It was not surprising, therefore, that the innocent occasion of a wedding became the setting for conspiracy. Nor was it surprising that though the conspirators shared a common aim they were wholly lacking in unanimity. The intransigent independence of the Magyars, which so frequently led them into rebellion, made rebellion itself too often ineffective since none would discipline himself to serve under another. Suspicion of Leopold was of too recent a growth to overshadow the more ancient rivalries of one family with another, and for three years the conspirators pursued a confused course of treachery, cowardice, delay and deceit. Moreover, they failed to win support abroad. Louis XIV, who alone might have given them practical aid, was at that time negotiating a partition treaty with Leopold[17] and judged the moment inopportune to embarrass him.

Lobkowitz, the man who had used the failure of the Bohemian revolt to destroy the liberties of the Letter of Majesty, waited until the conspiracy had worn itself out in futility and struck in 1669. Detachments of the Austrian army marched into Pressburg to augment the local forces, and a series of arrests was swiftly carried out. Four of the most prominent rebels were executed straightaway, and a fifth, Stefan Tokoli, was killed as he defended his castle against Imperialist troops. As in Bohemia, the punishment of treason was made an excuse to extend royal authority: 'The Magyars rebelled and therefore have lost all their privileges,' wrote one of the cameralists. 'Henceforward they must be treated as *armis subjecti*', or, as Lobkowitz put it, 'the Hungarians were to be put into Czech trousers'. A new governor, Caspar van Ampringen, was appointed to reduce Hungary to obedience by a reign of terror. The Magyars were not easily intimidated. Many fled into the northern valleys to fight under Imre Tokoli, Stefan's son, who combined the advantages of courage with those of birth, being related to all the victims of 1669. Within a few years it became clear that Tokoli was unlikely to be suppressed, especially since the issues confronting Leopold were not confined to Hungary alone. Because he had intervened in the Netherlands to save the Dutch in 1673 the French had declared their support for Tokoli and sent agents to recruit on his behalf in Poland, though in the event they did little harm as Sobieski was becoming increasingly obsessed with his vision of a crusade. More serious were the indications of a renewed Turkish attack which prompted Pope Innocent XI to take the lead in reconciling Leopold and Tokoli. As neither side could triumph over the other, they wisely agreed to a truce in 1679.

Peace was bought at a high price since Leopold was compelled to recall van Ampringen, declare an amnesty for both rebels and Protestants, and withdraw all German troops from Hungarian soil. Worst of all, he agreed to accept the decisions of a Diet held at Oldenburg in 1681, which gave new life to the time-honoured forms of Magyar government and administration, and freed the council in Pressburg of all control from the cameralists in

17 See Chapter VII, p. 337.

Vienna. Leopold was to some extent playing for time, and Imre Tokoli was not deceived. Boycotting the Diet of Oldenburg and opposing Leopold's choice of officials, he appealed to the Turks to recognise him as king of Upper Hungary in place of Leopold. In January 1682 the Turks accepted his proposal: the destiny of Hungary was thus once again thrown into the balance.

The Defeat of the Turks 1682–1721

The decision to support Tokoli was taken by Kara Mustafa who had succeeded his brother-in-law, Ahmed Köprülü, as Grand Vizier in 1676. The most ambitious of the Köprülü family, his contempt for Europeans blinded him to the possibility of defeat, and in his determination to outshine his predecessors by the capture of Vienna he made his plans with cavalier disregard for what the enemy might do to prevent him. When he heard of Tokoli's rebellion he decided not to wait upon the expiry of the Truce of Vasvar but to make immediate preparations for attack. In the spring of 1683 he mustered the Rumelian spahis at Adrianople, along with the professional Janissaries, and marched northwards collecting local levies as he went until finally he arrived with 250,000 men at Gran on the frontiers of Habsburg Hungary. Leopold was unready to meet him. Unwisely he had relied upon the Truce of Vasvar to secure him immunity until 1684, and had it not been for Montecucculi's foresight in retaining 30,000 men after peace had been made with Louis XIV at Nijmegen in 1679, the Austrians would have been entirely defenceless. Montecucculi himself had just died and it was Charles, the exiled duke of Lorraine, who faced Kara Mustafa's vast horde. After playing with the idea of striking the first blow by attacking Gran, he decided that it was his prime duty to keep his small army in being by not taking risks. In consequence, though he fought a creditable delaying action up the Danube, the harsh fact emerged that whatever he did nothing could stop the Turks reaching Vienna.

Leopold quitted his capital on July 7th leaving the Count of Starhemberg to defend it as best he could, and its capture would have been assured if the Ottoman army had stormed its walls within the week; but Kara Mustafa made slow progress. He arrived on the 17th and then rejected the idea of a direct assault

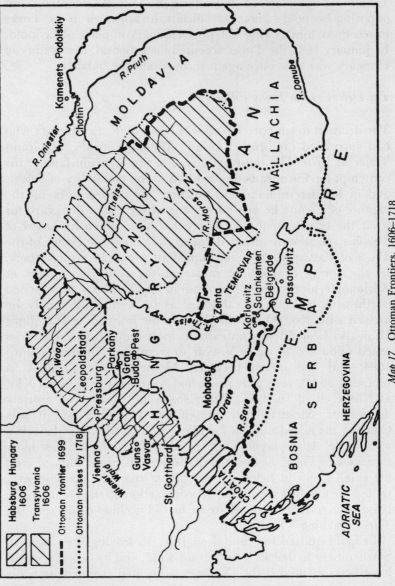

Map 17 Ottoman Frontiers, 1606–1718

in favour of reducing the city by attrition, thus preserving its value when taken. It was the wrong decision, though Kara Mustafa very nearly succeeded. By attempting to starve the city into submission he imposed considerable strain on his own army, whose lines of communication were stretched to their utmost, and whose commissariat, though the best in Europe, was scarcely capable of supplying a quarter of a million men for two months. The besieged, of course, were in a worse plight. They had over three hundred cannon but very little ammunition, and bread but little else; by the end of August dysentery and near starvation had seriously reduced their power of physical resistance. On September 12th the last stage was reached in a complicated series of sapping operations, and within twenty-four hours the explosion of the mines would have given the Turks access to the city.

While Charles of Lorraine used his small force to the full to defend Pressburg from attack by Tokoli and to harass the Turkish lines, a powerful army began to assemble under his direction behind the Wienerwald, the Alpine spur to the south-west of Vienna, overlooking the foothills and the plain which stretched to the city walls. The Elector of Saxony came in person with 9,000 men, the Elector of Brandenburg with 10,000, and the Circles of Franconia and the Upper Rhineland sent 9,000 more; most valuable of all was the arrival of 27,000 Poles under Sobieski. For him it was the fulfilment of his dream of striking a dramatic blow at the Turks, and since the February of 1683, at a time when the emperor was still refusing to take the Turkish threat seriously, he had been raising troops, corresponding with Charles of Lorraine, and denouncing the opposition of the French party in Poland. When news of Vienna's danger reached him he moved swiftly to its defence across three hundred miles of country with few roads and no bridges. To him Charles surrendered command of the army.

The Turks were well aware of this concentration of more than 70,000 men in the Wienerwald and a council of war on September 9th urged Kara Mustafa to attack it before it could reach the plain. Kara Mustafa rejected the advice: the city would fall within three days, and his contempt for European troops made him over-confident of success. Thus the relieving force was able to approach with no greater hindrance than the terrain it covered. Working from the map alone, Sobieski had imagined a gentle continuous slope from the Wienerwald down to Vienna, only to discover that the foothills were covered with woods and terraced vineyards; his plan of a swift dash by the cavalry had therefore to be laid aside and it was not until the critical day of 12 September that his army was in position for the final attack. At 4 a.m. the Austrians, led by Charles of Lorraine, advanced along the Danube while the Germans in the centre awaited Sobieski's final manœuvres to bring his cavalry over the last of the foothills on the army's right. The army, stretching from Sobieski in the west to Charles in the north, thus formed a wide arc which began to close in upon Vienna throughout the morning, until Sobieski gave his cavalry the signal to charge. The effect of 20,000 horses impetuously bearing down upon the Turkish lines was too much for an army which had done little but dig trenches for the past two months. Moreover, having turned to face the attack, the Turks were immediately harassed by sorties from Vienna itself, and by late afternoon their front was broken. Kara Mustafa was swept away in the headlong flight of his troops down the Danube valley, and the relieving army burst into Vienna.

For three days the allies and the Viennese celebrated their triumph, but by 14 September when Leopold arrived for the thanksgiving service the expressions of gratitude were beginning to wear thin. The Poles complained that they were denied fodder for their horses, the Germans claimed that the Poles had fought the least and seized the most, and the Elector of Saxony withdrew his men immediately after Leopold's arrival on the grounds that his Protestant troops were ill received by the Catholic population. Sobieski retired to sulk in his tent when Leopold, far from giving him praise and gratitude to which he felt entitled, and the hand of a Habsburg princess for his son, received him coldly and snubbed his son at their official meeting on the 17th. Jealous that Sobieski should have won the great victory that had always been beyond his own reach, Leopold had listened too intently to false rumours that the Polish king, who had after all been a French agent in the past, was seeking to win Habsburg Hungary for himself.

Dissensions of this sort prevented the allies from exploiting their advantage until the 18th when the chase was at last taken up. With the capture of Gran in early October, European troops entered a fortress which had been held continuously by the Turks since the first siege of Vienna in 1529. After this the coming of winter prevented any further campaigning and the armies went home. Meanwhile Kara Mustafa, having executed all those whose counsel he had foolishly rejected, was himself put to death by the sultan's orders.

The winter months gave Leopold time in which to come to a crucial decision: he could either abandon western Europe to Louis XIV in order to recover Hungary from the Turks, or he could settle for a truce with the Turks, like that of Vasvár, in order to return to the struggle against France. It was a complex problem: to attempt the conquest of Hungary meant accepting the *réunions* and the sacrifice of Spain to France; against this, Austria might become more of a match for France if her territories were united and her eastern frontier settled. In a historic decision Leopold agreed to all Louis XIV's demands in order to secure the Truce of Regensburg, and ordered Charles of Lorraine to renew his campaign in the Danube. One factor of great importance in nerving Leopold to a decision was the support of Innocent XI who formed a Holy League in 1684 in order to raise funds to recruit troops and, especially, to keep Poland in alliance with Austria. This was particularly important since Louis XIV had intensified his efforts to isolate Sobieski, a task made all the easier by Leopold's treatment of the Poles after the relief of Vienna. Innocent's appeal to Sobieski, however, kept that gallant crusader in the field, and even reconciled him, two years later, to making formal recognition of Russia's control of the left bank of the Dnieper, in order to win another ally against the Turks.

In the subsequent campaign Charles of Lorraine ignored the Turkish and Hungarian fortresses which commanded the numerous river valleys running down to the Danube since these were too strongly sited to be taken with ease. Instead he sought to hustle the Turks down the Danube valley itself and thus disrupt the lines of supply without which the fortresses could not long subsist. For four years (1684–8) the campaign went well. Buda, the ancient capital of Hungary, was taken in 1686 after a ten-week siege, and Tokoli, after successive defeats in the north, was expelled from the kingdom. In 1687 the nobles of Transylvania made their submission, and in a great victory near Mohacs Charles of Lorraine avenged the Hungarians who had been slain there in 1526: where the first battle of Mohacs had resulted in Hungary's conquest, the second was followed by its liberation. Finally, in 1688, Belgrade was taken by the Elector of Bavaria, its capture being singularly opportune since in that year Louis XIV invaded the Palatinate,[18] an act of aggression which Leopold as a member of the League of Augsburg could not overlook.

Since he had to strip the Danube army of its best men and commanders, leaving Louis of Baden hard-pressed to retain control of Hungary and Transylvania, it was a wise move for Leopold to assure himself of Sobieski's continued co-operation by at last offering to provide his son with a Habsburg princess and to guarantee that Moldavia, when liberated, should return to Poland. Once again Sobieski's determination to destroy the Turks proved of service to Austria, for the years during which Leopold had to turn against Louis XIV were marked by the rise to power of Mustafa Zadé, yet another member of the Köprülü family and the brother of the famous soldier Ahmed. Recovering Belgrade in 1690, Mustafa Zadé sent Tokoli into Transylvania to raise the Protestant nobility and seemed about to drive the Imperialists out of Hungary. In the late summer, however, the Poles won a major battle in Moldavia, and though Sobieski was not able to exploit his victory for lack of reinforcements from the emperor, Louis of Baden profited from this diversion to drive Tokoli from Transylvania. Finally, at Salankemen, the Turkish revival was abruptly ended by the death of Mustafa Zadé and the defeat of his troops by Louis. Unhappily for Sobieski his inability to follow up his Moldavian victory forfeited him support at home where he was fatally hampered by the influence of his wife who returned to her old love for her native country and who revived French intrigues among the nobility. In any case, it was only too obvious that Sobieski's efforts against the Turks, invaluable though they had been, had benefited Austria rather than Poland: Austria had been saved and had gained Hungary, whereas Poland had nothing more to show than the recovery of Kamenets Podolskiy. Sobieski died in 1696 without again taking the field against the Turks, and his disappointment at the results of his crusade was heightened by the Diet's refusal to elect his son as his successor. In his place it chose Augustus, Elector of Saxony.

Curiously enough, this too was of benefit to Austria rather

18 See Chapter VII, p. 351.

than to Poland since Augustus had succeeded Louis of Baden in command of the Danube army and had proved his incapacity as a soldier. Leopold, hesitant to dismiss him on account of his importance in Germany, seized the opportunity of his election to the Polish throne to replace him by Prince Eugène. Eugène's decisive victory at Zenta in the Theiss valley completed the work of reconquest begun after 1684, and with Imperial troops marauding as far afield as Bosnia and Herzegovina, Leopold called a halt in 1699. Well satisfied with the recovery of his territories, his mind was urgently occupied with the problem of the Spanish succession; accordingly, before the Turks were ready to counter attack, Leopold offered them terms at Karlowitz. This proved to be a general settlement:

(i) Transylvania and Hungary, with the exception of Temesvar, a small province in the south-eastern corner of the kingdom, was recognised as Habsburg territory, the new frontier being drawn along the lines of the Save and Theiss rivers at their junction with the Danube.

(ii) The Turks recognised the recovery of Kamenets Podolskiy by Poland.

(iii) Russia gained Azov in the Crimea.[19]

The Turkish empire was not destroyed but its existence was no longer a threat to Europe. Little attention was paid to it during the War of Spanish Succession, but once it was over Leopold's son, Charles VI, sent Eugène down the Danube in a successful bid to recover Belgrade (1717). The Treaty of Passarovitz which followed reaffirmed the terms of Karlowitz and added Temesvar, western Wallachia and parts of Bosnia and Serbia to the Habsburg dominions. The Danubian Monarchy had at last been established.

The cost of waging war on two fronts had far exceeded the revenues of the Viennese administration which had therefore been forced to borrow heavily. Many of its creditors were its own great nobles and officials who, inspired by patriotism rather than greed, lent vast sums — Count Tschernin advanced 1,200,000 florins in 1704 — at less than the current rates of interest. More expensive, and also available in much larger amounts, were the sums lent by the Jewish bankers in Vienna, and in particular by

[19] See Chapter X, p. 444.

the house of Oppenheimer. Like the Fuggers and Welsers of a previous age, the Oppenheimers, who, in the years 1695–1703 lent 30,000,000 florins at very nearly 50%, finally found their money locked up in the government and, being unable to pay their own debts, went bankrupt. This disaster, commented a contemporary, was 'so deadly a blow that France herself could not have contrived anything more advantageous to herself and harmful to the emperor.'

Eventually the Vienna State Bank was founded in 1706 which was administered by the city of Vienna whose credit was good and whose administration was efficient. The government revenues assigned to it enhanced its security and by the end of the wars the bank had successfully carried through a major funding operation, converting the government's short-term, high interest loans into long-term debts at lower rates. The bank proved to be the Habsburgs' most successful financial experiment in this period, but could not of course solve all the administration's problems. Austria ended the wars indebted to the extent of nearly seven years' revenues.

The integration of Hungary into the Danubian Monarchy

The Danube campaign was of paramount importance in the extension of Habsburg administration to Hungary since every defeat of the Turks was also a defeat for Tokoli and his followers. When the kingdom was occupied by an army of 44,000 Leopold became ruler by right of conquest and, as had happened in Bohemia, election promises and coronation oaths were powerless to protect the cause of local liberties. As early as 1685 when the relief of Vienna had demonstrated that the Turks were occasionally fallible, but when there was as yet nothing to presage their wholesale expulsion from Hungary, Leopold had none the less appointed a special commission to investigate means of effecting the integration of Hungary with his other territories. Significantly, its leaders were two experienced cameralists, Stratmann and Kinsky, the chancellors of Austria and Bohemia; men who regarded traditional liberties as concessions to anarchy, and feudal immunities as obstacles to effective administration, and whose recommendations were certain to favour the supremacy of Austrian bureaucracy.

A most difficult problem was the one of religion. Leopold's devotion to the Catholic Church precluded him from freely granting toleration to heretics, and it was an inescapable fact that the Holy League against the Turks should also be opposed to Protestantism. Moreover, the association of dissent and treason in Hungarian history was too close to be ignored. The cameralists, however, urged caution. They planned first to create an effective bureaucratic system which, having overridden political non-conformity, would then be able to eliminate heresy: until the first stage had been achieved, any precipitate attempts at conversion might cause rebellion. Consequently commanders were ordered to restrain their men from destroying Protestant churches, and the promises of 1681[20] were not broken outright.

By 1687, before the kingdom had been altogether cleared of Turks, the political plans of the cameralists reached fruition, and a Diet was summoned to Pressburg to receive their decisions. The Golden Bull of 1222 was amended by the abolition of the *jus resistandi*, and the monarchy was declared to be no longer elective but the hereditary possession of the Habsburg family: to symbolise this, Leopold's nine-year-old son, Joseph, was brought to Hungary and formally crowned. Though Hungary was thus reduced to the provincial status of Bohemia, the administrative revolution was carried through with caution and without the brutality which had occurred in the latter. Leopold desired to make his settlement acceptable, and since he could not liquidate the Magyar nobility he made them what few concessions he could. Though a Hungarian section was established in the *Hofkanzlei,* and though the fiscal administration too was reorganised to assess contributions in proportion to the kingdom's wealth, within the kingdom itself the administration of the edicts was left in the hands of Hungarian officials, and the nobility confirmed in their social and economic privileges as landlords.

Transylvania, where traditions of independence died hard, was allowed further concessions. By special arrangements drawn up in 1690 and 1691 the country was not merged into Hungary but governed directly from Vienna, which meant in practice that the local nobility retained their political pre-eminence, and the coexistence with the Roman Church of the various Protestant denominations was allowed to continue.

[20] See above, p. 430.

There was of course opposition to the ascendancy of Austria, no matter how moderately exercised. The new tax assessments were naturally unpopular, and the Protestants feared that the period of toleration was of uncertain length. Thus, when Francis Rackoczi led a rebellion to restore the guarantees of the Golden Bull he did not lack for recruits, and the government had to maintain 30,000 troops in Hungary in order to contain the insurgents until the War of Spanish Succession had ended. From that moment Rackoczi was doomed, though both Joseph I (1705–11) and his brother Charles VI (1711–40) were determined to pursue the policies of their father by avoiding undue violence. Rather than crush the entire rebel army, Charles won over the rebels individually until Rackoczi had been isolated. He was then allowed to escape into exile.

The final stage in the creation of the Danubian monarchy was reached in 1713 when Charles VI declared, in the Pragmatic Sanction, that the German, Bohemian and Hungarian possessions of the Habsburgs were to be regarded as a single state. The problems of the diversity of race, religion and culture persisted long after this date, indeed they were never solved, but the political structure of the empire had been established. The Austrian Habsburgs, no longer condemned to the impossible task of rejuvenating the obsolete Holy Roman Empire, emerged as a major European power whose diverse territories had been organised into one administrative unit. They had defeated the Turks; they had contained, and finally had helped to destroy, the French attempt to establish a Bourbon hegemony in Europe; they won possession of Milan, Tuscany, Naples and the Netherlands; and from the dangers and confusions of both the Thirty Years War and the war with the Turks they survived to create the great Danubian monarchy.

X

RUSSIA, SWEDEN AND THE GREAT NORTHERN WAR
1700—21

Russia and the West to 1700

The European civilisation of Kiev and Smolensk had been destroyed in the thirteenth century by Genghis Khan and the Tatars of the Gobi Desert, and for four hundred years Muscovy was isolated from the original sources of her culture. The refugees from Kiev made their way up the river Desna to the present site of Moscow, and there they attempted to preserve some continuity with the past by preserving the Orthodox religion they had received at the hands of Byzantium. Moscow, too, was overrun and Muscovy became a province of the Tatar empire, but her grand dukes were granted particular privileges as the tax-collectors of the Khans. As the centuries passed, the dukes began to extend their authority, and finally to strike at the heart of the Tatar empire. Ivan the Great (1462–1505) and Ivan the Dread (1533–84), no longer dukes but self-styled tsars, plunged further into Asia. Their colonists trekked across Siberia, reaching the Pacific about 1640, but the tsars were more interested in expansion to the south-east, through Kazan and Astrakhan, until it was only the power of Abbas the Great of Persia which checked their advance beyond the Caucasus.

At the same time Europe had not been entirely ignored. Ivan the Dread had made alliances with European princes — had even proposed marriage to Elizabeth of England — and European merchants had begun to trade through the port of Archangel. Western fashions and connections were subsequently discredited during the Time of Troubles, the period of civil war in which Sweden acquired Russia's Baltic coast but by the middle of the seventeenth century the tsar Alexis had succeeded in bringing Russia back into Europe by recovering Kiev and

Smolensk from Poland (see p. 424–6). Through contact with the Poles the Russians became aware of the professional, technical and military skills available in Europe, and foreigners with experience of metallurgy, mining, commerce, administration and warfare were recruited to such an extent that as many as 18,000 Germans, Scots, Dutch and English were to be found in Moscow.

It was typical of the ambivalence with which Russia regarded the West that the foreigners whose skills were respected by the government were nonetheless isolated from the rest of the city in what was called the German Quarter, as though they were carriers of a dangerous infection. In the opinion of the Russian Orthodox Church they were indeed a source of contamination, and no institution had been better placed to exert its tremendous authority to preserve the purity of the Russian soul. In the latter years of the seventeenth century, however, the Church was weakened by schism. The Patriarch Nikon, though conservative in all essential points, had attempted in 1667 to bring the Church back into line with the practices of the Greek Orthodox Church from which it had originated. His proposals antagonised many of the more ignorant clergy, who had come to believe that salvation was jeopardised if the worshipper departed by one word or gesture from the prayers and rituals to which they had become accustomed. These 'Old Believers', as they were called, were so exercised by the changes that they broke away from the Church, and although they were persecuted with rigour, the effect of their action diminished the Patriarch's authority throughout Russia and compromised his role as the champion of Russian values against the infiltration of European habits and ideas.

It also made it more difficult for the Patriarch to exercise the restraint which, traditionally, the Church had imposed on the authority of the tsars — a point of considerable importance since there was no other institution capable of doing so. The Assembly of the *Boyars,* the great territorial magnates, had been closed down by Ivan the Dread in the sixteenth century, and the *boyars* themselves had become accustomed to hold their vast estates on condition of service in the army or the administration. Throughout the nobility at large, indeed, each owner of an hereditary estate or *votchina,* who failed to fulfil his obligation of service forfeited his lands, which were then assigned to another as a *pomestye,* an estate granted solely for the performance of specified duties. In 1682, moreover, the tsar advanced his power significantly by abolishing the *mestnichestvo*, the right of boyars and nobles to refuse employment in his service if the rank associated with the task was below their own rank in the order of nobility. In practice the only effective restraint on the autocracy of the tsar was the lack of a bureaucratic apparatus to apply it uniformly and in every region. All that had been achieved by the end of the century was the creation of forty government departments, *prikazy*, but below this level local government was in the hands of military governors whose administration was characterised by brutality and inefficiency.

Many of the tsar's ministers therefore looked towards Europe with envy and admiration — Alexis' foreign minister, Nashchokin, was particularly impressed by the administrative efficiency of western states; he was also aware of the importance of commerce, of securing access to the Baltic and of establishing a Baltic fleet. His successor, Matvieef, married a Scotswoman and their adopted daughter, Natalie Naryshkin, was much influenced in her education by European customs and attitudes. She, in turn, became the second wife of Alexis, and the mother of the future Peter the Great. Alexis died in 1676, when Peter was four years old, and it was Feodor, the elder son of the first marriage, who ruled until his own death in 1682. Since Feodor's brother Ivan was an imbecile a group of nobles declared for Peter, but they had little chance against Ivan's determined sister Sophia who won over the *Streltsi*. The *Streltsi* were the officers of the palace guard who throughout the century had engineered a succession of palace revolutions, each marked by barbaric cruelty. On this occasion the unfortunate victims were Matvieeff and all those associated with the Naryshkin connection. The imbecile Ivan and the child Peter were proclaimed as joint Tsars, but Sophia was empowered to rule on their behalf as regent.

Peter was left to grow up in relative obscurity and, encouraged by his mother, spent a great deal of his adolescence in the German Quarter. Physically powerful, of massive build and of unstable temperament, he could be rebellious, uncouth and cruel: he was also capable of warm friendships and sustained enthusiasms. Of all the things which excited his imagination none compared with the vision of Europe he derived from conversation with the European doctors, traders, soldiers and engineers who lived in Moscow. It was a Dutchman, Timmerman, who first showed him how a boat could sail against the wind and took him to Archangel to see for himself the merchantmen arriving from Holland and England. He also studied ballistics and fortification and, raising two regiments, each 300 strong, from the sons of local nobles and peasants, drilled them and practised them in military manoeuvres.

These same regiments joined him in 1689 when Peter took refuge in the fortified monastery of Troitsa. Sophia had failed in a campaign against the Turks, and although a conspiracy against her had proved abortive she sought to strengthen her position by eliminating Peter — Ivan having died in 1686. This time however the *Streltsi* changed sides, and Sophia was committed to a nunnery. Peter's victory had been fortuitous and he himself was content to leave affairs of state in the hands of his mother, withdrawing once again to the German Quarter and his regiments until her death in 1694.

Peter's first task was to renew the war with his government's traditional enemy, the Ottoman Turks, but with an altogether novel objective. In 1695 he determined to seize possession of the Ottoman-held port of Azov, from where he could build a fleet to challenge the Turks in the Black Sea. If the campaign was a failure, the manner of it confirmed his view of sea power since it was from the sea that the Turks sustained the siege of Azov. Immediately Peter ordered the construction of his own fleet during the winter of 1695–6 at Voronezh on the Don. It was a good centre for shipbuilding, standing in the heart of pine forests and with access to the Black Sea, but the first ships to be launched there were in fact made four hundred miles away outside Moscow. There Peter had secured a Dutch galley to serve as a model; twenty-five copies were then shipped overland to Voronezh, and commissioned for action in the Sea of Azov. The first victory of the Russian navy was thus the successful blockade of Azov, which fell to Peter in July 1696.

Peter could no longer contain himself: the west had so much to offer that he took the unheard-of step of going there in person in 1697, not to see the stately splendours of Rome and Versailles, but to tour the dockyards of Holland and England. His journey, as Macaulay put it, 'is an epoch in the history not only of his own country but of ours and of the world.' Peter worked for some time in Amsterdam, in the yards of the East India Company, but finding the Dutch too empirical for his taste he crossed the North Sea to study the theory of shipbuilding in London. Apart from the great concourse of merchantmen which excited his admiration and envy, he was equally struck by the industry and invention of the craftsmen whose skills alone made commerce possible. It became vital to his plans to return not merely with European shipbuilders but with technicians of every kind. Among the thousand and more who accompanied him home were several Englishmen, among them John Parry, an expert in Hydraulics, to construct a canal between the Volga and the Don, and Henry Farquharson of Aberdeen University, who established a school of mathematics and navigation at Moscow. Peter intended to visit Venice, too, for he had heard of its famous arsenal and of the commercial prosperity of the lagoons, but his plans were suddenly changed by news of a revolt at home by the *Streltsi*.

Although the *Streltsi* had supported Peter against Sophia, they were outraged by his novelties, above all by his visit to Europe. Fortunately for Peter, he had left command in the hands of a Scot, Patrick Gordon, who, by his quick action in summoning the aid of loyal troops led by other foreign officers, suppressed the revolt. Peter returned to make a terrible example of the rebels. More than a thousand suffered torture and death, some at Peter's own hands as, in order to garnish a night of drunken revelry, he summoned them from their cells to be despatched with savage brutality among the trestles and the drinking-cups. The bloody orgies revealed the pathological blemish in his character; there was nonetheless, a political motive behind the slaughter. The *Streltsi* represented the most conservative, the most traditionalist, force capable of opposing Peter's reforms, and by eliminating them he made himself free to govern as he wished without the fear of palace revolutions.

If the European tour confirmed Peter's determination to set about the transformation of his backward and isolated country into a European state, it had a rather different consequence of equal importance. One major purpose of the tour had been to persuade the governments of Europe to join Russia in a major campaign against the Turks. Peter learned very quickly that this was not to be because of the difficulties arising over the succession to the Spanish empire. Instead, Peter was himself approached by Augustus of Saxony and others (see p. 448) with a view to joining their coalition against Sweden. The irresistible lure proved to be the opportunity to recover the Baltic Provinces lost to Sweden in 1617, and Peter immediately agreed. No sooner had he decided upon this change of front than he made peace with the Turks, recalled his troops from the Crimea and invaded Livonia in 1700. It was a decision made with characteristic impetuosity. It proved to be one of profound historic importance. The Livonian campaign projected Russia, firmly and for ever, into the sphere of European diplomacy and warfare.

Charles XII and The Great Northern War 1700–21

When Charles XI died in 1697 he left his fifteen-year-old son in the care of a council of regency. As Sweden had suffered too often from the misrule of nobles in the past, Charles had appointed the regents with care, selecting men who were wholly committed to his policy of *reduktion*. So loyally did they carry out his intentions that the nobles, who had looked for a respite from the persecution of their class, began to cast about for some means to get rid of them. In the *riksdag* they appealed to Charles XII to free himself from the council's control. The other three estates supported them, partly because of their innate suspicion of all regency government, partly because once the proposal had been made no one wished to be seen in opposition to it. Even the regents themselves, bearing in mind what had happened to their predecessors in Charles XI's reign, did not oppose the measure and within six months of Charles XII's accession they had surrendered their powers to him.

Charles XII had been brought up by his father in a regime of austere simplicity. Exercise, drill and hunting — he killed his first wolf when only ten — alternated with the study of languages and military history. His isolated childhood left him reticent and solitary; to observers he appeared 'shy as a nun', 'a peasant lad newly enlisted who kept his eyes downcast with rustic shyness'. His education had developed in him a stern passion for duty and a rather simple-minded notion of virtuous behaviour in politics, which led him to despise diplomacy as hypocrisy and deceit as the cardinal sin.

Map 18   The Great Northern War

Historians have differed widely in their view of him but there remains a substantial number who find in Charles XII a leader in the tradition of Norse Saga, a reincarnation of the untamed spirit of the Viking hero, choosing to fight because for him the sword was the best and the only argument. His powers of leadership, his disdain of personal suffering and his burning delight in war, won him the utter devotion of his men who fashioned a legend around his exploits and blindly followed him to the portals of Valhalla.

Charles was only fifteen when sovereignty was thrust upon him. Being reticent he did not freely discuss affairs of state with others; being obstinate it was difficult to persuade him when he was wrong. Above all he needed time to gain experience without the urgency of crisis to force his hand, especially since the Swedish crown had become so autocratic that his people's destiny depended upon his judgement alone. But his judgement was never given the chance to mature. No sooner was he established on the throne than a coalition of European powers threatened the entire Swedish empire.

The strengths and weaknesses of the Swedish empire in 1697 have been described (see p. 398). No matter what the achievements of Charles XI, however, the empire could not hope to withstand the simultaneous invasion by its major enemies of its settlements, conquests and bases strung out along the Baltic coastline. One man who attempted to engineer just that was John Patkul, the Livonian noble driven into exile for his opposition to the *reduktion* commission (see p. 399). On Charles XII's accession he appealed for a pardon but, in company with the Swedish nobles who too had looked for favours from the new king's hand, was brusquely repulsed. From that moment Patkul determined on nothing less than the destruction of the Swedish empire, and his pursuit of vengeance led him from one northern capital to another, fomenting jealousy of Sweden's power and inciting greed for her possessions.

Patkul's role as a catalytic agent in a volatile situation must not be exaggerated. It did not need anyone to awaken the appetites of Christian V of Denmark, of Peter the Great or of Augustus of Saxony who were all anxious to enlarge their territories at Sweden's expense, but what proved to be influential with Patkul's chief patron, Augustus, was his assertion that the moment he returned to Livonia at the head of an army the discontented nobility would rise immediately in revolt. Augustus of Saxony had a special interest in Livonia. In 1694 he had been elected king of Poland and he hoped that by recovering for Poland the territories lost to Sweden he would be rewarded with an hereditary title to the kingdom. His dynasty would therefore be established in considerable power over a vast domain, extending from Leipzig across Lusatia and Poland to the Gulf of Finland. In November 1699 therefore Augustus, with Patkul's aid, brought to a conclusion two years of negotiation with Russia and Denmark — with an agreement designed to ensure the simultaneous invasion of Livonia, Ingria and Holstein-Gottorp.

The duchy of Holstein-Gottorp had long been the thorn in Denmark's flesh and until it had been taken no invasion of the Swedish mainland could be contemplated. In the year of Charles XII's accession Christian V invaded the duchy in order to destroy the fortifications erected by its duke, but Charles had intervened, with the diplomatic support of England and the United provinces — guarantors of the treaty of Altona (see p. 398) — to secure their restoration. When Christian died in 1699 his son Frederick IV was as eager as his father to join the coalition against Sweden.

Only one potential ally stood aloof from the coalition, Frederick of Brandenburg. Like his father he wanted to drive the Swedes from Pomerania but he was a cautious man and, for the time being, preoccupied with his coronation as king in Prussia. Moreover, he could not afford to forfeit the subsidies he enjoyed from the emperor for his support in the coming conflict with France, and neither Augustus nor any other member of the coalition was prepared to buy him over.

While Danish forces invaded Gottorp in 1700, secure in the belief that their navy had the Sound, an Anglo-Dutch fleet entered the Baltic in order to fulfil its obligation under the treaty of Altona. Under its protection Charles XII landed wholly unexpected on Zealand with 11,000 men, but since the Maritime Powers were concerned to protect Gottorp but not to destroy Denmark they restrained Charles from attacking Copenhagen. By the treaty of Travendal, which Frederick gratefully accepted, they insisted only that Denmark withdraw from the coalition of Sweden's enemies.

Disappointed that he was unable to dispose of Denmark in a more lasting manner Charles XII swiftly transferred his army across the Baltic to meet the Saxons and Russians. Patkul, however, like many exiled leaders, had overestimated the warmth of feeling for him in his own country, and his arrival with the Saxon forces aroused none of the support he had anticipated. The Livonian gentry failed to join him, and the Swedish garrisons, having no local rising to contend with, swiftly expelled the invaders. Peter the Great was more successful. His army invaded Ingria, the most northerly of the Baltic Provinces, where, on the frontier with Estonia, it laid siege to Narva. Since Charles was presumed to be fully occupied in the west the outcome of the siege seemed assured, until it was learned that Charles had arrived on the Estonian coast with 7,000 men. Peter had no illusions about his army's fate. Though the Russians outnumbered the Swedes by five to one, they were dispersed in siege-works around the city and lacked experience of war; in fact they would never have been risked in a campaign at all had Peter anticipated that they would encounter Charles XII. With ruthless logic he promptly deserted them, taking with him those officers who might be useful in raising a new army. The outcome in fact was by no means as certain as Peter had imagined. Rehnskiold, the able Swedish general who had planned the landing on Zealand, was urged by Charles to risk the army in appalling weather conditions and complete a forced march of seven days with rations for only four. The march was nonetheless achieved. The Swedes arrived at Narva in a blinding snowstorm on November 20th 1700, to find the Russian army demoralised by Peter's departure. Within a few hours the city had been relieved, and the captured Russian artillery and stores taken in triumph within its walls.

Charles' first instinct was to press on immediately for Moscow but the army had to go into winter quarters and await reinforcements in the spring of 1701. The first thing to be done then was to march south because a Saxon army had returned to besiege Riga. Subsequently, when the Saxons had been driven off, Charles occupied Courland — despite the protestations of the Poles that though their king Augustus might as elector of Saxony be Charles' enemy they themselves were neutral. Charles XII had now to decide whether to pursue Augustus or Peter. A negotiated settlement was possible but Charles, though disposed to prefer military to diplomatic solutions, was probably correct to assume that neither of his enemies was to be trusted. There seemed in fact no other way to preserve the empire than by successive campaigns of intimidation.

If Charles had gone straight for Moscow in the summer of 1701 it is clear that Peter would have been hard pressed to stop him. Equally, Augustus would have been able to disrupt the Swedish lines of communication with Russia and occupy the Baltic Province. The Saxons, in fact, were militarily more formidable at that moment than the Russians and Charles' decision to attack them first was probably correct. What was mistaken was his contempt for Russia's recuperative powers, since he left only 15,000 men to guard a frontier over 600 miles long, and stripped the garrisons of their best men to strengthen his campaign to the south. Worse still, this campaign turned out to be more compli-

cated and long-lasting than Charles could ever have imagined —
indeed it occupied him fully for the next six years.

The problem for Charles was that Augustus ruled both Poland
and Saxony. To overrun Poland as Charles did quite brilliantly
in 1702, winning a major victory at Klissow, midway between
Warsaw and Cracow, did not destroy Augustus. To go further
into Saxony was to become involved in central European affairs
when Sweden's real enemy was marching back into the Baltic
Provinces. Moreover, the Maritime Powers in alliance with the
emperor were engaged in war with Louis XIV. They did not
want Sweden to upset the delicate balance of alliances within
Germany, and Charles could not afford to endanger Swedish
naval power by antagonising England and Holland. Although
the matter has been much debated by historians, it seems clear
that Charles, after the victory at Klissow, should have settled for
peace in order to turn on Russia, before Peter had time to
consolidate his hold over the Baltic Provinces. Charles, however,
was not to be deflected from what had now become a personal
vendetta.

In Augustus he faced an enemy whom he hated above all
others, an enemy who had concealed his hostile intentions up to
the very outbreak of war. Such duplicity Charles found intolerable and he refused to negotiate with him: 'It would put our glory
to shame if we lent ourselves to the slightest treaty accommodation with one who has so vilely prostituted his honour'.

Charles' first objective therefore was to depose Augustus from
the Polish throne. Many local families of great influence were
angry at the consequences of Augustus' policies and would have
united happily behind a rival, if only they could have agreed
upon one. In the event Charles XII selected Stanlislaus Leszczinski and, after a series of campaigns throughout 1703 and
1704, mustered enough support to have him crowned in 1705.

There was much to recommend the transformation of Poland
into a Swedish satellite but in the meantime the Russians had
taken the Baltic Provinces, the very bastions of the Baltic empire.
Livonia was devastated, Ingria — as a future Russian province
— carefully occupied, Narva captured and, at the mouth of the
Neva in May 1703, work was begun on the construction of St
Petersburg, an act of faith that the territory was to be permanently held by Russia (see pp. 467–8). At this crisis Charles XII

revealed the narrow rigidity of thought, almost the monomania, which blinded him to every consideration but the defeat and humiliation of Augustus. In 1706 he risked the displeasure of the Maritime Powers and invaded Saxony, where Augustus at last submitted. He recognised Stanislaus as king of Poland, withdrew from his alliances and handed over Patkul for summary execution.

Charles was at last prepared to turn against Russia, but not before provoking a conflict with the emperor Joseph over the persecution of Lutherans in Silesia. For the best part of a year the Swedish army encamped at Leipzig until the emperor became so incensed that it needed Marlborough's personal intervention to prevent open warfare between them. In order to concentrate on the struggle with France, Joseph reluctantly agreed to humour the mad young Swede, and at Altranstadt, 1707, he granted the necessary concessions to the Silesian Lutherans.

In September 1707 Charles at last left Silesia for Russia. Peter the Great had used every device to stave off an attack, even to the extent of offering Marlborough either Kiev or Smolensk, in addition to a pension of 50,000 *thalers*, if he would mediate between Sweden and Russia. Peter in fact was ready to surrender everything but St Petersburg, but Charles refused his offers. Ever since Narva he had had nothing but contempt for the Russians. 'There is nothing in winning victories over the Muscovites; they can be beaten at any time'. From Charles' point of view the time had now come, though others might suggest that it was already five years too late. Peter the Great retained an exaggerated respect for Charles' ability, as Charles undervalued Peter's, but their relative strengths had in fact been materially altered since Narva. Peter had created a new army (see p. 461), better trained than the old one, better led and better equipped. Moreover with the Baltic Provinces mainly in his control, he could interfere very easily with Charles' lines of communication and supply as the Swedish army advanced into Russia.

Confident of victory, nonetheless, Charles decided to ignore the Baltic Provinces and go straight for Moscow. He moved quickly. Crossing the Vistula on Christmas Day his army reached Grodno on the Niemen in January 1708, only two hours after Peter had withdrawn in haste. From there Charles struck out for the Dneiper and Smolensk. He had ordered a Swedish supply column — indeed a colossal mobile supply depot under the command of Levenhaupt to set out from Riga to join him en route, and he was in touch with Mazeppa, the leader of the Cossacks of the Ukraine.

The alliance of Viking and Cossack was a theme to excite the imagination, but Mazeppa was anything but romantic. The landowner of more than 19,000 farmsteads, he exploited his vast estates with the prosaic business acumen of a Dutch burgher and monopolised the mining of saltpetre in the Ukraine. As leader of the Dnieper Cossacks he was also a soldier, but he regarded wars as investments and selected his allies with the same shrewd care with which he chose his bailiffs. He had gone to Peter's aid at Azov, and had fought against Charles XII in Poland, but since then he had fallen foul of Peter and suspected him of attempting to integrate the Ukraine with Russia. Peter, for his part, suspected Mazeppa of intriguing with Charles. For the time being, however, Mazeppa played for time, determined to await the result of the encounter between Charles and Peter before revealing his own hand.

Charles left Grodno and successfully fought his way eastwards, winning what was to be his last great victory at Holowczyn on the river Drucz in June, 1708. He then advanced a further twenty-five miles to a point on the Dnieper, a little to the south-west of Smolensk. He was now in trouble. Peter's army, in retreat, had systematically destroyed everything along a wide front so that the Swedish army had nothing to confiscate and was running short of supplies. Levenhaupt meanwhile was delayed by heavy rains which hampered the progress of his bulky supply wagons. Charles therefore crossed the Dnieper and marched to the south-east, intending after a while to turn north and outflank the Russian army covering Smolensk. Peter however had foreseen this move and had already devastated the countryside in Charles' path. By September Charles could persist no longer. He sent orders to Levenhaupt to catch up with him as best he could and turned south towards the unravaged province of Severia. Everything went wrong for him. Levenhaupt was caught at Lesnáyà losing half his force of 11,000 and all the baggage train. Meanwhile a Russian column slipped ahead of the Swedish army and devastated Severia.

There was nothing for it but to press on further south to the

Ukraine. Unaware as yet of the news of Lesnáyà the troops were in high spirits, according to a British officer in Swedish service. 'We find ourselves at present with the hopes of coming into a country flowing with milk and honey, that Count Levenhaupt will soon reinforce our army with the addition of eleven or twelve thousand men and that General Mazeppa will declare for us'.

En route, however, the remnants of Levenhaupt's defeated troops joined up with the army which was then, to Charles' consternation, confronted by the arrival of Mazeppa, fleeing for his life with barely a thousand men and no supplies. Peter had wasted no time in sending troops into the Ukraine and Mazeppa's capital, Bakurin, was under siege.

With his army augmented but without the ability to feed it, Charles continued the march southward in a desperate search for supplies. He marched into the teeth of the worst winter of the century, when birds fell dead in flight from the cold. On the endless steppes of the Ukraine, where there was neither shelter nor food, the attacks of Russian troops were the least of all the perils. Exposure and starvation reduced the army from 44,000 to 20,000. Charles suffered the same privations as his men, and it was only his example and determination which held together the remnants of the army. But the terrible ordeal drove him yet further into insanity. The single-minded pursuit of vengeance which had characterised his campaigns, first against Augustus and then against Peter, became wholly obsessive. With the spring of 1709 his spirits lifted, and all his talk was of reserves to be raised in Poland and Sweden and of victory to be won against Peter. But the real problem was still that of survival, and the army still continued its march southward for supplies. In June it reached the town of Poltava on the river Vorstkla, fifty miles above its junction with the lower Dnieper.

Charles intended, by attacking Poltava, to tempt Peter into a major engagement, and Peter, remembering Narva, moved in cautiously to accept the challenge. He now had 45,000 troops to face Charles' 20,000; moreover they were well supplied with artillery and ammunition. Charles himself was wounded in the foot from a chance encounter with a patrol before the battle, and although he was carried hither and thither in a palanquin to survey the battlefield, the morale of the troops was affected and his commanders felt uneasy at exercising responsibility while he remained present. In the event the Russian artillery barrage took tremendous toll of the Swedish infantry, and there was no room in which to manoeuvre as the Russians, arrayed in a vast arc, closed in upon the town. The Swedish army was defeated.

After the battle Charles retreated south with about 15,000 men, many of them ill from the months of suffering, or wounded in the battle. He too was wounded and it was decided that he should be sent on with a small force to Turkey, where he planned to mobilise support for a campaign against Russia, while Levenhaupt and the survivors followed behind. In the event, and with Charles gone ahead, Levenhaupt lost confidence in the plan. Shaken by the defeat at Poltava, and as worried about meeting the Turks as allies as of avoiding the Russians as enemies, he found himself suddenly confronted at Perevolochna by a Russian army in pursuit and lost his nerve. Without any discussion with his officers he surrendered his entire force.

The Swedish empire was the artificial creation of the sword: when that sword was splintered at Poltava the empire collapsed. Swiftly Sweden's enemies began the work of partition. Augustus regained possession of Poland where Stanilaus Leszczinski thankfully abandoned the throne to him, while Peter seized Riga and Reval and launched the Russian Baltic fleet. Elsewhere, in one grim rearguard action after another, the Swedes clung desperately to their territories and a Danish invasion of Scania in 1709 was defeated at Hälsingborg in March 1710. The emperor and the Maritime Powers, anxious to keep the German princes committed to the war with Louis XIV, offered to guarantee Sweden's remaining possessions if Sweden would refrain from any attack on the enemies. The *riksrad* welcomed and accepted the proposal but when it was transmitted to Charles XII he repudiated it.

The refugee on Turkish soil would neither negotiate with his enemies nor return to fight them. Refusing to accept that his campaign to bring retribution upon Peter had ended at Poltava, he first caballed at the Ottoman court to remove a grand vizier who advocated peace with Russia, and then persuaded the sultan to attack. At the crossing of the Pruth the Russians were defeated in 1711, but when the sultan regained possession of Azov he decided not to push his luck too far and concluded a treaty of peace.

Far from accepting this as an occasion to negotiate with Peter, Charles settled down at his headquarters in Bender near the Russo-Turkish frontier to plan another campaign. In 1712 he ordered the *riksrad* to raise 16000 fresh troops and send them under the command of Stenbock to Pomerania; thence they were to invade Poland and join Charles at Bender. With a succession of bad harvests, made worse by the arrival of the plague in 1710, and expenditure exceeding revenue by a factor of three, it was an act of unparalleled loyalty for Sweden to rally to its king in this way. Stenbock landed successfully in Pomerania but as the transports were destroyed by the Danish Fleet the army was unable to advance as Charles had intended. Instead it was called upon to provide a last-ditch resistance in north Germany against Russians and Saxons in Pomerania, Danes in Bremen and Gottorp and Hanoverians in Verden. Eventually Stenbock was driven into Gottorp in 1713 and was there compelled to surrender.

Throughout all this Charles XII remained at Bender. His subjects begged him to return; his hosts urged him to depart; even his enemies wanted him back in order to negotiate a settlement in the Baltic, and Peter the Great offered him safe conduct across Russia. But Charles trusted no safe-conduct given by enemies and the route through Austria was closed at the frontiers because of an outbreak of the plague. Some historians (see e.g. R. Hatton in the Bibliography) interpret Charles' refusal to leave Bender in a sympathetic way, and even discern policy in it: an alternative opinion is to assume a degree of insanity dangerous in the rulers of kingdoms. On the whole, although Charles had good reason to distrust his enemies, he seemed obsessed with avenging Poltava, and determined to stay in Turkey until the sultan joined him in the venture. If the sultan chose to expel him then he would fight him too. This is what it finally came to. On 1 February 1713, while his subjects at home were at their wits' end to defend themselves, Charles with forty men, challenged an army of 12,000 Turks to remove him from his headquarters. 'The affray of Bender' became one more incident to add to the saga, the last stand of the Viking. It took eight hours to dislodge Charles and cost the lives of 200 Turks. Though Charles was still treated with courteous respect, the sultan insisted upon his departure. After many delays and false starts, indeed 15 months later, Charles left for home in September 1714, over five years since his escape from Poltava.

Charles arrived at Stralsund in November to find that things were worse than ever for his country. The population of barely one million had been reduced during the period of the Northern War by over 120,000: 30,000 had been lost in the war and the remainder died as a result of famine and epidemics at the end of the century and of the plague (1710–12). Russia had successfully invaded Finland and her Baltic fleet had shown its strength. The Finland invasion in fact had been made possible by the defeat of a Swedish fleet in 1713, and in June of 1714, off Cape Hangö, 20 Russian ships of the line accompanied by nearly 200 galleys defeated 21 Swedish ships after three hours of heavy fighting in which the Russian galleys rammed and grappled as though born to the Mediterranean tradition. Galleys in fact were particularly useful in the Baltic since they could get under way and man-oeuvre easily among the clustered shoals and islands, where lofty cliffs stole the wind from the sails of other ships. The victory at Hangö established Peter's dream of naval power, and he rightly celebrated it as great a triumph as Poltava.

All that remained to Charles outside Sweden was Stralsund, and there he proclaimed his defiance of all his enemies, who reformed in a new coalition comprising Russia, Poland - Saxony, Prussia, Denmark and Great Britain, through George I's connection with Hanover.

The allies were to some extent embarrassed by their own success. Denmark had excited the jealousy of Hanover and Saxony who disliked the prospect of her recovering control of Scandinavia, and the intrusion of Russia into European affairs was resented and suspected by all. Indeed, public opinion was more hostile to Peter than to Charles, and the Baltic Provinces were not only the very territories which Sweden most wished to recover but also the ones which the other powers wished to see denied to Russia. There was scope for fruitful negotiation, and indeed Charles declared his policy to be one of making settlements with his enemies individually in order to secure from them guarantees of support against Russia. That he failed cannot entirely be laid at his enemies' door.

In 1715 Charles ordered the blockade of all trade with the Baltic Provinces. The Maritime Powers however were as anxious

to continue their trade with Narva and Riga as Charles was to
intercept it, and not surprisingly a British fleet appeared in the
Baltic to protect its interests. Stralsund fell at the end of the year
after the Danes had successfully prevented Sweden sending aid
by sea, and Charles returned to Sweden after an absence of over
fourteen years. Immediately he launched an invasion of Norway
designed to strengthen his bargaining position, and to acquire a
base from which to invade Denmark. There was logic of a sort in
this, but with the Maritime Powers against him the chances of
invading Denmark were remote. He took Oslo in March 1716 but
withdrew to protect Scania from the threat of an invasion by
Danish and Russian troops, supported by the British fleet. In the
event Peter cried off, believing the risk to be too great and
antagonised all his allies by quartering his troops in Mecklenburg for the winter. Once again Charles had an ideal opportunity
to negotiate separately with his enemies, but again he made little
progress and again he returned to Norway. His death in the
trenches outside Frederickshald on December 12th 1718 came as
a relief to all the belligerents.

Charles' sister Ulrica succeeded him and speedily made peace:
The Treaties of Stockholm (1719 and 1720) ceded Bremen and
Verden to Hanover, and Stettin with most of Pomerania to
Prussia; the Treaty of Fredericksburg (1720) restored to Denmark
her right to tax Swedish shipping, and also gave her the
duchies of Holstein and Gottorp. Russia alone remained at war,
since Sweden could not be reconciled to the loss of the Baltic
Provinces until a series of damaging raids on her mainland
accelerated her decision to give way. At Nystad (1721) Peter was
granted formal recognition of his title to Estonia, Livonia, Ingria,
Kexholm, Viborg and part of Finland. It was the culmination of
twenty-one years of endeavour: 'Most apprentices generally serve
for seven years; but in our school the term of apprenticeship has
been thrice as long. Yet God be praised, things could not have
turned out better for us than they have done.'

In Sweden the spell of the saga was too powerful to be
dispelled: a hero king was enshrined in the national pantheon,
but his country was reduced to the rank of a third-rate power.
She was of course more powerful in 1721 than in 1621 because of
the acquisition of Scania, Bleking and Halland, and if imperial
glory was denied her in the eighteenth century, Sweden found

solace in happier activities. Her forests produced the timber for which the maritime powers competed, her iron mines were systematically exploited, and her overseas trade began to flourish. With the wealth thus gained, universities were founded at Lund, Uppsala and Stockholm, a great achievement for so small a country. The free peasantry survived the holocaust which had decimated their ranks, and the ideals of local liberty, good order, honesty and justice in the internal administration of Sweden were of permanent value, even though the pretensions to a *dominium maris balticae* had been irrevocably shattered.

Peter the Great and Russia 1700 – 25

Peter succeeded in bringing Russia into Europe: it was more difficult to bring Europe into Russia. Yet from 1700 to 1721 Russia was involved in a European war, and unless she herself became something of a European state herself she could not hope to survive against her more advanced opponents. To further the war effort Peter had to grasp whatever the west could offer, and as he copied European weapons of war so he proposed to adopt European techniques of industry and administration. Though the speed at which he moved was unparalleled, the direction he took was not altogether novel since western ideas were already entering the country and there were precedents for much of what he did. Nor was Peter's programme wholly revolutionary since he sought no alteration in the basic structure of Russian society.

What was novel was the extraordinary energy, the ruthless brutality and the enthusiasm with which he attempted to encourage the growth of European institutions and attitudes within a semi-Asiatic, Muscovite state which, at heart, preferred to remain self-contained and self-regarding. Without the pressure of two decades of warfare the task might have been undertaken more cautiously and to better effect. Without that pressure it might not have been undertaken at all. The Great Northern War, it can be argued, compelled Peter to adopt one expedient after another as he tried to make good the deficiencies not only of the armed forces but indeed of the entire government of Russia, so that the men, the munitions and the money he required in unprecedented quantities could be mobilised for the defeat of Sweden.

Map 19   Russia in the Reign of Peter the Great

The defeat at Narva left Russia humiliated and defenceless and there would have been no opportunity to make any changes at all had not Charles XII preoccupied himself with Poland and Saxony for the next five years. During these precious years Peter recreated his army and took the first steps to make it indestructible by tapping the vast reserves of Russia's manpower. One recruit was demanded from every twenty peasant households, and depots were established in every recruiting area to train the reserves and to make good the losses caused by death, mutilation and desertion. 168,000 men were raised in this way during the critical years 1705–09, and by the end of the war Peter had over 200,000 trained men in the field, assisted by 100,000 Cossacks and other irregulars. As for the artillery and munitions destroyed or captured at Narva, Peter imported new weapons from Europe but wasted no time in setting up factories (see below) to imitate them. By the end of the reign the army was munitioned mainly from Russian resources, no small arms were imported after 1712 and a Prussian observer in 1713 estimated that the Russians had over 13,000 iron and brass cannon of their own.

Narva destroyed some of Peter's confidence in his foreign officers. Many were retained in service since he could not do without them but a Russian, Sheremetieff, was appointed to command and the proportion of Russian to European officers was increased. After the destruction of the *Streltsi*, Peter's Guards, the regiments raised during his adolescence, became the *élite* of the army and its training school since officers were required to serve in the Guards as common soldiers before receiving commissions in other regiments. In addition schools were established to train military engineers, artillerymen and medical officers. All in all Peter's military reforms proved to be successful, and the eulogy of the Funeral Oration was not far off the mark. 'He was your Samson...Finding an army that was disorderly at home, weak in the field, the butt of the enemy's derision, he created one that was useful to the fatherland, terrible to the enemy, renowned and glorious everywhere'.

Equally essential, if Russia were to fulfil the ambitions which Peter entertained, was the creation of the navy. Before he left for Europe Peter had drawn up plans which despite their ruthless innovation were remarkably fulfilled in his absence. Twenty thousand men from the Ukraine were drafted to build a town and a harbour on the shores of the Sea of Azov at Taganrog, while the fleet which was to ride at anchor there was swiftly constructed at Voronezh. Every landowner was required to provide one ship for every 10,000 serf households attached to his estates, the Church a ship for every 8,000 households, and the lesser landlords were taxed in proportion. Peter's government supplied the timber at Voronezh, but everything else had to be provided by the reluctant patrons down to the last item of rigging. Skilled labour was secured by importing fifty shipbuilders from Europe in the first half of 1697, and, a radical innovation of great importance, by sending Russians to Europe for training.

But the Voronezh fleet never sailed upon the Black Sea. Instead, Peter transferred his ambitions to the Baltic where his achievement was wholly remarkable. Apart from the creation of St Petersburg as a naval base (see below) he launched 48 ships of the line before 1725, giving Russia more men of war on the Baltic than either Sweden or Denmark. In addition there were the 800 galleys, including those whose victory at Hangö was as significant in its way as that of the army at Poltava. It was not, however, to be so long lasting in its effect. Although serfs were conscripted to the dockyards and to serve aboard the ships, Peter remained almost entirely dependent upon foreign recruitment to provide his officers: the navy attracted little enthusiasm outside Peter's own circle and it was allowed to decline after his death.

The expansion of the army and navy was paid for out of taxation. Allowing for inflation, to which the government contributed by its debasement of the coinage at considerable profit to itself between 1700–03, income from taxation was increased threefold in real terms between 1680 and 1725. Indirect taxes traditionally provided two-thirds of government revenue and these were exploited to the full, including new taxes on beards and Muscovite dress, but as the reign progressed more than half the revenue came from direct taxation. Since the household was the unit of taxation, large numbers of peasants evaded its incidence by merging several households in one. In 1718, therefore, Peter imposed a poll tax on all males, and ordered a census to be taken every twenty years. The intention was that the local community would have to make good the taxes lost from those who left the village between censuses, and the net result was to limit the peasants' freedom of movement.

To collect taxes and to conscript labour for his public works and his armies, Peter required a more efficient administration than that evolved by his predecessors. No one questioned the absolute authority vested in the tsar, but, arbitrary and despotic though he might be, it was often impossible to secure compliance with his orders. For one thing the very vastness of Russia was bewildering: stretching 1,500 miles from Archangel to Azov, 1,200 miles from the Dnieper to the Urals, with another 3,000 miles across Siberia to the Pacific, Russia presented an administrative problem which would remain insoluble until the age of the telegraph and the railway. Inspector-generals and Guards officers assigned to investigate particular problems were given powers as arbitrary as those of their sovereign, and their irruptions into provincial life invariably resulted in the wholesale dismissal, and frequently the execution, of incompetent and dishonest officials. Local government was thus temporarily galvanised into unusual activity, but visitations of this sort were spasmodic, short and all too few.

Since the forty or so government departments (*prikazy*) failed in their perennial task of supplying him with money and recruits, Peter tried to solve the problem in 1708 by decentralising the administration. Eight provincial governments were created, each to be responsible not only for collecting taxes but also for spending them locally on recruitment, training and billeting. In this way time-wasting reference back to the *prikazy* was to be avoided, but the areas under the control of the new authorities were too vast, even when subdivided later in districts, and decentralisation without effective direction from the centre merely caused confusion and the abdication of responsibility.

In 1711 Peter remedied this by creating a new institution, the senate, whose functions were to make policy and to supervise its execution by the *prikazy*. Seven years later the *prikazy* were replaced by nine colleges run on Swedish lines, each with its own president answerable to the senate. Bureaucracy of this sort was an innovation of which few Russians had had any experience and the collegiate system resulted too often in the employment of five men to do the work of one. Consequently the colleges had to be staffed by foreigners, Swedish prisoners of war were especially useful, but when, by 1722, Peter began to weed them out in order to establish Russian control of the administration, the collegiate boards became merely nominal organisations with real power in the hands of the presidents. Nevertheless the colleges relieved the senate of much detailed work, leaving it freer to co-ordinate and to direct the administration as a whole. In the senate the appointment of a Procurator-General in 1722 strengthened the work of centralisation. The Procurator-General had his own procurators in each of the separate colleges, presided over the senate in Peter's absence, and had charge of the revenue officials in the provinces. He thus became the central figure in the administration, combining knowledge of Peter's intentions with

detailed information not only of the colleges but also of the
provincial government.

Yet for all the innovations and reforms the Russian administration was not a success. Some of Peter's work was invalidated
by passive resistance, concealed behind a front of incompetence
and assisted by the difficulty of communication. More deep-
rooted than this was the general tradition of peculation. What
was commonplace throughout Europe had grown out of hand in
Russia, where never more than a third of estimated revenues
reached the treasury. Peter took violent action against known
offenders, and introduced special agents, the *fiscals*, to check on
dishonesty; but it was an *ober-fiscal* Nesterov, who had ordered
the hanging of a governor of Siberia, who was himself executed in
1717 for taking bribes. As one official reported to Peter, 'In the
end you will have no subjects at all for we are all thieving.' What
finally compromised Peter's achievement was the fact that even
his most loyal officials were wholly disinclined to assume responsibility for anything. Departmental decisions were referred to
higher authorities; 'the official was kept like a child,' said Peter,
'swaddled in long, meticulous edicts, and on each new unforeseen
occasion the grown child asked for instruction'. Unfortunately
the root cause was irremediable. Peter was held in such terror by
his subordinates that there were few who dared to assume
responsibility, especially as the pace of Peter's innovations and
reforms obliterated the conventional landmarks of their experience.

The great days of the boyars, the territorial magnates, had
ended long before Peter's reign. By 1700, indeed, the *votchiniki*
(see above p. 442), the traditional landowning class, had entered
government service in order to retain their estates, and Peter
simply made more onerous the obligations demanded of *votchiniki*
and *pomestyes* alike. Two-thirds were required to serve a term in
the armed forces, and one-third were called upon to man the
mushrooming offices of the central and provincial administrations. In 1722 a new Table of Ranks recognised fourteen grades
of service in the military and civil fields, with the top eight grades
in each field qualifying for the privileges of nobility. By and large
the Russian nobility benefited from Peter's reign, provided its
members fulfilled their obligations. There was in any case no
rival class to make its career in government service, and the effect

of Peter's various reforms was to strengthen and confirm the essential divisions of Muscovite society into tsar, noble and serf. Since the lowest unit of administration for the purposes of taxation and conscription was the landed estate, the noble was then made more powerful than ever since his serfs had to obey him not only as landlord but also as the agent of Peter's government. As a result, the old legal and economic distinctions which had preserved a variety of grades of peasant status lost much of their relevance, and the general reduction of the peasantry to the status of serfdom, a process begun in the sixteenth century, was significantly advanced by the end of Peter's reign.

The preservation of the Muscovite social order had an adverse effect on Peter's plans for the industrial development of his country. Technical schools were set up at home and groups of Russians sent abroad to complete their technical education, but Russia lacked the principal driving force of the English and Dutch economies, an ambitious middle class equipped with capital, skill and enterprise. For this the social structure of Russia was to blame. There was no free labour market, no free migration from country to town, since the entire labour force was bound in serfdom to the soil. So jealous were the nobles of their privileges that none but themselves might own land or purchase serfs, and it was only with great difficulty that aspiring industrialists could assemble a labour force. What aggravated the problem was that most of the middle classes were resigned to their difficulties. Even when trade was opened up with Europe during the seventeenth century they let it fall into European hands. This was not due, as many have claimed, to the lack of a Protestant ethic, but to lack of numbers: they constituted barely 3 per cent of the population, they enjoyed no social prestige, and were utterly lacking in self-confidence. They had no idea at all of the wealth and position enjoyed by their class in other countries and, in their isolation, they too easily gave way to the forces and conventions which inhibited their expansion.

It was scarcely surprising that the burden of promoting industrial expansion fell principally upon the government. Three quarters of all industry established between 1695 and 1709 was owned by the state, and all of it was promoted by the state to supply the armed forces with small arms, cannon, gunpowder and uniforms. Most of these state enterprises foundered after 1724, deprived of Peter's direction and encouragement, and without the artificial demand generated by war for their products. Only the mining and metallurgical industries prospered to any great extent. This was not novel: the Demidovs, a famous family of ironmasters, had built up a tradition over several generations, and since they had been ennobled they were no longer denied the right to employ their own serfs to work the furnaces and mines, but private enterprise generally had to be supplemented by the state. Peter wrote, 'our state is richer than other countries in metals and minerals which until now have never been used' — and the reason for neglect was self-evident. The iron deposits of the Ural Mountains were hundreds of miles from the coal mines and from the principal centres of population. It needed the resources of the state to exploit them. Technicians were recruited abroad in vast numbers — so that Great Britain, for example, passed special laws to prevent the loss of its craftsmen — while unskilled labour was conscripted from the serfs. As a result, 5,000 tons of pig iron were produced in 1700, 20,000 in 1725, and Russia became the third largest iron exporter after Sweden and Great Britain.

Many of Peter's reforms were concerned with the superficial imitation of western habits. Peter was not so foolish as to believe that clothes could transform a Russian into a European, but he persisted with his insistence on apparently trivial points because he realised that the customs he sought to change had acquired an aura of traditional, even of religious, associations which retarded the acceptance of western ideas in general. For this reason he abolished the Russian calendar, brought the New Year from September to January, and abandoned the tradition of dating events from the Creation which had resulted in a discrepancy of eight years between Russian and European calendars. Above all he struck at the beard, forcibly shearing his own courtiers should they be obdurate, and supplying all customs posts along the roads with pairs of scissors to deal with travellers. Ivan the Dread had expressed the Muscovite veneration of the beard: 'To shave the beard is a sin that the blood of all the martyrs cannot cleanse. Is it not to deface the image of God created by men?' Peter's attack on beards and the calendar was a stroke at the heart of Russian tradition, and caused trouble with the clergy, the most reactionary body in Russia.

This might have been a serious matter since the Orthodox Church has always possessed a very great influence in political affairs but, luckily for Peter, the Church itself was then divided over the reforms initiated by the Patriarch Nikon (see p. 442). The Church Council of 1666–7 had deposed Nikon and declared the precedence of the temporal power over the spiritual but there was always the danger that the Patriarch, whose authority and prestige made him second only to the tsar, might precipitate a quarrel between Church and State. Peter scotched this by letting the patriarchate lapse in 1700 and, after twenty-one years, by putting it into commission under a layman, the Procurator of the Holy Synod. In a way Peter's policy resembled that of Henry VIII of England: his concern was political not doctrinal, and having won control over the church he could not resist encroaching upon its wealth by secularising its land, a process completed in 1764. What angered the clergy most, however, was his abandoning of Holy Moscow, centre of 'the old and ancient faith, of holy orthodox Rus', for St Petersburg.

The building of St Petersburg was the greatest novelty of Peter's reign. Here on the delta of the Neva he resolved to establish a great naval base: here, in a harbour less remote and less ice-bound than Archangel, Russia might compete in the commercial enterprises which underlay the power of European civilisation: here could be the window on the west from which to intervene in Europe, and through which European ideas might illuminate Muscovy. It was an enthralling prospect, but in 1703 it seemed scarcely attainable. The delta was a waste of swamps and islands, frequently flooded, with no local stone and no local labour. Thousands of serfs were conscripted from elsewhere, and, though they perished in their thousands from exhaustion, exposure and disease, though Swedish raiding parties hampered the work of construction, though Russia had to be ransacked for stone and Europe for technicians and craftsmen, the city began to rise. In 1703 the Peter and Paul fortress was completed on the island dominating the delta. In 1704 the foundations of the Admiralty were laid, and then of the docks and the warehouses. All would have been in vain had Charles turned north from Grodno in January 1708, but his long march into Russia, ending at Poltava, saved the city: 'Now', said Peter, 'the final stone has been laid of the foundations of St Petersburg.'

After this date the city could be embellished. A decree of 1712 forbade any construction in stone elsewhere in Russia so that St Petersburg should not run short of its raw material, and a second tour of Europe in 1717 raised a new army of architects and engineers, since it was only fitting that the window on the west should be constructed in western style. A French architect, Le Blond, prepared a master plan for the whole capital, with terraces, palaces and gardens on a scale to dwarf Versailles, but the project was not to Peter's taste. He was not aping Louis XIV nor did he think that France provided the best models. 'I have been in France myself', he wrote to a group of Russian architects visiting Europe, 'where they have no decoration in architecture and do not want it. They build smooth, straight and very heavily, and only in stone not brick. I have heard quite enough about Italy and already have three architects who have studied there. But the conditions of building here are similar to those in Holland. Therefore you must stay in Holland and learn about the Dutch manner of building, especially of laying foundations which are so essential here.' The buildings which have remained from Peter's reign indicate his preference for the simple burgher's houses with curly gables and plaster decoration which he had seen in Amsterdam. Though the city was not completed before his death in 1725, its purpose was fulfilled. From St Petersburg Russia became a naval power in the Baltic, through it passed the commerce and the techniques to speed the internal development of Russia, in it was established the new capital of the new Russia looking firmly to the west.

The measures adopted by Peter did not go wholly unopposed. The Don Cossacks rebelled in 1706–08, the Cossacks of the Ukraine joined Charles XII of Sweden in 1709 and there was religious opposition behind the rising in Astrakhan in 1705–06. Within Russia itself, however, none dared to resist. The peasants, the principal victims of Peter's reign, could escape the burdens imposed upon them only by flight to the Cossacks or to the thinly-populated frontier areas of the east. 200,000 cases of peasant flight were recorded between 1719 and 1727, and many thousands more went unrecorded.

More serious in Peter's eyes was the danger that all his achievements might be undone after his death by his son Alexis.

Alexis showed no interest in warfare, no enthusiasm for St Petersburg and no admiration for Europe. Too timid to challenge his father, he unwittingly became a focal point for all those disaffected by Peter's actions. 'It is well known to everyone' complained Peter 'that you detest the work I do for my people, without any consideration for my health, and that after I am gone you will be its destroyer'. Alexis fled to Europe in 1716, taking refuge in Naples, but after a long correspondence in which Peter promised that no harm would come to him Alexis returned in 1718. Within a few months he was tortured to death.

The violence of Peter's anger against his son betrayed his anxiety that none of his reforms would have lasting effect, and to some extent it is true, as Frederick the Great commented, 'that Peter worked upon Russia like nitric acid upon iron, merely scarring the surface.' In spite of all the changes, the essential characteristics of the old regime — arbitrary despotism, the service nobility and serfdom — remained entrenched for generations to come. The dead hand of tradition, the centuries of isolation, the inertia of the people and the enormous size of the country could not be overcome by one man alone. Ivan Pososhkov, one of Peter's economic advisers, commented: 'the tsar pulls uphill with the strength of ten but millions pull down hill'.

Peter moreover, was preoccupied throughout his reign with waging war against a powerful enemy : indeed, many of his reforms were improvised responses to the challenges generated by the war, lacking both coherent planning and sustained supervision. 'After all the pains which have been taken to bring this country into its present shape', wrote Daniel Finch, the British ambassador in 1741, 'I must confess that I can yet see it in no other light than as a rough model of something meant to be perfected hereafter, in which the several parts do neither fit nor join, nor are well glued together'.

Although the comments of Finch, and of Frederick the Great, can be substantiated, it is nonetheless misleading to interpret the events of Peter's reign as if they constituted nothing more than a series of impromptu and short-lived expedients designed to secure the defeat of Sweden. Most of the changes brought about by Peter were already in train. What was revolutionary in this respect was not the direction Peter took but the inexhaustible energy, the overriding enthusiasm and the stubborn determination he brought to the task of speeding up an evolving process. The creation of the navy, the choice of St Petersburg as capital, the education of Russians abroad and the abolition of the patriarchate were indeed startling innovations without precedent, but of all his other actions as tsar it can be said that 'he opened wider, with sledge-hammer blows, fissures which had already been spreading in the half century before 1700'. (B.H. Sumner)

BIBLIOGRAPHY

GENERAL HISTORIES
Best, G. M. *Seventeenth Century Europe* London, 1982)
Friedrich, C. J. *The Age of the Baroque, 1610–1660* (New York, 1952
Lossky, A. *The 17th Century* (New York, 1967)
Maland, D. *Europe at War, 1600–1650* (London, 1980)
Mousnier, R. *Histoire Générale des Civilisations*, vol iv, *Les 16e et 17e Siècles* (Paris 1964)
New Cambridge Modern History
    vol iii, Wernham, R.B. (ed), *The Counter-Reformation and the Price Revolution, 1559–1610* (Cambridge, 1968)
    vol iv, Cooper, J. P. (ed), *The Decline of Spain and the Thirty Years War, 1609–1648/59* (Cambridge, 1970)
    vol v, Carsten, F. L. (ed), *The Ascendancy of France, 1648–1688* (Cambridge, 1961)
    vol vi, Bromley, J. S. (ed), *The Rise of Great Britain and Russia, 1688–1715/25* (Cambridge, 1970)
Nussbaum, F. L. *The Triumph of Science and Reason, 1660–1685* (New York, 1953)
Parker, G. *Europe in Crisis, 1598–1648* (London, 1979)
Stoye, J. *Europe Unfolding, 1648–1688* (London, 1969)
Trevor-Roper, H. (ed), *The Age of Expansion* (London, 1967)
Williams, E. N. *The Ancient Régime in Europe: Government and Society in the Major States, 1648–1789* (London, 1970)
Wolf, J. B. *The Emergence of the Great Powers, 1685–1715* (New York, 1951)

THE SEVENTEENTH CENTURY BACKGROUND
Barker, E., Clark, G. N., and Vaucher, A. (eds), *The European Inheritance*, vol ii (Oxford, 1954)
Clark, G. N. *The Seventeenth Century* (Oxford, 2nd ed., 1947)

ECONOMIC, SOCIAL AND POLITICAL STUDIES

Aston, T. (ed), *Crisis in Europe, 1560–1660* (London, 1965)

Braudel, F. *Capitalism and Material Life, 1400–1800* (London, 1967)

Cipolla, C. M. (ed), *The Fontana Economic History of Europe*, vol ii (London, 1974)

Cipolla, C. M. *Before the Industrial Revolution: European Society and Economy, 1000–1700* (London, 1976)

Clark, G. N. *War and Society in the Seventeenth Century* (Cambridge, 1958)

Goubert, P. *The Ancien Régime* vol i (London, 1973); vol ii (Paris, 1973)

Jones, W. T. *Masters of Political Thought*, vol ii, *Machiavelli to Bentham* (London, 1947)

Kamen, H. *The Iron Century* (London, 1971)

Merriman, R. S. *Six Contemporaneous Revolutions* (Oxford, 1938)

Parker, G. and Smith, L. M. (eds), *The General Crisis of the Seventeenth Century* (London, 1978)

Plamenatz, J. *Man and Society* vol i (London, 1963)

Polisensky, J. V. *War and Society in Europe, 1618–1648* (Cambridge, 1978)

Rich, E. E. and Wilson, C. H. (eds), *The Cambridge Economic History of Europe* vol iv (Cambridge 1967); vol v (Cambridge 1977)

Sabine, G. H. *A History of Political Theory* (New York, rev. ed., 1950)

Shennan, J. H. *The Origins of the Modern European State, 1450–1725* (London, 1974)

Vries, J. de *The Economy of Europe in an Age of Crisis, 1600–1750* (Cambridge, 1976)

Wilson, C. H. *The Transformation of Europe, 1558–1648* (London, 1976)

SCIENCE, PHILOSOPHY AND RELIGION

Anglo, S. (ed) *The Damned Art* (London, 1977)

Bréhier, E. *The History of Philosophy: the 17th Century* (Chicago, 1966)

Butterfield, H. *The Origins of Modern Science* (London, 1949)

Cragg, G. R. *The Church and the Age of Reason* (London, 1960)

Crombie, A. C. *Augustine to Galileo*, vol ii (London, 1959)

Dampier, W. C. *A History of Science* (Cambridge, 1948)

Dijksterhuis, E. J. *The Mechanisation of the World Picture* (Oxford, 1961)

Flew, A. *An Introduction to Western Philosophy* (London, 1971)

Goldmann, L. *The Hidden God* (London, 1964)

Hall, A. R. *The Scientific Revolution, 1500–1800* (London, 1954)

Hall, A. R. *From Galileo to Newton* (London, 1963)

Hampshire, S. *Spinoza* (London, 1951)

Hazard, P. *The European Mind, 1680–1715* (translation, London, 1964)

Kenny, A. *Descartes: a Study of His Philosophy* (New York, 1968)

Knox, R. A. *Enthusiasm* (Oxford, 1950)

Koestler, A. *The Sleepwalkers* (London, 1959)

Mesnard, J. *Pascal* (London, 1952)

Meyer, R. W. *Leibnitz and the Seventeenth Century Revolution* (Cambridge 1952)

Ranke, L. von *History of the Popes* (translation, London, 1907)

Russell, B. *History of Western Philosophy* (London, 1946)

Toulmin, S. and Goodfield, J. *The Fabric of the Heavens* (London, 1961)

Webster, C. *The Great Instauration: Science, Medicine and Reform, 1626–1660* (London, 1975)

Willey, B. *The Seventeenth Century Background* (London, 1934)

Wolf, A. *A History of Science, Technology and Philosophy in the Sixteenth and Seventeenth Centuries* (London, 1950)

Yates, F. *The Rosicrucian Enlightenment* (London, 1972)

ART AND ARCHITECTURE

Blunt, A. *Art and Architecture in France, 1500–1700* (London, 1953)

Dickens, A. G. *The Courts of Europe. Politics, Patronage and Royalty, 1400–1800* (London, 1977)

Gerson, T. and Kuile, Ter *Art and Architecture in Belgium, 1600–1800* (London, 1960)

Gombrich, E. H. *The Story of Art* (London, 1956)

Hempel, E. *Baroque Art and Architecture in Central Europe* (translation, London, 1965)

Highet, G. *The Classical Tradition* (Oxford, 1949)

Kitson, M. *The Age of the Baroque* (London, 1966)

Kubler, G. and Soria, M. *Art and Architecture in Spain, Portugal and their American Dominions, 1500–1800* (London, 1959)

Maland, D. *Culture and Society in Seventeenth Century France* (London, 1970)

Millon, H. A. *Baroque and Rococo Architecture* (London, 1963)

Pevsner, N. *An Outline of European Architecture* (London, 1963)

Price, J. L. *Culture and Society in the Dutch Republic during the Seventeenth Century* (London, 1974)

Tapié, V. L. *The Age of Grandeur: Baroque and Classicism in Europe* (translation, London, 1960)

Wittkower, R. *Art and Architecture in Italy, 1600–1750* (London, 1958)

Wölfflin, H. *Renaissance and Baroque* (translation, London, 1964)

NATIONAL HISTORIES, MONOGRAPHS AND BIOGRAPHIES

France

Ashley, M. *Louis XIV and the Greatness of France* (London, 1946)

Bonney, R. J. *Political Change in France Under Richelieu and Mazarin* (Oxford, 1978)

Briggs, R. *Early Modern France* (Oxford, 1977)

Brown, W. E. *The First Bourbon Century* (London, 1971)

Buisseret, D. *Sully and the Growth of Centralised Government in France* (London, 1968)

Cole, C. W. *Colbert and a Century of French Mercantilism* (Columbia, 1939)

Coveney, P. J. (ed) *France in Crisis, 1620–1675* (Totowa, New Jersey, 1977)

Erlanger, P. *Louis XIV* (London, 1970)

Goubert, P. *Louis XIV and Twenty Million Frenchmen* (London, 1970)

Hatton, R. *Louis XIV and his World* (London, 1972)

Hatton, R. (ed) *Louis XIV and Absolutism* (London, 1976)

Kierstead, R. K. (ed) *State and Society in Seventeenth Century France* (New York, 1975)

Lloyd Moote, A. *The Revolt of the Judges: the Parlement of Paris and the Fronde, 1643–1652* (Princeton, 1971)

Lough, J. *An Introduction to Seventeenth Century France* (revised ed., London, 1969)

Lublinskaya, A. D. *French Absolutism – the Crucial Phase, 1620–1629* (Cambridge, 1968)

Mousnier, R. *La Vénalité des Offices sous Henri IV et Louis XIII* (2nd ed., Paris, 1971)

Ranum, O. *Richelieu and the Councillors of Louis XIII* (Oxford, 1963)

Rule, J. C. *Louis XIV: The Craft of Kingship* (Ohio, 1969)

Wedgewood, C. V. *Richelieu and the French Monarchy* (revised ed., London, 1962)

Wolf, J. B. *Louis XIV* (London, 1968)

Spain and the United Provinces

Baxter, S. B. *William III* (London, 1966)

Boxer, C. R. *The Dutch Seaborne Empire, 1600–1800* (London, 1975)

Davies, R. T. *Spain in Decline 1621–1700* (London, 1957)

Den Tex, J. *Oldenbarnvelt* (Cambridge, 1975)

Elliott, J. H. *Imperial Spain* (London, 1965)

Elliott, J. H. *The Revolt of the Catalans* (Cambridge, 1965)

Geyl, P. *The Netherlands in the Seventeenth Century,* vols i and ii (London, 1961, 1964)

Geyl, P. *Orange and Stuart, 1641–1672* (London, 1969)

Haley, K. D. *The Dutch in the Seventeenth Century* (London, 1972)

Kamen, H. *The Spanish Inquisition* (London, 1965)

Livermore, H. V. *History of Portugal* (Cambridge, 1947)

Lynch, J. *Spain under the Habsburgs,* vol ii (London, 1969)

Nada, J. *Carlos the Bewitched* (London, 1962)

Ortiz, A. D. *The Golden Age of Spain, 1516–1659* (London, 1971)

Parker, G. *The Army of Flanders and the Spanish Road* (Cambridge, 1972)

Parker, G. *Spain and the Netherlands, 1559–1659* (London, 1979)

Parry, J. H. *The Spanish Seaborne Empire* (London, 1965)

Rowen, H. H. *John de Witt* (Princeton, 1978)

Germany, Austria and Eastern Europe

Benecke, G. *Germany in the Thirty Years War* (London, 1978)

Carsten, F. L. *The Origins of Prussia* (Oxford, 1954)

Carsten, F. L. *Princes and Parliaments in Germany* (Oxford, 1959)

Chudoba, B. *Spain and the Empire 1598–1625* (Chicago, 1952)

Cook, M. A. (ed) *A History of the Ottoman Empire to 1730* (Cambridge, 1976)

Crankshaw, E. *The Habsburgs* (London, 1971)

Evans, R. J. W. *Rudolf II and his World* (Oxford, 1973)

Evans, R. J. W. *The Making of the Habsburg Monarchy, 1550–1700* (Oxford, 1979)

Holborn, H. *History of Modern Germany,* vol i (New York, 1959)

Koenigsberger, H. G. *The Habsburgs and Europe* (Cornell, 1971)

Macartney, C. A. *The Habsburg and Hohenzollern Dynasties in the Seventeenth and Eighteenth Centuries* (London, 1970)

Mann, G. *Wallenstein* (London, 1976)

Pagès, G. *The Thirty Years War* (London, 1971)

Polisensky, J. V. *The Thirty Years War* (London, 1971)

Schwarz, H. F. *The Imperial Privy Council in the Seventeenth Century* (Cambridge, Mass., 1943)

Spielman, J. P. *Leopold I of Austria* (London, 1977)

Steinberg, S. H. *The 'Thirty Years War' and the Conflict for European Hegemony* (London, 1971)

Tapié, V. *The Rise and Fall of the Habsburg Monarchy* (London, 1971)

Vaughan, D. M. *Europe and the Turk, 1350–1700* (Liverpool, 1954)

Wedgwood, C. V. *The Thirty Years War* (London, 1938)

Sweden and Russia

Anderson, M. S. *Peter the Great* (London, 1978)

Andersson, I. *A History of Sweden* (London, 1955)

Bengtsson, F. G. *The Life of Charles XII* (London, 1960)

Grey, I. *Peter the Great, Emperor of All Russia* (London, 1962)

Hatton, R. *Charles XII of Sweden* (London, 1968)

Klyuchievsky, V. *Peter the Great* (London, 1958)

Lisk, J. *The Struggle for Supremacy in the Baltic 1600–1725* (London, 1967)

Pares, B. *History of Russia* (revised ed., London, 1965)

Roberts, M. *Gustavus Adolphus 1611–1632* vols i and ii (London, 1953, 1958)

Roberts, M. *Essays in Swedish History* (London, 1967)

Roberts, M. *Sweden as a Great Power 1611–1697* (London, 1968)

Roberts, M. *Sweden's Age of Greatness 1632–1718* (London, 1973)

Roberts, M. *Gustavus Adolphus and the Rise of Sweden* (London, 1973)

Sumner, B. H. *Peter the Great and the Emergence of Russia* (London, 1950)

Sumner, B. H. *Peter the Great and the Ottoman Empire* (London, 1950)

Vernadsky, G. *The Tsardom of Moscow, 1547–1632* (Yale, 1969).

INDEX

477